Luke

Luke

Gospel to the Nameless and Faceless

W. Mark Tew

WIPF & STOCK · Eugene, Oregon

LUKE
Gospel to the Nameless and Faceless

Copyright © 2012 W. Mark Tew. All rights reserved. Except for brief quotations in critical publications or reviews, no part of this book may be reproduced in any manner without prior written permission from the publisher. Write: Permissions, Wipf and Stock Publishers, 199 W. 8th Ave., Suite 3, Eugene, OR 97401.

Wipf & Stock
An Imprint of Wipf and Stock Publishers
199 W. 8th Ave., Suite 3
Eugene, OR 97401
www.wipfandstock.com

ISBN 13: 978-1-61097-734-0
Manufactured in the U.S.A.

All scripture quotations, unless otherwise indicated, are taken from the Holy Bible, New International Version®, NIV®. Copyright ©1973, 1978, 1984 by Biblica, Inc.™ Used by permission of Zondervan. All rights reserved worldwide.

"Certain Scripture quotations contained herein are from the Revised Standard Version Bible, copyright © 1946–52, 1971, by the Division of Christian Education of the National Council of Churches of Christ in the U.S.A., and are used by permission. All rights reserved."

It is with cherished memory and loving appreciation this book is dedicated to the members of the Koinonia Sunday School class of Siloam Baptist Church, Marion, Alabama. Weekly they were the recipients of this work's premise. Their encouragement to undertake such an endeavor proved that a detailed examination of the text reveals truths that are not completely understood until proclaimed. To them remains a debt of love I can never repay.

And

To my parents, Earl and Juanita Tew, whose loving hands God used to weave the fabric of my life.

Contents

Preface ix
Acknowledgments xiii
Abbreviations xv

1 The Galilean Beginning 1

2 Journey to Jerusalem 146

3 Jerusalem and Beyond 261

Bibliography 313
Scripture Index 315

Preface

Growing up in the Rocky Ridge community just "over the mountain" from Birmingham, Alabama, we all knew a few things were certain. We knew there would be college football in the South, Christmas break would never be long enough, and there most definitely would be Vacation Bible School during the summer.

Accompanied by a parade, including the fire engine from the local fire district, the festivities started the weekend before the beginning of the two-week-long VBS. Volunteers walked alongside the siren-blaring truck, handing out fliers and enrolling families by writing the parents' names and addresses along with the children's names and grade levels on carbon paper duplicate forms. Teachers prepared their rooms in advance, and a portion of Sunday School that weekend was dedicated to finding where each class was located, thereby enhancing the coordination of the first day of Vacation Bible School. It was a grand event!

Then the first opening assembly arrived and every student wanted the same thing. Everyone wanted to carry a flag or the Bible for the procession and pledges. It was an accomplishment indeed to be deemed serious enough to be chosen for this honor. We stood, saluted, and pledged allegiance to the American flag, the Christian flag, and finally the Bible.

Taken predominately from Psalm 119, the pledge to the Bible stated, "I pledge allegiance to the Bible, God's Holy Word; and I will make it a lamp unto my feet, a light unto my path; and I will hide its words in my heart that I might not sin against Thee."

Many years have followed those formative days filled with important lessons and happy memories. While most of the names of teachers and students have faded, a few details from VBS remain ever present. God's eternal message revealed through Scripture is both a light and lamp capable of sufficient direction in even the darkest times. Furthermore, when the truths of Scripture are hidden in the heart like a treasure, the follower of God lives a victorious, sin-conquering life.

In the preface to his translation of the Greek New Testament, Erasmus wrote of Scripture: "These holy pages will summon up the living image of His mind. They will give you Christ Himself, talking, healing, dying, rising, the whole Christ in a word."[1] Such was the common conviction among the leaders of the protestant reformation. They believed providing Scripture in the vernacular to the laity would fundamentally change the nature of the church. History indicates they were right. Both the radical and the magisterial reformations swept Europe. Newfound religious liberty led to spiritual formation across the Atlantic in the "new world" as well. Soon the modern mission movement began attempting to evangelize the globe. And the list of accomplishments related to the "unchained" Word of God could go on.

Yet over four centuries after vernacular translations began being read in Europe there is an all too often a lack of effective proclamation of Scripture to the people of God. This phenomenon is occurring at a time when there are more resources, books, and electronic search capacities than ever before. The Scriptures have been and are being provided to every conceivable ethnic dialogue by dedicated groups of Bible translators and Bible society members. Software packages provide instant information regarding the grammatical properties of both the Greek and Hebrew texts. Propagation of the biblical message should be greater now than at any time in history. Why, with all of these available resources, should a breakdown ever occur of the basic hermeneutical process of presenting the meaning of an ancient text into a contemporary expression?

In his book *The Strange Silence of the Bible in the Church*, James D. Smart suggested at least two reasons for this reality. One occurs when the biblical scholar has applied scientific objectivity in interpreting the Bible to the extent of rendering explanations that have little or no contemporary application. I once heard Dr. P. Landrum Leavell II, president of New Orleans Baptist Theological Seminary, disparage such efforts as "going down deeper and coming up dryer" than anyone could image possible! One needs only to peruse a few critical commentaries to understand the point. While it is hard to fathom, it appears greater detail has led to less understanding by more people than ever before.

---

1. Robertson, *A Grammar of the Greek New Testament*, xix.

Yet the failure of the hermeneutical process cannot be laid solely at the feet of the biblical exegete. Smart continued by acknowledging the vital connection between hermeneutics and homiletics. "The preacher is dependent on the scholarly interpreter. But what is equally true but much less frequently recognized is that there are depths of meaning in the text of Scripture which remain hidden from the scholar until the text is preached."[2] What Smart was discussing is what I describe as the "immediacy of preaching." While critical scholarship is absolutely necessary, there is an indescribable clarity that occurs during the preaching event that somehow elucidates the text of Scripture in ways that neither the biblical scholar nor the biblical proclaimer, regardless of the extent of preparation, could have anticipated. In a less-educated age, this may have been described simply as "unction." It is to this dilemma the present volume was written. *Luke: The Gospel of the Nameless and Faceless* is an attempt to close the hermeneutical divide by bridging the gap between biblical interpreter and biblical proclaimer.

To accomplish this task, a fresh translation of the biblical text was necessary. Only a careful reading of the text could do justice to the conviction that inspired Scripture holds within itself a revelation of the nature and character of God. Accordingly, examination of the text included literary analysis, vocabulary choice, and grammatical syntax. As a result, all Scripture passages presented in italics are the author's translation. Scripture appearing in quotation marks are from the King James Version unless otherwise indicated.

But a detailed examination of the text was only the beginning of the process. Equally important is the presentation of the lessons learned from the text in such a fashion as to communicate the full and rich meaning of the biblical message. While this volume is not a series of sermons, its presentation does reflect that Scripture was designed to be proclaimed. The "sermonic" nature of any thorough explanation of the meaning of Scripture is inevitable. Anything else will fall short.

Accordingly, *Luke: The Gospel of the Nameless and Faceless* was written for two different audiences. The reader with the capacity to work with the original language will find in the narrative reference to technical issues of style, grammar, and syntax that could prompt additional study and evaluation. Yet the narrative presents the information in such a manner that the absence of advanced linguistic ability will not hinder understand-

---

2. Smart, *The Strange Silence of the Bible in the Church*, 33.

ing the depth of meaning found in God's eternal Word. Regardless of prior ability, *Luke: The Gospel of the Nameless and Faceless* will bring the reader into a new and fresh encounter with the God of all creation.

Acknowledgments

A GREAT MANY PEOPLE deserve expressions of my appreciation for this volume. Given the premise that interpretation of Scripture starts with a detailed analysis of the text but is incomplete until the message is proclaimed, it would be inappropriate indeed not to mention first the Koinonia Sunday School Class of the Siloam Baptist Church in Marion, Alabama.

During the early stages of manuscript preparation, dedicated friends offered observations on the work's merits. They include Robert Marcus and John Baugh of Marion, Alabama, and Meridian, Mississippi, and Bill Fishback, Jim Nance, Drs. Carol and Rance Boren, and Dr. Robert Tucker of Brownwood, Texas. Their encouragement sustained the project in its uncertain, developmental period.

Three educators deserve particular note in this endeavor, although none would ever claim credit. Dr. Bill Cowley of Samford University cared enough to take the time required to start a friendship that God used in moving and shaping my life as a young adult. Without his involvement I would not have met, worked for, and learned from Dr. James L. Heflin and Dr. R. E. Glaze, Jr., both of New Orleans Baptist Theological Seminary. Dr. Heflin was my preaching professor and Dr. Glaze my Greek professor. Working as a graduate assistant for both, I learned more than the lessons they delivered to their classes. I learned their heart. I learned their passion for teaching and preaching God's Word. I learned that neither the command of the Greek text nor any amount of human eloquence could ever substitute for the presence and work of the Holy Spirit in the effort to understand and proclaim God's eternal Word. In a formative way, they shaped the conviction that led to this effort.

Four individuals were pivotal to this book's development. Also a member of the Koinonia Class, Dr. Doug Halbrooks, DVM, undertook the laborious task of proofreading section by section the entire work in its original, rough-draft format. His was a labor of love that was unmatched and for which I will be eternally grateful. Dr. Bill McKee of Nashville, Tennessee, educator, fellow researcher, and mentor never ceased to insist on the importance of bridging academic and inspirational material in the present publication. Carolyn Gregory of Hendersonville, Tennessee, willingly participated as the final copy editor, bringing a polish to the work that my lack of objectivity caused by too many hours of association with the manuscript could never have achieved. Dr. Lane Nutt, OD, of Bolivar, Missouri, unknowingly provided the inspiration for this volume's title through his life of humble and obedient service to God and the kingdom of Heaven on earth. He is a contemporary example of the Nameless and Faceless who through immeasurable ways daily propagate the gospel. I am honored to call them my friends.

Finally, these acknowledgments would be incomplete without mention of my wife who is my closest companion, my God-given soul mate, my source of constant encouragement, and without whose presence, my life's journey would be far less than everything God had intended. To Annie Ruth: "Be ye stedfast, unmoveable, always abounding in the work of the Lord, forasmuch as ye know that your labour is not in vain in the Lord" (1 Cor 15:58).

Abbreviations

BBC   *The Broadman Bible Commentary.* 12 vols. Edited by Clifton J. Allen. Nashville: Broadman, 1969–72.

BDAG   Walter Bauer, Frederick W. Danker, W. F. Arndt, and F. W. Gingrich. *Greek-English Lexicon of the New Testament and Other Early Christian Literature.* 2nd ed. Chicago: University of Chicago Press, 1979.

IDB   *The Interpreter's Dictionary of the Bible.* 4 vols. Edited by George Arthur Buttrick. Nashville: Abingdon, 1962.

KJV   *King James Version.* 1611.

RSV   *The Revised Standard Version.* Cambridge: Cambridge University Press, 1971.

TDNT   *Theological Dictionary of the New Testament.* 10 vols. Edited by Gerhard Kittel and Gerhard Friedrich. Translated by Geoffrey W. Bromiley. Grand Rapids: Eerdmans, 1964–76.

TWOT   *Theological Wordbook of the Old Testament.* 2 vols. Edited by Robert Laird Harris. Chicago: Moody, 1980.

WPNT   Robertson, A. T. *Word Pictures in the New Testament.* vol. 2. Nashville: Broadman, 1930.

1

The Galilean Beginning

LUKE: THE GOSPEL OF THE NAMELESS AND FACELESS

> *Luke 1:1–4*
> ¹*As many have taken in hand the task of compiling a narrative of all the events accomplished among us,* ²*and even as those who from the beginning were eyewitnesses and servants of the Word delivered the same to us,* ³*it seemed appropriate to me also to write to you, most excellent Theophilus,* ⁴*so that you may know a true report concerning that which you have been informed.*

MANY THINGS CAN BE and indeed have been said about the introduction to Luke's Gospel. Scholars appropriately call attention to the identity of the author: Luke, the beloved physician and traveling companion of Paul.[1] The fluid literary Greek style, among the best in the New Testament, is noted along with the author's attention to historic detail while remaining true to the unique genre of gospel: a sermonic form that is part narrative, part polemic, part apology. The occasion and date are frequently and properly tied to the initial recipient, a Gentile given the title of "Your Excellency" and called by the name Theophilis. Luke wanted this one named "lover of God" to understand that the good news of God's kingdom was the culmination of Judaism, a recognized and legal religion, and, as such, was nonthreatening to governmental and civic order. Furthermore, the gospel's proponents were all law-abiding citizens of the Roman Empire, intent only on extending the understanding

---

1. See Colossians 4:14 and the "we sections" of Acts 16:11–18.

of God's love and acceptance to all. Though addressed to a governmental official, the story began with the poorest of the social order and continued to include the outcasts of society. Sinners; tax collectors; women; shepherds; lepers, and the lame, sick, and dying all found inclusion through the work of the Holy Spirit that dominates the unfolding story. The pervasive nature of Luke's Gospel clearly demonstrates the larger audience: Gentile readers both with and without Jewish backgrounds who lived in the expanding Roman Empire of the Mediterranean world.

It is to this nameless and faceless crowd that the Gospel of Luke is intended and, with regard to his sources, also indebted. After indicating that others had transmitted the Gospel information orally and in written form, Luke subtly acknowledged the importance of his sources as being *those who from the beginning were eyewitnesses and servants of the Word*. The beauty of Luke's word choice should not be overlooked. The word translated "servants" or "ministers" of the Word is ὑπηρεται (*hupēretai*), a word that predates the New Testament era. Mathew, Mark, and John used the term in a military capacity describing an *officer* of the court (Matt 5:25; 26:58; Mark 14:54,65; John 7:45; 18:3,12,18,22; 19:6). Jesus also described his *servants* in a hypothetical military fashion when he said his servants would fight for him if his kingdom were of this world (John 18:36). Luke alone in the Gospels used the word to describe an *attendant* who facilitates worship, an application seen clearly in the only other reference in the Gospel. In Luke 4:16, Jesus inaugurated his public ministry by reading from the prophet Isaiah. Upon completion, Jesus handed the scroll to the attendant, ὑπηρεται (*hupēretai*). Paul used the word only once. When addressing the Corinthians he said, "This is how one should regard us: as *servants* of Christ and stewards of the mysteries of God" (1 Cor 4:1, italics added).

A compound word, ὑπηρεται (*hupēretai*) would be translated literally as "under rower." Unsuccessful attempts have been made to link the resulting translation of servant to the lower tier of oarsmen in the trireme, a class of warship common to the Mediterranean Sea in the centuries before the birth of Christ. As the name of the vessel implies, three sets of oarsmen—thranites, zygites, and thalamites—were located in vertical banks to the starboard and port of the ship. More likely is the explanation offered by L. J. D. Richardson who related the word meaning not to an oarsman's position but to the oarsmen's cooperation in a group effort. Richardson held that "the word ὑπηρέτης came into use as soon as the number of ἐρέτας reached a point when it became necessary to have on board a 'time keeper' or controller, in other words a κελευστής. All the oarsmen now became 'under-rowers' in respect of this coxswain, taking their time, orders, etc., without question from him."[2] This understanding led to Richardson's position that the under rower rendered "unquestioning service in response to another's authoritative bidding."[3]

With this background, Luke's description of his literary sources takes on new life. These eyewitnesses and servants were not merely reporters of fact. They were not omniscient narrators untouched by the reality of their message. They were attendants, working together to achieve a common goal, abdicating individualism and recognizing as they did the essential task of following one leader.

Three characteristics should be attributed to these "servants of the Word." (1) These servants of the Word were participants in the gospel. The evangelist John delivered to the readers of his epistles "that which was from the beginning, which we have heard, which we have seen with our eyes, which we have looked upon, and our hands have handled" (1 John 1:1). Additionally, John wrote in the prologue of his Gospel, "And the Word was made flesh, and dwelt among us (and we beheld his glory, the glory as of the only begotten of the Father), full of grace and truth" (John 1:14). But Luke had no such personal experience with the resurrected Christ. Like the author of Hebrews, Luke was a second generation Christian,[4] dependent on the experience and report of others. Servants of the Word must experience the message to which they attend.

(2) These servants of the Word faithfully delivered their experiences. Without their willingness to share, the gospel message would have faded into lost details of societal memory. The servants of the Word are required not only to experience the message but to propagate the same. Spiritual illiteracy is never further away than one generation.

(3) These servants of the Word were perfectly content to be anonymous in their service, to call no attention to themselves, and to focus all glory on Christ. These first-century heralds of the good news were indeed nameless and faceless.

2. Richardson, "ΥΠΗΡΕΤΗΣ," 58.

3. Ibid.

4. Hebrews 2:3 indicates the message of Christ was "spoken by the Lord, and was confirmed unto us by them that heard him." The author clearly indicated receiving the message from a source other than directly from Christ.

ZACHARIAH AND ELIZABETH

Luke 1:5-6

⁵*During the days of Herod, King of Judea, there arose a priest of the course of Abijah whose name was Zachariah, and whose wife, a daughter of Aaron, was named Elizabeth.* ⁶*Both Zachariah and Elizabeth were righteous before God and blameless, constantly observing the commandments and decrees of the Lord.*

In the *Antiquities of the Jews*, the Jewish historian Josephus repeated the details of 1 Chronicles 24 where King David divided all of the descendents of Aaron into twenty-four sections.⁵ This took place as David described the details of his vision for the temple to his son Solomon (1 Chron 28:11-19). These divisions, courses, or sections were necessary due to the large number of direct descendants of Aaron, specifically, thirty-eight thousand Levites thirty years of age or older (1 Chron 23:3). Two of Aaron's sons, Nadab and Abihu, did not survive their father, while their brothers, Eleazar and Ithamar did. David organized the direct descendants of Eleazar and Ithamar into twenty-four groups, each bearing the name of the various sons of Eleazar and Ithamar. Although it is an argument from silence, Ezra implied that descendants of all twenty-four sections either did not survive the Babylonian deportation or did not return when released. Only Jedaiah, Immer, Pashur, and Harim, along with the Number of their descendants are recorded (Ezra 2:36-39). Nehemiah seemed to have reordered all twenty-four as they have reappeared in the New Testament era (Neh 13:30). Josephus asserted that the each section served in the temple from Sabbath to Sabbath, or eight days.⁶ If this is accurate, the only biblical reference would be when the high priest Jehoiada engaged the sections as body guards for the boy King Joash (2 Chron 23:8).

Luke introduced the first key figures of the Gospel as Zachariah, a priest from the section of Abajah. Furthermore, the story is heightened by the identity of Zachariah's wife, whose name was Elizabeth. Marriage was sacred to the Jewish people. Racial purity was of utmost importance in the post-deportation culture. Elizabeth was not only a Jew but she was

---

5. Josephus, *Antiquities*, Book 7, Chapter 14, verse 7.
6. Ibid.

also the daughter of Aaron. Far from being trivial details, Luke initiated the story of the Messiah grounded firmly in established Judaism, as it had been practiced since Zerubbabel rebuilt the temple. What is more, Luke showed this heritage to be inclusive of women. Far from being illegal or seditious, this Gospel message is reputable and inclusive of all social orders.

Not to be overlooked are the attributes of these two people who were privileged to initiate the story of God's kingdom on earth. (1) Zachariah and Elizabeth were described as righteous before God. Keeping in mind Luke's intent to convey the non-seditious nature of the gospel to the Roman official Theolphilis, it comes as no surprise that the first adherents of the faith are described as righteous before God. A word with rich history in classical and *Koine* Greek literature, δίκαιος (*dikaios*) means "to be upright and just" when applied to people. In a secular sense, a righteous person always conforms to the law of the land, be that religious or civic in nature. Luke accordingly showed the forbearers and followers of Christ to be upstanding citizens of God's kingdom and of the social order. In so doing, Luke depicted the nature of the Christian life for subsequent readers as people living in harmony with God and man.

(2) Not only were Zachariah and Elizabeth righteous but they also were blameless. The English prefixes *a, non,* and *un,* are negating prefixes that rephrase a word to its antonym. Friendly and unfriendly, political and nonpolitical, moral and amoral are only a few examples. The Greek language achieves the same mechanics with the alpha privative. In this passage, ἄμεμπτοι (*amemptoi*) means "blameless." The prefixed Greek *alpha* negates the root word μεμπτός (*memptos*), which means "a reason for complaint." The apostle Paul used μεμπτός (*memptos*) when he urged the Colossian Christians to forgive the one against whom they had a reason for complaint (Col 3:13). Zachariah and Elizabeth were flawless in their character, giving no one a reason for complaint.

(3) Zachariah and Elizabeth were constantly abiding in the commandments and decrees of the Lord. Matthew captured the essence of the word πορευόμενοι (*poreuomenoi*) when he recorded the directions of Jesus, "As you go, proclaim saying, the kingdom of heaven is at hand" (Matt 10:7). Translated as "*go, proceed, or travel,*" πορευόμενοι (*poreuomenoi*) gathers together the journey of life as a collective expression of how one lives. Additionally, πορευόμενοι (*poreuomenoi*) is a present

active participle, describing a continuous act or process. The resulting meaning is to show how Zachariah and Elizabeth carried out their daily routines and responsibilities. Specifically, they were constantly abiding in the ordinances and decrees of God. These two concepts are tied together grammatically as to avoid separation.[7] Luke was not distinguishing the law of God from the statements of God. Rather, Luke's intention was to characterize Zachariah and Elizabeth as completely dedicated to everything that came from God (Deut. 8:3). Far from only depicting the character of these two heretofore unknown first-century Jews, Luke presented a paragon for all who would be used by God to introduce the Holy Spirit into a lost and needy world: righteous, blameless, and always abiding in the presence of God.

ANNOUNCEMENT OF JOHN'S BIRTH

Luke 1:7–17

[7] They had no child because Elizabeth was barren and both were well advanced in years. [8] Now it happened that while Zachariah was serving as priest before God, [9] duties directed of his priestly section, that according to the priestly custom, the lot fell to him to enter the house of the Lord and offer incense, [10] and all the multitudes of people were outside praying at the hour of the incense offering. [11] Just then, there appeared to him an angel of the Lord, standing to the right of the altar of incense. [12] Seeing this, Zachariah was troubled and fear came upon him. [13] But the angel said to him, "Do not fear, Zachariah, because your prayers have been heard. Your wife, Elizabeth, will bear to you a son, and you will call his name John. [14] He will be a joy to you and many will be made glad on account of his birth. [15] He will be great in God's sight. He will never drink wine or strong drink, and he will be filled with the Holy Spirit from his mother's womb. [16] And he will turn many sons of Israel to the Lord their God. [17] He will go before him in the spirit and power of Elijah. He will turn the hearts of the fathers to the children and the disobedient to the understanding of the righteous. To make ready for the Lord a people having been prepared."

---

7. See Zerwick and Grosvenor, *A Grammatical Analysis of the New Testament*, 59.

The Galilean Beginning 7

Details from the lives of Zachariah and Elizabeth continue to dominate Luke's presentation of his Gospel. The couple was a model example of Judaism. Zachariah was a priest of an order that traced its heritage to the golden days of King David and before. He remained true to his Jewish customs and married not only a Jewish woman but a daughter of Aaron, a prominent person in her own right. Furthermore, Zachariah's life-long dream of serving in the temple was being fulfilled.

But one detail of their life cast a shadow on all the rest. Elizabeth was barren. The term στεῖρος (*steiros*) means "barren," "childless," and even "sterile." No attempt is made via this term to designate a specific reason for the resulting condition. Luke alone in the Gospels employs the term for childlessness.[8] His use of the concept tied so closely to the recognition that both were beyond childbearing years should be viewed as Luke's continuing to champion the cause of the social outcast. Certainly the lack of posterity placed both in a less than enviable social position.

But to the hopeless, God brings hope. The means God used to accomplish his purposes should not be overlooked. (1) God brought hope when and where Zachariah was serving. It was in the temple that God revealed the divine image. Zachariah had prepared for this moment his entire life. He knew every aspect of his responsibility. He was involved in the things God had directed. Too often the church casts doubt on the motives and actions of the devout Jew of the first century. One should not forget that all the Old Testament saints were devout Jews. Peter, Paul, and the Twelve all were Jews. Out of Judaism came God's Messiah. Zachariah believed God's promises and worked to perfect the customs of the priesthood, trusting in the God whose presence those same procedures were designed to highlight. Zachariah was involved in the things of God, and God brought hope out of his service.

(2) God brought hope in response to Zachariah's petitions. Verse 13 indicates Zachariah's petitions had been heard. The word δέησις (*deēsis*) is a petition or entreaty directed almost exclusively to God. Accordingly, the idea of prayer developed from the concept of making a request of deity. Uncertain in this passage is the connection between the phrases *your prayers have been answered* and *your wife will bear a son*. Furthermore, what is the connection to the preceding phrase in verse 10 that *all the people were outside praying*? Were the worshipers that day so in tune

---

8. See also Luke 1:36 and 23:29. The only other New Testament reference is found in Galatians 4:27 where Paul quoted the Septuagint (LXX) wording of Isaiah 54:1.

with Zachariah's and Elizabeth's plight that they were asking for a barren woman and her aging husband to have a child? More likely is that the worshipers and Zachariah were praying in one accord for the coming of the Messiah. It is to that issue the messenger said, *Your petitions have been heard*. It was to the longing for the kingdom of heaven that the response came *your prayers have been answered*. What is more is that the birth of the child was the means of answering the request for God's presence, not to fulfill Zachariah and Elizabeth's familial desires. The child to be born was to announce the coming of Messiah. God's work on earth brings great fulfillment to the church, but typically in ways that propagate the gospel first.

(3) God's hope prompted reverence and awe. Zachariah's first response was that of trepidation. The angel said, "Stop being afraid." The construction of the statement, the Greek negative μη (*mē*) with a present imperative, prohibits the continuation of action. Zachariah was afraid, and the angel said, "Stop It!" There always exists a fine line between respect and fear. Zachariah responded appropriately with awe. The human nature in us will move quickly from embracing with proper respect our Creator and Designer to fearing a God who knows us at our worst. Such actions will cause the Christian to hold God at arms' length, not willing to come into the presence of a holy being. Yet the hope that God brings grows precisely at that point. Ours is a responsibility to trust and not to fear, neither of which are normal human traits.

Luke also detailed the first description of John the Baptist via the message of the angel. Pivotal in Luke's portrayal of John is the introduction of the exclusively Lucan phrase, *filled with the Holy Spirit*. Three times in Luke (1:15,41,67) and six times in Acts (2:4; 4:8,31; 9:17; 13:9,52), Luke recorded events when God interrupted history in such a significant manner that the world would never again be the same. These watershed moments, these lines of eternal demarcation, are signaled by Luke's use of the phrase *filled with the Holy Spirit*.

Although the use of the phrase is limited to Luke and Acts, one should not assume that the presence of the Holy Spirit is a New Testament phenomenon. In King David's repentant Psalm 51 he said, "Create in me a clean heart, O God; and renew a right spirit within me. Cast me not away from thy presence; and take not thy holy spirit from me. Restore unto me the joy of thy salvation; and uphold me with thy free spirit" (Ps 51:10–12). The prophet Isaiah recounted God's steadfast love for his people and their unfaithful ways when he wrote, "But they rebelled, and vexed his holy Spirit: therefore he was turned to be their enemy, and he fought against them. Then he remembered the days of old, Moses, and his people, saying, Where is he that brought them up out of the sea with the shepherd of his flock? where is he that put his holy Spirit within him?" (Isa 63:10–11).

In addition to these direct references, God's Holy Spirit is identified in more general terms through Scripture. Before the universe was created, God's spirit moved upon the face of vast emptiness and spoke all into existence (Gen 1:2). When mankind sinned, God said his spirit would not strive with them forever (Gen 6:3). When Joseph interpreted Pharaoh's dreams and encouraged warehousing the produce of the bountiful years, Pharaoh said, "Can we find *such a one* as this *is*, a man in whom the Spirit of God *is*?" (Gen 41:38). The Spirit rested on the seventy elders and caused them to prophesy (Exod 11:25–29). The Spirit of God came upon Balaam and directed him to bless Israel (Num 24:2). Moses anointed Joshua at God's command as Joshua was "a man in whom *is* the spirit" (Num 27:18). Throughout the period of the Judges, Scripture repeats the phase "Then the spirit of the Lord came upon him." Likewise, in the Samuel and Kings material, the spirit of God is seen as the agent of intervention, enabling God's chosen servants to accomplish mightily in God's name. God's trinitarian nature was preexistent in its totality as the prologue of John's Gospel clearly demonstrates. All that God is—Father, Son, and Holy Spirit—has always worked in complete harmony to create, sustain, and save.

These facts should not lessen the significance of Luke's reference to being filled with the Holy Spirit; rather, the facts should call attention to the significance of the moments and matters at hand. In the Acts materials, the filling of the Holy Spirit occur at unparalleled events in the life of the early church or during moments of significant conflict with the powers of the world. At Pentecost, the disciples were filled with the Holy Spirit and proclaimed the message of God's salvation via the resurrected Christ in known human languages (Acts 2:4). The presence of the Holy Spirit validated the experience. After healing the crippled man at the Beautiful Gate, Peter and John were arrested by the priests, the captain of the temple, and the Sadducees, a first for the new Christian movement. The established authority was annoyed by Peter and John preaching openly that one who was recently crucified by the Romans (at the hands of the Jewish establishment) was now resurrected and possessed the power to heal and to save (Acts 4:8,31). The church was thrust into open conflict with the world, and the Holy Spirit validated the experience. When the fullness of time took the gospel beyond the boundaries of Judaism, God placed his hands on Saul of Tarsus to be the spokesman to the Gentiles (Acts 9:17). The church faced ethnic and religious barriers, and the Holy Spirit validated the experience. Two times on the first missionary journey the ministry team came into open conflict with those who would prevent the gospel from taking hold. Paul and the disciples rose to the occasion, powerfully articulating the message of salvation (Acts 13:9,52). In all the challenges the church met, the Holy Spirit indwelled them and validated the experience.

Each event details developments within the early church. As a precursor to the coming of Christ and the subsequent birth and growth of the New Testament church, the Holy Spirit validated the authenticity of the events surrounding John's birth. Luke indicated that Zachariah was filled with the Holy Spirit at John's birth (Luke 1:67), as was John to be from his mother's womb (Luke 1:15), and as was Elizabeth at the sound of Mary's voice (Luke 1:41). Everything about the announcement and conception of John was unique. The Holy Spirit placed its seal of approval on the birth of John as a divine intervention into time and space. Nothing would be the same after these events. God was fulfilling the eternal plan to create, redeem, and enjoy a people.

Furthermore, the indwelling presence of the Holy Spirit was demonstrated specifically in John's life. (1) John was to be a source of joy. When the Christian is filled with the Holy Spirit, one distinctive attribute is the display of joy. The psalmist said, "Thou wilt shew me the path of life: in thy presence is fulness of joy; at thy right hand there are pleasures for evermore" (Ps 16:11). Paul included joy among the fruits of the spirit when he said, "But the fruit of the Spirit is love, joy, peace, longsuffering, gentleness, goodness, faith, meekness, temperance: against such there is no law" (Gal 5:22–23). Both references position the one demonstrating the joy as being in close relationship to the Spirit.

(2) John was to be dedicated to God's service. The description of John's dietary restrictions is reminiscent of the Nazirite vow. Described only in Numbers 6 and Judges 13, the Nazirite vow could be taken for a specific time period or for a lifetime from birth. The conditions of the vow included the prohibition of wine, strong drink, or even eating the

fruit from the vine, letting the hair grow without being cut by a razor, and the complete avoidance of touching a corpse or carcass. These three components of the vow would make the adherent noticeably different, which was in fact the purpose of the vow. The one who had taken the vow was to be set apart for God's use. Far from mere ostentatious behavior, the Nazirite was dedicated to God and God alone. Persons characterized by the filling of the Holy Spirit are to carry themselves with the same devotion to deity.

(3) John was to be honored by God. As a result of the presence of the Holy Spirit and the noticeable separation from the world's standards to follow the call of God placed on their lives, those who are filled by the Holy Spirit receive God's favor.

(4) John was to accomplish his task of getting ready a prepared people. Filled with joy, set apart for service, and honored by God's favor, the one indwelled by the Holy Spirit is called to a great destiny: to prepare a people for God. But this text indicates the people of God are not simply a collection of followers. Those to whom John was called were to be prepared. The marvelous nature of the Spirit-filled Christian is that he or she is always being used by God to propagate the gospel of Jesus Christ.

ZACHARIAH'S RESPONSE

Luke 1:18–25

^{18}Zachariah said to the angel, "How will I know this? For I am an old man and my wife is advanced in her days." ^{19}The angel answered and said to him, "I am Gabriel, the one standing before the face of God. He sent me to speak to you and to bring this good news to you. ^{20}Now behold, you will be silent, unable to speak until this day arrives, because you did not believe my words, which will be fulfilled in their time." ^{21}Now the people were expecting Zachariah and wondered about his delay in the temple. ^{22}Coming out of the temple, he was not able to speak to them and they knew that a vision had appeared to him while he was in the temple. He motioned to them, but remained silent, unable to speak. ^{23}When the days of his service were fulfilled, he went to his own house. ^{24}After these days, his wife Elizabeth conceived and

> she hid herself for five months, saying, ²⁵"Thus the Lord did to me in the days when he looked upon me and he removed my disgrace before men."

Notable in the story of Zachariah is his reaction of disbelief. Rather than casting a shadow on his character, the details of the story serve to emphasize Luke's assertion regarding the humble and nonthreatening nature of those involved in the Gospel story. When told that he and his wife were to be used by God in a unique manner, Zachariah could not believe what was happening. His questioning Gabriel demonstrated the human nature common to all. At this very early stage of the Luke's Gospel, comprehension is not a requirement for inclusion. Later in his Gospel, Luke developed the concept that faith transcends understanding. Early in his Gospel, Luke told all who disbelieve that they can still be used by God to accomplish his eternal purposes.

Yet one should notice the location of the announcement to Zachariah about the divine plan. Zachariah was in the temple of God, attending to the service of God, and ministering to the people of God. One aspect of the new concept of the "filling of the Holy Spirit" that Luke introduced is that proximity to the otherwise known attributes of God presents greater likelihood of understanding the heretofore unknown attributes of God.

THE ANNOUNCEMENT OF JESUS' BIRTH

Luke 1:26–38

> ²⁶*In the sixth month, the angel Gabriel was sent by God* ²⁷*to a city of Galilee, specifically Nazareth, to a virgin who was engaged to a man named Joseph, who was of the house of David. The virgin's name was Mary.* ²⁸*The angel came to her and said, "Hail to thee, greatly favored! The Lord is with you."* ²⁹*But she was disturbed by the words and wondered what sort of greeting this was.* ³⁰*And the angel said to her, "Stop being afraid, Mary. You have found favor with God.* ³¹*Behold, you will conceive in your womb, and you will bear a son. His name will be called Jesus.* ³²*He will be great, and he will be called the son of the most high. The Lord God will give to him the throne of his father David.* ³³*He will rule over the house of Jacob forever, and of his kingdom there will be*

> no end." ³⁴But Mary said to the angel, "How can this be as I have not been with a man?" ³⁵The angel replied, "The Holy Spirit will come upon you and the power from on high will overshadow you. Therefore, the one to be begotten will be called Holy, the Son of God. ³⁶Furthermore, your relative Elizabeth has conceived a son in her old age. This is the sixth month of pregnancy for a barren woman. ³⁷With God, nothing is impossible." ³⁸Mary replied, "I am your servant; do to me according to your word." And the angel left her.

Luke identified three pivotal issues in the announcement of Jesus' birth: (1) Grace is expanded beyond a greeting and is elevated to its New Testament usage as the vehicle for salvation. (2) Luke provided formative Christological statements upon which the church would build its understanding of the person and work of Christ. (3) Luke declared openly the previously sequestered concept of the virgin birth.

Grace. Three times in the announcement of Jesus' birth the angel Gabriel referred to grace. The greeting translated hail is the Greek word χαίρω (*chairō*). This root verb literally means "to be glad, to be joyful, to be full of hope."⁹ This is the parent verb for several other verbs, nouns, and adjectives, including the participle that continues the greeting, κεχαριτωμένη (*kecharitōmenē*), which is translated literally "having been highly favored." Redundant in its literal translation, Gabriel's statement, "Grace to you, one who has been highly graced" signals an intentional emphasis. The thought is extended as the angel declared that Mary had found favor, or grace, with God. A third word, the noun χάριν (*charin*) means again "favor, grace, free favor." Though viewed here in a formative setting, the concept of grace expanded throughout the early years of the church to mean the activity of God that is based on who God is, not what mankind does. All of salvation will come to be understood by means of God's character of grace. Mankind will find redemption only in the character of God that acts on humanity's behalf rather than on humanity's merit. This definition is no clearer demonstrated than in the proper understanding of the incarnation. God interrupted human history and intervened on our behalf, not because we deserved such activity but because God chose to demonstrate divine love to us. Mary represents no special merit other than being the recipient of God's pleasure. The threefold grace declaration highlights this event.

---

9. See also Matt 2:10; 5:12; 18:13; Mark 14:11; Romans 12:12.

Christology. Beginning with its New Testament origins, the church has returned repeatedly to statements like this to identify and articulate its belief in the divine incarnation. The study of the person and work of Christ depend on the statements of its first faith recipients. Luke recorded this early Christological formula via the prediction of the angel. The Christ would be great and called the Son of the most high. God would give him the throne of his father David. He would rule the house of Judah, but his kingdom would know no end. Reminiscent of the Davidic throne promised in 2 Samuel 8 and Isaiah 7, this stylized hymn could well have been a first-century litany of the worshiping church. Embedded within this confession is the belief of Christ's preexistent deity (son of the most high), his human incarnation (receiving and ruling Judah via the messianic expectation), and rising in exaltation having conquered death, his kingdom never to be overpowered (will see no end).

Miraculous Conception. In his introduction to the infancy narrative of Luke, A. T. Robertson said, "The supernatural aspects disturb only those who do not admit the real Incarnation of Jesus Christ and who are unable to believe that God is superior to nature and that the coming of the Son of God to earth justifies such miraculous manifestations of divine power."[10] Such a statement portrays the full array of opinion on the subject of the virgin birth of Jesus. While it is clear from his work that Robertson unequivocally accepted the scriptural position that the earthly mother of Jesus bore the incarnation without human agent, the statement also indicates the undeniable presence within scholarship that questions the virgin birth, choosing rather to attribute the story to the efforts of the early church to deify its heroes. Yet just such arguments miss the point Luke was seeking to make, specifically God's power to intervene in the course of human events.

Frank Stagg correctly chose to discuss the miraculous conception, not the virgin birth. For Stagg, the virgin birth places the emphasis on the condition of Mary while the miraculous conception indicates the power and ability of God.[11] Discussions about the condition of Mary are easily sidetracked into theological debates such as those that gave way to the Immaculate Conception. Seeking to articulate Mary's sinless nature, the Catholic doctrine of the Immaculate Conception holds that the Holy Spirit blocked the biological transmission of sin in the conception

---

10. Robertson, *Luke*, 7–8.
11. Stagg, *Studies in Luke's Gospel*, 19–21.

of Mary, making her the sinless vessel through which the incarnation could take place. This was necessary to get a sinless Jesus. According to the doctrine of the Immaculate Conception, if Mary were not sinless, the best that the Holy Spirit could produce would be a half sinless deity.

If, however, the discussion concerns Jesus' conception, the focus becomes the miraculous nature of Jesus' incarnation. The entirety of the point is summarized in Mary's response to the angel. Even though she did not understand a concept already demonstrated in the life of Zachariah, Mary obediently submitted when told, "All things are possible with God."

Here is the point for the church today: Jesus' miraculous birth can be a point of intellectual argument or it can be a transformational event. Far more than accepting intellectually the fact of Jesus' virgin birth, the miraculous conception can become real to the individual Christian who accepts that God intervenes into our lives and accomplishes divine purposes we cannot achieve. Ability doesn't matter. Elizabeth was barren, Mary was a virgin. Heritage doesn't matter. The prominence of Zachariah's priestly appointment created no privilege. Even comprehension doesn't necessarily matter. Both Zachariah and Mary expressed an inability to understand what God was doing. But regardless of ability, background, and intellectual ascent, the virgin birth becomes real when Christians trust God to work miraculously in their midst, accomplishing the seemingly impossible.

MARY, ELIZABETH, AND THE WORK OF THE HOLY SPIRIT

Luke 1:39–45

39 In those days, Mary got up and went with eagerness into the hill country, to the city of Judah 40 and entered the house of Zachariah and greeted Elizabeth. 41 When Elizabeth heard the greeting of Mary, the infant in her womb leaped, and Elizabeth was filled with the Holy Spirit. 42 She then exclaimed with a loud shout and said, "Blessed are you among women and blessed is the fruit of your womb. 43 Why has the mother of my Lord come to me? 44 For behold, when the voice of your greeting happened to my ears, the infant in my womb leaped because of extreme joy. 45 Blessed are you, the one having believed that all that had been spoken about her from the Lord would come to pass."

With the words of the angel lingering in the air, Mary went with haste to visit her cousin, Elizabeth. Luke offered no explanation for this trip. No doubt Mary had heard about Elizabeth's conception and perhaps sought a sympathetic ear for her own incredible story. But these are not the details Luke recorded. What is presented is the dynamic between persons of faith who trusted the Holy Spirit to lead in their lives.

Upon arrival at Elizabeth's home, Mary must have offered a customary greeting. But before she could tell Elizabeth about what had happened, Elizabeth knew that Mary was bearing the Messiah. "Why has the mother of my Lord come to visit me?" Elizabeth asked. Mary must have listened with amazement as Elizabeth explained that the child in her womb leaped for joy and she was filled with the Holy Spirit simply at the sound of her voice. While this was marvelous on its own, Luke conveyed that Elizabeth also knew from the series of events the level of trust Mary placed in the Holy Spirit. Not only did Elizabeth proclaim that Mary and her unborn child were blessed because of what God had done but Elizabeth said Mary was blessed because she believed God.

While the birth of the Messiah and the birth of the Messiah's announcer certainly were unique circumstances in the span of human history, the understanding of God's activity between persons of faith should never be a rare experience. When faith is placed in what God is doing, the body of Christ bears witness to its credibility. They understand, and blessings are the result.

THE MAGNIFICAT

Luke 1:46–56

⁴⁶And Mary said, "My soul magnifies the Lord ⁴⁷and my spirit praises in the God my Savior, ⁴⁸because he has looked with care upon his humble servant. Behold, from now on, all generations will call me blessed. ⁴⁹For the one who is able has done great things for me, and his name is holy. ⁵⁰His mercy extends to generation after generation of those who fear him. ⁵¹He demonstrates might in his arms. He scatters the arrogant in the imaginations of their heart. ⁵²He tears down the mighty from their thrones and lifts up the humble. ⁵³The hungry he fills with good things, while the rich he sends away empty. ⁵⁴Remembering mercy, he helps his child

> *Israel, just as he spoke to our fathers,* ⁵⁵*to Abraham, and to his descendants unto the ages."* ⁵⁶*Mary stayed with her three months and then returned to her home.*

Named by the first line of Mary's song as translated in the Vulgate, *Magnificat anima mea Dominum*, the *Magnificat* is one of three "hymns" taken from the infancy narrative of Luke. The three are the *Magnificat*, Luke 1:46–56; *Benedictus*, Luke 1:68–79; and *Nunc Dimittis*, Luke 2:29–32. Used as part of the Liturgy of the Hours,[12] these hymns are presented along with psalms and other readings to compose a significant portion of the public prayers of the liturgical traditions. While the reference to "all generations will call me blessed" certainly is part of Catholicism's honor of Mary as the bearer of God, it is important to note what Mary's comments communicate about the praise of God.

(1) God is to be praised because he changed the standard by which believers are measured. Mary said she praised God because he took notice of her lowly estate and transformed her to one whom all generations would bless. No longer was Mary just another Jewish maiden growing up in first-century Palestine. No longer was she just another face in the crowd at the temple rituals. Through no merit of her own, Mary was now blessed. God changed the standard by which she would be measured.

(2) God is to be praised because he acts on the believer's behalf. Mary indicated that God, the Mighty One, had done great things for her. Specifically, he showed mercy to her because she feared God. This same mercy was and is available to all who, out of reverence and respect, obediently honor God.

(3) Finally, God is to be praised because his interaction with people is not based on appearance. Two illustrations are given of groups that by the normal course of evaluation would be afforded great success. With each, God awarded the blessing to those whose appearance would not commend them. God has brought down rulers and exalted the humble. God has fed the hungry and sent the rich away with nothing to eat. Rather than basing divine action on the deceptiveness of appearance, God judges the inmost thoughts of mankind.

---

12. The Liturgy of the Hours is a series of prayers and scripture readings designed to assist the participant's effort praying without ceasing. The Liturgy of the Hours is offered throughout the day also in an effort to consecrate the entire day as holy.

JOHN'S BIRTH

Luke 1:57-80

⁵⁷When the time was fulfilled for Elizabeth to give birth, she bore a son. ⁵⁸When the people of the area and her relatives heard that the Lord had extended great mercy to her, they rejoiced with her. ⁵⁹And it happened on the eighth day that they went to circumcise the child and were about to name him after his father Zachariah. ⁶⁰His mother answered and said, "No, his name will be called John." ⁶¹They said to her, "None of your relatives are called by that name." ⁶²They then made signs to the child's father as to what he desired the name to be. ⁶³Zachariah asked for a tablet and wrote saying, "His name will be John." And they were all amazed. ⁶⁴Immediately, Zachariah's ability to speak returned and he began praising God. ⁶⁵As a result, fear came upon all those living nearby, and throughout the hill country of Judea these words were spoken from mouth to mouth. ⁶⁶All the ones hearing these things lay them up in their hearts saying, "What then will this child be? For surely the hand of God is upon him." ⁶⁷Zachariah, his father, was filled with the Holy Spirit and prophesied saying, ⁶⁸"Worthy of praise is the Lord, God of Israel, for he visited and redeemed his people. ⁶⁹He lifted up a horn of salvation on our behalf in the house of David his servant ⁷⁰(just as he spoke from the mouth of his holy prophets from the ages) ⁷¹so that we would be saved from our enemies, from the hands of those who hate us. ⁷²Showing mercy to our fathers and remembering his holy covenant, ⁷³the oaths that he swore to our father Abraham ⁷⁴to grant us, having been delivered from the hand of our enemy, to serve him without fear, ⁷⁵in holiness and righteousness, all the days of our lives. ⁷⁶But you, child, will be called the prophet of the most high. For you, yourself, will go before the face of the Lord; to make ready his way; ⁷⁷to give knowledge of salvation to his people through the remission of sins; ⁷⁸moved by the compassion of our God when the dawn from on high shall appear to use; ⁷⁹to give light to those in darkness and to those sitting in the shadow of death, to guide our feet in the way of peace." ⁸⁰And the child grew and became strong in the Spirit, and he was in the Spirit until the day of his public appearance to Israel.

The circumstances of John's birth were described by Elizabeth's relatives as God's extended mercy. Every child should be endowed with just such posterity that he or she is an expression of God's mercy. Sadly in our society, children are thought of as everything but an extension of God's mercy. In the agrarian economy of the nineteenth century, children were assets to be employed in the family enterprises. During the re-industrialization of the twentieth century, children shifted from being assets to being liabilities. Latch-key kids came along and largely raised themselves, only to give way to the soccer mom children who seem always to be in need of entertainment. Too often these systems miss the prime issue: Children are a gift from God, an underserved expression of divine mercy. Every child should be cherished. My wife and I were blessed with three perfect daughters. When our first child was born, a colleague gave us the following poem stitched in needlepoint and beautifully framed.

> *Cleaning and Scrubbing can wait till tomorrow.*
> *For babies grow up we've learned to our sorrow.*
> *So quiet down, cobwebs;*
> *Dust, Go to Sleep!*
> *I'm rocking my baby,*
> *And babies don't keep.*
> *(Anonymous)*

Notice next the irony of how what God intended as a blessing quickly became a curse. The family is instituted by God and designed to produce happiness, belonging, security, and a forum for the continuation of the faith. Perhaps no clearer example of godly leadership of the family exists than of Joshua's statement, "Choose you this day who you will serve . . . But as for me and my house, we will serve the Lord" (Josh 24:15). Yet in the example of Elizabeth and Zachariah's extended family, these two were being thwarted in their efforts to do all that God had commanded. When choosing a name, the family wanted to follow custom and tradition rather than God's direction. Culture will substitute its own agenda for that of God's at every occasion, robbing in the process what God intended as a blessing.

The crowed reacted with amazement to Elizabeth's assertion about the child's name. When Elizabeth said the child was to be called John, a name not associated with the family, the onlookers turned to Zachariah and began gesturing to him in signs as though he could not hear what was going on! When visited by the angel, Zachariah lost his ability to speak, not his ability to hear. He must have thought, "You idiot people! Mind your own business! If I could talk, I would tell you a thing or two! Oh, and by the way—I Can Hear You"!

Of greater significance than these details is the result of Zachariah's obedience. (1) When Zachariah obediently confirmed Elizabeth's statement, he received his voice. The ability to speak returned when he desired to communicate everything God had said. The ability of the Christian should always flow from what God has directed.

(2) When Zachariah obediently confirmed Elizabeth's statement, fear spread throughout the region. Nothing may be more powerful than a good story. People are drawn to the details of the narrative like no other instrument. A well-told story engages the listener, and both speaker and hearer are tied together in communication. As the story spread about John's birth, his naming, and the recovery of Zachariah's voice, fear spread to all who heard. Robertson noted correctly that this was "not terror, but religious awe because of contact with the supernatural."[13] Such is the case in Luke 7:16 where the crowd's response to the raising of the widow of Nain's son was that they glorified God and proclaimed Jesus as a prophet in their midst. Unswerving obedience on the part of the Christian still causes the world to stop and ask questions about such a person, about obedience, and about God.

(4) Finally, when Zachariah obediently confirmed Elizabeth's statement, John was marked by the community of faith as a unique instrument of God, destined to accomplish unique service. Too little must not be made of this point. Those looking on in bewilderment about the geriatric birth, the non-familial name, the miraculous recovery of speech, and the fear and awe of God all took a very specific action. They validated for the community at large that this child was different. More than self-fulfilling prophecy, the community engaged in accomplishing all that God intended for John. While the details of John's early life are even more scarce than those of Jesus, John must have lived his formative years under many a watchful eye. By the time of his retreat to the wilderness, John was thoroughly indoctrinated with the story of his birth and in his inevitable service. The community of faith helped shape the one who would prepare the way for the Lord. The church retains this responsibility today. Perhaps more so now with society's fractured nature, this

---

13. Robertson, *Luke*, 18.

imperative remains: The body of Christ must be involved in calling out those whom God has singled out.

Following the return of his speech, Zachariah responded with a hymn of adoration. In his song, Zachariah accomplished two tasks. First, he explained why God was worthy of praise. Second, he described what is involved in the service of God.

Often translated "Blessed be the Lord God of Israel,"[14] the Greek text can be read as *Worthy of praise is the Lord God of Israel*. If the latter is selected, note the smooth transition to an explanation of why God is worthy of praise.

(1) God is worthy of praise because he visited his people. The verb ἐπεσκέψατο (*epeskepsato*) carries the meaning of looking in on a person or a situation with the specific intention of giving aid and assistance. Here and in Luke 7:16 the setting was the same—the crowds were amazed at a miraculous event and subsequently praised God for his visitation. A more descriptive occurrence of the word's meaning is found in its use in Acts and the general epistles. In Stephen's martyrdom sermon he described the setting when for Moses "it came into his heart to visit his brethren" (Acts 7:23). After the Jerusalem Council and before the departure on the second missionary journey, Paul said to Barnabas, "Let us go again and visit our brethren in every city where we have preached the word of the Lord, and see how they do" (Acts 15:36). James described well-intentioned, sincere religion as "to visit the fatherless and widows in their affliction, and to keep himself unspotted from the world" (James 1:36). Finally, the writer of Hebrews described the incarnation of Jesus by quoting the psalmist who asked, "What is man, that thou art mindful of him? or the son of man, that thou visitest him? You madest him a little lower than the angels; thou crownedst him with glory and honour, and didst set him over the works of thy hands" (Heb 2:6–7). Clearly, in each of these instances, the presence of the speaker, human or divine, was not simply chance or casual observance. Moses was concerned about his people and wanted to ease their burdens. Paul was concerned about the fledgling churches and wanted to see them mature. The main point of James's argument is that being a "hearer" of the word and not a "doer" of the word is a contradiction of faith. Finally, God's incarnation in Christ certainly was not an absentee moment. According to Paul, "God was in Christ, reconciling the world unto himself" (2 Cor 5:19). Zachariah

---

14. Luke 1:68, KJV.

believed that God was worthy of praise because he visited his people, coming to them in their time of need, intent on interceding on their behalf.

(2) God is worthy of praise because he redeemed his people. There has never been a time when God did not intend to redeem his creation. Nothing in the garden was a surprise to God. When Adam was created, God knew his new creation would follow a path of destruction. In the words of Robert Robinson's 1757 hymn, "Prone to wander, Lord I feel it, Prone to leave the God I love." Given this knowledge, a lesser god would have not created man. But God wanted to have fellowship with his creation, a divine desire that necessitated free choice.

(3) God is worthy of praise because he is true to his people. God is immutable. God never changes. The modern church long has sung God's praises in hymns of faith. One such hymn that clearly articulates the reality of God's constant, dependable nature is *Great is Thy Faithfulness* by Thomas O. Chisholm.

Luke closed his first section with a magnificent parenthesis. While it should be remembered that chapter and verse designations were very late in the process of the transmission of the text, every section of Scripture has its own literary character, imposed by God who directed the abilities of the writers. Luke continued his introduction of his Gospel by providing unique information about the birth of Jesus, but not before he paused to reiterate important themes of his work via a masterful literary style. The parenthesis is seen in the pairing of the concept of service as worship in Luke 1:1–4 with the concept of serving without fear that is heard from the prophecy of Zachariah in Luke 1:73–79. The overarching message deals with the heart of the Christian's relationship to Christ. All are to be servants of God, under rowers who answer without hesitation to the one who directs our efforts. When Christians approach their lives in this manner, all serve without fear. This is further identified as serving without fear, in holiness and righteousness. Noted by Robertson as "not a usual combination," holiness and righteous only appear together four times in the New Testament.[15] The phase carries the implication of right conduct both with God and with man. The Ephesians reference certainly bears this out with its emphasis on not lying to and stealing from a neighbor, as well as not grieving the Holy Spirit and forgiving as

---

15. Robertson, *Luke*, 19. See also Luke 1:75; Ephesians 4:24; Titus 1:8; and 1 Thessalonians 2:10.

God forgives. Again, Luke's message here parallels that of the opening verses, assuring the outside reader of the absence of sedition in the new Christian movement as depicted by right relationship in a civic community setting.

But more than a polemic about the early church, service without fear that is holy and righteous should describe all the church continues to do in today's world. (1) When the church serves without fear in holiness and righteousness, it prepares the world for an encounter with Christ. (2) When the church serves without fear in holiness and righteousness, it conveys to the world the knowledge of Christ. (3) When the church serves without fear in holiness and righteousness, it engages in God's redemptive forgiveness. (4) When the church serves without fear in holiness and righteousness, it illuminates a dark and dying world, guiding the way to the path of peace.

JESUS' BIRTH

Luke 2:1–7

¹It happened in those days that a decree went out from Caesar Augustus that all the Roman Empire should be enrolled. ²This was the first census when Quirinius was governor of Syria. ³Everyone went to be enrolled in their home town. ⁴Joseph also went up from Galilee, out of the city of Nazareth, to Judah, unto the city of David, called Bethlehem, because he was of the house and ancestry of David; ⁵to be enrolled with Mary, his betrothed, herself being pregnant. ⁶It happened during these days that it became the time for her to be delivered. ⁷She gave birth to her first son. They wrapped him in soft clothes and laid him in a manger, because there was no room in the inn.

Mary and Joseph lived in Nazareth of Galilee. Jesus' birth took place in Bethlehem of Judea. The relocation was due to the census of Quirinius, governor of Syria. Placing specific dates on events described in the Old and New Testaments is a difficult task. Reference points are limited and often debated. Some have taken the mention of Quirinius as problematic. This should not lead one to question the historicity of the Luke and Acts material. While it is believed Quirinius was not governor until approximately AD 6, too late to reflect an accurate statement by Luke, the data that dates his political reign is equally suspect. In short, Jesus birth took place up to two years before King Herod's death in 4 BC Augustus was emperor, and in the quiet little town of Bethlehem, an event took place that changed history.

Two recurring themes should be observed in the birth narrative recorded in Luke. First, adherents to the Christian faith, even its progenitors, were law-abiding citizens, carrying out the obligations of their lives with duty and responsibility. Second, no royal entourage gave fanfare to the birth of God's Son. Mary and Joseph witnessed the angel's promise fulfilled in the most modest of surroundings. As such, the message of the gospel is not reserved for the wealthy and well-to-do. All may kneel at the manger.

JESUS' BIRTH ANNOUNCED

Luke 2:8–14

⁸And there were shepherds living in the fields, keeping watch at night over their sheep. ⁹The angel of the Lord appeared to them and the glory of the Lord shown around them, causing them great alarm. ¹⁰And the angel said to them, "Stop being afraid and pay close attention! I give you great joy that will be for all people everywhere. ¹¹Born to you today in Bethlehem was the Savior, Christ the Lord. ¹²Furthermore, this is the sign to you: You will find the baby wrapped in soft clothes and lying in a manger." ¹³Suddenly there was with the angel a plethora of heavenly host, all praising God and saying, ¹⁴"Glory to God in the highest and on earth, peace to men of God's good will."

As with Elizabeth, Zachariah, and Mary earlier in the story and now with the shepherds on the hillside, the gospel message involved the lowest of the social strata. The shepherds were out in the night, simply doing their jobs, when the announcement came that the world would forever be changed. The message that was entrusted to them is nothing short of revolutionary. Divided into two parts, the message is composed first of the angel's announcement and second of the reverberation of praise by the heavenly hosts.

No doubt the flood of light into the dark was enough in itself to frighten the shepherds. The angelic command to stop being afraid certainly is understandable. They were terrified! The angel knew, however, that the content of the message was so glorious that the shepherds would gladly receive it. "Stop being afraid–because." The reason given is so magnificent that they will no longer fear. The shepherds were about to receive good news of great joy. Furthermore, the shepherds needed to stop being afraid because the message was not just for them. The message was for all people everywhere. The lowly shepherds were being entrusted with a message of remarkable content. They did not need to have a spirit of fear but of excitement and exuberance. It is as if their station had suddenly been elevated. No longer were they the dredges of society but rather its chief messengers. Furthermore, the angel explained, the joyful message intended for all people was that the Savior had finally arrived. Born in Bethlehem, the city of David, was Christ the Lord. The long-awaited Messiah had arrived. The messianic hope had been realized.

As if the first message had not been sufficient, the angel was joined by the heavenly host who proclaimed God's glory. As with the filling of the Holy Spirit in chapter 1, the heavenly anthem served to punctuate the event, giving it one more validation of authenticity. This was not a fluke vision by one or two blurry-eyed shepherds. The skies were filled with God's praise. In keeping with the presentations of the Holy Spirit, the angelic choir called attention to God's greatness and nothing else. "Glory to God," they sang over and over. It was to God that glory was due, and it was from God that peace was given.

Luke 2:14 presents difficulty in its translation. The King James Version reads, "Glory to God in the highest, and on earth, peace, good will to men." The problem with this translation is that the best texts do not support this reading. The best textual evidence changes the beauty and poetry of the King James Version to the more awkward reading *and on earth, peace to those of his good will*. The difference between the two in the Greek text is one letter—a final sigma. Included in the standard procedures of textual criticism[16] is that it is easier to explain why a text was

---

16. Textual criticism is the term used for the study of ancient manuscripts. Literally thousands of manuscripts and portions of manuscripts, all handwritten, have survived to modern times. None are believed older than the papyrus fragment, P52, which dates to the second century, perhaps as early as AD 135. P52 is a fragment of John 18. Because there are no extant autographs, the first recorded documents, the biblical scholar must establish the best text. While a masterful translation that provided the scripture to the masses in their vernacular language, the King James Version of the Bible is based primarily upon 10th century texts and in some cases used the Latin Vulgate to supply

26 LUKE

dropped than to explain why text was added. The King James Version, "Good will to men," translates εὐδοκία (*eudokia*). Modern translations change the word to a possessive and read "men of good will" because the earlier and more reliable texts recorded the word εὐδοκίας (*eudokias*). Before the discovery of the Qumran Scrolls, the phrase "men of his (God's) good pleasure" was an unknown Hebraism (Hebrew vernacular expression).[17] With the growing understanding of the language and its uses, the biblical scholar can judge appropriately between the two spellings.

As time passed while Scripture was being hand copied, transcription errors occurred. Reading from one copy and writing on another, it is easier to explain that a copyist accidentally omitted a final sigma than to explain that a copyist purposefully added a letter to the text. The resulting meaning of the translation adds to the credibility of the decision to accept the earlier text. Furthermore, Jesus' birth did not bring nirvana to earth. Jesus would spend a great part of his earthly ministry attempting to dismantle such a belief. His messianic rule was not what many in popular culture of the day were expecting. Matthew alone recorded Jesus as he said,

> Think not that I am come to send peace on earth: I came not to send peace, but a sword. For I am come to set a man at variance against his father, and the daughter against her mother, and the daughter in law against her mother in law. And a man's foes shall be they of his own household. He that loveth father or mother more than me is not worthy of me: and he that loveth son or daughter more than me is not worthy of me. And he that taketh not his cross, and followeth after me, is not worthy of me" (Matt 10:34–38).

While the angels' proclamation did not announce the arrival of earthly bliss, it should be noted that it is mankind who is the object of God's pleasure. The Savior, Christ the Lord, who was born of lowly means and heralded to the outcasts of society, came with singular intent: to redeem a lost humanity that he had created in eternity and for which he would be willing to suffer and to die. God's glory in the highest had

---

translations for missing sections of text. Accordingly, as textual criticism progressed and more, older and more reliable manuscripts were discovered, the era of the modern translation of Scripture began.

17. Metzger, *A Textual Commentary of the Greek New Testament*, 133.

descended into incarnate form in order to demonstrate the depths to which God's love would bend.

SHEPHERDS' ADORATION AND MARY'S AMAZEMENT

Luke 2:15–20

15So it happened as the angels departed from them into the heavens, the shepherds said, one to another, "Let us indeed go to Bethlehem and let us see this thing that has taken place, which the Lord has made known unto us. 16So they went quickly and after searching diligently, found Mary and Joseph and they found the baby lying in the manger. 17Having seen these things, they made known what had been spoken about the child 18and everyone who heard them was amazed by what the shepherds told them. 19But Mary stored up safely all these things in her heart, and was herself amazed and perplexed. 20Then the shepherds returned, glorifying and praising God for all that they had heard and seen, just as it had been told to them.

There are two separate and distinctive narrative strands that compose Luke 2:15–20. There is the reaction of the shepherds to the angelic message and Mary's pondering of the events.

When the angels proclaimed Jesus' birth, their announcement was made to the outcasts of society. This has been clearly established as one of Luke's dominant themes both in this volume as well as many other scholarly works. What is easily overlooked is the reality of the shepherds' reaction. More than simple sequence, Luke's presentation of the shepherds' reaction was chronological and replete with personal fulfillment. Had Luke been composing fiction, a reviewer of novels would have called this "character development."

Notice the details of the story. The shepherds were on the hillside minding their business. The night sky erupted with heavenly anthems announcing to them, of all people, that the Savior of all the world had arrived and they were the first to know. After the angels departed, the shepherds made a very telling statement. The grammar of the text includes intensive language that describes more than a series of events.

More than a mere suggestion, the hortatory subjunctive[18] διέλθωμεν (*dielthōmen*) is a polite command or exhortation.

In the early days of commercial television, viewers watched with great humor the characters of *The Andy Griffith Show*. A regular to the show was Jim Nabors, who portrayed the role of Gomer. In 1964 Aaron Ruben cast a new setting for Nabors' character and Gomer Pyle, PFC, became the troublesome, but lovable and dependable private in the United States Marine Corp, who was sure to make his drill leader, Sergeant Vince Carter (Frank Sutton), regret the day Pyle joined the Corp. Private Pyle, living in San Diego, met and courted his sweetheart, LouAnn Poovie (Elizabeth MacRae). A much anticipated exchange between the two pictured the two in friendly banter attempting to make plans for the evening. "It is OK with me, if it is OK with you, LouAnn," Gomer would say politely, only to be countered by "Well, it is OK with me if it is OK with you, Gomer." This comic routine of classic inability to make a decision is the very antithesis of the hortatory subjunctive. "Let us go to Bethlehem" was not a take-it-or- leave-it suggestion, it was an imperative!

Additionally, the grammar suggests more insight into the shepherds' psyche. The shepherds knew they had become privy to something above their normal status. The intensifying particle δὴ (*dē*) added more drama and urgency to the statement as translated above, "Let us indeed go." Perhaps the best illustration of the intensifying particle is found in 1 Corinthians 1:12 where Paul sought to communicate dramatically the negative effect of the party factions at Corinth. A literal rendering of the verse would be "I, indeed I, I am of am Paul. I, indeed I, I am of am Apollos. I, indeed I, I am of am Cephas. I, indeed I, I am of am Christ." Paul's repetition and use of the intensifying particle made the point well! The shepherds had no casual interest of verifying the facts. Rather, they knew that *they* should go. This reality is expanded in the details of their rationale. "Let *us indeed* go even to Bethlehem, and see this great thing that has come to pass, which was *told to us!* It was not hearsay or the latest rumor. We did not learn about it in the usual manner, with us being at the bottom of the food chain. *The angel told us!*"

---

18. All finite Greek verbs have tense, mode, voice, person, and Number. The mode is the manner of affirmation, declarative (statement of fact), imperative (command), subjunctive (contingency/ uncertainty). The tense of a finite verb describes the kind of action and the time of action. For example, a present tense verb describes continuing action in the present time. The aorist subjunctive is often, but not always, translated as a hortatory, or exhortation. The common translation is "let us."

Furthermore, the urgency of their new, elevated identity had a direct impact on the manner in which they discharged their responsibilities. Their behavior effectively was changed as a result of the encounter. Two descriptors are given.

(1) They went with haste to Bethlehem. The phrase ἦλθαν σπεύσαντες (ēlthan speusantes) is a verb and a participle and is translated literally as "they went, being hasty." A smoother translation that takes into consideration Luke's literary style would consider the second word of this construction as a participle of simultaneous or concomitant action. Although a Greek participle expresses its adjectival properties predominantly as a rule, this construction emphasizes the verbal qualities of the participle. As such, the King James Version is quite accurate: "They came with haste." More important than the mechanics of linguistics is what Luke sought to convey via the grammar. When faced with the intersection of eternity and their time-bound existence, the shepherds dropped what they were doing and went quickly to participate in an event that would never be repeated.

(2) The text indicates that when the shepherds made their hasty departure, they sought diligently before they found the Christ child. A compound word, ἀνεῦραν (aneuran) comes from the root verb εὑρίσκω (euriskō), which means "I find." Prefixed by the preposition ανα (ana), the resulting meaning is to find after a diligent search. Only two references in the New Testament include the expression; here in Luke 2 and again in Acts 21:4. In the latter, Paul had left Ephesus en route to Palestine. At Tyre, Paul sought out the disciples and spoke to them there. The search was not casual as Paul was deliberate in finding the members of the body of Christ who were in the area. Of interest is that Luke observed this event, as this is one of the "we sections" of Acts. Luke would have experienced firsthand the intensity of Paul's search to find these individuals. Clearly, Luke was intent on showing that the shepherds added conviction to conduct as they sought out the child.

When the shepherds found Jesus, the text indicates they did three things. (1) They told what they knew. The Gospel's dependence on the nameless and faceless for its propagation is again repeated as a dominant theme in Luke. Throughout the recorded history of the church, the shepherds have remained anonymous. Yet they are among the gospel's first emissaries. No special ability was required. They simply told what they knew. Saint Frances of Assisi was once asked for a definition of evangelism, to which he responded, "It is one beggar telling another beggar where to find food." The shepherds told what they knew.

(2) The shepherds returned to their obligations. Note that after finding the child and telling what they knew, the text indicates the shepherds returned to their flocks. They may never have looked at the night sky the same again, but Scripture indicates these lowly outcasts of society went back to work. Luke never backed away from asserting this fundamental character of the early church. The earliest participants of the gospel were law-abiding, ethical, hard-working people who were the fabric of society even though they would never have a name or a moment of fame.

(3) The shepherds glorified and praised God for what they had experienced. Do not forget, the shepherds had no background that could commend them. They had no education, station, or rank. Yet they glorified and praised God because they had experienced and worshiped God. Can the same be said of the church today? Do we routinely share what we have been given? Do we take God into our daily routines, demonstrating that our calling from God demands we be people of integrity, honesty, and dignity? It has been said that many people cherish their religion so deeply that they do not take it with them to work for fear they will lose it! Is the church today a nameless and faceless army that glorifies and praises God for what they have experienced and for what they have seen God do? The shepherds went, looked, told, returned, and praised, and in so doing pointed the way for the Christian church of every age.

The second narrative strand is found in verse 19 and can be easily overlooked. The key to understanding Mary's pondering is linguistic and literary.

From a linguistic standpoint, the meaning of two words influences the proper understanding of this text. The words are συνετήρει (*sunetērei*) and συμβάλλουσα (*sumballousa*), which are translated in this volume as *stored up safely* and *was herself amazed and perplexed* respectively.

A compound word, συνετήρει (*sunetērei*), is built upon the word meaning "to guard" or "to watch protectively," prefixed by the preposition that carries the idea of combining or grouping together events or subjects. The resulting idea is "to gather together items and then keep close watch over them." Translated here as "stored up safely" the word group is used to describe protecting or preventing from loss the new wine that must be placed in new wineskins (Matt 9:17, Mark 5:38). Mark also used the word "group" to describe the protective custody into which

Herod Antipas placed John the Baptist (Mark 6:20). Luke used the word only here in the infancy narrative to describe Mary's thought process. The King James Version and the Revised Standard Version translate the word as "kept" and the New International Version prefers the word "treasured." While both accurately serve the text, there seems to be more meaning inherent in Mary's actions. All the events, all the emotions, all the possible ramifications of her actions are rolled together. Luke's use of συνετήρει (*sunetērei*) seems to carry the force of Mary gathering together all of these matters and holding them close, keeping careful inventory of each item, each sequence of events, making sure not to lose one particle of the experience.

The second linguistic or lexical consideration regards the meaning of συμβάλλουσα (*sumballousa*). The word has the literal meaning of to throw together. Unique to Luke and Acts, the uses of the word in the New Testament are varied. Jesus' parable regarding the kingdom of heaven asked what king would not count the cost before *engaging together* in battle (Luke 14:31). When Peter and John were taken before the council for healing the lame man at the temple gate called Beautiful, the council *conferred* with each other about the incident (Acts 4:15). The word can simply mean meet or help as in Acts 20:14 and 18:27, respectively. However, the word also means to draw into a debate or discourse, as in Paul's encounter with the Stoics and Epicureans at Mars' Hill (Acts 17:18).

Given the breadth of application of this word, Christians today should consider what things, issues, and realities were being *thrown together* that Mary "pondered them in her heart" (Luke 2:19). What concepts were being debated in her mind? What events were colliding in her thinking? What among the items that she stored up safely were being thrown together in battle, in conflict, in discourse?

It is at this point that the linguistic intersects the literary. The modern reader can easily write off as natural Mary's pensive mood. Seemingly at the end of the birth narrative, as the shepherds returned to the hillside, Mary pondered these things in her heart. But note carefully the sequence of events. Mary and Joseph delivered the Christ child. The angel made the announcement to the shepherds followed by the heavenly vibrato. The shepherds were moved by their inclusion in such a miraculous event and sought diligently until they found the blessed family. Upon finding Mary, Joseph, and Jesus, the shepherds told everyone everything the angels had told them. Then Mary stored up safely all these things—things that were thrown together in unanticipated fashion, things that were moved with such force of their own that they collided in her mind, leaving her to wrestle and to debate in her own being everything that had happen and that would most surely take place from that time forward.

Only after this clash of great ideas and events took place did the shepherds return, praising God. Luke did not place the description of Mary at the conclusion of the infancy narrative but rather awkwardly interrupting the flow of the shepherds' tale. It is precisely this interruption that signaled a key issue for Luke. Mary had quite some time to get use to the virgin birth part of this miracle. She had come to find Joseph a decent and honorable man.[19] That much was settled. And besides, they were away from Nazareth, a young couple with their first baby; no one would expect anything bizarre. Nothing about them looked out of the ordinary.

But then the shepherds showed up, and Mary did not know what to do. They began telling everyone around the little courtyard area about the angels, about the message, about the Savior, and Mary's anonymity was forever gone. The shepherds told their story with such joy and excitement that she knew this was only the beginning for her and her family. Mary knew that the shepherds' exuberance was generated by a genuine encounter with God, one about which they would not be silent. Her experience had been a remarkably private one to this point. Only her closest of friends and family had heard the remarkable and arguably unbelievable story of the miraculous conception and the virgin birth. But suddenly people were coming up to her, knowing about her role in the Messiah's incarnation. Mary pondered these things because they were unexpected, because things were not happening the way she had planned.

Yet participation in the church and kingdom of God frequently take just such a pattern. What we expect is not what God has in store. Others know what we thought only we knew. Unexpectedly they stand in our presence, wanting to participate in Christ's kingdom. Our joys and sorrows, our troubles and triumphs, as much as we would cherish them as personal, truly are not as unique as we believe. When our preconceived ideas of how and when God should act collide with the providential reality of God, the true disciple will take that which we have stored up safely

---

19. The reader is dependent on the infancy narrative of Matthew for details of Joseph's character and reaction.

and offer it to God in an act of praise and adoration, humbly saying as did Mary, "I am your servant, do with me as you will."

LAW-ABIDING FAMILY MEETS LAW-BELIEVING SAINTS

Luke 2:21–40

²¹*The child was circumcised after the eighth day had been completed, and he was called by the name Jesus, the name that he had been called by the angel from before he was conceived in the womb.* ²²*When the days of their purification had been fulfilled according to the law of Moses, they brought him to Jerusalem, presenting him to the Lord,* ²³*(just as it is written in the law of the Lord that every male that opens the womb will be called holy to the Lord) in order* ²⁴*to offer the sacrifice according to what was spoken in the law of the Lord: a pair of turtledoves or two pigeons.* ²⁵*Now there was in Jerusalem a man named Simeon. He was righteous and devout, looking for the consolation of Israel. And the Holy Spirit was upon him.* ²⁶*It was revealed to him by the Holy Spirit that he would not see death before he saw the Lord's Christ.* ²⁷*He came, led by the Holy Spirit, to the temple. When the parents of the child Jesus had brought him in to do all that was customary regarding the law,* ²⁸*he took him in his arms and blessed God, saying,* ²⁹*"Now you may release your servant, Lord, according to your word, in peace,* ³⁰*because my eyes have seen your salvation,* ³¹*the one that was prepared for all people to see;* ³²*a voice of revelation to the Gentiles and glory of your people Israel."* ³³*His mother and father were amazed at what was being spoken about him.* ³⁴*Simeon blessed them and said to Mary, the child's mother, "Behold, this one is placed for the fall and rise of many in Israel; unto a sign of controversy.* ³⁵*He will pierce your own soul as with a sword; so that the thoughts of many hearts may be revealed."* ³⁶*Anna was there, a prophetess, a daughter of Phanuel, of the tribe of Asher. She was advanced in days, having lived in wedlock for seven years from the time of her marriage,* ³⁷*and from then, eighty-four years as a widow. She was constantly not leaving the temple, worshiping night and day with fasting and prayers.* ³⁸*At that moment, she began giving acknowledgment to God and was speaking to everyone who was eagerly waiting for the redemption of Israel.* ³⁹*And when they had completed all ac-*

> *cording to the law of the Lord, they returned to Galilee, unto the city of Nazareth. ⁴⁰The child grew and became strong, becoming full in wisdom. And the grace of God was with him.*

That Luke continued to emphasize the law-abiding commitments of Mary and Joseph comes as no surprise to the astute reader of the narrative. This will remain a dominant theme in Luke. The infancy narrative opened with the child's parents complying with civil authorities and continued with them complying with religious authority.

But Luke was demonstrating more than civil and religious tranquility. Luke showed the Messiah to be in conformity with God's redemptive plan. Mary and Joseph brought Jesus to the temple in order to make the required Mosaic sacrifices. Specifically, they were making the redemption sacrifice. God had said through Moses, "Sanctify unto me all the firstborn, whatsoever openeth the womb among the children of Israel, both of man and of beast: it is mine" (Exod 13:2). The importance of the first-fruit offering was that the first produce or the first off-spring indicated that the crop or specific livestock was in fact fertile, capable of reproducing. Thus the first-fruit was a pledge of sorts that more certainly was to follow. As such, the firstborn of all cattle, sheep, and goats were to be sacrificed and their blood sprinkled on the tent of meetings.

This was not the case with respect to the firstborn child; he or she was to be redeemed. Although the firstborn male was to be considered holy to God, he was not to be sacrificed for an offering. The parents were to pay an estimation and buy back or redeem their child (Num 18:15–18). Mary and Joseph dutifully fulfilled their obligation. But much more than legalism was being demonstrated. God intended from the beginning of time to have fellowship with his creation. This was not possible if the human race did not have free will. The problem with giving humans the ability to choose is humanity invariable seeks its own way and chooses wrongly. Humans always seek to supplant the authority of God in favor of their own ability. Thus with sin marring his creation, God would redeem that which had been intended as perfect but which had strayed and became lost. In short, mankind was created to be redeemed, and God demonstrated the same even with his own Son.

Following the theme of law-abiding citizens, Luke returned to the emphasis of the Holy Spirit. Two examples were given of how to be used by the Holy Spirit, specifically, Simeon and Anna.

The text indicates the Holy Spirit had revealed to Simeon that he would not die before seeing God's Anointed One. This setting in itself is a beautiful statement of what life in the Spirit can mean. Simeon was in such harmony with the presence of God in the world that he could receive this wonderful revelation: He would observe God's salvation unfold.

Several character traits abounded in Simeon that created this fertile, receptive personality. Simeon was righteous and devout, expectant and obedient. That Simeon was righteous, *dikaios*, meant he observed God's laws and kept God's commandments. But more than simple compliance, Simeon's righteousness meant he was pleasing to God. Simeon also was devout. The Greek word translated "devout" is εὐλαβής (*eulabēs*) and "means taking hold well or carefully (*eu* and *labein*) and so reverently, circumspectly."[20] It is used only by Luke in the New Testament. The Jews living in Jerusalem were chosen to participate in the first Pentecost were devout, as were those who buried Steven and Ananias, whom God used to minister to Paul during his conversion (see Luke 2:25; Acts 2:5; 8:2; 22:12). All these individuals can be described as people who were going about their daily business but with an awareness of God's presence around them. These were people who consistently discharged their responsibilities reverently and circumspectly. They were neither flighty nor vagrant. They were stable, dependable, upstanding people. Righteous and devout described people who pleased God and were trustworthy. Such people can be used by the Holy Spirit.

Furthermore, Simeon was expectant and obedient. Notice Luke's description: Simeon was "looking for the consolation of Israel." The word προσδεχόμενος (*prosdexomenos*) is a present middle participle. The word introduces an adjectival phrase that describes Simeon. The phrase modifies what Simeon was, not what he was doing. This is an important distinction to understand. *Looking for the consolation of Israel* was what Simeon was. He was an expectant person. Simeon certainly did many things because he was expectant. He no doubt prayed. He no doubt studied Scripture. He no doubt lived his life as not to be inconsistent with his beliefs. All these activities were born out of his being an expectant person.

While living in Marion, a rural town in west central Alabama, I would frequently walk our dogs, Menno and Matthew, on the immaculate and impressive campus of Judson College. Both dogs were mutts; both

20. Robertson, *Luke*, 27.

chased squirrels. Matthew awoke to a brand-new world every day. Every day he chewed the newspaper, not remembering from the day before that there was nothing particularly palatable in the local print. Matthew would see squirrels, give chase, never getting very close. Menno, on the other hand, always came close, and occasionally won his contest. I loved both of these pets dearly for they truly had their own personalities. The secret to Menno's frequent success was this: He always began running *before* he saw the squirrel! Being expectant has its advantages.

Additionally, Simeon was obedient. Verse 27 indicates that he came "in the spirit" to the temple. The prepositional phrase ἐν τῷ πνεύματι (*en tōi pneumati*) indicates the cause of the main action—in this case, Simeon's traveling to the temple. Sensitive to the leadership of the Holy Spirit, Simeon obeyed the impulse of the Spirit and complied. What would have been the result of a delay? Mary and Joseph had limited time in the temple. Their business completed, they would have returned home, and Simeon would have missed the opportunity to have seen the Messiah. Righteous and devout, expectant and obedient, Simeon had positioned himself to be used by the Holy Spirit.

Far from receiving only a personal reward, Simeon was used to convey important truths regarding the nature of Messiah. (1) Simeon indicated the Messiah would be for the rise and fall of many in Israel. "This is a strange and a hard saying but it is true. It is not so much God who judges a man; a man judges himself; and his judgment is his reaction to Jesus Christ."[21] The same concept is repeated in John 3 where judgment is defined as choosing darkness over light. A person relegates himself or herself to the shadows of God's great desires rather than embracing fully all that God is and all that God seeks to accomplish. (2) Simeon indicated the universal mission of the Messiah. In addition to demonstrating the law-abiding practices of the Gospel's adherents, in addition to demonstrating the inclusion of the social outcasts, Luke specifically demonstrated that the Messiah had come to save the entire world, not just the Jewish people. Simeon said that the Messiah had been prepared for all people (Luke 2:31) and a light of revelation for the Gentiles. Luke clearly positioned the church to continue the mandate of Christ to evangelize the entire world.

---

21. Barclay, *The Gospel of Luke*, 21.

Either a widow of 84 years or an 84-year-old widow,[22] Anna was a Jewish woman of noble birth. The text makes an unusual assertion about Anna that is difficult to capture in modern English translations. Verse 37 indicates that she "departed not from the temple" (Luke 2:37, ASV, KJV) or that she "never left the temple." (Luke 2:37, NASB, NIV).

What these translations gain in smooth English, they lose in accuracy. The Greek text, οὐκ ἀφίστατο τοῦ ἱεροῦ (*ouk aphistato tou hierou*), uses an imperfect tense verb that expresses continuous action in past time. A literal translation would render the phrase *kept on not leaving the temple*. There should be no doubt that Luke intended this awkward construction to emphasize the situation. Not being involved in service to God was in no way an option for Anna. Furthermore, anyone desiring to be used by God's Holy Spirit should constantly not be leaving God's presence. That she was in the temple, worshiping through fasting and prayers, positioned her to catch a glimpse of God's eternal plan. Upon seeing Jesus, she burst into the conversation with uncontrolled praise of God. Found almost exclusively in the Books of Luke and Acts, ἐφίστημι (*ephistēmi*) and its related word forms can be translated literally as *place upon* or *stand by*. In use the word group conveys urgency or sudden action as when the angel appeared to the shepherds (Luke 2:9) or when Martha, frustrated over Mary's lack of assistance, burst into the conversation to question why her sister felt no domestic obligation (Luke 10:40). Anna's perception of God's activity led her to engage in speaking about Christ enthusiastically.

THE ADOLESCENT JESUS

Luke 2:41–52

[41] It came to pass that every year Jesus' parents went to Jerusalem for the Passover Feast. [42] When he was twelve, they went up, as was their custom. [43] When the days of the feast were completed, the boy Jesus remained during their return. But his parents did not know it. [44] Supposing him to be in the company, they went a day's journey and then began searching for him among the relatives and acquaintances. [45] Not finding him, they returned to

---

22. It is impossible to tell from the grammar of the text if Luke intended to count consecutively or cumulatively.

> *Jerusalem, still looking everywhere for him. ⁴⁶It happened that on the third day they found him in the temple, sitting in the midst of the teachers, listening to them, and asking them questions. ⁴⁷All who heard him were astounded by his understanding and his answers. ⁴⁸Seeing him, they were overwhelmed and his mother said to him, "Child, why have you treated us in such a manner? Look at me! Your father and I have been frantically seeking you." ⁴⁹And he replied, "Why were you seeking me? Did you not know that it was essential that I be in my father's house?" ⁵⁰But they did not understand the words that he had spoken to them. ⁵¹He went down with them and went to Nazareth and he was submissive to them. His mother stored up safely all these things in her heart. ⁵²Jesus progressed in wisdom, grew physically, and gained more and more grace with God and his fellow man.*

Perhaps one of the more misunderstood passages in Scripture, the challenge of interpreting Jesus' journey to Jerusalem at age twelve revolves around the humanity of Jesus. Modern Christianity has little problem grasping the divinity of Christ. The church easily places Jesus together with the father creating all things before time began. The church readily sees Jesus miraculously walking on water and controlling the forces of nature as he commanded the storm to cease. In truth, the church rarely has a problem understanding Jesus as divine but often fails to grasp his humanity. Out of respect, fear, admiration, and awe, the church fails to ascribe to Jesus the fullness of humanity as he was born, grew, and eventually died. The church ascribes Jesus' power to his divinity rather than understanding the potential of a person who is in a complete unfettered relationship with God the Father.

Much of this dilemma can be traced to the misunderstanding of Luke 2:41–52. This section of Scripture is the only glimpse of Jesus' adolescent years. Part of a devout Jewish family, Jesus attended the feast of the Passover with his parents. No attention is given to the time spent in Jerusalem while at the feast. Instead, the narrative focuses on the departure from Jerusalem. Both parents assumed incorrectly that Jesus was with the other. Not until evening when Mary and Joseph were together did they realize what had happened. Jesus' earthly parents immediately began backtracking their steps in hopes of finding their "lost" son. The text indicates Mary and Joseph did not find Jesus until the third day.

Logic would dictate they spent one day (or most of a night) returning to Jerusalem, leaving an unprofitable search for two more days and nights.

Then after three days, Jesus was found in the temple. It is here, in verses 46, 47, and 49 that the controversy of this event truly centers. Jesus was in the temple, engaged in dialogue with the Jewish scholars, and said when questioned by his mother, "Didn't you know that I would be in my father's house?"

A very traditional view on the meaning of these verses contributes to the misunderstanding of Jesus' humanity by the modern church. The view would not be uncommon that ascribed to Jesus divine knowledge about all things godly and scriptural. Accordingly, young Jesus was there in the temple, setting straight the Pharisees' errant views of the law, the prophets and the writings. This view is supported by his reply to his mother that revealed his knowledge of his true identity—not the son of a carpenter as everyone had been led to believe for twelve years but the son of God.

However, if this were true, why did Jesus grow? Why would it have been necessary for Luke to record verse 52: "Jesus progressed in wisdom, grew physically, and gained more and more grace with God and his fellow man"? What other possible explanation could there be for Jesus' self-acknowledged special filial relationship to God? The answer to these questions grasps the full meaning of the incarnation and affirms that Jesus was in fact human, that he did in fact suffer the normal frailties as a member of the human race, and that he grew and matured just like everyone else.

Note the following: According to ancient sources, a typical Hebrew boy would begin to study Scripture at age five by learning to read Hebrew, using as his primer selections from the Old Testament. At age ten he would begin reading the Mishna. This was the oral law, also known as the tradition of the fathers. The Torah would be studied at age thirteen and Talmud[23] studies at fifteen. The final level of scholarship would be professional studies that were not available to the entire population. This would begin at eighteen, the age of normal marriage.[24]

Given this understanding, the verses in question take on the description of ideal maturation. In verse 46 Luke depicted Jesus as "sitting

---

23. The Talmud was the codified Mishna and Gamarah (the commentary on the Mishna). These volumes were regional. During the first century there was a well-established Palestinian Talmud as well as an Alexandrian Talmud.

24. McCasland, "Education, NT," 36.

in the midst of the teachers, listening to them, and asking them questions." Unlike the Gnostic Gospel of Thomas where Jesus silenced the teachers and elders and began instructing them regarding the true nature of God, Luke's narrative reveals nothing supernatural in the progression of Jesus' development—certainly advanced, clearly remarkable, but not supernatural. One should expect that Mary and Joseph, knowing Jesus' true identity, were at least as attentive to the normal educational customs and values incorporated into the cultural expectations of other devout Jews of the day. Accordingly, by the time Jesus went to the temple at age twelve one may expect that Jesus had in fact learned to read Hebrew, had learned the stories of the patriarchs, had learned the Torah, and also progressed to studies of the Talmud. If one is committed to reading the biblical text, not reading into the text, the clear picture begins to emerge. Luke indicated nothing except that Jesus was in the temple, listening to the scholars and asking them questions. A. T. Robertson pointed out that they were "probably on the terrace where members of the Sanhedrin gave public instruction on Sabbaths and feast-days."[25]

Luke continued the description in verse 47 where he said all were amazed at his understanding and at the questions he asked. Rabbinic argument frequently followed the course of posing hypothetical questions that routinely begged a stock response. This response would then be used as the basis for the next question and so on. Additionally, precedence for arguments would be established by calling a well-traded series of questions that had been coined by a revered elder of the past. What was remarkable to those observing was not that Jesus presented any new argument but that he demonstrated a command of biblical knowledge that was advanced for his age. If in fact Jesus had already begun Talmud studies at age twelve and not at eighteen, people would have marveled. Such has always been the case of a child prodigy. Nothing in the text indicates Jesus' comprehension exceeded that of the teachers of the law.

Finally, great concern is often expressed over the phrase in verse 49, "Did you not know that it was essential that I be in my father's house?" While the literal translation reads *Father's things*, which explains the King James Version rendering of "Father's business," study of Lukan Hebraism indicates that "Father's House" is in fact the correct translation.[26] Certainly those who wish to articulate the deity of Christ at the

---

25. Robertson, *Luke*, 33.

26. A similar construction is found in Genesis 41:51 (LXX) where Joseph referred to the naming of Manasseh with the expressions "For God hath made me forget all my

expense of his humanity will point to this verse as the inauguration of Jesus' earthly ministry by asserting Jesus' self-acclaimed identity as referenced by being in his Father's house.

The mistake this interpretation makes is that it completely discounts what should be viewed as a normal outcome of the caring, nurturing, teaching environment in which Jesus was raised. When Jesus acknowledged the importance of being in his Father's house, was he revealing a special filial consciousness that mandated a personal obligation to fulfill the will of God? Without a doubt! Should there be any less filial consciousness and sense of obligation to fulfill God's will for any child of God who was raised in a Christian home and nurtured through biblically oriented, Christ-centered instruction? None whatsoever! For the incarnation to be valid, God must have emptied himself of divinity in the person of Jesus and become completely human, subject to the limitations of maturation and constraints of the human condition. As such, Jesus' experience provides for us a model after which we must strive. If through love, diligence, and consistent instruction Jesus grew in his understanding that God was placing demands upon his life, through Christian homes and God- honoring churches, we can bring a new generation of children to the same place of life-changing commitment to God and to Christ's kingdom.

THE MESSAGE OF JOHN THE BAPTIST

Luke 3:1-6

> ¹*The word of the Lord came to John the son of Zachariah in the wilderness in the fifteenth year of Tiberius Caesar, when Pontius Pilate was governor of Judea, Herod was tetrarch of Galilee, Herod's brother, Philip, was tetrarch of Ituraea and Trachonitis, Lysanias was tetrarch of Abilene,* ²*and Annas and Caiaphas were high priests.* ³*John went into all the region of Judea, proclaiming baptism unto the remission of sins.* ⁴*As it had been written in the Book of Isaiah the prophet: A voice crying in the wilderness; Prepare the way of the Lord, make straight his paths.* ⁵*Every valley will be made full and every mountain and hill will be made low. The crooked will be straight and the rough places smooth,* ⁶*and all*

---

toil, and all my father's house."

flesh will see the salvation of God.

Following a typical Lucan description of the historic setting,[27] the Gospel returns to the development of a character already introduced. John the Baptist reemerged into the plot following the infancy and adolescent narrative of Jesus. No other details of John's life are presented. The story moved from his birth by the aged Elizabeth and Zachariah to his ministry. John simply appeared in the region of the Jordan, delivering the message of an itinerate preacher.

It is John's message that is unique in Luke, not his description of clothing and diet that is seen elsewhere in the Synoptic Gospels (Matt 3:4). Luke presented John as "proclaiming baptism unto the remission of sins." This is a stark contrast to the angels' message delivered to the shepherds. Rather than the heavenly host's declaration of εὐαγγελίζω (*euangelizō*), literally translated "good news," John *proclaimed* repentance was necessary to enter the kingdom. "Proclamation," κηρύσσω (*kērussō*) is distinguished from "good news" in that the message delivered by the communicator could be positive or negative. Jesus proclaimed a positive message when he quoted Isaiah 61: "The Spirit of the Lord *is* upon me, because he hath anointed me to preach the gospel to the poor; he hath sent me to heal the brokenhearted, to preach deliverance to the captives, and recovering of sight to the blind, to set at liberty them that are bruised, To preach the acceptable year of the Lord" (Luke 4:18–19).

However, the proclamation of the gospel also necessitates confrontation and even condemnation. While the angelic message of inclusion that was so prevalent in εὐαγγελίζω (*euangelizō*) was continued in this declaration, Luke used the proclamation of John to set the stage for a shifting reality: The kingdom of heaven is at hand, and it is unlike anything that has gone before.

The stipulation for kingdom entry that John presented was baptism unto the repentance of sin. The Jews practiced ritual purification. These baptisms were intended to keep the participants ceremonially pure. Other evidence in the New Testament suggests that John may have

---

27. Luke's time frame includes the following: fifteenth year of Tiberius (AD 14 to AD 37); Pontius Pilate, governor of Judea (AD 26 to 36); Herod Antipas, tetrarch of Galilee (4 BC to AD 39); Herod Philip, the half-brother of Antipas, tetrarch of Northern Trans-Jordan region (4 BC to 33/34); Lysanias of Abilene (Dates extant); Caiaphas, high priest (AD 18 to 36). All these dates range from BC 4 to AD 39. The fifteenth year of Tiberius narrows the focus of these ranges to AD 28/29.

lived in one of the Essene communities in southern Judea, similar to the Qumran community. Tremendous insight into first-century Judaism has been learned from studying the manner in which these separatist Jews practiced their religion, including the ways they intentionally withdrew from the accepted practices of orthodox Jews. It could well be that John arrived in the Jordan area after spending much of his adult life in one or more of these extreme religious practices. Having seen the abuses of the mainstream and of the radical right, John proclaimed only one way into God's presence, that being baptism that involved not ritual purification, not customs and ceremonies, but true repentance.

Luke defined the concept of repentance in four ways. (1) John proclaimed his message of repentance in terms of the hope expressed in Isaiah 40:3–5. In his wonderful work on Isaiah in *The Cambridge Bible for Schools and Colleges*, Skinner said, "This is a passage of singular beauty, breathing the spirit of new-born hope and enthusiasm with which the prophet enters on his work. The announcement of a miraculous restoration of the exiles to their own land is the central theme of his prophecy, and the point around which all the ideas of the book crystallize."[28] Skinner captured the hope that is born within repentance. Assuming his audience would hear these beloved words with the same emotion and identification, John called people to return from the exile of sin and despair to the new kingdom God had prepared—a kingdom of hope and inclusion that required a change of heart.

(2) The phrase "prepare the way" means to remove all obstacles from a path. Such was the case when Laban invited Eliezer into his home (Gen 24:31). Such was the case when the high priest examined the home of the leper who had been healed (Lev 14:36). Such was the case in Malachi's messianic expectation of the return to the temple (Mal 3:1). Each of these examples illustrates the importance of removing obstacles that would prevent the event at hand. Each deals with significant, life-altering moments where the individual would never be the same again, a watershed point to which people could return in their minds over and over again.

(3) Repentance is a complete reversal of identity, of way of life, and of behavior. Each of the examples of the poetic prophecy involved a complete turnaround: valleys, mountains, crooked and rough are re-

---

28. Skinner, The Book of the Prophet Isaiah Chapters XL-LXVI, 1.

versed. The word for repentance, μετανοίας (*metanoias*), literally means "to change one's mind."

(4) Finally, Luke showed the penitent to be incapable of accomplishing the end results of repentance on their own. While personal responsibility certainly is not to be ignored, one should note that the mountains do not level themselves, the valleys do not fill themselves. Rather, both are made level and made full. In its final reality, repentance enables people to be changed, not to change themselves.

JOHN AND CONTEMPORARY RELIGION

Luke 3:7–14

⁷John said to the crowds that were coming out to be baptized by him, "You offspring of vipers! Who warned you to flee from the coming wrath? ⁸You should produce fruit worthy of repentance and do not start saying to yourselves, 'We have Abraham as our father.' For I say to you that God is able to raise children of Abraham out of these stones. ⁹Indeed, already, the ax has been laid to the root of the tree. Every tree that does not bear good fruit is being cut down and is being thrown into the fire." ¹⁰And the crowds were asking him saying, "What, therefore, are we to do?" ¹¹He answered them saying, "The one having two coats should hand over one to he who has none. The one having food do likewise. ¹²Tax collectors came to him to be baptized and said to John, "Teacher, what should we do?" ¹³And he said to them, "Not one thing more than you are commanded are you to exact." ¹⁴Even those in military service asked, "And we, what are we to do?" And he said to them, "Extort money neither by force nor false statement and be content with your wages."

Following the poetic description of John's message of repentance is the stinging reality of the inevitable confrontation between the expectations of a righteous God and the excuses of a religious humanity. No doubt a term of derision, brood of vipers could be translated "generation of snakes." The word for generation, γεννήματα (*gennēmata*), has a technical sense found neither in Luke nor the rest of the New Testament. John the Baptist may have intended a play on the concept of Abraham's generation. Regardless, John showed no preferential treatment simply due to ethnic background.

Rather than heritage, John insisted on genuine and sincere responses to the message of repentance. The aorist passive infinitive, βαπτισθῆναι (*baptisthēnai*), indicates purpose of action. "To be baptized" was the reason for the crowds coming up to John. Yet John clearly stated that baptism without conviction, remorse, repentance, and response was inappropriate. Only repentance had efficacy. John called for a life-changing event that could be demonstrated by tangible means— bear fruit worthy of repentance. Without genuine change, the self-trusting, religiously minded could expect one thing: destruction. The ax was laid to the root. John's image is not that there will be loss but destruction. Beginning with the root and moving out, there would be complete destruction.

What follows are four indicators that true repentance has occurred. Two are viewed in the reactions of the people while two are taken from John.

(1) The inquiries of the penitent were repetitious. Luke indicated that the crowds "were asking" what was required of them. The imperfect tense verb ἐπηρώτων (*epērōtōn*) could be translated "they were repeatedly asking" or "they kept on asking." The imperfect tense carries the meaning of continuous action in the past tense. Many parents can look back on tenacious two-, three-, and four-year-olds and understand the meaning of the imperfect tense. They were (past time) always (continuous action) up to something! John's followers heard his declaration of God's demands and were touched at the very core of their beings. Nothing would do but to take the next step. They would not stop asking what had to happen next. The cavalier attitude of the modern world may reflect insecurity, but sadly it also reflects a lack of urgency when the message of Christ is delivered.

(2) Not only was the truly penitent's response repeated but it also was a direct result of the message. There was no bait and switch. There was no false impression or misunderstanding, only true conviction. The people were continuously asking "What, *therefore*, are we to do?" A. T. Robertson identified this construction as a deliberative aorist subjunctive.[29] Specifically, even though there was uncertainty as to their future action (subjunctive mode), the insertion of the οὖν (*oun*), a particle that simply shows sequence or consequence, makes the phrase deliberative.

---

29. Robertson, *Luke*, 39.

There was an action to follow as a result of what they had heard. At the time, they were not sure what action, but something was about to happen. The particle οὖν (*oun*) may be translated "therefore." Luke's point was that all that they heard, therefore, pressed them forward. "So, what are we to do now?" One identifying characteristic of true repentance is that the message internalized becomes the driving force for future action.

(3) When confronting the superficial attitudes of the contemporary religious crowd, John asked, "Who warned you to flee the coming wrath?" "Warned" is an interesting word choice. Used only once outside of Luke and Acts, the word ὑπέδειξεν (*hupedeixen*) is found in Matthew's rendering of this same incident (see Matt 3:7). In the sermon on the plain, Jesus prefaced his description of the man who built his house on the rock as *I will show you what everyone coming to me and listening to my words and practices doing them is like* (Luke 6:47). Luke used the word only four other times. Specifically, after directing disciples not to fear the religious leaders who could incarcerate them, Jesus said, *I will show you how to fear: fear him who condemns the body and soul* (Luke 12:5). When God directed Ananias to visit Paul, he said, "I will show him what great things he must suffer for my name's sake" (Acts 9:16). Finally, at the conclusion of his sermon to the Ephesian elders, Paul said, "I have showed you all things, how that by working you ought to support the weak, and to remember the words of the Lord Jesus, how he said, It is more blessed to give than to receive" (Acts 20:35). Clearly John's "who warned you" comes from the message and not the medium. The Pharisees had not been warned. They had been informed of what was happening out in the Judean wilderness. John asked, "Who told you that you better flee the coming wrath?" The warning is implied. True repentance comes as the message carries its own consequences.

(4) Finally, true repentance changes a person's relationships. Note carefully the fruits that are described by John as worthy of repentance. Give shelter to those less fortunate than you. Provide food for those who are without food. Do not use your influence to take advantage of others simply because you can. Be content with what you have, and see that you use your resources to lift the lives of others. John was forcing the penitent to acknowledge the needs of others. All around them that day must have been real people with real needs. One clear example of fruits worthy of repentance was to care for others more than self.

JOHN TESTIFIES ABOUT JESUS

Luke 3:15–20

¹⁵*Now all the people were in expectation and so they all began wondering in their hearts whether or not John was the Christ.* ¹⁶*John answered every one of them saying, "I indeed baptize you in water, but he who is coming is mightier than me; one whose sandal I am not worthy to loosen. He will baptize you in the Holy Spirit and fire.* ¹⁷*His winnowing fork is in his hand to clean his threshing floor and to gather his wheat into his barn, but the chaff will be burned with unquenchable fire."* ¹⁸*With many other encouragements, he delivered good news to the people.* ¹⁹*But Herod the tetrarch, having been rebuked by John on account of Herodotus, his brother's wife, and on account of all the other misdeeds Herod had done,* ²⁰*Herod added all these things together and put John in prison.*

John never compromised the message that caused people to come in droves seeking baptism of repentance. They knew there was something different about John's message. They knew it was not the same old, tired and empty insistence on ceremony and ritual. They knew there was new life in the message, even as difficult as it was. John never wavered regarding the demands of the gospel but added good news.

Notice in the life of John the consequence of adding good news to the insistence on repentance. People wondered if John was the Messiah. Modern readers should not be quick to write off as uniformed and misguided the Jewish anticipation of "the coming one." Theirs was a deep and sincere longing for God to intervene in their lives and usher in divine control. The modern church should be so anticipatory! Two millennia have caused hearts to grow cold. Affluence has caused expectations to wane. Yet oppressed people are always given over to hope and eager anticipation. The Jews had endured centuries of oppression and wanted God to act on their behalf.

In their expectation, they did, however, mistake the message of John as the message of Messiah. They knew the Messiah would represent God. They knew the Messiah would tell them all things. They knew the Messiah would usher in a new world order. And they heard these things in John. When Christians stand in the midst of the lost and dying world and proclaim good news without compromising repentance, they too will be identified with Christ. But the converse of this truth must not be ignored. When the lost world does not hear in our words the message of Messiah, when they do not see in our actions the methods of the Messiah, it is time for the church to re-examine both its methods and message. The church always must adapt its methods to meet the needs of society without altering the message of salvation grace through faith.

THE BAPTISM AND GENEALOGY OF JESUS

Luke 3:21-22

²¹And it happened when all the people were baptized and Jesus had been baptized and was praying that the heavens opened ²²and the Holy Spirit, in a bodily form like a dove, descended upon him. A voice came from heaven, "You are my beloved Son. In You I am well pleased."

At least two approaches can be taken to the baptism of Jesus. (1) Jesus knew himself to be the unique Son of God. As such he was sinless and did not need John's baptism of repentance. Given this understanding, the reader may understand Jesus' actions as both validation and identification. By his action Jesus validated John's message. This makes Jesus' baptism an endorsement of John's entire message. Furthermore, Jesus' baptism was intended to identify his activity with the work and ministry of John, or more specifically, to identify Jesus' actions with the kingdom of God on earth as preached by John. This approach fits well with those who see in the adolescent narrative a fully formed understanding on the part of Jesus of his unique relation to the Heavenly Father. At age twelve, Jesus knew himself to be the sinless Son of God. Accordingly, he was to be about his Father's business. However, this view does leave the reader without an answer to the question regarding Jesus' activity during the intervening eighteen years if in fact Jesus knew at age twelve what he was to do.

(2) Luke gave his readers a glimpse of the "coming of age" of the Messiah. In this case, there are several high watermarks in Jesus' own understanding of who he was. Rather than a supernatural existence where he knew at age twelve that he was immortal God, Jesus demonstrated how every believer learns of God's perfect will. Through time

spent with God, the believer begins to understand his or her true relation as a child. Jesus' understanding was advanced, to be sure. But taken without augmentation, Luke presented Jesus in the temple, expressing a longing for the things of God he did not yet know, an innate comprehension that was present yet mysterious. Luke portrayed Jesus hearing the message and ministry of John and being strangely drawn to the same. When he heard the message, Jesus too knew he was to be involved in what God was doing. Far from simply joining the emotive hysteria of the crowd, Jesus somehow knew he was on the right path. Luke omitted John's objection of Jesus' request for baptism (Matt 3:14) and so offered no explanation to his readers for whom Jesus' lack of need for a baptism of repentance would not have been an issue. To this point in the narrative, Jesus was a God-fearing Jew, raised by law-abiding, religiously attentive parents. Jesus had shown a perception of God that was beyond his years and was responsive to the message that a new means of serving and worshiping God was near. According to Luke, Jesus was starting to understand who he was and what God expected of him, an identity that would come into sharper focus via the temptation in the wilderness.

What is not open for debate is the heavenly response to Jesus' action. Regardless of Jesus' intention in requesting and receiving baptism, the heavens opened with a visible display and an auditory affirmation. The Spirit, taking the form of a dove, descended and rested on Jesus. In that moment, Jesus' identity came into focus on hearing the heavenly affirmation. "You are my Son," said the voice. If Jesus was uncertain before that moment, he was no longer.

LUKE'S GENEALOGY OF JESUS

Luke 3:23–38

²³Jesus began his ministry when he was about thirty years old, being the supposed son of Joseph, the son of Heli, ²⁴the son of Matthat, the son of Levi, the son of Melchi, the son of Jannai, the son of Joseph, ²⁵the son of Mattathias, the son of Amos, the son of Nahum, the son of Esli, the son of Naggai, ²⁶the son of Maath, the son of Mattathias, the son of Semein, the son of Josech, the son of Joda, ²⁷the son of Joanan, the son of Rhesa, the son of Zerubbabel, the son of Shealtiel, the son of Neri, ²⁸the son of Melchi, the son of Addi, the son of Cosam, the son of Elmadam, the son of Er, ²⁹the son of Joshua, the son of Eliezer, the son of Jorim, the son of Matthat, the son of Levi, ³⁰the son of Simeon, the son of Judah, the son of Joseph, the son of Jonam, the son of Eliakim, ³¹the son of Melea, the son of Menna, the son of Mattatha, the son of Nathan, the son of David, ³²the son of Jesse, the son of Obed, the son of Boaz, the son of Sala, the son of Nahshon, ³³the son of Amminadab, the son of Admin, the son of Arni, the son of Hezron, the son of Perez, the son of Judah, ³⁴the son of Jacob, the son of Isaac, the son of Abraham, the son of Terah, the son of Nahor, ³⁵the son of Serug, the son of Reu, the son of Peleg, the son of Eber, the son of Shelah, ³⁶the son of Cainan, the son of Arphaxad, the son of Shem, the son of Noah, the son of Lamech, ³⁷the son of Methuselah, the son of Enoch, the son of Jared, the son of Mahalaleel, the son of Cainan, ³⁸the son of Enos, the son of Seth, the son of Adam, the son of God.

Unlike Matthew's genealogy that related Jesus to Joseph, Luke showed Jesus' ancestry related to Adam. Clearly Luke intended to convey that salvation is available for all people through the person and work of Christ, not only the Jews who had been in relationship with God for centuries. Gentiles too could be secure in their faith because of the life and work of Jesus.

JESUS' TEMPTATION IN THE WILDERNESS

Luke 4:1-13

¹Now Jesus, filled with the Holy Spirit, returned from the Jordan and was led by the Spirit ²into the wilderness for forty days, being tempted by the Devil. He ate nothing during those days. When the days were finished, he was hungry. ³The Devil said to him, "If you are the Son of God (and we both know you are), command these stones that they become bread." ⁴Jesus answered him, "It is written: not by bread alone will man live." ⁵Then leading him up, he showed him all the kingdoms of the world in a moment of time. ⁶And the Devil said to him, "I will give to you the authority of all of these, and their glory; because they have been delivered to me and I may give them to whomever

I desire. ⁷If, therefore, you bow down before me, it will all be yours." ⁸Jesus answered and said to him, "It is written: You will worship the Lord your God, and him only will you serve." ⁹ Next he took him to Jerusalem and stood him on the highest point of the temple and he said to him, "If you are the Son of God (and we both know you are), throw yourself down from here. ¹⁰For it is written: His angels will be given charge concerning you, to preserve you from harm; ¹¹they will lift you in their hands so that you will not strike your foot against a stone." ¹²Jesus answered and said to him, "It has been spoken: You are prohibited from testing the Lord your God." ¹³When all these temptations were finished, the Devil left him until a significant moment.

Jesus' temptation in the wilderness occurred immediately after the baptism experience. The reader is correct to connect Jesus' becoming aware of his unique relation to the Father with the temptation experience. This is not two stories (baptism/temptation) but rather one continuous event where Jesus grew in his understanding of who he was and who God expected him to be.

Luke transitioned into the next phase of the baptism/temptation event by connecting these stories via the theme of the indwelling Holy Spirit. Prominent in the stories of Elizabeth and Mary, Zachariah and John, the Spirit was present again in Jesus' baptism and the temptation. Regarding the former, the visible presence of the Spirit announced Jesus' identity and the Father's approval. With the latter, Jesus was led by the Spirit into the wilderness. Specifically, Luke employed the imperfect tense to convey continuous action in past time. Additionally, the passive voice of ἤγετο (ēgeto) renders the translation "was being continuously led." With the occurrence of Jesus' self-awareness and confirmation of the temptation, Jesus was shown to be constantly under the guidance of the Spirit. From this point on in the narrative, Luke depicted that Jesus was led continuously by the Spirit, always garnering his Heavenly Father's approval.

The sequence that follows is important in understanding Luke's articulation of Jesus' self-identification as Messiah. Unlike Matthew's depiction that implies the temptations were at the conclusion of the 40 days, Luke stated that Jesus was being led and tempted for 40 days. It is impossible to know if these are the only temptations during this period or if these were merely selected samples of Jesus' experience while in the wilderness. What is clear is that these are the events that Luke chose to make his point. Again, taken as a continuation of the identification as the Son of God at the baptism, the temptation event continued to pull back the veil on Jesus' understanding of his role in the Father's plan. As such, the specificity of the temptations reveals Jesus' thoughts and concerns.

In addition to the importance of Luke's choice of events is his grammatical depiction of the dialogue between Jesus and Satan. In verse 3, Satan posed the temptation via a first class conditional sentence. There are four classes of conditions in Greek grammar, each with a *protasis* and an *apodosis*. The *protasis* is the "if" clause or condition. The *apodosis* is the "then" clause or conclusion. In the first class conditional, the *protasis* is introduced by the conjunction *ei*, followed by any tense in the indicative mode in the *protasis* and the *apodosis*. The importance of this issue is that the first class conditional sentence assumes the condition is fulfilled; the statement of the if clause, or condition, is factually true (or at least assumed true). Accordingly, the translation becomes *If you are the Son of God, and we both know that this is true, then command these stones to become bread*. Again, Luke clearly intended to demonstrate Jesus' awareness of his divine self-identity. The mastery of Luke's Gospel is that this assertion of Jesus' identify is couched in the narrative that unquestionably maintains the importance of Jesus' humanity. God/Man was now the central figure of the gospel; the good news that was proclaimed by angels, anticipated by those who longed for God's control, and set in opposition to the hypocritical religious establishment yet necessary as the only means of achieving redemption in God.

Before addressing how Jesus' temptations defined his self-proclaimed identity as the God/Man, several matters should be observed.

(1) Satan tempted Christ with good things. In order, the temptations were to turn stones to bread, to rule the world, and to demonstrate God's power and glory. In other words, these three addressed first food, clothing and shelter, followed by esteem, and finally self-actualization. Familiar to many as Maslow's Hierarchy of Needs, the pyramid can be described in a variety of ways. All carry the same force; no one is concerned with higher issues when basic needs have not been met. As one moves upward, the needs become loftier and less tangible. Certainly the temptations follow this process. "Turn these stones to bread. You are a man. You must be hungry," said Satan. Next Satan turned to Jesus' desire to rule in the hearts

of mankind. In an instant, he showed Jesus all the kingdoms of the world. Used only here in the New Testament, στιγμῇ (*stigmē*) indicates Jesus saw the entire inhabited world in a moment of time, an instant, a split second. Nothing was held back. Satan offered Jesus everything. Finally, even Jesus' desire to glorify his Heavenly father was placed in the crucible of temptation. "Throw yourself down and realize your ultimate self-awareness as God's son whom God has sworn to protect," chided Satan.

What the temptations attacked were elements of basic human character. We all need basic necessities of life. There is not only nothing wrong with providing these needs but they are also often commanded in Scripture. Paul told Timothy that anyone who did not provide for his family was worse than an infidel (1 Tim 5:8). Jesus' choice of activities he used to describe his followers was that he was naked and they clothed him and hungry and they fed him (Matt 25:35–36). Furthermore, influencing the hearts of men and glorifying God represent not only noble but also desirable qualities and normal human desires. Satan attempted to take what was good and decent and twist them into something evil. The nature of all temptation is viewed in this point. God gives all things for good; Satan perverts what God intends to be pleasing and rewarding. One need look no further than human sexuality to see the perfect example. God created man and woman and gave them the ability and inclination to enjoy each other. The evil of the world has taken what was given as pleasing, substituted a different context, altered the motivations, and created a trap that ensnares the inattentive.

(2) Jesus battled temptation by quoting Scripture. An element of his earlier years was evident in that Jesus had the mental discipline to memorize Scripture. Growing as a child, Jesus heard the Scriptures taught, memorized them, later read them, and as a result, learned the Scripture and applied the same to daily life. Most importantly, Jesus did so in such a manner that when the need came to trust God, he was prepared. "Study to show thyself approved unto God," Paul said to Timothy (2 Tim 2:15). "Thy word have I hid in mine heart that I might not sin against thee," David said (Ps 119:11). Joshua commanded, "This book of the law shall not depart out of thy mouth; but thou shalt meditate therein day and night, that thou mayest observe to do according to all that is written therein" (Josh 1:8). The Christian today should be no less diligent.

(3) When Jesus resisted, Satan left him, but only until a more significant moment. Two distinctively different lessons must be understood

from this portion of Jesus' temptation story. The first is that Satan left. "Resist the Devil and he will flee from you" (James 4:7). "There hath no temptation taken you but such as is common to man: but God *is* faithful, who will not suffer you to be tempted above that ye are able; but will with the temptation also make a way to escape, that ye may be able to bear it" (1 Cor 10:13). Jesus is our model. When we resist temptation with God's help, we will have victory over sin.

The second issue is regrettably inevitable; Satan never stays away. In American cinematography, there have been momentous films where actors and actresses caught a moment so perfectly that the performer became tagged with the phrase. Mae West shocked society in the 1933 film *She Done Him Wrong* with her suggestive phrase "Why don't you come up and see me some time?" *Casablanca* included Humphrey Bogart's "Here's looking at you, kid." Film making forever changed following Clark Gabel's portrayal of Rhett Butler with his controversial profanity. Much later, Renee Zellweger captured the romantic moment in *Jerry McQuire* with "You had me from hello."

For different reasons, another unexpected memorialized phase sprung from the lips of Arnold Schwarzenegger, former governor of the great state of California. Perhaps because of his heavy Austrian accent the young Mr.-Olympus-turned-actor had few spoken lines in MGM's film, *The Terminator*. In his debut as the futurist cybernetic organism sent through time to execute the mother of the soon-to-be opposition leader, the character delivered a line that became his trademark. A phrase that would be repeated in jest and in parody in many of his later works, the Terminator said, "I'll be back."

While temptation is not to be trivialized, demonic destruction and devastation always come back. As long as Christ's return is delayed, Christians will struggle to overcome human nature and its inclination to sin. Furthermore, the text specifically indicated Satan left until "an opportune moment." Not without purpose and not without specific intent will temptation return. At the moment of greatest weakness, the temptation will return. At the most inappropriate event, temptation will return.

(4) Finally, the temptation of Jesus is direct dialogue. No one was there to observe the event, save Jesus himself. Christians through the ages have possessed these pivotal stories not because the early church recognized their importance, which certainly was true. There were no twelve disciples there to chronicle what happened and thereby preserve

the oral tradition. Rather, the church cherishes to this day these extraordinary events because one day Jesus turned to those around him and said, "Let me tell you what happened to me. Let me share how I overcame that problem. Let me help you understand the nature of God seeking to find expression in sinful flesh. And oh, by the way, if I can do it, so can you."

Given these observations, the picture comes into focus regarding the self-identification of the God/Man.

(1) Jesus was completely human, capable of sinning and thereby falling out of fellowship with the Father. Note specifically the second temptation: "If you bow down and worship me." The grammar presents a third class conditional sentence. Unlike the first class mentioned previously, the third class states the condition is undetermined but with possibility of fulfillment. In the first class, the reader understood that Satan and Jesus both knew Jesus was God. *If you are the Son of God, and we both know you are, command these stones to become bread.* This temptation is followed by the next, *If you will worship me, I will . . .* The grammar of the sentence mandates the conclusion that the outcome of the condition was unknown. Neither Satan nor Jesus knew the outcome of the temptation prior to Jesus' response. Failing the temptations was a real possibility. This was not an exercise in futility. For the Scripture to be inspired, one must allow that Jesus could have sinned. The only way this could take place was that his humanity was real. One should not ignore his divinity. But one must accept his humanity. To fail to believe the former robs humanity of a God who is willing to do anything to redeem his creation; to fail to believe the latter is to relegate that same humanity to a diminished capacity without the hope of possible success. We lose having an example to follow if Jesus was immune to temptation. Hebrews clearly indicates that Jesus was tempted in all ways like a man. But he did not sin (Heb 4:15). The fact that he did not sin was not because he was God but because he depended on God, not because his divinity trumped his humanity but because his humanity trusted deity.

(2) The temptations indicate the kind of God/Man Jesus was going to be. Jesus came to rule the hearts of all men but was committed to accomplishing that only though fellowship, not coercion. He came to glorify God but gave the ultimate example of how that is done—not by tricks and sensationalism that had a determined and safe outcome but by giving his life as a ransom for many.

GALILEAN MINISTRY

Luke 4:14–30

¹⁴*Jesus returned to Galilee in the power of the Spirit. And reports concerning him went out into all the surrounding regions.* ¹⁵*And he was teaching in their synagogues and he was being glorified by all.* ¹⁶*And he went to Nazareth where he had been raised. And he went into the synagogue on the Sabbath day according to his custom and he stood up to read.* ¹⁷*The book of the prophet Isaiah was given to him and he opened the book to the place where it was written:* ¹⁸*"The Spirit of the Lord was upon me because he has anointed me to bring good news to the poor. He has sent me to proclaim release to the captives and recovery of sight to the blind, to set at liberty those who have been broken in captivity,* ¹⁹*to proclaim the acceptable year of the Lord."* ²⁰*Closing the book and giving it back to the attendant, he sat down. Then all the eyes in the synagogue were focused upon him.* ²¹*He began to say to them, "Today, this writing has been fulfilled in your hearing."* ²²*Everyone bore witness to him and were amazed at the gracious words coming from his mouth, for they said, "Is this not Joseph's son?"* ²³*And he said to them, "No doubt you will say me this parable, 'Physician, heal thyself.' What we heard happened in Capernaum, do even in your own country."* ²⁴*And he said, "A prophet is not acceptable in his own country.* ²⁵*But in truth I say to you, there were many widows in Israel during the days of Elijah when the heaven was shut up for three years and six months, when there became a great famine upon all the land,* ²⁶*but Elijah was sent to none of them, except to a woman who was a widow in Zarephath of Sidon.* ²⁷*And there were many lepers in Israel during the time of the prophet Elisha but he cleansed none of them except the Syrian, Naaman."* ²⁸*And the ones hearing this in the synagogue were filled with anger.* ²⁹*Getting up, they forced him out of the city and they took him to the edge of the hill so that they may throw him down the cliff on which the city had been built.* ³⁰*But passing through their midst, he departed.*

In his beautifully concise manner of writing, Barclay separated verses 14 and 15 from 16 through 30. His intent seemed to be to contrast the reaction between Jesus' initial ministry and what followed. But Luke's narrative seems to place the events much closer, even though the contrast is obvious. The acceptance of the crowd quickly gave way to their rejection because the message of inclusion challenged their predetermined assumptions of God's work and way.

Used only twice in the New Testament, φήμη (*phēmē*) means "fame." The same word is used in Matthew's account of the healing of Jairus's daughter (Matt 9:31). At its root, the word means to talk. Given the demonstration of the Spirit's power and the initial acceptance of those worshiping in the synagogue, everyone was "talking up" Jesus. His fame spread abroad. The reaction is not uncommon. People inherently recognize the hand of God. Because humanity is created in God's image, there is a natural affinity to kingdom activity. Unfortunately, people do not disconnect from the message of God because of lack of perception but from a lack of willingness to change.

This passage presents a typical Lukan feature: historical reduction. Simply stated, Luke often collapsed history in way as to condense large blocks of time. Far from fictitious, Luke simply glossed over details unnecessary to the narrative, leaving visible only the thread that was required. Following the temptation, Jesus began ministering, a series of events that prompted public notoriety. Subsequent to the actual inauguration of his ministry was the public appearance in Nazareth. However, Luke's smooth transition from verse 15 to 16 causes the events to seem immediately sequential.

This condensing of history helps explain many of the details of the story. Jesus' reputation caused the worship facilitator to offer him the opportunity to read Scripture. Furthermore, the rapt attention of the hearers depicts a scene where all in the synagogue were amazed that this popular figure was in their midst. Finally, they were not disappointed in their expectation as they were astounded by his gracious words.

As Jesus stood to read, he opened the scroll, selected Isaiah 61:1, and added Isaiah 58:6. Reminiscent of the year of Jubilee that was to herald a new and hope-filled day (Lev 25:8–17) Jesus' text signaled the nature of his messianic duty. Following on the conclusion of the temptation, Luke's narrative reinforces this theme: What kind of Messiah would Jesus become? His self-proclaimed identity now included the following: good news to the poor, sight to the blind, release to the captive, and healing to the broken. The absence of the article in each of these cases indicates no particular individual was being described. Each is intended to be descriptive of groups of people. Luke's theme of including the hopeless was furthered as Jesus proclaimed that it was to these nameless and faceless outcasts that the Messiah was sent.

Although the message Jesus proclaimed depicted God providing each with their particular need, the crowds turned on Jesus as they realized the worldwide nature of his intent. While those in the synagogue certainly knew the stories of the widow of Zarephath (1 Kings 17:8) and of the Syrian army officer Naaman (2 Kings 5), today's reader cannot know if those present that day had ever made the connection Jesus made of these events in the lives of Elijah and Elisha. Specifically, Jesus demonstrated that God never intended to bless only the Hebrew people. God intended from the beginning to bless all peoples, regardless of their ethnicity. Filled with rage, those who sang his praises turned their intent gazes into stares of contempt. The stage was set: Jesus was Messiah to all, starting with the Jew, seeking to lead them to understand all that their heritage of faith was intended to communicate but while never excluding those outside the camp.

One additional note must be observed in the masterful literary style of Luke's narrative. Following John the Baptist, Jesus was led by the Spirit, ἐν τῷ πνεύματι (*en tōi pneumatic*), into the wilderness (4:1). After the temptation, as Jesus entered his public ministry, he went up in the power of the Spirit, ἐν τῇ δυνάμει τοῦ πνεύματος (*en tē dunamei tou pneumatos*), into Galilee (4:14). While there is no actual difference in the presence of the Holy Spirit in our lives, there is perceived difference from our perspective of the weakness of the flesh. We resist temptation by being led in the Spirit. But after resisting temptation we begin proclaiming the good news in the power of the Spirit.

WHAT TO ME AND TO YOU?

Luke 4:31–37

³¹*And he went down to Capernaum, a city of Galilee. There he was teaching them on the Sabbath.* ³²*And they were overwhelmed with astonishment concerning his teaching because of the authoritative nature of his words.* ³³*There was in the synagogue a man who was having the spirit of an unclean demon, who shouted in a great voice,* ³⁴*"Jesus of Nazareth! What does this have to do with*

you and us? Have you come to destroy us? We know who you are; the Holy Son of God." ³⁵ *Jesus rebuked him saying, "Be silent and come out of him!" After the demon had thrown the man down in full view of everyone, he came out of him, having done the man no harm.* ³⁶ *All became amazed and spoke to one another saying, "What words are these that in authority and power he commands the unclean spirit and he came out?"* ³⁷ *After this, rumors went out about him unto every place in the surrounding areas.*

On the surface, this text accomplishes several purposes. Luke showed movement in Jesus' ministry. Jesus continued moving through the communities of Galilee. Luke also demonstrated Jesus' continued pattern of taking the message of hope to the Jewish people. Again, Luke revealed Jesus' popularity with the general public. The teachings of the Messiah are always recognized as authoritative.

In addition to continuing these themes, a new element is introduced in the story of the demoniac who was disrupting the synagogue worship. Unlike Mark's Gerasene demonic (Mark 5:1–20) who acknowledged Jesus' identity as the Son of God after Jesus had commanded the demon to leave his host, the Galilean synagogue demonic announced Jesus' true identity before the verbal interchange. With a loud voice the demoniac cried, "Hey! What business do we have together? We know who you are. You are the Son of God! Have you come to destroy us?" While much of the dialogue can be heard in other Scriptures, there is one very specific phrase that must be considered to understand fully Luke's intent. That phrase is τί ἡμῖν καὶ σοί *(ti ēmin kai soi)*, "What to us and to you?"

Other than the change in person and Number from first singular to first plural, the phrase is not unique to Luke. At least two other incidences shed light on the expression. The first occurred in the period of religious and nationalistic fervor, inspired by the child king Josiah. After finding a copy of the law, probably a Deuteronomy scroll, King Josiah caused revival to occur throughout his kingdom. Seeking to establish military security, Josiah interfered with the plans of Pharaoh Necho of Egypt who was traveling through Palestine to war against Syria at Carchemish. Josiah knew that if either Syria or Egypt fell, the other would become stronger and be an imminent threat to Judah. Accordingly, Josiah refused passage through his land. Pharaoh was incredulous. Necho sent word to Josiah and said, τί ἡμῖν καὶ σοί *(ti ēmin kai soi),*—"What to me *and to you?"* (Septuagint, 2 Chron 35:21). Again, at the wedding feast in Canaan, Mary seized upon the potential embarrassment of the wedding host who ran out of wine to propel Jesus into the spotlight of traditional messianic expectation. In a seemingly terse statement Jesus said, "What to me and to you?" (John 2:4). Both incidences convey the same sentiment. Both say, "This is none of our business," "this is not our affair," or to use southern vernacular, "We don't have a dog in this hunt!"

Assuming the same meaning is to be conveyed in the story of Jesus and the Galilean synagogue demoniac, the interpreter is left to determine the levels of the conversation. There must be the surface issues to which the casual observer in the narrative is privileged. Additionally, there must be the second tier conversation that is the real meaning of the conversation. Given this assumption, the former must be the details of the demon possession and the disruption of worship; the latter must be the conversation between Jesus and Satan. "This man has nothing to do with us," said Satan. "He is just a pawn. You and I have an eternal score to settle. I told you I would come again to tempt you at a more pivotal moment."

The problem with this scenario is that the man *did* matter to Jesus. "I don't separate time and eternity," said Jesus. "I will not fall into your trap of thinking that mortality is separated from the eternity of God. All the Father and I created is good, and when any of my children come to terms with their true identify, they also see themselves as eternal. Leave this man alone! Be gone!"

The result of the exchange was that Jesus' authority was made known throughout the region. There is no substitute for the authority of God, which transforms and identifies the hearers with God's eternal purpose and always with the same results. God is glorified.

A PRIVATE MIRACLE

Luke 4:38–39

³⁸Leaving the synagogue, He entered into the house of Simon. Now Simon's mother-in-law was being afflicted with a great fever, and they asked him about her. ³⁹Standing over her, he rebuked the fever, and it left her. At once she got up and served them.

Departing from the narrative pattern of public demonstrations of power, Jesus entered the private home of a friend and there found tragedy.

Peter's wife's mother was sick with a fever. Specifically, she *was going on being sick with a fever*. The grammar of the phrase, ἦν συνεχομένη πυρετῷ (*ēn sunexomenē puretōi*), uses a state of being verb with a participle,[30] in this case, an imperfect participle. The importance of the tense of the participle is that the imperfect conveys continuing action in past time. The woman was constantly being afflicted by the fever, her disease being chronic.

Jesus went to her side and quietly performed a life-saving miracle. The beauty of the narrative continues as she "immediately" got up and served her guests. Having endured a chronic fever, one would expect her to be weak, in need of convalescence for some time. But Jesus' healing power was so complete that no lingering effects were found.

Finally, note the private nature of the miracle. There were no crowds present. No one marveled at Jesus' authority. No one went out proclaiming Jesus' authoritative words. Jesus' ability to heal was not predicated on public applause. Jesus healed her, and she went back to work. The Gospel of the nameless and faceless added one more member to its unassuming ranks.

HEALING AND TEACHING

Luke 4:40–44

> [40] *At sunset, anyone who was having those with various illnesses brought them to him. He was placing his hands upon each one of them and healing them.* [41] *Demons also came out of many, crying and saying, "You are the Son of God!" He rebuked them, commanding them not to say that they knew him to be the Christ.* [42] *When it became day, he went out early to a lonely place. The crowds were looking for him and went out to him to try to keep him from leaving.* [43] *But he said to them, "I must deliver the good news of the kingdom of God to the other cities as well, for unto this reason I was sent."* [44] *And he was preaching in the synagogues of Judah.*

Luke concluded the description of the first Galilean ministry with the introduction of the kingdom of God. John proclaimed repentance and preparation. Jesus proclaimed a new reign on earth.

---

30. Called a periphrases or periphrastic construction.

This introduction coincides with another incidence of Jesus prohibiting the spread of his identity. The adjacent position of these two events was intentional. Jesus first had to explain the kingdom before he could explain the messianic role in that kingdom. Jesus first had to move the masses from temporal and particular to eternal and pervasive. In so doing, Jesus shifted them from self-centered nationalism that existed to further a flawed notion of superficial service to God to a heaven on earth citizenry whose actions of serving others was born of a sincere desire to love as God loves. Without the right understanding of how the Messiah would rule, it was pointless to talk about the Messiah at all.

FROM FISHERMEN TO FISHERS OF MEN

Luke 5:1-11

¹When the crowd was pressing Jesus to hear the word of God, he was standing by the Lake of Gennesaret. ²He saw two small boats tied along the shore of the lake, but the fishermen had gotten out of them and were mending their nets. ³Getting into one of the boats, the one that was Simon's, he asked him to shove off from the shore a short way. Sitting down, he taught the people out of the boat. ⁴When he stopped speaking, he said to Simon, "Push out into the deep water, and let down your nets for a catch." ⁵Simon answered and said, "Master, we have worked hard all night and have caught nothing. But upon your word, I will let down the nets." ⁶Doing this, they caught a great abundance of many fish. Even their nets were being torn. ⁷They waved to their partners in the other boats to come and help them. They came and filled both boats to the point of sinking them. ⁸Seeing this, Simon Peter fell at the knees of Jesus and said, "Depart from me, Oh Lord, for I am a sinful man." ⁹This was because he was astonished at the catch of fish they had taken. ¹⁰All who were with him were astonished as well, including James and John, the sons of Zebedee who were his partners. Jesus said to Simon, "Stop being afraid! From now on, you will be catchers of men." ¹¹When they brought their boats to shore, they left all and followed him.

As chapter 5 opens, Jesus has shifted his ministry away from the synagogue. Because of the growing animosity of the official religious leaders,

Jesus avoided the urban areas and was more visible in rural settings. But one fact remains: The crowds were always there. The crowds of people were described in verse 1 as being eager to hear the word of God. Throughout Christian history, this fact remains true. Wherever the gospel is presented in sincerity and in truth, people respond. Inside every person is an individual created in the image of God, an aspect of humanity that cannot be ignored, the reality of which creates a need met in only one way—fellowship with God.

The scene at the lake provides several important details. There are three names used in Scripture for this body of water: the Sea of Galilee (Matt 4:8), the Sea of Tiberias (John 6:1), and the Lake of Gennesaret. Only Luke referred to the large inland sea as a lake. Furthermore, as Luke broke from the Marcan Priority,[31] the reader should seek to understand the literary nuance of Luke's intent. As Jesus already had gathered his disciples by this point in Luke's narrative, the retelling of the call to be fishers of men fits another purpose for Luke. As the story unfolds, Luke's intent appears to be the reinforcement of Jesus' ministry to all people, not just the religious elite of the day. Even though Jesus moved from the synagogue to the sea shore, both the common person in the crowd and the inner circle of the disciples realized they were in the presence of God incarnate.

Notice the results of such a revelation. (1) God always acts with purpose. After teaching the crowds that had assembled, Jesus directed Peter to push out into the deep waters. While many sermons have encouraged stepping out into the darkness in faith based on Jesus' statement to move out into the deep, it was not the danger of the event that was the subject of Luke's attention. Peter was not reluctant because he was being asked to do something that would threaten life and limb. Peter was reluctant because he was being asked to do something that he thought was a waste of time. Jesus said to push out, let down your nets, for the purpose of collecting a "catch of fish," εἰς ἄγραν (*eis agran*). There was intent in what Jesus said. He was not hoping to catch fish. He did not say, "Why don't we try over there? That looks like a good spot. How about it, guys?" Jesus acted with purpose. Ironically, it was Peter's ability, not his sensibility, that could have prevented the demonstration of Jesus' purpose. "Master," Peter said, "we have toiled all night and taken

---

31. Reference used to describe the dependence of Matthew and Luke on Mark for the basic historic framework or narrative of the Synoptic Gospels.

nothing. We are professional fishermen. We do know what we are doing. You go right ahead with the religious stuff and leave the real work to us! But, if you insist, we will. Just don't blame us if this turns out to be a wild goose chase!" What the disciples would learn was that God always has a purpose. Understanding God's purpose requires the believer to trust God, not self.

(2) God uses his purpose to prepare believers for worship. No other direct use of the incident appears in Luke's narrative. Jesus made no application to his nature. The number of the fish is not stipulated. No one but the disciples witnessed the event. The only thing that takes place as a result of the catch of fish is that Peter fell to his knees and worshiped Jesus. Two aspects of Peter's worship are noteworthy. First, God's greatness in Jesus brought Peter's own identity into sharp contrast. God's presence always forces a comparison between Holy God and sinful man. Second, Peter's realization of his inadequacy resulted in fear. Jesus said to Peter, "Stop being afraid." The use of the negative μη (*mē*) with the imperative verb φοβοῦ (*phobou*) conveys the command to discontinue an action that has already begun. Peter was afraid because the event demonstrated so clearly that he was a sinful man, one not deserving of God's favor. Most importantly, while these two components can lead one to avoid worship, they also are what provide the greatest opportunity of worship.

(3) The demonstration of God's purpose leads to preparation of worship and concludes with participation in service. "Stop being afraid," Jesus said. "From this point on, you will be catchers of men." Belief in Jesus is not for the ultimate purpose of introspection but for kingdom growth. Be a fisher of men! When given the opportunity, the disciples left everything and followed Jesus. Participation in what God is doing is worth everything.

KNOWING AND BELIEVING

Luke 5:12–16

¹²*Now it happened that while he was continuing in a city that there suddenly appeared a man covered with leprosy. Seeing Jesus, he fell before him, and begged him saying, "Lord, if you desire, you are able to cleanse me."* ¹³*Reaching out his hand, he touched him, saying, "I do so desire. Be clean." Immediately the leprosy*

> left him. ¹⁴*Jesus gave him strict orders to speak nothing of the event, saying, "Go show yourself to the priest, taking the sacrifice for cleansing, just as Moses command as evidence to the people." ¹⁵But immediately, the leper was spreading a great word about him, so much that large crowds were gathering together to hear him and be healed of diseases. ¹⁶But he withdrew to a desert place and was praying.*

Several aspects of the story of the leper whom Jesus healed are typical of Luke's literary style. For example, the narrative champions the plight of the weak, the downtrodden, and the oppressed. Leprosy was a horrible and debilitating disease in the first century. Known today as Hansen's Disease, leprosy is a treatable dermatological and neurological infectious disease that robs its victims of the sense of feeling. In that lay the problem for the first century. Cuts and abrasions to the skin would go untreated because there was no noticeable discomfort to the injury. In a dirty environment without the advantage of sanitary conditions, these wounds became infected and began to cause necrosis.

With no understanding of the infectious disease process and no effective treatment option, lepers were simply isolated from society. Mosaic law commanded that torn clothes be worn, that hair be unbraided and free, that all afflicted with the disease live outside the camp and shout "unclean, unclean" upon seeing anyone in the vicinity (Lev 13:45–46). While intended for overall public safety, the procedure rendered the patient completely isolated. Also repeated from previous points in Luke's narrative was Jesus' ministry of healing. This is not the first healing miracle. Nor is this the first command to keep the miracle quiet. Neither is this the first time that Jesus demonstrated he was well versed in Old Testament law.

What is new is that Luke began at this point in the narrative to give his readers insight into the objects of Jesus' attention. Notice two important aspects of the character of the leper. (1) He suddenly burst on the scene. While rudeness maybe considered uncouth by the respectable crowd, this matter is far beyond manners and social etiquette. The leper did not break socially approved morays; he broke the law. Punishment could have been death by those who sought protection through enforcement of the lifestyle restrictions thrust upon the victim. But the man did not care. Desperate to see Jesus, the leper abruptly entered the crowd.

Demonstrated in this act is nothing short of complete singleness of mind. He was willing to risk everything for a moment with the Master.

(2) The words of the leper provided Luke the opportunity to pull back the curtain on the mind of those in his society. "If you desire to cleanse me, I know that you are able to cleanse me," said the leper. The manner in which Luke articulated this statement is important. The use of ἐάν (*ean*) with a subjunctive verb, θέλῃς (*thelēs*), constitutes a third class conditional sentence. The condition, or if clause, describes a future eventuality that while it is likely is still uncertain to the speaker. In this case, the protasis indicates the leper was uncertain, not about Jesus' ability but about Jesus' willingness to heal him. Luke let his readers understand that while news of Jesus' ability was well established, his motivation remained a mystery. The public was flocking to Jesus to hear him talk about the kingdom of God (Luke 5:1). News of Jesus' power to heal was widespread (Luke 4:37). But despite Jesus' statement about delivering the good news of the kingdom (Luke 4:18–19), people still did not understand why he had come. As a result, Luke recorded this very telling statement about knowing that Jesus had power but not being sure Jesus was willing to use the power. The leper knew Jesus was able to heal. No other reason could explain why he would risk all by breaking the law and coming into the general population. For the leper, there was no turning back. Unfortunately, while the leper believed Jesus could, he wasn't sure Jesus would.

This is a combination that will spell disaster for the church today. Christianity knows who God is and what God is capable of doing. The church has witnessed God's power for two millennia and can articulate the nature and character of God better than any generation throughout human history. Yet if the church will not expect God to act, all the knowledge will be in vain. Unless the church expects Jesus to reach out and touch the hurting, no power will flow. Unless the church becomes the hands through which Jesus acts, no power will flow. But if the church will believe God has power to change lives today and the faith to expect that God will, then we too will hear the words and feel the touch that were heard and felt by the leper.

WHICH IS HARDER TO DO?

Luke 5:17–26

[17] Now it happened on a certain day that Jesus was teaching, and sitting there were Pharisees and teachers of the law, having come from every village in Galilee, Judah, and Jerusalem; but the power of the Lord God was present upon him in order for him to heal. [18] And behold, men were carrying a man on a pallet who had been paralyzed and they sought to bring him in and to lay him before Jesus. [19] But not finding a way to bring him in through the crowd, climbing upon the roof, they lowered him on the pallet through the roof tiles to the middle of the crowd before Jesus. [20] Seeing their faith, Jesus said, "Man, your sins are forgiven to you." [21] The scribes and Pharisees began arguing, saying, "Who is this that is speaking blasphemy? Who is able to forgive sins if not God alone?" [22] But knowing their thoughts, Jesus answered them and said to them, "Why do you ponder such things in your hearts? [23] Which is easier to say, 'Your sins are forgiven to you,' or to say 'Rise and walk'? [24] But, so that you may know that the Son of man has authority on earth to forgive sins," he turned and said to the paralytic, "I say to you, Rise! Pick up your pallet and go to your house." [25] Immediately he rose before them, took up that which he had been lying upon, and went to his house, glorifying God. [26] And they were overcome with amazement and were glorifying God and were filled with fearful respect, saying, "We have seen something incredible today."

The healing of the paralytic who had been lowered through the roof is common to all of the Synoptic Gospels. Even the details are highly stylized with only the author's literary style making distinctive difference. In its basic form, the story is a vehicle to communicate Jesus' power. Each Synoptic Gospel has the paralytic arriving on his pallet, carried by compassionate acquaintances. Each lowered the man through the roof. All three recorded the same response from Jesus at observing their faith. In all accounts Jesus forgave the man's sin, knew of the disapproving thoughts of the religious elite, and countered their thoughts with the same reversal of words. Key to the narrative is Jesus' assertion that if he were in fact the charlatan the Pharisees supposed him to be, what would he say that would perpetuate his deceit? Would he not pose his ruse in a manner that would go undetected, specifically, forgiving sins? No one knew but God if sins were forgiven, so the cat would stay in the bag. The fraud would be complete. That would have been easier! But the Synoptic Gospels recorded the same response, "In order that you may know that the Son of man has authority on earth to forgive sins, I will do the harder," said Jesus. "Young man, get up, take your bed, and go home." In so doing, Jesus demonstrated by performing the genuine undeniable work that he could also do what was neither detectible nor observable.

Yet the settings chosen by the three Synoptic writers are remarkably different. Matthew placed Jesus in a boat, arriving from the other side of the sea to "his own city" (Matt 9:1). Immediately the narrative of the story began with the paralytic being carried in by his friends. Mark indicated that Jesus returned to Capernaum following an itinerate ministry of an undermined amount of time throughout Galilee (Mark 2:1). The story commenced only after crowds had time to gather as to prevent entry to the room by the friends carrying their disabled comrade. Luke alone prefaced the story of the lame man lowered through the roof with two wonderful verses that set the tone of the well-known tale with beautifully crafted Lucan finesse.

Whatever the biblical translator could choose for a title to this paragraph of Luke's Gospel, the subtitle could easily be "The Conflict Begins." Subtle to this point, Luke drew a bold line in the sand and announced the open hostility to Jesus on the part of the religious elite. Designated in the narrative as the Pharisees and teachers of the law, they were gathered to see and to hear what Jesus would do and say. In the body of the narrative, Luke followed the Marcan order. Specifically, the religious leaders objected to Jesus forgiving the sins of the paralytic, asserting that only God could forgive sins. Clearly they demonstrated their bias that they did not believe Jesus to be one with the Father. Furthermore, that lack of belief is the reason or motive for their presence. The leaders of the day had heard these incredible stories about a miracle worker. The uneducated public, easily fooled and often led astray, were already proclaiming the "Day of the Lord." *Could this be Messiah?* they wondered as word spread abroad. It was up to those for whom religious orthodoxy was a way of life to protect the weak and simple from any who would come to proclaim they spoke for God. After all, the Pharisees and their associates were the ones who read Scripture. They were the ones through whom

God spoke. If the word of God did not originate with them, then surely its authenticity must be questioned.

With this understanding of Luke's depiction of the roof-breaking paralytic, one can understand the preceding verses. Present at the teaching event of Jesus were the highest of the social strata. They had arrived from all regions of Palestine, three to be exact. They came from Galilee, from Judah, and from Jerusalem. In modern terms, to use Judah and Jerusalem would be redundant for Jerusalem is located in Judah. If you are from Birmingham, you are also from Alabama. Yet Jerusalem carried its own designation, its own prestige. But their motive was not to learn but to leer. They were there to gather information to be used against Jesus.

The adversative use of the conjunction καί (*kai*) helps to draw the contrast. The self-righteous religious crowd was there to test Jesus. But the power of the Lord was on Jesus. In this verse, Luke introduced a remarkable term. "The power of the Lord," δύναμις κυρίου (*dunamis kuriou*), is a phrase found only twice in the New Testament—here and in 1 Corinthians 5:4–5. Paul directed the church at Corinth to deliver the church member with abhorrent behavior to Satan for the destructions of his flesh and resulting salvation of his soul. This act of tough love was to be administered by the "power of the Lord." Both in the case of Luke and Paul, the settings were laced with conflict. In these settings of suspicion and defiance, the power of the Lord was required for resolution.

Were these the only two incidences of strife in the New Testament? Were there no other occasions of difficulty within the fledgling church? Obviously not. But were these two incidences unique in their basic elements? Perhaps Paul clearly stated that the egregious act of the man having sexual relations with his stepmother was not to be tolerated. Paul stated clearly that such immorality was unknown even in the pagan world. Paul signaled the emergence of the power of the Lord in a setting that was unique to the New Testament. Perhaps Luke sought to describe the condescending mind games of the religious leaders of his day with the same level of disgust. Perhaps Luke felt their subterfuge was equally as offensive.

What cannot be refuted is that in both pressing circumstances the presence and power of the Lord were engaged. Luke added a strong purpose or final clause in his construction of the sentence. Specifically, the use of εἰς τό (*eis to*) with an infinitive indicates purpose. In some instances, the same construction conveys result rather than purpose, with the difference being the intent of the subject. A clear example of both is in Matthew 20:19 where Jesus indicated he would be delivered to the Gentiles in order to be mocked, scourged, and crucified. The Jewish leaders' intent is clear. Of interest in this verse is Matthew's continuation to say "and on the third day to be raised." Clearly this was not the Sanhedrin's intended purpose. The result of the action is, however, made very clear. Luke indicated that in the presence of unique and groundbreaking events, the power of the Lord was present in order to heal. Even today, healing with kind words or careful interaction, the church is called on to be the power of the Lord.

LEVI

Luke 5:27–32

²⁷After these things, Jesus went out and saw a tax collector named Levi sitting at the tax booth, and he said to him, "You follow me!" ²⁸Levi got up, left all, and followed him. ²⁹Levi then made a great banquet for him at Levi's house, and there was a large crowd of tax collectors and other sorts sitting at the banquet table. ³⁰The Pharisees and scribes were grumbling about them to Jesus' disciples saying, "Why does he eat and drink with tax collectors and sinners?" ³¹Jesus answered and said to them, "The healthy have no need of a physician, the badly sick do. ³²I have not come to call the righteous but sinners to repentance."

When he saw Levi sitting at the tax collector's booth, Jesus issued the call, "Come. Follow me." The call of Levi to be a disciple follows closely the Marcan order. One cannot help but see Luke's desire to emphasize the inclusive nature of the gospel. All were invited to participate in the new kingdom that had come on earth. Even the dreaded tax collector could participate.

It has been said that only two things in life are certain: death and taxes. Accordingly to Barclay, the first century had an overabundance of taxable events. There were two general categories: stated taxes and duties. The stated taxes during the time of Jesus included the poll tax, ground tax, and income tax. Duties included a fee to travel via roads and waterways. Vehicles were taxed via the number of wheels and the number of animals pulling the vehicle. Additionally, import and export tariffs abounded that were item specific.[32]

But the occurrence of the tax was only part of the problem. The administration of the tax collection system gave way to graft in its ugliest form. Local governments in the Roman Empire were left largely undisturbed when conquered. This was an effort to maintain law and order more than any magnanimous gesture toward thought of indigenous pride or effort to foster nationalism. The Romans maintained roads for commercial benefits and kept the peace so that trade would flourish. To accomplish public works, the people were taxed. The job of collecting the tax went to the highest bidder. This provided the collector the opportunity to charge anything in excess of the demand for personal gain. The Romans were hated in Palestine because they were Gentiles and had defeated the Jewish people. Their presence was a constant reminder of these facts. Jews willing to work with or for the Romans were considered traitors to their faith.

Given this, it is not hard to understand the Jewish reaction to Jesus' call of Levi. To make matters worse, Jesus not only associated with those most hated by society but he also associated with them during a meal. While Mark indicated that Jesus ate with the tax collectors, both Luke and Matthew added "and drank" with the same. Ritual purity was difficult to maintain if meal etiquette was not followed strictly. The exchange of bodily fluids made one unclean. Thus the use of common utensils provided the means for this transfer. By all obvious observations, Jesus identified with and thereby assumed the liability of those among the lowest in society.

Yet note Jesus' reaction. Knowing the thoughts of the Pharisees and scribes and knowing they were murmuring among themselves about his activity, Jesus answered their thoughts. When Jesus' disciples were asked why their teacher engaged in such unacceptable practices, Jesus answered in two parts. First, Jesus made a declaration that could not be questioned. Jesus stated that the healthy had no need of a physician but the unhealthy did. The statement cannot be debated. It is a statement that is true on its own merits. The interesting aspect of the statement is that Jesus acknowledged the Pharisees' bias in the way that he responded. "You know, fellows; you are right. These tax collectors really are the scum of the earth." The merit of this response is in meeting his

---

32. Barclay, *The Gospel of Luke*, 61.

adversaries half way. Jesus soon enough antagonized those who refused to understand. But by engaging those who were there, Jesus may have brought at least one Pharisee to the point of personal identification with the assistance Jesus was offering, as they too were in need of salvation.

Second, Jesus provided a clear statement of his ministry's purpose—to call sinners to repentance. Luke already recorded Jesus' sermon in Nazareth (Luke 4:16–21). There Jesus indicated he came to preach good news to the poor, to release the captives, and to bring sight to the blind. That was the "what" of Jesus' purpose. It was not until his encounter with the Pharisees at Levi's banquet that Jesus revealed the "how." John came on the scene proclaiming baptism of repentance for the forgiveness of sins (Luke 3:3). For the first time in Jesus' conversations and for only the second time in Luke, repentance was again the subject of conversation. "I have come," Jesus said, "to call sinners to repentance." Again, as with the use of the need for a physician, Jesus used an analogy that would lead the arrogant astray. The righteous do not need repentance. They are in fact righteous. But who that day under the sound of Jesus' voice were the righteous? Who were the sick in need of a physician? No doubt, many who thought they were righteous, who thought they were healthy, were the very ones Jesus came to save. Sadly, many walked away that day unchanged by the event. In their turning away, their false assumptions about their standing before God forever cemented their fate. Yet there always is hope that one stayed, that one listened, that one questioned under the convicting power of the Holy Spirit, "Am I in need?"

SAVING OLD WINESKINS

Luke 5:33–39

³³And they said to him, "The disciples of John fast often and make prayers even as the Pharisees, but yours eat and drink." ³⁴Jesus said to them, "You cannot make the wedding guests of the bridegroom fast while the bridegroom is with them, can you? ³⁵The days are coming when the bridegroom will be taken away from them and then in those days they will fast." ³⁶Then he said to them in a parable, "No one tears a piece of new garment and places it upon an old garment. If indeed he does, he will tear the new and the piece from the new will not match the old. ³⁷Neither do you cast new wine into old wineskins. If indeed he does, the new wine will burst the old wineskins and it will be poured out and the wineskins destroyed. ³⁸*Rather new wine is placed in new wineskins.* ³⁹*Furthermore, no one drinking old wine desires the new; for he says, 'the old is good.'"*

Luke continued the theme of the established leaders voicing complaints against Jesus' unconventional methods by including three examples. The Pharisees complained Jesus' disciples were not reverent enough, that they were never somber, and that their piety was not obvious in their spoken prayers and outward expressions of worship. The sequence of the preceding events certainly gives rise to the conflict—the lavish meal at the home of the tax collector. There Jesus drew a line in the sand and said, "Here is where I stand." In response to the question about why his disciples did not behave like others, Jesus gave not one answer but three.

(1) You cannot expect the wedding party to grieve while the bridegroom is still present. The picture of the Jewish wedding was intended to evoke feelings of joy and happiness. The Christian life is intended to be full and meaningful. While it is true that growing closer to God causes the worshiper's heart to break over that which breaks God's heart, still the consequence of an abiding presence of God is joy.

(2) You cannot expect a new patch to stay on an old cloth. The sewing analogy depicts the incompatibility of the two materials. The reason that Jesus' disciples did not behave like other disciples was that the relationship they had with God was like no other. Systems and procedures and means of achieving results that worked before will no longer reach their intended audiences. Jesus came to introduce a new kingdom that was completely different from the old.

(3) Finally, the same point is repeated for a third time with the new wine in old wineskins. Fermentation of wine caused effervescence to occur. If the wineskin did not possess the ability to expand, the skins would burst and the contents would spill. The old system was not capable of containing the new revelation of God's kingdom on earth. Taken together, especially following immediately the calling of Levi and the subsequent banquet at his house, these narratives convey a radical shift in what God was doing and how God was going to accomplish his purposes. With reference to this passage, Barclay said, "Nothing moves more slowly than a Church. The trouble with the Pharisees was that the whole religious outlook of Jesus was so startlingly new that they simply could

not adjust themselves to it. The mind soon loses the quality of elasticity and will not accept new ideas."[33] Furthermore, Stagg said, "Man often is more impressed with the antiquity of religious practice than with its validity."[34] These statements are born out in Luke's closing of the narrative that is unique to the Synoptic Gospels. Left unchallenged, people will prefer the old, the tried and true, the comfortable. As Jesus said, "No one drinking old wine desires new; 'the old is good,' they say."

Yet the church is not to be written off as having no hope. If condemnation was the purpose, that message could have been accomplished with much greater dispatch. Even the Pharisees who were condemned by John as having the ax already laid to the root were given the opportunity to do works worthy of repentance. Works worthy of repentance? What does that mean? Could it be interpreted as being saved by works? Repentance remains the overriding theme of the section. The irony of the section is that while numerous dichotomies were offered (i.e. healthy or sickly, righteous or sinner, wedding party member or outsider, old cloth or new patch, new wine or old, new wineskin or old), all are in need of that which only God offers. None achieve on their own merits but all are called to walk worthy of the gospel. None measure up, but all are given the opportunity to receive God's grace and favor.

SABBATH LAW VIOLATIONS

Luke 6:1–5

¹Now it happened on a Sabbath that as he was going through a grain field, his disciples were picking and were eating wheat, having rubbed the heads of grain in their hands. ²Some of the Pharisees said, "Why are you doing what is not allowed on the Sabbath?" ³Jesus answered them and said, "Have you not read what David did when he was hungry and those with him? ⁴How he entered into the house of God and taking the bread that had been offered to God he ate it and gave it to those with him, which no one is allowed to eat except the priest?" ⁵Then he was saying to them, "The Son of man is Lord of the Sabbath."

---

33. Barclay, The Gospel of Luke, 64–65.
34. Stagg, Studies in Luke's Gospel, 51.

Luke's presentation of the Sabbath law violations served two purposes. First, Luke continued to show the lengths to which the religious leaders were willing to go to discredit Jesus. It is possible that the observation of the infraction was spontaneous; the disciples were plucking and eating, as described by the continuous action of the imperfect verbs ἔτιλλον (*etillon*) and ἤσθιον (*ēsthion*). What seems more probable is that Jesus' every move was being watched. Luke's purpose was served by showing the petty manner in which Jesus was treated. The complaints that would ultimately rise to the level of charges of treason began by a casual activity that would normally go unnoticed.

To be sure, Sabbath restrictions had their origin in biblical mandate. God created the universe, including the earth and its inhabitants, and then rested from his creative work (Gen 2:2–3). In the Ten Commandments, the Sabbath was reinforced by the admonition to remember and keep holy the same. Furthermore, God's creative work was recounted and the logic forwarded that because God rested from his creative work on the Sabbath so should God's creation rest from all work on the Sabbath (Exod 20:8–11). Accordingly, Moses prescribed the sentence of death for those who violated the prohibition to work (Exod 35:2–3).

However, as was the case with all aspects of legalism, a hedge ultimately was built around the law to protect the law. Beginning out of fear, respect, and a genuine desire to comply with regulations, people often create a law around the law. As children, we were not allowed to play in the street. That was a pretty good law! Enforcing this law was, however, somewhat problematic. In order to achieve compliance with the real law, stay out of the street, the new hedging law became stay out of the side yard near the street. The logic was simple: If we as children never went in the side yard, we could never get in the street. Prohibition-based rule systems almost always begin because of a hedging process. One rule is created to prevent the violation of another. Then another, and then another, and so on it goes.

Upon returning from the Babylonian deportation, post-exilic Judaism developed just such a hedge around the law. The Talmud is composed of Mishnah and Gamarah. The former is the codified version of the oral traditions. The latter is commentary on the former. For example, in order to remember the Sabbath day to keep it holy, devout Jews would cease from their labor. But to ensure that no one ever worked on the Sabbath, work had to be defined. When Jesus and his disciples passed through the grain fields, they violated four different work laws. Specifically, they harvested, they threshed, they winnowed, and they cooked (prepared food). All of these were prohibited actions on the Sabbath. Whether the observation was intentional or truly casual, the Pharisees finally had Jesus right where they wanted him—in violation of Sabbath law. What Jesus had not done and what the Pharisees had failed to appreciate was to violate the intention of the Sabbath law.

Luke also used the event to continue defining what kind of Messiah Jesus came to be. Jesus demonstrated that his concern was for people, not process. His open defiance of established customs was intended to correct a misunderstanding. Specifically, Jesus sought to explain that the law was given as a means of understanding God, not as a god in itself, and that people were more important than the law. Luke used the event to explain that the Son of man was Lord of the Sabbath, not the other way around. Jesus came to fulfill the law, meaning in part to emphasize obeying the spirit of the law and not the letter of the law.

TO SAVE LIFE OR DESTROY IT

Luke 6:6–11

⁶It happened on another Sabbath that Jesus entered the synagogue to teach. There was a man there with a withered right hand. ⁷The scribes and Pharisees were watching this man closely for themselves to see if Jesus would attend him on the Sabbath, possibly to find an accusation to bring against him. ⁸But Jesus knew their thoughts and said to the man with the withered hand, "Get up! Stand in our midst!" Getting up, he stood. ⁹Jesus said to them, "I put a question to you. Is it allowed on the Sabbath to do good or to do evil, to preserve life or to destroy it?" ¹⁰Looking around at all of them, he said to him, "You stretch out your hand!" He stretched out his hand, and it was restored. ¹¹But they were filled with rage and were discussing with each other what they might do with Jesus.

Luke continued with the theme of Jesus redefining the meaning of Sabbath law and of the negative reaction by the religious elite of his day by including this story about the man with the withered hand. Keep in mind that Luke's intent was to present the followers of the gospel as innocent of civil violation. Accordingly, Luke began this narrative simply enough with Jesus entering the synagogue on the Sabbath to teach. No harm, no foul. Judaism was a recognized religion in the Roman world and synagogue instruction certainly was a legitimate part of that process. Luke was careful to indicate Jesus' innocence in these Jewish conflicts.

As Luke revealed the plot, he made clear the sinister motives imbedded within the actions of the scribes and Pharisees. Notice the cascading effect of their activity as it built momentum toward its ultimate conclusion: open animosity and hostility toward Jesus.

(1) In verse 7, Luke indicated that the Pharisees *were watching*. The verb παρετηροῦντο (*paretērounto*) is in the imperfect tense. The force of the imperfect is that it states continuous action in past time. Descriptive of an unknown period of time, the opponents of Jesus were lying in wait like a predator stalking its prey, constantly watching, constantly waiting, and constantly hoping for an opportunity to attack Jesus.

(2) The Pharisees *were watching closely*. The word παρετηροῦντο (*paretērounto*) is a compound word that occurs only four times in Luke and Acts and only six times in the New Testament. The root word τηρέω (*tēreō*) means "to watch, observe, or guard" but usually in a protective manner. When Herod imprisoned Peter, sentries also guarded the doors (Acts 12:6). The angelic messenger used τηρέω (*tēreō*) to mean "guard, protect, keep, or heed" when he said to John in the apocalypse, "Blessed is he that readeth, and they that hear the words of this prophecy, and keep those things which are written therein: for the time is at hand" (Rev 1:3). Furthermore, Jesus connected observing the Word of God with eternal life when he said of his disciples, "Verily, verily, I say unto you, if a man keeps my saying, he shall never see death" (John 8:51).

The addition of the preposition παρά (*para*) intensifies the root word, altering the meaning to "observing, watching, guarding," but with the additional element of considerable suspicion. In addition to the reference here and its parallel in Mark 3:2, Luke used a form of παρετηροῦντο (*paretērounto*) to describe the Pharisees watching Jesus on the Sabbath in Luke 14:1 and who also were said to be watching and spying on Jesus in Luke 20:20. Furthermore, Luke used παρετηροῦντο (*paretērounto*) in Acts 9:24 to describe the Jewish attempt on Paul's life in Damascus. Finally, Paul used παρετηροῦντο (*paretērounto*) to convey a derogatory statement about the Judaizers "keeping" dietary regulations in Galatians 4:10. Clearly, the emphasis of παρετηροῦντο (*paretērounto*) is not gently guarding or protecting. The force of the word is to watch with malicious intent. Not only were the Pharisees engaged in waiting and watching but also their devious vigil had no good end in sight.

(3) The Pharisees *were watching closely for themselves*. Deviating from the Marcan narrative, Luke changed the voice from Mark's imperfect indicative active voice verb παρετήρουν (*pareteroun*) to the imperfect indicative middle voice verb παρετηροῦντο (*pareterounto*). This is a subtle but important distinction. English verbs have lost the middle voice in favor of the reflexive pronouns *yourself, myself, ourselves, themselves*. With the active voice, the subject does the action of the verb, which often is extended to an object. With the passive voice, the subject is acted upon by the object, thereby receiving the action of the verb. With the middle voice, the subject both does and receives the action. In other words, the subject acts on its own behalf. Luke indicated the Pharisees were *watching closely for themselves*. Their motives were not pure. They had selfish motives and intentions and were looking to further their own plans at any cost. They were intent on preserving their system of religion that exercised control of God and kept the masses in abeyance.

(4) Finally, the Pharisees *were watching closely for themselves to see if he would attend to the man*. This last action may present the most insidious of all as it furthers the Pharisees cause at the expense of the weak. The Pharisees took advantage of those who were incapable of taking care of themselves. The use of personal pronouns in this phrase forces the reader to make assumptions about the intended reference or antecedent of the pronouns. A literal translation of verse 7 would be, *Now the scribes and Pharisees were watching 'him' closely for themselves whether on the Sabbath 'he' would cure, in order to find an accusation to bring against 'him.'*

With each of the third person personal pronouns, the reader must determine if the reference is to Jesus or to the man with the withered hand. Clearly, the second and third instances refer to Jesus. No one thought the afflicted man would suddenly begin working miracles, nor was the man with the withered hand the subject of the Pharisees accusatory tone. What is not as clear is who the Pharisees were watching.

While there are no hard and fast syntactical rules for determining antecedents, context and contiguity are rules of thumb commonly used in translating. By using context, the reader could substitute Jesus or the man for the first him and the story would still make sense. Accordingly, using context alone will not provide the identity of the antecedent.

Although the Greek language is not dependent on word order, antecedents often are placed in a contiguous fashion to the pronoun. If the reader focuses on verse 7 alone, contiguity may push the antecedent to Jesus. If, however, the reader follows the flow of the narrative beginning in verse 6, the closer antecedent is in fact the man with the withered hand. Accordingly, verse 6 opened with the declaration that there was in the synagogue a man with a withered hand. Verse 7 continued with another declarative statement, specifically that the scribes and Pharisees were watching him—the man with the withered hand.

Given the plausibility of this rendering as grammatically correct, the reader finally should ask if the interpretation fits what else is known about the writer, specifically style and purpose. With this, the final piece falls into place. Without question, Luke would not have hesitated to reveal the religious leaders for what they were: self-righteous, control seeking members of an exclusive, legalistic system who were bent on destroying Jesus by any means necessary. The resulting translation that conveys clear meaning would be: *Now the scribes and Pharisees were watching the man with the withered hand closely for themselves whether on the Sabbath Jesus would cure, in order to find an accusation to bring against Jesus.*

Luke used this story to close a section that dealt with the Jewish response to Jesus' redefining of the rules. The man with the withered hand stands at the end of a series of encounters between Jesus and Jewish authorities. Luke's formulaic approach includes the following in each event in the series: a setting, a challenge of traditional position, Pharisaic murmuring, and a restatement of the critical issue by Jesus. With the paralytic through the roof, Jesus forgave the man's sin, the Pharisees murmured that only God could forgive, to which Jesus said the Son of man had authority to forgive. In the calling of Levi, Jesus ate with sinners, which prompted the Jewish leaders to ask why he would defile himself with such a base sort, causing Jesus to explain that he came to call sinners to repentance. When the disciples of Jesus were not fasting, the Pharisees questioned why Jesus did not insist on religious observance of traditional customs, to which he said via the wedding, the patch and the wine that a new set of traditions were now here. The grain field incident caused the religious elite to ask why Jesus' disciples did what was not allowed on the Sabbath, prompting Jesus to say he was the Lord of the Sabbath. With the final twist of Luke's narrative section, the man with the withered hand demonstrated the opponents' willingness to trap Jesus. Rather than taking the bait, Jesus turned their words against them when he asked, "Is it allowed on the Sabbath to do good or to do evil?"

While each story maintains numerous common elements, the last two build with particular crescendo, as emphasized by the phrase what is allowed or what is lawful to do. Already noted was Luke's propensity to bracket material by an opening and closing parenthesis. Luke used this mechanism again beginning in 5:17 and concluding with 6:11. When questioned about forgiving sins, Jesus said, *But, so that you may know that the Son of man has authority on earth to forgive sins* (Luke 5:24). In this sentence, Luke used the phrase ἐξουσίαν ἔχει (*echousian exei*) to mean "have authority." While this is the usual translation in the New Testament for the Greek expression, ἐξουσία (*echousia*) is a derivative word from the parent group ἔξεστι (*echesti*), which has the root meaning of something that is possible. Accordingly, Jesus' word to the crowd with the paralytic in their midst could have been, "So that you know that the Son of man is *capable* of forgiving sins." Capability ultimately questions permission and permission authority. Understanding the relation of these Greek words allows the English reader to see the important connection Luke was making between both the grain field incident and the man with the withered hand. Luke began the parenthesis talking about authority-*echousia,* and closed the parenthesis talking about what was allowed-*echesti.* This explains why the Jews were filled with rage. Nothing angers a person more than to be confronted with his own assumptions and proven to be wrong. Jesus said, "Your sins are forgiven." The Jews said, "You are not able to do that." Jesus responded, "I am not only able, I am allowed. You seek to limit people by telling them that they are not allowed. But I am here to say doing good is allowed. I have come to introduce something new. I have come to invite repentance and to offer redemption. I have come to usher in something new that cannot be contained in the old. I have come to be Lord of the Sabbath and to explain the true meaning of the law. I have come to fulfill the law, not destroy it. You can decide if you want to be part of what God is doing on earth, or you can choose to follow the Sabbath with its exclusive, endless laws, or you can follow the Lord of the Sabbath and have life. You choose!"

LEARNERS BECOME AMBASSADORS

Luke 6:12–16

¹²*It happened in those days that he went out to the mountain to pray, and he spent the entire night praying to God.* ¹³*When it became day, he called to his disciples and he chose from them twelve, and he named them apostles.* ¹⁴*The twelve were Simon, who he called Peter and Andrew his brother, and James and John and Philip and Bartholomew* ¹⁵*and Matthew and Thomas and James the son of Alphaeus and Simon, being called the Zealot* ¹⁶*and Judas the son of Jacob and Judas Iscariot, who became a traitor.*

The calling of the disciples may seem out of place. After all, Luke had already presented to his readers several stories involving the disciples. In order of appearance, there were disciples at Simon's mother-in-law's home (Luke 4:38–39). Next Simon, James, and John were fishing when Jesus led them to the miraculous catch, followed by his invitation to become fishers of men (Luke 5:1–11). Following these events, Jesus called Levi (Luke 5:27–28), the disciples were criticized for not fasting (Luke 5:33–39), and finally there was the grain-field incident of violating the Sabbath laws. Clearly Luke demonstrated the nature of his Gospel, namely an edited literary work that compiles factual material from numerous sources, intending to convey a particular message. As such, his Gospel often gains meaning at the expense of chronology.

What was important for Luke at this point in the narrative was not creating a blow by blow commentary on the life of Jesus. More important than bibliography was insight into Jesus' motive and actions. Two issues conveyed in this text far outweigh the exact sequence of Jesus' calling of his disciples.

(1) Jesus prayed before calling the disciples. This detail is unique to Luke's account of the naming of the disciples. Matthew omitted the reverence to the mountain, choosing rather to include the delivering of authority over demonic influence and illness (Matt 10:1–4). Mark included the mountain but omitted the prayer of Jesus (Mark 3:13–19). Luke alone showed Jesus anguishing in prayer over the decision to choose his disciples. But Luke didn't just indicate Jesus prayed over the decision. Luke indicated Jesus prayed all night. The phrase ἦν διανυκτερεύων (*ēn dianuktereuōn*) means literally "continued throughout the entire evening."

Only when the new day began was Jesus ready to make the decision. In a world of instant information, introspection often is lost. Only with discipline will the Christian take the time to bathe decisions in prayer.

(2) Jesus chose apostles from the disciples. Luke made clear the distinction between the two groups in this passage. As indicated previously, Jesus had a following for some time. Ever since he entered the synagogue to deliver his good news to the poor sermon, Jesus had a following. This group of individuals easily could be described as his disciples, people who identified with Jesus' teachings, were blessed by his healing power, or even just wanted to see what would happen next. This group of disciples represented a wide variety of backgrounds and levels of commitment. All these factors went into Jesus' decision. Who had showed promise? Who was responding to questions? Who had demonstrated willingness to commit by actually experiencing present sacrifice? Who would have staying power? Jesus had to decide because the next step was significant. Jesus came down the mountain and selected apostles from the body of disciples. Jesus selected from the group of learners those who would be sent out with Jesus' own authority to do the work of the kingdom. Those that were ready were chosen. How sad, how tragic it must have been to be on the periphery. Yet those who had prepared, those who were ready to accept the challenge, were used in a dynamic way.

This is a process that continues today. God calls, and his people respond. They respond with different levels of intensity and integrity. They respond with different understandings of commitment. But one thing is sure. While Christians cannot manufacture God's call in their lives, they can increase the likelihood of being used. God calls apostles out of disciples.

SERMON ON THE PLAIN: SETTING

Luke 6:17–19

¹⁷Coming down with them, he stood upon a plain with a great crowd of his disciples and a multitude of people from Judea and Jerusalem and from the coastal district of Tyre and Sidon, who came in order to hear him and to be healed by him from all illness; ¹⁸also those being troubled with unclean spirits were cured. ¹⁹All the crowds were trying to touch him because power came from him and healed all.

Immediately following the call of the apostles is the Sermon on the Plain. The reason for the change of venue from Matthew's more familiar Sermon on the Mount has been the topic of much scholastic debate. Positions vary from Luke presented a different sermon to attributing the various vantage points of the sources (i.e. there was a flat meadow on the side of hill). As with other material, these differences accentuate the nature of gospel as a literary form. Neither Matthew nor Luke were interested in recording details as in a police blotter. Both wrote from specific theological perspectives, intent to communicate specific messages. Matthew's and Luke's sources of information were accurate, and no question of authenticity should be entertained. Rather, the interpreter should seek to understand the unique perspectives that both have to offer.

Although the physical geography of the introductions differs, the political geography between Matthew and Luke was almost identical. In Matthew 4:24 through 5:2, Jesus' reputation was responsible for the sick, diseased, and tormented coming to him to be healed. When he saw the multitude, Jesus ascended the mountain and began teaching. Here in Luke, the same crowd was present for healing. Moreover, the aorist infinitives ἀκοῦσαι (*akousai*) and ἰαθῆναι (*iathēnai*) were used to indicate the intended purpose of the crowds. Specifically, the crowds came *in order to hear* and *in order to be healed*. It is important to understand that the world inherently knows it is in need. Furthermore, there is a longing on the part of those in the world for the things of Christ, even though they do not always correctly identify their need. The text indicates they came in order to hear him and in order to be healed of all their diseases. A cheap substitute would not do. The lost world knows when we are acting as the apostles who have been called out from the disciplines and when we are acting out of other motives. When the church moves with the authority of God, the world comes to hear from Jesus and to be healed by his power.

SERMON ON THE PLAIN: BEATITUDES

Luke 6:20–26

²⁰And lifting his eyes to his disciples, he said, "Blessed are the poor because yours is the kingdom of God. ²¹Blessed are the ones hungering now because you will be satisfied. Blessed are the ones

> *weeping now because you will laugh.* ²²*Blessed are you when men hate you and ostracize you and reproach you and throw out your name as evil because of the Son of man.* ²³*Rejoice in that day and leap for joy, for listen, your reward is great in heaven. In such a manner they treated the prophets who were before you.* ²⁴*Woe to the rich, because you have received your comfort.* ²⁵*Woe to you, the ones being satisfied now, because you will be hungry. Woe to the ones laughing now because you will mourn and weep.* ²⁶*Woe to you when all men speak well of you. In such a manner their fathers treated the false prophets."*

Upon comparing the Sermon on the Mount and the Sermon on the Plain, one immediately notices the abbreviated format of Luke, as well as the absence of the formulaic style of Matthew. Instead of "Blessed are the poor in spirit: for theirs is the kingdom of heaven" (Matt 5:3), Luke said, *Blessed are the poor, for yours is the kingdom of God*. Instead of "Blessed are they which do hunger and thirst after righteousness: for they shall be filled" (Matt 5:6), Luke quoted, *Blessed are the ones hungering now because you will be satisfied*. In the place of "Blessed are they that mourn: for they shall be comforted" (Matt 5:4), Luke wrote *Blessed are the ones weeping now because you will laugh*.

But what Luke lost in symmetry and poetry, he gained in clarity and personal affinity. No doubt, the formal style presented by Matthew goes to the needs of his identified audience—Jews or Jewish Christians wanting to understand Jesus in light of Old Testament fulfillment. For that setting, Matthew was magnificent.

Luke, on the other hand, had a different approach. Luke's readers did not share the same need for formalized religious expressions. Their context, a Gentile world filled literally with a pantheon of religions choices, had failed. They knew how completely ineffective religion could be. They had viewed the aimlessness of the anonymous crowd and had felt the emptiness that such expressions produce. To them, Luke became very personal. *Yours is the kingdom of God, you will be completely satisfied*, and *you will laugh*, were the words of Jesus that Luke knew his audience needed to hear.

To the church today, two messages should become abundantly clear. (1) In many ways, Christians are called on to live, work, and minister in Luke's world even today. The opening narration to *Dragnet*, a radio show (1949–1957) and subsequent television production (1951–1959 & 1967–1970), was always the same. "The story you are about to hear is true. The names have been changed to protect the innocent." The absence of meaning in life felt by modern culture is as real as it was in the first century, only the names of the empty crowd have changed.

(2) The difference between Matthew's Sermon on the Mount and Luke's Sermon on the Plain should reinforce that while the church's message is timeless, the methods needed to communicate the message must always change. Understanding the needs of the people to whom we are sent and adjusting our delivery in proper accord in no way waters down the gospel of Jesus Christ. To a synagogue full of people, Jesus quoted Isaiah. From a woman shunned by society, he requested a drink of water. To a hungry crowd, he multiplied fish. To a small group of panic-stricken disciples, he calmed the sea and walked on water. Regardless of the situation, Jesus always found a way to meet the eternal needs of people and simultaneously tell them about the love of God.

Luke continued the "Beatitude" section with a statement about how the follower of Jesus will be treated by the world. The word μακάριοι (*makarioi*) means "happy" or "blessed." Jesus was telling the crowd, most of whom would not have been accepted by the world's standards, that they could have fulfillment, that they could find contentment. The force of Luke's Beatitudes is that the poor, the hungry, and the weeping have the opportunity to be happy or blessed, not because they are poor, hungry, and weeping but because they have the kingdom of God. These will be satisfied and will laugh. What God was offering them transcended the physical limitations of their time-bound existence in favor of the expanded reality of God's reign. The same was true of their relations with others in society. They were blessed in the face of outward persecution, not because they were being persecuted but because the presence of persecution placed them in the company of God's servants.

To describe the situation, Luke used four aorist verbs. Jesus said, "Blessed are you when men hate you, when men exclude you, and when men insult and cast out your name." While there are in fact four separate verbs in the phrase, the use of conjunctions and personal pronouns seems to imply only three actions. Specifically, the repetition of the second person plural personal pronoun, leads the reader to gather up the last two verbs, *revile and cast out* into one action. Jesus knew his disciples would face opposition from the Jews. The hatred would come first from their Palestinian kindred. The reality of this hatred would lead to expulsion from the synagogue and the derision even of the follower's name. The result, however, for the believer of this persecution will be great joy. Luke added the phrase "Rejoice and leap for Joy!"

Breaking from the common material with Matthew, Luke moved into the unique counterstatement of woes. In Matthew and Luke, the poor, hungry, and sorrowful are encouraged with promise of relief in the new order of the kingdom. Luke alone added the condemnation to those who in society were rich, satisfied, and filled with laughter. Far from being a polemic against wealth, nutrition, and happiness, Luke's woes condemn the person who is unaffected by those in need. Those who hoard wealth in the midst of poverty, those who fill their own stomachs while others about them are hungry, and those who laugh in the midst of sorrow will ultimately experience the opposite. The teaching here parallels that of Matthew 25, where one's true attitude toward Christ is shown to be reflected in his attitude toward the hungry, the sick, and the friendless.[35]

SERMON ON THE PLAIN: LOVE YOUR ENEMIES

Luke 6:27–36

[27]*"But I say to you who are listening, love your enemies. Do good to those who hate you.* [28]*Bless those cursing you. Pray for those mistreating you.* [29]*To the one striking you on the cheek, you turn the other. From the one taking your outer garment, even your inner garment, do not withhold.* [30]*Give to everyone begging from you and do not ask again of those taking from you.* [31]*Just as you desire that men should do to you, you do to them in the same manner.* [32]*And if you love the ones loving you, what credit is that to you? For sinners in fact love the ones loving them.* [33]*If you do good to the ones doing good to you, what credit is that to you? Even sinners do such.* [34]*If you lend only to those from whom you expect to receive, what credit is it to you? Even sinners lend to sinners in order to receive the same.* [35]*But love your enemies and do good and lend, expecting nothing in return. Your reward will be great and you will be sons of the most high, for he is kind to the ungrateful and the wicked.* [36]*You be merciful just as your father is merciful."*

---

35. Stagg, Studies in Luke's Gospel, 57.

The beginning lines of this passage draw obvious contrast from the section that preceded it. The unique Lucan woes focused attention on negative example. Those who pursue the pleasure and fulfillment of this world to the exclusion of social responsibility and civic accountability have received all that they will receive. Jesus sharply countered with the command, "But you should love your enemies." What follows is a series of imperative verbs[36] that command specific action of the disciple of Christ. Jesus' followers are to love, do good, bless, pray, turn the other cheek, not withhold from those in need, give, don't ask back, and do unto others as they would have others do unto them. After an intervening section comparing the action of sinners and the righteous, Jesus returned to his imperatives, concluding the section with commands to love, do good, lend, and be merciful. Clearly the ethical demands put forward in this portion of Jesus' teaching were unparalleled. Adherence to these behavioral standards extended the law far beyond its first-century bounds. Jesus was in the process of establishing a new citizenry of a new kingdom that found earthly expression in the hearts of mankind, both in their actions and in their intents.

Included in this section is what Christendom (and perhaps even all of western culture) has termed "The Golden Rule." Jesus told his disciples, *Just as you desire that men should do to you, you do to them in the same manner.* (Luke 6:31). Unlike most legal codes both before and after Jesus' day, this command and the accompanying ethical demands of Jesus are stated positively. Barclay listed in his *Daily Study Bible* on Luke the following examples of negatively stated commands. One of the famous Jewish pairs of scholars and teachers, Hillel, summarized the entire law by saying, "What is hateful to thee, do not unto another. That is the whole law and all else is explanation." The Jewish historian and philosopher Philo who lived in Alexandria said, "What you hate to suffer, do not do to another." The Greek orator and writer Isocrates said, "What things make you angry when you suffer them at the hands of others, do not you do to other people." A stoic motto was, "What you do not wish to be done to yourself,

---

36. Greek verbs have one of four moods that indicate the manner of affirmation. The indicative states a fact and is used in a declarative sentence. The imperative mood makes a command. The subjunctive adds an element of contingency. A special use of the aorist tenses with the subjunctive mood can be used as a command. Luke's list of commands includes both imperatives and aorist subjunctive. Greek grammars use mood and mode interchangeably.

do not you do to any other." Confucius taught his disciples, "What you do not want done to yourself, do not do to others."[37]

When Jesus indicated he had come to fulfill the law (Matt 5:17), one of the things he meant by this statement was that the old law was restrictive and interested in prohibiting action rather than prescribing action. Jesus said in the Sermon on the Plain, "Here is what you should do. Here is what you should be. Here is how you should relate to your neighbor." If participation in the kingdom introduced nothing else, it changed this aspect of religious expression within society.

Due to the overwhelmingly positive tone of Jesus' teaching on this subject, one should stop to consider carefully the insertion into the list of positive ethical demands of three prohibited actions. Specifically, Jesus said not to withhold your inner garment from one taking your outer garment (v. 29), not to ask the poor to give back assistance after it was rendered to them (v. 30), and not to expect anything in return for a loan (v. 35). These three prohibitions center around property issues. Jesus described a world order where control of things and the acquisition of property were secondary to compassion for people. Jesus was not issuing a polemic against either personal property or wealth. He was saying that wealth and possessions are blessings that should be shared and not hoarded. A kingdom person should not resist with violence if robbed. A kingdom person should be willing to give to the poor and not expect to receive the gifts in return. A kingdom person should not lend and exact usury in return. All three examples show how not to behave. It is interesting that Jesus knew material possessions would bring out the worst in people, a situation that would mandate prohibition, when what Jesus wanted to do was spend time telling us how we should live.

Finally, this section includes a comparison between the behavior of the world and the desired behavior in the kingdom of heaven. Jesus drew a contrast that said if all you do is behave correctly to those who are of like mind and who will treat you with reciprocity, you have no favor with God. Jesus said that is how the world treats itself. What Jesus expected of kingdom participants was to treat people by the new standard, whether they would reciprocate or not. What Jesus was describing was the issue of unconditional love. When a person enters into a social contract, he or she relies on the socially acceptable conventions that dictate an unspoken rule: I will treat you a certain way if you will respond in kind.

---

37. Barclay, *The Gospel of Luke*, 77.

This "I will love you, if . . ." aspect of a social contract can simply and appropriately be called conditional love. We depend on this in social circles. We trust that everyone will know and follow the same rule. I will respond courteously and politely if you will respond the same. So we extend that courtesy, that pleasant talk, that genteel spirit, because we all are agreeing to the social contract that dictates conditional love.

But Jesus was introducing a new social contract. "What grace do you have with God," he asked, "when you act the way the nonbelievers act? when you enter into social contract that depends on conditional love?" What Jesus was demanding was an unconditional love of which the world knew nothing. Jesus said to treat others the way you want to be treated, regardless of how they will treat you, regardless of the social contract of conditional love. Jesus said to treat people with unconditional love. "Then," Jesus said, "you will have grace with God." Jesus was not saying we can merit salvation by the good deeds we do to others. Jesus was saying this is how God acts, and if you want to share grace with God, begin by sharing grace with others.

STOP JUDGING

Luke 6:37–42

37 "Stop judging so that you may not be judged, and by all means, stop condemning so that you may not be condemned. Forgive, and you will be forgiven. 38 Give, and it will be given to you; good measure, having been pressed down and shaken, continuing to be overflowing, poured out into your lap; for the amount you measure out will be measured back in return to you." 39 Then he told them a parable. "A blind man is not able to lead a blind man. Will they not both fall into a ditch? 40 The disciple is not greater than the teacher; however, having been fully trained, the disciple will be as his teacher. 41 Why do you see the splinter in your brother's eye but cannot notice the log in your own eye? 42 How are you able to say to your brother, 'You should allow me to take the splinter out of your eye' when you are not seeing the log in your eye? Hypocrites! First cast out the log from your eye, then you will see clearly to remove the splinter out of your brother's eye."

Jesus presented four commands; two positive, two negative. First Jesus issued two prohibitions against ongoing action. The words κρίνετε (*krinete*) and καταδικάζετε (*katadikazete*) are both present imperative verbs translated "you judge" and "you condemn" respectfully. Both verbs are preceded by the negative particle μη (*mē*). The negative with the imperative verb in Greek renders a command to cease an action, a prohibition against continuation. The resulting understanding was that the disciples were in fact involved in judgmental, critical, even condescending activities. Jesus told them to cease and desist. These negative commands were followed by two positive commands, ἀπολύετε (*apoluete*) and δίδοτε (*didote*), which mean "forgive" and "give," respectfully. In each of the four instances, Jesus stated the inevitable consequences of the prescribed action. Specifically, if the disciples would stop judging, stop condemning, start forgiving, and start giving, then the disciples would not be judged, not condemned, would be forgiven, and would receive.

One should be careful not to read into these sayings of Jesus an unspoken transactional religion. One does not forgive in order to be forgiven but rather forgives because it is the right thing to do. One does not refrain from criticism in order to avoid criticism but because refraining from criticism is the right thing to do. Furthermore, Jesus was indicating the act of forgiving opens a person to receiving forgiveness. When we exercise these qualities in how we treat others, we condition ourselves to receive the same.

These four commands and four promises are then summarized by the statement of reciprocity: The measure you give is the measure you get. While only one of the imperatives mentions giving specifically, all four should be understood in the principles of this conclusion. What Jesus was saying was that how we treat others will dictate how we are treated.

Introduced as a parable, Jesus taught his disciples by saying that the blind cannot lead the blind. Nothing more than the inherent logic of the sentence is intended. Jesus was saying you need to understand whom you are following. The disciples were not greater than their master. If they assumed they were, they would come up short. The very fact that Jesus had to direct the disciples to stop judging and stop condemning could mean that they had let their newfound position in Jesus' new world order go to their heads. They were about the business of setting the world straight. Jesus called them hypocrites, which means actor. Stop acting and start being genuine. Don't think you can solve the world's problems when you cannot solve your own.

FRUIT

Luke 6:43–45

⁴³"A good tree does not bear rotten fruit, neither again does a bad tree bear good fruit. ⁴⁴For each tree is known by its own kind of fruit. For they do not gather figs from a thorn bush, neither do they pick grapes from brambles. ⁴⁵The good man brings forth good out of the good treasure of his heart. And the evil man out of evil produces evil; for his mouth speaks out of the abundance of his heart."

Jesus used a common-sense agrarian illustration to teach his disciples about the thoughts and intents of the heart when he said, *Each tree is known by its own kind of fruit.* More than straight didactic narrative, the symmetry and poetic turn of phrase give this passage its beauty. Both the preceding and succeeding analogies add color and definition to the statement. Specifically, good plants do not produce bad fruit and good people do good things. Furthermore, the passage may be analyzed through two approaches.

First, the passage can be explained linguistically. The literary explanation is rather obvious. The teaching of Jesus states that practice is consistent with principle, that actions follow attitudes. What we do defines who we are.

This same point is made grammatically. Luke used the genitive case to say a tree is known ἐκ τοῦ ἰδίου καρποῦ (*ek tou idiou karpou*). The phrase means literally "out of its own fruit." The genitive case is the case of specificity. For the most part, the genitive case is used to designate the possessive noun. Unlike English that depends on word order for the grammar of the sentence, words in the Greek language change their spelling to indicate their grammatical function and relationship within the sentence. Jesus was saying that the kind of fruit specifies the kind of tree. What we produce demonstrates what we are. Finally, Jesus made the point very personal by applying the logic of the first analogy to people in general. Evil people only do evil, not good. Good people do good, not evil. Out of the things that are treasured in a person's heart come the attitudes and actions of their lives.

HEARING AND DOING

Luke 6:46–49

⁴⁶"Why do you call me Lord, Lord, but do not do what I say? ⁴⁷ I will show you what everyone coming to me and listening to my words and practices doing them is like. ⁴⁸ He is like the man building a house that dug down, and going deep laid a foundation upon the rock. When the floods came and the river rushed against the house, it was not able to shake the house because it had been built well. ⁴⁹ But the one who heard and does not practice doing is like the man building a house upon the ground without a foundation, against which the rivers rushed and the house immediately collapsed and ruin of the house was great."

The story of the house built on a solid foundation stands at the conclusion of both the Sermon on the Mount and the Sermon on the Plain. The differences are minor and usually are explained by the geographic assumptions about both audiences. Matthew added the adjectives wise man and fool, as well as the rain and wind preceding the floods. Furthermore, Matthew's wise man built upon a rock, whereas Luke's man who heard, listened and practiced God's Word dug down to get to the rock. Matthew's fool built on sand; Luke's built on the earth without a foundation. Clearly, Matthew was describing the flash floods that occur in Palestine during the rainy season when torrents of water rushes down the wadis of southern Palestine. The soil is either solid rock or shifting sand. No digging would be required. Luke's more generalized description could be applicable to almost anywhere in the Mediterranean world.

The similarities of the stories are important to understanding the intended meaning. First, both stand at the conclusion of the sermons. With the wide variety of selections and order that a comparison of the two sermons presents, the reader should conclude that this commonality is highly intentional. Something about this parable brings Jesus' teachings to an appropriate conclusion. Second, the basic analogy is one of planning. In both sermons, one person took the time to plan the construction and made the effort to do what was right. The person who took the easy path ultimately received calamity. Jesus was saying that the kingdom of God is worth the effort. Everything described about God's kingdom on earth was new, was radical, and a departure from the conventional, but it was worth it. Finally, the persons in the analogy who achieved safety and stability were those who heard and did. Blindly following custom would not merit God's blessing. Empty ritual and repetitive motion without meaning would not be the descriptors of the person entering the kingdom. Those who heard God's words and practiced God's teachings would enter. Jesus would bless those who heard his teachings and took them to heart. Only by doing the will of God would one draw closer in fellowship. Only by letting Jesus' teaching change a person's life at a foundational level would there be salvation.

FAITH OF A GENTILE

Luke 7:1–10

[1] After Jesus completed all his words in the hearing of the people, he entered into Capernaum. [2] Now there was a centurion whose servant was near death, having been greatly ill (the servant was very dear to him). [3] Hearing about Jesus, the centurion sent Jewish elders to Jesus asking that he come and heal his servant. [4] The ones coming to him beseeched Jesus earnestly saying, "He is worthy of you doing this; [5] for he loves our nation; he himself built our synagogue!" [6] Jesus was going with them, when not far from the house, the centurion sent friends to Jesus, saying to him, "Lord, do not trouble yourself. I am not worthy of your coming under my roof. [7] Nor did I consider myself worthy to come to you, but you speak the words and my servant will be healed. [8] For you see, I too am a man put under authority, having soldiers set under me. To this one I say 'go' and he goes, and to another 'come' and he comes, and to my servant 'do this' and he does it." [9] Hearing this, Jesus was filled with amazement and turning to the ones listening in the crowd he said, "I say to you, not in all of Israel have I found such faith." [10] When the ones who had been sent returned to the house, they found the servant well.

The lessons from this passage for the church today are twofold: How does the world perceive us and how does Jesus perceive us? Unlike most of the events in the Gospels that center on him, Jesus is not the primary subject of this story. Certainly Jesus was present. Certainly he healed the servant remotely. But the story is not about Jesus. Rather, the story is about the centurion, the qualities of his character, and the reactions of the Jews and Jesus to this most interesting person.

First, notice the characteristics of the centurion. (1) He was a generous man. The Jews indicated he had built their synagogue. The Roman position on indigenous religion was one of toleration, not support. Accordingly, any community effort made by the centurion would have been as a private citizen, not in any official capacity.

(2) He was compassionate. The text indicates his slave was very dear to him. A person of wealth could have owned many persons. Mistreatment of slaves was common in the Mediterranean world. Yet the centurion's response was one of provider and caregiver. Furthermore, the comment by the Jews was that he loved the Jewish people. While the term ἔθνος (*ethnos*) rarely denoted Israel, the context clearly implies that the Jews are intended and Luke's Gentile audience, as well the universal appeal of the gospel, account for the use of such a circumspect term.

(3) He was humble. When Jesus approached the centurion's house, the centurion said, "I am not worthy of your presence, neither in my home, nor in a public venue." Far from hollow flattery, the centurion conveyed a sincere appreciation of Jesus' statue in the community. The fact that the centurion's actions were based on his received report indicates his willingness to accept the word and urging of others. A less humble person would not have believed any of the hype that was circulating about this Galilean miracle man.

Each of these characteristics caused the Jews to hold this Roman citizen in high regard. Rather than the normal animosity, the Jewish people were loyal and responsive. The text indicates the Jewish elders gladly interceded with Jesus on the centurion's behalf. Not only did they *beseech* Jesus on his behalf but they also *eagerly beseeched* Jesus, commending the centurion's character as worthy of Jesus' attention. One should not overlook the irony in Luke's story. Not only is there absence of hostility between two parties that openly hated each other but Jewish elders, a group with whom Jesus had experienced little appreciation, were making an appeal for Jesus' assistance! The question should be ever before the modern church that if the social order is turned upside down when amoral people do basically godly things—exercise generosity, compassion, and humility—how much more could society be influenced by godly people behaving godly! The Christian today should carry away from this brief encounter the realization that the world does notice our deportment, our behavior, and whether or not we live lives that are consistent with our message.

But even more exciting to the Christian is to realize that God notices and enjoys exemplary behavior. Key to understanding this passage is Jesus' reaction to the centurion's words. The text indicates Jesus *was filled with amazement*. The use of the word for marveled or be filled with amazement, θαυμάζω (*thaumadzō*), is well established in the New Testament. When Jesus calmed the sea, the disciples marveled that even the wind and rain obeyed Jesus (Matt 8:27). When Jesus forgave the sins and healed the malady of the "roof-breaking paralytic," the people marveled and glorified God (Matt 9:8). When Jesus cursed the fig tree and it withered, the disciples were filled with amazement and wondered how the tree was destroyed (Matt 21:20). Pharisees attempting to entrap Jesus about taxes marveled and went their way when he told them to render to Caesar what belonged to him (Matt 22:22; Mark 12:17; Luke 20:26). At Jesus' trial, Pontius Pilate marveled that Jesus said nothing in his own defense (Matt 27:14; Mark 15:5). In Luke and Acts, the people marveled at the delay of Zacharias in the temple, and they marveled when Zacharias wrote on a tablet that his son was to be named John (Luke 1:21, 63). Mary and Joseph were amazed by the statement of Simeon about Jesus (Luke 2:33). Those listening at Pentecost were amazed they were hearing multiple foreign languages from Galilean fisherman (Acts 2:7) and Annas, the high priest and his council marveled at Peter and John when they saw their boldness but perceived their uneducated background (Acts 4:13). Finally, the apostles marveled that Jesus spoke to the woman at the well (John 4:27), and the crowds were filled with amazement following his teachings at the festival of booths (John 7:15). To summarize the New Testament use of θαυμάζω (*thaumadzō*) the reader can say the disciples marveled, the religious and governmental officials were amazed, and the crowds were filled with wonder, all about things that Jesus said or did.

But in order to understand fully the story of the centurion, the reader must observe one very important fact. Only twice in Scripture did Jesus marvel. Furthermore, in both instances, faith, πίστις (*pistis*), was the subject of Jesus' amazement. When Jesus preached in Nazareth, the people were indignant, questioning Jesus' authority. After all, they knew who he was and from where he had come. They knew his parents and his siblings. Who did he think he was? Scripture records Jesus' response as "And he marveled because of their unbelief" (Mark 6:6). Quite to the contrary, in Luke Jesus was filled with amazement by the centurion's statements and responded by saying, *Not in all of Israel have I found such faith.*

What is it about faith, or the lack of the same, that caused Jesus to marvel and be filled with amazement? The answer lies in one detail common to both stories. The people of Nazareth questioned Jesus' authority, and the centurion accepted it. Notice carefully the centurion's statement. As Jesus was approaching the centurion's house, he sent word to Jesus that there was no need for Jesus to come to his home. The explanation that followed was nothing short of remarkable. "Like you," the Roman official said, "I am under authority from another. Like you, there are those under my responsibility who do what I say do, not because of inherent authority but because of the authority of the one that sent me. I know that my commands will be discharged. You, yourself, need do nothing more than say the word!" The reader should be clear on this. The faith that impressed Jesus was not exemplified in the notion that Jesus could heal remotely. The faith that amazed Jesus was demonstrated in an understanding of Jesus' authority.

As with the first aspect of this story, today's Christians should pause to ask: How is our faith? Does our demonstration of our belief cause the world to notice our character? Do our generosity, compassion, and humility garner their loyalty and respect? More importantly and more fundamentally, does God marvel at our faith? Does God see us channel his authority, causing him to say, "Well, isn't this something!"? If not, we are failing at our task—to draw near to God and to lead others to experience the same.

RESURRECTION AND RECOLLECTION

Luke 7:11–17

¹¹Soon it came to pass that he entered a city named Nain and his disciples were going along with him in a great crowd. ¹²As he approached the gate of the city, a man had died and was being carried out. He was the only son of his mother, who was a widow. A considerable crowd from the city was with her. ¹³Seeing her, the Lord had compassion for her and he said to her, "Stop weeping."

> ¹⁴*Approaching it, Jesus touched the funeral stretcher, the pallbearers standing still, and he said, "Young man, I say to you, get up!"* ¹⁵*The dead man rose and began to speak and Jesus gave him to his mother.* ¹⁶*Fear seized all and they were glorifying God saying, "A great prophet has arisen among us! God has visited his people!"* ¹⁷*And this word concerning him went out to all Judea and the surrounding region.*

Perhaps no greater literary technique exists than the double entendre. Whether presented in written form or spoke in dialogue or soliloquy, who can resist the tug on the emotions, running from sadness to sheer exuberance, that arrives at the moment of understanding the double meaning? The pun, the play on words, the hidden meaning that is left hanging subtly in the mind of the communicants is one of language's great achievements. If one looks closely, he or she will see Jesus, a man of language, longing for just such double meaning.

On the surface, raising the widow of Nain's son is just another miracle in the Gospels. All the ingredients are here. Jesus was with the crowd, probably teaching as they made their way. There was human emotion that stirred Jesus' compassion, specifically that the only son of a disadvantaged person, a widow, had died. These elements are commonplace in Luke's presentation of his Gospel. Jesus routinely and tenderly ministered to the outcasts, the downtrodden, and the misfortunate of society.

The story continues with predictable formula. Jesus helped the needy. He stopped what he was doing and refusing to accept the circumstances of being limited by time and space, acted on behalf of the bereaved. After raising the young man, the crowd adopted their routine position. Fear, awe, and respect were fostered. Praise was attributed to God, and Jesus' reputation again was renowned.

But was that all that happened? In Longfellow's epic poem of the Revolutionary War, he penned a line that draws in the hearer. "Listen my children and you shall hear of the midnight ride of Paul Revere." In similar fashion, greater insight awaits the reader who is willing to see past the predictability of the narrative and come face to face with the personality of Jesus.

Have you ever started out in one part of your house or place of employment to fetch something from the other room or another part of your dwelling only upon arrival to have forgotten what you were attempting to retrieve? If you have, don't feel bad. It happens to all of us! Probably you did the other thing that is common. By returning to the starting point of your journey, you mysteriously remembered the object of your recent memory lapse. The mind relates well to familiar context, and the setting triggers your recollection.

In this lies the key to understanding the story of the widow of Nain. It has already been established that Jesus studied Scripture as a child.[38] Accordingly, it is not too great a leap to assume that Jesus had read and knew the details of when Elisha raised from the dead the son of the woman from Shunem, a town only a few miles from Nain (2 Kings 4:18–37). Triggered by proximity and the presence of similar underlying conditions—the wailing funeral procession of a broken-hearted woman whose only son had died—Jesus' mind went back to the particulars of the Elisha story, the similarities between the stories being too striking to ignore.

Recall for a moment the pertinent facts of 2 Kings 4. Elisha frequented the town of Shunem. The woman of the story perceived Elisha was a prophet of God and provided him a room for his sole disposal. Appreciative of her care, Elisha blessed her. Even though she was childless and her husband advanced in years, Elisha told her she would bear a son. The woman did in fact give birth, only for the child to die later in adolescence. Going to the prophet's abode, she fell at his feet and said that the child was her entire life and that Elisha should not have blessed her if only to have the child taken away in death. Elisha returned to her home and resurrected the dead child. These are the facts.

How Jesus processed these facts is a different matter. Given the emotionally charged moment of the seeing the widow who had lost her only son, being in Nain near Shunem, Jesus' reaction was understandable. Notice the sequence of events taken by Jesus and the similarity to the sequence of events taken by Elisha.

(1) Both Jesus and Elisha were moved with compassion. In verse 13, Luke used the word ἐσπλαγχνίσθη (*esplagchnisthē*) to describe Jesus' emotional state. Literally, the word describes an upheaval of the internal organs. The colloquial expression of being torn up inside begins to describe the inner stirring of the emotions. Common in the Synoptic Gospels (Matt 9:36; 14:14; 15:32; 18:27; 20:34; Mark 1:41; 6:34; 8:2; 9:22),

---

38. See the discussion of Luke 2:41–52.

Luke used the word only three times. Here Jesus displayed the emotion. The other two incidences were the Good Samaritan (Luke 10:33) and the Parable of the Prodigal Son (Luke 15:20). Notice that in all three the emotion was prompted by a person in great need who demonstrated outstanding concern for the less fortunate: Jesus for the widow, the Samaritan for the victim, and the father for his wayward son. Notice also that in all three cases, the emotion prompted specific action. Jesus raised the dead child, the Samaritan provided care for the injured traveler, and the father reinstated the lost son. True compassion is never just an emotion. True compassion prompts action and intervention.

(2) Both Jesus and Elisha gave life twice. In the case of Elisha, the Shunammite woman's delivery was the result of the prophet's blessing. Therefore, the raising again to life of the boy who died of what sounds like a cerebral hemorrhage was the second time Elisha gave life to the lad. Likewise, Jesus gave life twice to the widow's son. John's prologue indicates Jesus was the agent of creation of all things, both past and present. While intermediary agents certainly are involved in procreation, one cannot observe the miracle of life and not attribute the same to God. Though at the time of the Nain incident Jesus was God incarnate, his growing understanding of his unique relation to the father certainly warrants the assertion that Jesus gave life twice.

(3) Both Jesus and Elisha caused God to be glorified. With this third double coincidence, Jesus most certainly was connecting the two events in his mind. The Shunammite woman fell at Elisha's feet when her son was brought back to life. Luke's account of the story indicates that the people ascribed to Jesus the status of Great Prophet and his presence was evidence God had visited his people with the intent to help.[39] The exuberance of the praise and adoration of God must have propelled Jesus forward in the analogy with the widow of Nain and the woman of Shunem. But unfortunately, here is where the comparison stopped.

(4) Both Jesus and Elisha wanted a place to dwell. The details of the story must have stirred a longing in Jesus' heart. He knew the narrative. He saw a contemporary retelling of the events unfold before him, and he must have thought, "How wonderful to have a dwelling placed prepared!" In fact, the uniqueness of the setting and its comparison to historic events must have forced Jesus to assess his own feelings and desires. He had demonstrated compassion many times before. He had engaged

---

39. See discussion of "God visiting his people" in Luke 1:68 and 1:78.

that compassion without hesitation. He had even seized the teachable moment of such events to gradually bring along his disciples. But the one thing he had never experienced was the one thing he wanted most: a place to dwell in the hearts of his people. Returning to the premise of this interpretation, the reader should recognize the irony and understand the pivotal nature of the same with regard to God's plan for redeeming his creation. God can experience compassion and intervene as a result of his compassion. God can bring life to a person physically and even a second time in the form of a spiritual rebirth. God can position people and events that cause the divine name to be glorified. But God will not force a person, nonbeliever or believer, to enter into fellowship. We alone control the one thing God wants the most—a place to dwell with his people.

JESUS AND JOHN AND THE FORGOTTEN BEATITUDE

Luke 7:18–23

[18] Now John's disciples told him all these things. [19] Calling two of his disciples, John sent them to the Lord saying, "Are you the coming one, or do we continue looking for another?" [20] Going to him, these men said, "John the Baptist sent us to you saying, 'Are you the coming one or do we continue looking for another?'" [21] That same hour, Jesus cured many of illnesses, diseases, evil spirits, and many blind were given the ability to see. [22] Jesus answered and said to the two disciples of John, "Go and tell John what you see and hear: the blind are seeing, the lame are walking, lepers are being cleansed, the deaf are hearing, the dead are being raised up and the poor are having the gospel preached. [23] And blessed is the one who is not offended by me!"

Luke's use of source materials was well documented in his introduction to Theophilis (Luke 1:1–4). This story about the emissaries from John represents one of Luke's sources. Comparison to Matthew 11:2–6 reveals literary dependency by both Matthew and Luke on a common source other than the Gospel of Mark. This source has been dubbed "Q" from the German word *Quella*, which means source. Matthew and Luke used Mark, Q, and special material unique to each. There special sources have been aptly named M and L for Matthew's unique source and Luke's unique source. As is seen in this passage, Q is primarily a collection of Jesus' sayings or teachings.

Omitted from both Matthew and Luke is the historic background of this passage. While Mark did not record the conversation between Jesus and John's disciples, he did provide details of John's imprisonment (Mark 6:17–29). Matthew paralleled Mark's account (Matt 14:3–12), and Luke provided a far more concise rendering (Luke 3:19–20).

The subject matter of the passage revolves around John sending messengers to Jesus with a probing question: "Are you the Messiah, the one that was promised, the one for whom we have been waiting in longing anticipation?" Implicit in the question is John's perception of what the Messiah was to do. So John sent from his prison cell a communiqué. "I thought you were the coming one, but I haven't seen any evidence of your kingdom. I admit, I am somewhat stuck right now, but I am sure I would have heard about your big move. So tell me. Are you the One?"

While Jesus heard the question being asked, he also knew exactly what John really wanted to know. If John had been asking, "Are you the Messiah?" a simple yes would have sufficed. But Jesus' answer was more than an affirmation. Jesus gave the evidence of this messianic role—the real question John had asked. The reply via the messengers answered the larger question. "Tell John what you are experiencing, what you are seeing and hearing. Give him the following evidence of my messianic reign. The blind see; the lame walk; the leper is cleansed; the deaf hear; the dead are raised; and the poor are having the gospel preached." The first and last evidences were particularly pointed as they were drawn from Jesus' first sermon in the synagogue at Nazareth. These are the testimonies he had said would validate his kingdom on earth.

But as if that were not enough, Jesus concluded his comments about the role of Messiah by adding the forgotten Beatitude. *And blessed is the one who is not offended by me!* This is further evidence that John had misunderstood the role Jesus was to fulfill. Jesus was saying to John that those who accept him and do not question his plan and his means of accomplishing his plan are truly blessed.

JESUS PRAISES JOHN

Luke 7:24–35

²⁴As the messengers from John were leaving, Jesus began to speak to the crowd about John. "What did you go into the wilderness to see—a reed being shaken by the wind? ²⁵What did you go out to see—a man having been dressed in soft clothes? Listen to me! The ones existing in fancy and luxurious clothes are in the royal palace. ²⁶What did you go out to see—a prophet? Yes, I tell you, and much more than a prophet. ²⁷He is the one about whom is it has been written: Behold, I am sending my messenger before your face, who will prepare the way before you. ²⁸I tell you, no one born of woman is greater than John. But, the least in the kingdom is greater than he." ²⁹Hearing this, all the people and tax collectors acknowledged the righteousness of God by being baptized with John's baptism. ³⁰But the Pharisees and Jewish lawyers rejected the purposes of God for themselves by not being baptized by him. ³¹"To what may I compare this generation of men and what are they like? ³²They are like children sitting in the market, calling to one another saying: 'We played the flute for you but you did not dance, We lamented but you did not weep.' ³³But John the Baptist came neither eating bread nor drinking wine and you say, 'He has a demon.' ³⁴The Son of man came eating and drinking and you say, 'He is a glutton and a drunk, a friend of tax collectors and sinners.' ³⁵Yet wisdom is justified by all her children."

Following the departure of John's disciples, Jesus turned to the crowd and began talking about John's character. Jesus first engaged the people with a series of rhetorical questions. The reed shaken in the wind probably described a common expression about common everyday things. Reeds blowing in the wind were abundant along the marshy areas of the Jordan River and the Sea of Galilee. "You didn't go to the wilderness to see something ordinary, did you?" Jesus asked. From that reference point, Jesus continued to say there was nothing ordinary about John. The Old Testament quotation in Malachi 4:5–6 equated John with the great prophet Elijah. "Behold, I will send you Elijah the prophet before the coming of the great and dreadful day of the Lord: And he shall turn the heart of the fathers to the children, and the heart of the children to their fathers, lest I come and smite the earth with a curse."

This was not the first time these words had been used to describe John. In Luke 1, the messenger to Elizabeth said John would have the spirit of Elijah. Identifying John with the historic figure Elijah helped to clarify John's role in the kingdom of heaven on earth. The Old Testament prophet served two functions—one primary and one secondary. The latter was to predict what God would do. This normally was delivered in the form of a warning if selected behavior did not change. But the predictive function was not primary. The predominant role was to deliver the message of God. The prophetic formula "thus says the Lord" reveals the prophet's main responsibility. Telling forth the message was more important than foretelling the future. Jesus made the declaration of John's importance very clear when he reiterated the angelic message: "Listen to John! He is God's messenger sent to prepare you for what is coming."

Yet even with the prominence of John's responsibilities, the least in the kingdom was to be considered greater than John. The Jews placed high importance on social order. Already in Luke's Gospel the reader has seen that family origin was an important Jewish delineator. But Jesus introduced a new social order: The greatest will be least, and the least will be the greatest. What was important to human nature was not necessarily valued in the kingdom. A new world order was in store for those who would serve.

Caution must be urged at this point. Intentional service for the sake of gaining reputation would be and still is insincere. But when a person's motive is pure, God will reward his or her service. Jesus said to the Jews, "Stop playing your petty children's games. You said John was demon possessed because he didn't eat and drink. You said the Son of man was a glutton and a drunk because he did. Stop this tomfoolery and get with it! Listen to what God says is important and get engaged in what God is doing."

ALABASTER OINTMENT

Luke 7:36–50

³⁶One of the Pharisees asked Jesus to eat with him, so Jesus entered into the Pharisee's house and sat down to eat. ³⁷Behold, a sinful woman of that city, learning that Jesus was dining at the house of the Pharisee, brought an alabaster ointment ³⁸and positioned behind him at his feet was weeping tears and began to moisten his feet and was wiping them with the hair of her head and was kissing his feet and was anointing them with the ointment. ³⁹Seeing this, the Pharisee who had invited Jesus said to himself, "If he were a prophet, he would know what sort of woman was touching him, because she is a sinner." ⁴⁰Jesus answered and said to him, "I have something to say to you." Response—"Yes, Teacher, speak." ⁴¹"A lender had two borrowers; one owed five hundred days wage and the other fifty. ⁴²Neither being able to repay the lender, he forgave both. Who loves him more?" ⁴³Simon answered saying, "I suppose by the one who owed more." Jesus said to him, "You have judged correctly. ⁴⁴Turning to the woman, he said to Simon, "Do you see this woman? I came into your house and you did not pour water for my feet. But she moistened my feet with tears and wiped them with her hair. ⁴⁵You gave me no greeting, but since entering, she has not stopped kissing my feet. ⁴⁶You did not anoint my head with olive oil, but she anointed my feet with perfume. ⁴⁷Because of this I say to you that though her sins are numerous, they are forgiven, because she loved greatly. But the one being forgiven little, loves little." ⁴⁸Then Jesus said to her, "Your sins are forgiven." ⁴⁹The ones gathered for the meal began saying to each other, "Who is this that forgives sins?" ⁵⁰Jesus said to the woman, "Your faith has saved you. Go in peace."

No direct parallel is found in Matthew and Mark of the woman who anointed Jesus' feet while at the house of a Pharisee. There is a similar passion episode involving a woman at Bethany (Matt 26:6–13; Mark 14:3–9). But here in Luke, the event took place during the Galilean ministry; it was the host and his other guests who questioned Jesus about his accepting attitude of the sinful woman and not a criticism by the disciples for wasting money that could have fed the poor. Most importantly, only here is the parable told along with its interpretation of the forgiving creditor.

When invited to the Pharisee's home, Jesus responded as graciously as he had when invited to Levi's home. While at the Pharisee's home, a woman who was known to be sinner wept at Jesus feet, anointing him with a costly ointment. The host was quietly indignant, concluding that Jesus was no prophet, arguing that if he were, he would have known what sort of woman was touching him, knowledge that certainly would have caused Jesus to insist she desist. Perceiving his thoughts, Jesus told a parable about a creditor who forgave the debts of two men. A simple formula was presented. Both were forgiven, but the one who was forgiven more had more to appreciate. When her sins were forgiven, Jesus commented that she loved much because she had been forgiven much. Self-sufficiency frequently will rob people from understanding their need of Jesus. Such people believe they can take care of themselves and accordingly, do not request help. The sinful woman knew who and what she was but did not care. She loved greatly because she had been forgiven greatly.

A further twist to this story was that the sinful woman did what the host should have done. Custom of the day demanded that a guest be allowed to freshen up. Water should have been provided to wash his face, hands, and feet. A kiss, the customary greeting, should have been given. Also, olive oil should have been prepared for anointing. The host did none of these things. The sinful, outcast woman did everything the host should have done. One lesson not to be overlooked is that God's plan is not thwarted when those who know to do right fail to do it. God will find someone else to advance his kingdom!

Finally, Jesus drew the conversation to a close with the statement *Your faith has saved you. Go in peace.* The word for peace is εἰρήνην (*eirēnē*). Although it is not a new term in Luke, this is the first of only three times Jesus spoke of peace in direct discourse. When the women with the internal bleeding touched his robe, Jesus said to her, "Daughter, be of good comfort: thy faith hath made thee whole; go in peace" (Luke 8:48). Also, after the resurrection, Jesus appeared to the disciples in the upper room and said, "Peace be unto you" (Luke 24:36). Jesus' command to have peace was associated in these three passages with the newness of forgiveness and grace. Both women were praised for their believing spirit. Also, the disciples were at an obvious threshold of new possibilities as they prepared to embrace their new mission. However, all three events occurred in settings that were highly charged with great emotion, fear, and tension. The peace that God brings is not the absence of struggle or a world void of difficulty. The fact of the matter is that God frequently asks his children to do the most difficult things. It is the presence of God in the midst of trying circumstances that produces the calm that constitutes the peace of God.

JESUS AND WOMEN

Luke 8:1–3

> [1] *It happened soon after this that Jesus was going about the villages and towns preaching and delivering good news of the kingdom of God. The Twelve were with him* [2] *and certain women who had been cured of evil spirits and illnesses, including Mary, the one being called Magdalene, out of whom seven demons had gone.* [3] *Also, there was Joanna, Chuza's wife, the steward of Herod, and Susanna, and many others, such as provided for them by their own means.*

That Jesus had a following of women should come as no surprise to the reader of the Gospel narrative. Jesus championed the oppressed at every turn. In the first century, women would have been prominent on the list of those less fortunate. The women mentioned specifically had been the recipients of Jesus' healing ministry. Demon possession and illness are specifically mentioned as previous conditions. Mary Magdalene is said to have been the host of multiple demons. All of these issues were past, due to the compassion of a loving God that included even women in the kingdom.

Having been blessed, these women followed Christ without hesitation. Notice their commitment. (1) The text indicates they served others. Specifically, διηκόνουν (*diēkonoun*) means to provide for someone's needs. This is the same word Luke used to describe the actions of Simon's mother-in-law who rose from her fever and served Jesus and his disciples (Luke 4:39). The implication is one of rendering service without any ceremony. The purest of motives are attached to actions that are anonymous and driven by the needs of the recipient, not the ego of the provider.

(2) The women served out of their own means. Little if any clue is presented about the extent of their personal means. For Luke to make an issue of their wealth or lack thereof would in fact undermine the message he was conveying. What should be understood is that whatever they possessed, they shared.

(3) The women served at their own expense and at their own peril. By following Jesus and assisting those with whom he associated, these women were running the risk of bringing derision upon themselves. But again, no price was too great to pay to show gratitude for the manner in which their lives had been changed. They were willing to serve all, to give all, and to risk all.

THE SOWER AND THE GOOD EARTH

Luke 8:4–15

⁴*As a great crowd assembled with people from town after town, Jesus spoke to them in a parable.* ⁵*"A sower went out to sow his seeds. When he was sowing the seeds, some fell upon the path and were trampled and the birds of the heavens ate them.* ⁶*Others fell upon rocks and grew but dried up because they had no moisture.* ⁷*Others fell among the thorns, and the thorns growing with them chocked out the seeds.* ⁸*Others fell into the good earth and they grew, making fruit one hundredfold." As he said this, he was calling out, "He who has ears to hear, let him listen."* ⁹*His disciples were asking him what the meaning of the parable may be.* ¹⁰*Jesus said to them, "To you has been given to know the mysteries of the kingdom of God. But to the people, parables, so that seeing they may not see and hearing they may not understand.* ¹¹*Here is the parable. The seed is the word of God.* ¹²*The seeds along the way are the ones hearing, but then the Devil comes along and takes the word out of their heart, so that they may not believe and may not be saved.* ¹³*The ones upon the rocks are those who respond with joy when they hear the word. These, having no root, believe for a time but fall away in a period of temptation.* ¹⁴*As to those who fell among the thorns, after hearing, they choke themselves by means of the cares and riches and pleasures of life and do not grow to maturity.* ¹⁵*But the ones upon the good earth are they that hearing the word hold it fast in a noble and good heart and produce fruit in endurance."*

Luke's recording of the Parable of the Sower is strikingly similar to the passages in both Matthew and Luke. All three are more about soil conditions than about a sower who went out to sow his seeds. All three have the basic narrative—a sower casts seeds that land on a variety of soils, the condition of which determines the receptivity and rate of germination. All three Gospel accounts include the same soil conditions—the hard path, the rocky soil with its lack of depth and moisture, the area laden with thorns that ultimately lead to the demise of the fledgling growth, and finally good soil that produces abundantly. All three Gospel accounts include an intervening statement about Jesus' use of parables followed by the disciples' request for an explanation.

Furthermore, the explanations of the parable are closely patterned to each other. The basic thrust is the same. Satan snatches away the word of God from anyone whose heart is hard like the walking path along the edge of a field. The rocky soil describes one who received with joy the word of God but who does not grow because there is no depth, no encouragement. The seeds sown in the thorns are choked out like a person whose concern for God is less than that for earthly possessions and worldly passions. Finally, the good soil produces fruit in abundance. Again, viewing the broad strokes used to paint these word pictures, one barely discerns any difference between all three Synoptic versions, leaving the reader with the common interpretation that mere sowing of seed is no guarantee of its success. Other conditions and actions by outside influences can rob a person of the appropriate response to the shared gospel.

It is not until one analyzes closely the distinctions found in the interpretation of the parable that Luke's unique message may start to be understood. There are four.

(1) There is satanic deterrence. While all three Synoptic Gospels attribute the analogy of the birds taking the seed off of the hard path to the role of Satan taking away the word of God, Luke alone recorded the further explanation via the phrase ἵνα μὴ πιστεύσαντες σωθῶσιν (*hina mē pisteusantes sōthōsin*). Translated *in order that they may not believe and be saved*, Luke made two very important assertions. First, Luke identified faith and belief as the means of salvation. Luke already made the connection between faith and healing (Luke 7:9–10) and tied faith to forgiveness (Luke 5:20). The Parable of the Sower is one of four instances where Jesus addressed the relationship between faith and sal-

vation. These passages include the Parable of the Sower, the woman who anointed his feet with ointment and tears (Luke 7:50), the woman with the hemorrhage (Luke 8:48), and later to the blind beggar outside of Jericho (Luke 18:42). In the parable, Jesus indicated that Satan took the word of God away from the would-be believer, preventing both belief and salvation. Second, Luke presented unbelief as the direct result of a deliberate, malicious act. Satan is depicted as removing the word of God for the intended purpose that a person would not believe and consequently not be saved. The satanic deterrence is the cause of the unbelief. The satanic deterrence interrupts what would otherwise be considered normal—the seed germinating, rooting, growing, and bearing more fruit. Yet when the word is removed from that process, what is normal is completely reversed. When the word of God is absent, the heart grows cold and hard, and unreceptive to God's leadership.

(2) There is standing-off from the Divine. With this soil condition the parable moved from a dichotomy of believer/nonbeliever to a dichotomy between growing, maturing, productive Christian as opposed to one whose development is thwarted or arrested. The basic analogy stated some seeds fell on rocky soil that allowed initial growth that was doomed to failure. The unique Lucan contribution is seen in the description of what causes the growth of a new Christian to halt. Matthew indicated that "when tribulation or persecution ariseth because of the word, by and by he is offended" (Matt 13:21). Mark, likewise, applied the analogy to the Christian who is offended "when affliction or persecution ariseth for the word's sake" (Mark 4:17). Both Matthew and Mark used the term σκανδαλίζονται (*skandalidzontai*), which means "to be offended" or "to stumble in an offense." Matthew and Mark indicated that when a new Christian's faith is put to the test, many will stumble. Their failure is due in part to not having support, not having the background that would enable them to hold up under the persecution.

Luke, however, used the term ἀφίστανται (*aphistantai*), which means "to stand off from," instead of σκανδαλίζονται (*skandalidzontai*). Additionally, rather than persecution causing the offense, Luke said periods of temptation cause the Christian to stand off from God. Luke described a Christian holding God at arm's length, standing off from the presence of the Divine. Luke's narrative implies this act of stepping back from a trusting position that embraces God is caused by a condition described as rocky soil that has no moisture or depth. The comparison conveys a situation where what is needed for growth—moisture and soil—is not present. Accordingly, what is needed to resist temptation is not present. Luke depicted Jesus resisting temptation by praying, quoting Scripture, and by leaning on fellowship with the Father. When these basic rudiments of the faith are not present, Christians are doomed to fail via temptation. Instead of drawing closer to God, they hold God at arm's length. They fail to approach the very source that can provide victory in times of trial.

(3) There is self-destruction. Jesus' parable indicated seeds fell among the thorns. The same soil that gave nourishment and moisture to the thorns provided the seeds the opportunity to grow. At fault in this setting was not the soil but the surroundings. The thorns choked the fledgling plants. The explanation of the parable was that the thorns were identified as the cares, riches, and pleasures of life.

All three Gospel accounts are similar except for the voice of συμπνίγονται (*sumpnigontai*), the main verb of the sentence. Matthew and Mark both said the cares of the world and the delight of riches choked the new plants as they grew.[40] Luke changed the verb from the active voice used by Matthew and Mark to the middle/passive form of the same verb. On the surface this appears to make little difference. By changing to the passive voice, Luke would have changed nothing in the eventual meaning of the sentence. There is no difference between saying the cares of the world choked the seed or saying the seeds were choked by the cares of the world. The cares are doing the choking either way. What can be said is that the use of the passive voice is weak, lacking direct force. It is difficult to explain why a person of Luke's literary mastery would purposefully communicate with such a poor style.

Assuming Luke would not have used the passive voice and he intentionally changed Mark's active voice does provide an answer to the dilemma: Luke intended to use the middle voice. All finite verbs Greek have three voices: active, passive, and middle. Unfortunately for the interpreter, there is rarely a difference in spelling[41] between the middle and passive voice. The interpreter must use the context of the sentence or verb to determine if the middle voice is intended. The English language has lost the middle voice, using instead the reflexive pronoun. What the middle voice does in Greek is indicate the action the subject completes

---

40. Mark also added the desire for things to the subject of the sentence.
41. Also called inflection.

in its own behalf. As such, the subject does and receives the action of the verb.

If this is correct and Luke's intention was to use the middle voice, the meaning of the passage becomes obvious. Matthew and Mark both accurately indicate the cares of the world with its riches and pleasures corrupt the natural maturation of the Christian. Luke, however, laid the fault of these distractions squarely at the feet of Christians themselves! If the middle voice is intended, the translation changes from the seeds are choked by the thorns to the seeds choke themselves by means of the thorns—the cares, wealth and pleasures of this age. In words similar to Franklin Roosevelt's "The only thing we have to fear is fear itself," we as Christians have no one to blame but ourselves. God sows the seed into our hearts. We take that with joy and begin to grow, only to allow sin and its associates room to grow alongside. Rather than rooting out the causes of temptation, we become enamored with the world, tolerant of its deviance, and slowly anesthetize ourselves to the perils of an environment that is hostile to ways of Christ.

(4) There is sustained determination. As with Matthew and Mark, Luke's presentation indicates the seed that fell on good soil produced abundance. While all three use the same word for bear fruit, καρποφοροῦσιν (*karpophorousin*), Matthew and Mark have the stylized phrase thirty-, sixty-, one hundredfold. Luke deviated from the pattern at this point to say the seed that fell on good soil bore fruit with endurance. Luke clearly was seeking to communicate a message beyond that of productivity. All three carry the same emphasis: When everything works as it is designed, there is a great harvest. But Luke seems to have had an additional agenda.

The idea of endurance is communicated by the word ὑπομονή (*hupomonē*). A compound word, ὑπομονή (*hupomonē*) means "to remain under the load." Writing to a primarily Gentile audience, Luke could have been saying with the apostle Paul, "Let us not be weary in well doing: for in due season we shall reap, if we faint not" (Gal 6:7). Knowing the challenges the struggling church was to face, Luke was instructing them to stay the course. Harvest does not come immediately upon planting the seed. Luke seemed to pull together all the preceding elements of the parable into this final concluding statement. Do not allow circumstances to rob you of your faith. Let the word of God take hold in your life. Don't yield to temptation. Change the aspects of your life that give rise to temptation. Provide the environment for growth and maturation. Do not blame other people or other situations when you yield to temptation. Put the blame where it belongs, with the one who has cultivated the receptivity to the stimuli. And when all that has been done, just hang on! In the words of pop culture, when you get to the end of your rope, tie a knot and hold on. God will cause you to grow and produce abundance.

REFRAIN TO A PARABLE

Luke 8:16–18

> [16] *No one, after lighting a light, hides it in a container or places it under a bed, but rather places it on a lamp stand so that everyone entering in may see the light.* [17] *For nothing is hidden that will not become visible, nor is anything secret that will not be made known and come into the open.* [18] *Be careful how you listen: For to whomever has it will be given and to whomever has not even what he thinks he has will be taken away from him.*

From a cursory reading, one could conclude Luke only rearranged material that belonged to the Sermon on the Plain or Matthew's Sermon on the Mount. But like the refrain to a revival tune that repeatedly brings the worshiper back to the anchor message of a beloved song's lyric, this passage underscores Jesus' intent in speaking in parables.

Echoing the phase from the parable, "he who has an ear to hear let him hear," Jesus told his disciples to listen carefully. Sandwiched between the parable and the interpretation of the parable was Jesus' warning that the disciples had been trusted with the mysteries of the kingdom. Others heard the parable and did not comprehend its meaning—seeing they did not see and hearing they did not comprehend. Jesus further explained to the disciples that more would be given to those who had and that the little that others possessed would be taken away from them. While his statements were both poetic in style and figurative in nature, Jesus in reality was criticizing the religious insiders who had failed to understand the true nature and character of God. They had continued to perpetuate hollow rituals and an empty religion as the objects of worship rather than allowing worship to point to the true object of devotion. Consequently, they would continue in darkness.

To the contrary, the disciples would see, hear, and understand. Furthermore, the disciples, and all Christians after them, would spread the good news they had received. The analogy of the light on the light stand clearly demonstrates the gospel was to be shared. The "mysteries" of God should be understood as sarcasm. Jesus was saying religious establishments may conceal in darkness and shroud in secrecy the true meaning of God, but the informed disciple of Jesus would declare openly that which had been held privately.

While Jesus' disciples were blessed to be included in God's mission, they also received a warning. The disciples were to understand they too could one day lose the privilege of understanding the mysteries of God. What happened to the Pharisees could one day happen to them. This message is no less appropriate to the modern church. God will always have a people who will be willing to share the good news. When systems and programs begin to cloak the message of salvation in proprietary terms, God will take away the light and give it to someone else! The light is intended to reside on a lamp stand, shedding its beams on all who will come.

JESUS' FAMILY

Luke 8:19–21

¹⁹The mother and brothers of Jesus came to him and were not able to get near him through the crowd. ²⁰A message was delivered to him: "Your mother and brothers are standing outside desiring to see you." ²¹Jesus answered and said to them, "My mother and brothers are the ones hearing and doing the word of God."

Mary and Jesus' earthly brothers went to see him but could not gain access. A message was given to Jesus that they were outside and could not get in. Luke did not explain why Jesus' earthly family sought an audience. Placed here, the narrative seems to be less about Mary and her sons than it does about characteristics of the new family of God. As the Son of God, Jesus had a new family. Entry into that family was a matter of hearing and doing the will of God. The grammar of the text draws a contrast between Jesus' physical and spiritual families. Jesus was told his mother and brothers desired to see him. Specifically, Luke used the definite articles with both nouns: "the mother of you" and "the brothers of you." When Jesus responded with the identification of all who hear and do God's will as being his mother and brothers, the articles were not present. An accurate, how be it awkward, translation would be that those who hear and do the will of God are motherly and brotherly of me. Luke's dropping of the articles in the Jesus' comments causes the phrase to lose a degree of specificity and become more adjectival, describing the characteristics of a group rather than identifying specific individuals.

Of interest is what this story conveys about the generally held public view of Jesus and his background. While Mary obviously knew Jesus' background, the crowd who saw the events unfold believed the entourage to be Jesus' *real* brothers and sisters. Though absent in Luke, Mark's representation of the event was an effort to prevent Jesus from continuing to embarrass the family (Mark 3:19-22). "They think you are crazy down at the lodge. You have got to stop this Messiah talk," they must have said. "Come on home, and we will put you back to work in the shop. You will not even need to speak to the public. One of us will do that!" Nowhere in the Gospels is there any evidence that Jesus' miraculous conception was ever public knowledge during his earthly life and ministry.

WHERE THERE'S A WIND, THERE'S A WAYWARD HEART

Luke 8:22-25

> ²²*It happened one day that Jesus got into a boat with his disciples and said to them, "Let us cross to the other side of the lake." So they shoved off.* ²³*While they were sailing, Jesus fell asleep. Just then, a wind storm came down on the lake so that they were being filled and were in danger.* ²⁴*Going to Jesus, they woke him saying, "Master, Master! We are perishing!" Getting up, Jesus rebuked the wind and the waves of water. The wind and waves stopped and became still.* ²⁵*Then Jesus said to them, "Where is your faith?" Fearing, they were awestruck, saying one to another, "Who is this that commands even the winds and water and they obey him?"*

"Where there is a will, there is a way." The vernacular expression holds wide acceptance and understanding. The sentiment speaks to the unquenchable nature of the human spirit. When encouraged, there is nothing a person cannot do. The certainty of success clearly is stated by the logic of the phrase: A person who determines to do a thing and perseveres, even against immeasurable odds, will find ultimate victory. Such a story was retold in Walt Disney's 1994 historic fiction film about the 1917, 522-mile dog-sled race from Winnipeg, Manitoba, to St. Paul, Minnesota. The young hero of the story, Will Stoneman, battled incredible odds from the elements, from his competitors, and from his own fears in order to save the family farm and fulfill his deceased father's ambition. Capturing the hopes and hearts of the spectators and the general public from two nations, young Stoneman soon was dubbed "Iron Will."

Unfortunately, such an indomitable spirit is not always visible in matters of faith. What causes a person to lose heart? What causes faith to wane? What events transpire in a believer's life to precipitate doubt? All too often it appears that the least amount of difficulty will shatter a Christian's confidence; with the slightest wind comes a wounded, wayward heart.

These are the central issues of the story of Jesus' calming the sea. Not only did Luke reveal to his readers why a person's faith can falter but he also provided through the words of Jesus the understanding to prevent doubt and to cultivate an unshakable faith.

"Where is your faith?" was the question Jesus asked as he woke from rest in the boat to find the disciples battling the elements and fearing for their lives, their faith being all but gone. Though in the middle of the story, Jesus' question holds the key to understanding the meaning of the events that took place that night on the lake. But notice these events first in sequence.

In all three Synoptic Gospels the events unfold about the same (Matt 8:23–27; Mark 4:35–41). Jesus and the disciples entered the boat to go to the other side of the lake. While Jesus slept in the boat, a storm suddenly appeared, threatening the safety of all on board. In a panic, the disciples woke Jesus. In Matthew and Luke, Jesus reprimanded them for their lack of faith. In all three accounts, Jesus calmed the storm. Finally, all three stories end with the disciples being amazed at Jesus' ability. From these details, one can understand what causes doubt and also how to prevent doubt.

Doubt occurs because of uncertainly. Fear sets in when people feel they have lost control, when circumstances move with apparent aimlessness, all too often in a downward spiral. Such was the case with the disciples. Luke indicated that a *storm of wind came down upon the lake.* Matthew and Mark indicated by other means the same suddenness of the inclement weather. Without warning, the disciples were in peril. Luke used the terms συνεπληροῦντο (*suneplērounto*) and ἐκινδύνευον (*ekinduneuon*) to describe their condition. The first is a term used only by Luke in the New Testament. More important than its definition is the verb's passive voice. The issue was not that there was water in the boat, a condition most certainly to be avoided! The real issue was this undesirable circumstance was not only not their fault but it also was beyond their control. Their boat was being filled completely with water by an outside force, and they had no ability to change the situation! Understanding the force of Luke's word choice for the first term helps explain the second term. They were being filled up and consequently were continuing in jeopardy. The second term is used only here in the Gospels and limited use by Paul. Perhaps the most illustrative reference is found where Paul described his ordeals in propagating the gospel. He said, "In journeyings often, in perils of waters, in perils of robbers, in perils by mine own countrymen, in perils by the heathen, in perils in the city, in perils in the wilderness, in perils in the sea, in perils among false brethren" (2 Cor 11:26). The imminent danger to the disciples was real, it was certain, it was inevitable, and what is more, they knew it.

These conditions led to doubt on the part of the disciples. Jesus already knew their answer when he asked, "Where is your faith?" Their faith was gone. The circumstances had robbed them of their confidence in God's divine protection. In the same way, Christians today lose heart and their faith grows cold. Circumstances force on them a reality they would neither choose nor care to endure. The difficulties are real, and they are lasting. Furthermore, their problems are caused by someone or something else. The economy causes employment problems. Health complications prevent full and meaningful quality of life. Worry about a family member snatches away all comfort from the God who once felt so close. Jesus asks the same question today, "Where is your faith?"

Thankfully the passage is not without hope. Jesus did not leave the disciples in despair; nor will he leave us in despair. Notice carefully the disciples' statement. In Matthew and Mark, the disciples responded in awe and wonder upon observing Jesus' great power. The disciples commented, "What manner of man is this, that even the winds and the sea obey him!" (Matt 8:27). Luke, however, revealed not only Jesus' ability but also his intention when he recorded the disciples' reaction as *"Who is this that commands even the winds and water and they obey him?"* That the elements obeyed Jesus is common to all the Synoptic Gospels, but Luke clarified that Jesus commanded the elements and they obeyed. By adding that Jesus commanded even the wind and the water and they obeyed, Luke stated that Jesus always was in control of the situation. Far from splitting grammatical and theological hairs, Luke clarified why Jesus was astonished at the disciples' lack of faith. If Jesus was in control of stopping the storm when he awoke, why would the disciples assume he was not in charge of starting the storm before he went to sleep? Jesus was saying to all disciples, then and now, that nothing comes the disciple's way that is not ordained of God nor intended to be used to glorify God. No event surprises God. God never says, "Oops! I sure didn't see that one coming." God is always in control. Faith should position us to live lives that reflect such confidence, a position from which we never should falter.

GERASENE DEMONIAC—POWER OR PERMISSION

Luke 8:26–39

²⁶*They sailed into the region of Gerasene, which is on the shore opposite Galilee.* ²⁷*As Jesus disembarked, a man with demons from the city met him. For a considerable time, the demoniac had neither put on himself clothes nor lived in a house but among the tombs.* ²⁸*Seeing Jesus, he fell down shouting before Jesus and said with a loud voice, "What business do you and I have between each other, Jesus, the Son of the most high God? I know who you are—Stop torturing me!"* ²⁹*(Jesus had command the unclean spirit to come out of the man. For many times the demon seized the man and even though he was guarded, being bound with chains and leg irons, he would break the bonds and be driven by the demon into the wilderness.)* ³⁰*But Jesus asked him, "What is your name?" He responded, "Legion"—because many demons entered into him.* ³¹*And they begged Jesus not to command them to enter into the abyss.* ³²*Now there was a considerable Number of swine rooting around for food on the hillside. The demons begged Jesus to let them enter into the swine. Jesus allowed them.* ³³*Leaving the*

man, the demons entered into the swine. The herd rushed over a steep bank into the lake and drowned. ³⁴Seeing what happened, the herdsmen ran and told the story in the city and in the country. ³⁵So they went out to see what had happened and came to Jesus and found the man from whom the demons had left. He was sitting at the feet of Jesus, clothed and in his right mind. The people were terrified. ³⁶The ones who had seen the events told how the man had been possessed. ³⁷All the people from the region of Geresene asked Jesus to leave them, for they were overcome with great fear. Getting into the boat, Jesus began to return. ³⁸But the man out of whom the demons had left begged Jesus to be with him. But Jesus sent him away saying, ³⁹"Return to your home and tell all what God has done to you." So he left, proclaiming throughout the city all that Jesus had done for him.

Luke's recording of the healing of the Gerasene demoniac follows the basic Marcan outline while maintaining undeniable Lucan characteristics. The story is replete with nautical terms used only in Luke and Acts. Translated above as *shove off, on the shore opposite Galilee,* and *disembarked* are terms Luke used to relate a high degree of understanding of the seafaring arts. Furthermore, Luke's medical background cannot be suppressed, noticing details not unlike those on a modern medical patient intake form. For example, the demoniac was not just naked; he had not been able to dress himself for an extended period of time. Furthermore, his domicile was not the basic shelter of a house. Rather, the demoniac endured the elements, unprotected from their harsh reality. Finally, Luke's empathy for the downcast is seen throughout the account as aid is rendered to a poor, diseased, social outcast who was in need of help. But as typical as the presentation is, the Lucan Gerasene demoniac story is not about receiving Jesus' power but about receiving Jesus' permission.

Luke's telling of the Gerasene demoniac story is in keeping with Jesus' authority to control the seas, demonstrated in the previous passage. At Gerasene, three different groups or persons asked Jesus' permission to do a particular thing. Inherent within the very request is the belief by the petitioner that the person to whom the request is made has the power to grant the request. Otherwise, why would permission be sought?

Furthermore, Luke frequently emphasized his unique message by stating things differently from the Synoptic Gospels. Specifically, Mark used παρακαλέω (*parakaleō*), meaning to beg or beseech, for all three requests—by the demons, by the indigenous population, and by the former demoniac. Luke, however, changed this series and used three different synonyms. The demons begged, παρακαλέω (*parakaleō*). The local population begged, ἐρωτάω (*erōtaō*). The man healed also begged, δέομαι (*deomai*). No great lexical definition can be ascribed to these three terms, a fact that could lead one to conclude this simply is an example of Luke's fluid literary style. However, a careful reading of Luke recognizes these shifts are purposeful and demonstrate Luke's intentions. To that end, notice the request, the reason there is an expectation of fulfillment, and the resulting manner in which Jesus gave each what they requested.[42]

(1) The demons asked permission to leave the possessed man and enter the pigs rather than being consigned to the depths of the abyss. The demons recognized Jesus' true identity and power and knew Jesus could send them anywhere he pleased. Perhaps consignment to the abyss would mean they could do no harm to others as it was held to be the abode of malicious spirits only. Entering the swine gave them one last opportunity to create disorder in the created order. The demons were willing to destroy themselves in order to destroy others.

Such is the nature of sin in world today. Misery loves company, and disharmony breeds discord. Before much time has elapsed, the absence of good in a situation will cause wrong to grow exponentially and the innocent are damaged along with the guilty. While this is a sad reality for all, it is tragically so for those who should understand the character of God and respond accordingly. The nature of sin is the same regardless of one's relationship to the Father. Self-destruction appears to be inevitable, even among God's children.

(2) The local townspeople asked Jesus permission for his departure. Where the demons were motivated by the uncontrollable desire for random destruction, the townsfolk were motivated by fear. They saw in Jesus something they had never seen, something they could not explain and could never control. They saw in Jesus the ultimate upheaval of their

---

42. The reader should exercise care to remain within the confines of Luke's narrative. Little if any productive results will be gained from analyzing the issues of whether or not the demon possession was real or just a mental disorder. The reader should hear the details of the narrative and respond to the intended meaning of the text.

entire way of life, and they were terrified by the prospect of such change. Overcome by this fear, they asked Jesus to depart from their midst. Sadly, in the face of their fear, Jesus granted their request; he left. Perhaps one of faith's greatest challenges is overcoming fear. Trust and doubt cannot survive together. Faith and fear are mutually exclusive.

(3) The formerly possessed man asked permission to be with Jesus. At first blush, the former demoniac seems to be denied his request. But a closer examination reveals a truly beautiful lesson. The demons wanted to destroy themselves, and Jesus granted their request, sending them into the ill-fated swine. The local population wanted to live in their fear, and Jesus granted their request by departing from their shores. But the man, clothed and sane, asked permission to be with Jesus, a request that drew a seemingly negative answer. "Stay here," said Jesus, "and tell others what God has done." What seemed to be a denial in fact was the greatest affirmative response in the narrative. Luke continued the narrative to indicate the man traveled through the entire city, proclaiming the message of release from captivity, from fear, from isolation, from aimlessness. What better way to be with Jesus!

TWO COMMANDS AND A PROMISE: JAIRUS'S FAITH STORY

Luke 8:40–42a, 49–55

⁴⁰Upon his return, the crowd welcomed Jesus, for they were all waiting for him. ⁴¹Then a man named Jairus, who was a ruler of the synagogue, came to Jesus and falling down at Jesus' feet begged Jesus to come to his house ⁴²ᴬbecause he had only one daughter, twelve years old, who was dying.

⁴⁹While Jesus was still speaking, a leader from the synagogue came saying, "Your daughter is dead. Trouble the teacher no longer." ⁵⁰Hearing this Jesus answered, "Fear not, summon your faith, and she will be saved." ⁵¹Reaching the house, Jesus would not let anyone enter except Peter, James, John, and the father and the mother of the child. ⁵²All were crying and mourning her. But Jesus said, "Stop crying! She is not dead, only sleeping." ⁵³They ridiculed him, knowing she was dead. ⁵⁴Taking her hand, he called saying, "Child, get up." ⁵⁵Her spirit returned to her, and she rose at once.

> Jesus gave orders that she be given something to eat. ⁵⁶ Her parents were amazed. Jesus commanded them to say nothing of what had happened.

Too often the story of the synagogue ruler named Jairus is told from the perspective of his death's doorstep child—Jairus's daughter—or even more likely from the perspective of the intervening episode of the woman with the internal hemorrhage. While it is true that Luke followed the Marcan order of the narrative and that Mark routinely depended upon the A'B'A' literary pattern—Jairus's daughter, woman with hemorrhage, Jairus's daughter—to make a point about the entire sequence, Luke was pursuing a different goal. Simply stated, the story of Jairus's faith cannot be summarized as a healing story of either the child or the woman. The story of Jairus's faith presents all who hear it with an identification of a basic human reality that when addressed by divine intervention yields comfort and hope.

The story is well known. Jairus, a ruler of the synagogue, had a sick child. Great respect was paid to Jesus in the very request for assistance, a detail Luke certainly wanted his Roman governmental reader to know. While going to Jairus's house, a crowd followed. A woman broke through the crowd, touched Jesus, was healed, was discovered, and following a fearful confession, was affirmed by Jesus. Following the interruption, the Jairus narrative was reestablished with the sad news of the child's death. Yet Jesus did not give up. Upon arriving at Jairus's home, Jesus raised the child from death, her life returning to her deceased body.

The flow of the narrative as presented by these details is easy enough to follow. However, to understand the intent of the narrative one must understand the force of the two imperative verbs used in the story. After the woman's healing, Jairus was told, "Your daughter is dead. Why are you still troubling the master?" It is at this moment of heightened tension in the narrative that the primary meaning is revealed. Jesus responded to Jairus with two imperatives and one promise: "Stop being afraid, summon your faith, and she will be saved."

(1) The first imperative Jesus issued to Jairus was, "Stop being afraid." The force of the phrase μὴ φοβοῦ (*mē phobou*) can be overlooked easily in English translation. This phrase is rendered as "Fear not" in the King James Version and the American Standard Version, as "Do not be afraid" by the New American Bible, New American Standard Version,

New Jerusalem Bible, and New King James Version, as "Don't be afraid" by the New International Version and as "Do not Fear" by the English Standard Version, the New Revised Standard Version, and the Revised Standard Version. However, the negative μή (*mē*) used with the present imperative conveys the idea of discontinuing an action already in progress. Jesus commanded Jairus to stop being afraid.

The reasons for Jairus's fear are very understandable; his only daughter was ill and at the point of death. But more pervasive than one father/daughter struggle with sickness, Jesus' statement indicated an important aspect of human nature: We all fear. Being afraid is a natural, all-too-human condition. It is driven by appropriate and inappropriate stimuli. It never goes away; it is relentless. Fear clutches us in the cradle with our first experience of separation anxiety and refuses to relinquish its control until death eases its icy grip. Fear comes in all shapes and sizes and most often is highly personalized. While the specifics of fear differ widely, the results are very focused: Fear immobilizes its victims and captures their joy, incarcerating their victory in self-made prisons.

(2) But fear need not have the final word. Jesus commanded Jairus to summon his faith. While it defiles the constraints of grammar, faith is intuitively both a verb and a noun. Jesus instructed Jairus to reach inside himself and to bring up the thing called faith, to position faith in the presence of fear, and then to demand that faith do what it was designed to do—allow a person to trust God to take control. This is precisely why acts of faith are so difficult for many people. In fear, they cling to the erroneous perception that they are actually in control of their circumstances. True wisdom enlightens the soul regarding the issue of control and accurately debunks the concept entirely. We are never in control! But God is.

Of what are you afraid? Are you afraid of spiraling gas prices, the weak dollar, and a fragile economy? Are you afraid there will be too much month at the end of the money, too many retirement days at the end of the retirement dollars? Do you fear being alone? Are you afraid your children will never be successful, stand on their own, and leave home? Or are you afraid your children will be successful, they will stand on their own, and they will leave home? To all of these Jesus said, "Stop being afraid! Summon your faith! You will be made whole."

There is a fear that everyone in the church has experienced though for many of us it was long ago. There is the fear the lost feel as they face the uncertainty of eternity without Christ. Many do not even know what it is they fear. They cannot articulate this fear, but it is real and they know it. To them we need to carry the words of Jesus: "Stop being afraid! Summons your faith! You will be saved."

THRONGED OR TOUCHED

Luke 8:42b-48

⁴²ᴮWhile he was going, the crowd pressed hard against Jesus. ⁴³A women who had a hemorrhage of blood for twelve years, having spent her entire livelihood on physicians, and they were not able to heal her in the least, ⁴⁴came from behind and touched the hem of Jesus' garment and immediately her hemorrhage of blood ceased. ⁴⁵Jesus said, "Who touched me?" When all denied, Peter said, "Master, the crowd is surrounding you and pressing you." ⁴⁶But Jesus said, "Someone touched me, for I know that power went out from me." ⁴⁷But the woman, knowing that she was not hidden, trembling, came and fell before him, telling all the people the reason she touched him and how she was healed immediately. ⁴⁸Then Jesus said to her, "Daughter, your faith has saved you. Go in peace."

Three characters are prominent in the story of the woman with the internal hemorrhage. There is, of course, the woman herself, representing a stereotype for Luke. She stands for all the outcasts of society who try though they may, can never take control of circumstances that negatively affect their lives. Through no fault of her own, she was penniless, without standing in her culture, and for all practical purposes, without hope. She represents one other characteristic for Luke; she reached out to Jesus when all else had failed.

The second character is the crowd. Taken collectively, the crowd represents the oppressor. Though they did not know they were guilty of such, an all too often and tragic reality of the human condition, the crowd overlooked the woman. That was their role. The harsh fact of their oversight proved the point of her nonexistence. She didn't matter. They were busy furthering their own agenda, which on the surface seems rather high toned and fancy; they wanted to be near Jesus. But as the plot will reveal, they were further from Jesus' attention than the one who to them was invisible. In an ironic twist, Peter actually became the spokesperson for the crowd, proving that callous disregard for the true needs of humanity is one characteristic of human nature and can be displayed by anyone at any time. Anyone can get caught in man's inhumanity to man.

Finally, there was Jesus. He remained sensitive to the Holy Spirit's leading, even in the midst of commotion. Even without his intention, he was used as a conduit for the ongoing work of God's kingdom.

As the narrative unfolds, the plot contrasts the socially acceptable crowd with the socially outcast woman. The scene opens with an awkward statement that seems out of place: *While he was going, the crowd pressed hard against Jesus.* The Greek word συνέπνιγον (*sunepnigon*) is translated here as "pressing hard." The King James Version indicates the crowd "thronged" Jesus (Luke 8:42b). Unique to the Synoptic Gospels, the term is used only in the Parable of the Sower and here in the story of the woman with the issue of blood. In all three Synoptic Gospels the term is used to describe the manner in which the thorns crowd out the seed. But only Luke repeated the word in description of the crowd surrounding Jesus. For Luke, the crowd pressing Jesus was the same as the thorns pressing the seed. As a result, Luke's narrative depicts the crowd mindlessly seeking its own agenda, with no regard for the health and well-being of another. The woman is literally and figuratively shoved aside.

Unfortunately this comes as no surprise to the astute reader of Luke's Gospel. As stated before, the woman plays a predictable role. But Luke demonstrated more than how society devalues the weak. Luke showed that heaven values the weak. "If I can only touch the hem of his garment," she said to herself, "I will be healed." Completely self-effaced, she thought nothing of her own ability. All rested with reaching Jesus, who had the resolution to her problem.

This faith position prefaces one of the most beautiful confessions in Scripture. Luke departed from Mark's narrative to set the stage for her statement. Mark recorded that the woman, "knowing what was done in her" (Mark 5:33), came and fell before Jesus. Luke revealed an additional quality when he said, *Knowing that she was not hidden*, she came and fell down trembling at the feet of Jesus. Unlike most of the crowd who wanted a public encounter with Jesus, she was happy to be changed quietly. There was no pretense, no ambition for fame or glory; there was only recognition that Jesus alone could do what she needed to be done.

Furthermore, the sincerity of her response was obvious. After breaking the bounds of anonymity, there was a flood of confession. What Mark described simply as "she told him all the truth" (Mark 5:33), Luke described in much greater detail. (1) The woman made her proclamation to all who were present. There was no reluctance on her part anymore. She no longer felt the stigma of social rejection. She no longer believed she was less than human, not even deserving a voice. Rich and poor were there that day, but wealth did not matter. What she had to tell, she proclaimed to all. (2) The woman proclaimed the reason she touched Jesus. Though Luke did not elaborate on her reason, the reader certainly is to imply at least two driving factors: She had a need, and she believed Jesus could meet her need. Beginning with human need is always appropriate in communicating the gospel. In fact, perception on the part of the individual that no need exists is often the first hurdle in the conviction process. Who among us has not heard "Well I certainly am as good as old so and so"? The woman knew her need and what is more, knew she could do nothing about meeting her need. Furthermore, she obviously was motivated by a conviction that Jesus was both able and willing to act on her behalf. (3) Following her reason was the result of her actions. She was healed. Not only was she healed but she was healed immediately. The truth of testimony that can never be denied is what Jesus has done for you.

In 1968, Ben Haden became the eleventh pastor of First Presbyterian Church of Chattanooga, Tennessee. A former attorney and newspaper editor, Haden was noted for his conversational delivery of his sermons. An Old Testament and a New Testament text prefaced typically one story. These stories were taken from real world events of everyday happenings of real people who had one thing in common: Jesus had changed their lives. "Changed Lives" became the media ministry of Haden that was continued even after his thirty-one-year tenure as pastor concluded.

The woman with the internal hemorrhage had a testimony that could not be doubted because it was her personal story. She declared publicly to all who were present what was the reason for her action, why she took the action, and what happened to her, how her life was changed, because of her action.

POWER TO DO GOD'S WORK

Luke 9:1–6

¹*Calling together the Twelve, Jesus gave them power and authority over all demons and power and authority to heal illness* ²*and he sent them to proclaim the kingdom of God and to heal the sick.* ³*And he said to them, "Take nothing on the way; neither a walking stick nor a pack, neither bread nor money, and do not take two garments.* ⁴*Enter whatever house you come to, remain there, and depart from there.* ⁵*If anyone does not receive you, leaving that city, shake the dust from your feet as a testimony against them."* ⁶*Going out, they traveled through the villages, proclaiming the good news and healing.*

In the small community outside of Birmingham, Alabama, where I was raised, there lived a retired schoolteacher, Miss Lucille Watkins. She served as our church clerk. I would marvel during business meetings at the poetic sameness in her record and in her vocal tone as she read the minutes of our church's business. She and her sister, Mary, lived in a frame house with two enormous magnolia trees in the front yard. As I grew older, I gradually stopped yielding to the beckoning challenge to climb and began listening instead to Miss Mary and Miss Lucille as they recounted stories of life and of lessons learned.

Upon my commencement from undergraduate studies, I was presented with a gift from Miss Lucille: a handwritten volume of southern expressions, words of wisdom, and of sage advice. What a treasure! I have read and reread this "composition notebook" again and again. It draws me back to another day—to internalized values that function even without being called on to do so. One such entry summarizes perfectly what I believe Jesus intended when he commissioned his twelve disciples. "*Honest work bears a lovely face, for it is the father of pleasure and the mother of good fortune. It is the keystone of prosperity and the sire of fame. And best of all work is relief from sorrow and the handmaiden of happiness.*" The time had arrived for the disciples to go to work.

In order to engage the disciples fully, Jesus prepared them in three ways. Jesus' instructions addressed empowerment, entitlement, and encouragement. (1) Jesus gave the disciples direction and empowerment. Specifically, Jesus sent the disciples to preach the kingdom of God and to heal the sick. Still within the confines of the Galilean ministry, the reader should understand the nature of the message to be proclaimed. Luke's use of the phrase "proclaim the kingdom of God" was not necessarily "good news." While inclusion and forgiveness certainly were mainstays of the message, the idea of a new kingdom with new requirements would not have been embraced fully. The difficulty of this message, however, was in fact softened by the accompanying compassion for human well-being. In addition to proclaiming the kingdom, the disciples were sent to heal the sick. Genuine concern for the total person always characterized Jesus' ministry.

The disciples were not only given direction but they also were empowered. Three methods accomplished this task. First, they were given power over demons and power to heal the sick. Second, Luke emphasized the empowerment via redundancy. The word for power used by Mark and Matthew was ἐξουσίαν (*exousian*), which means "authority over someone or something." The resulting idea often is that of authority over a certain situation. Luke, however, related that Jesus gave δύναμιν καὶ ἐξουσίαν (*dunamin kai exousian*), "power and authority." No clear distinction between the two terms is intended. Luke's literary style frequently includes synonyms to strengthen the statement. Finally, Luke changed Mark's and Matthew's vocabulary choice for "called unto him" (Mark 6:7 and Matt 10) to "called together." The difference between προσκαλεῖται (*proskaleitai*), "called to himself," and συγκαλεσάμενος (*sugkalesamenos*), "called together," is slight from a lexical standpoint. However, Luke's vocabulary again opens a key to understanding the historic significance of the situation. Not until the commissioning of the seventy in the Judean ministry were the disciples dispatched two by two. A detail the language of Matthew and Mark glosses over is that the Galilean mission charge was as a group. Did Jesus sense the tentative preparation of the disciples? Did he know they were not ready for the pressure of relative isolation? If so, the directions were a warning of pending danger or difficulty. Accordingly, Jesus called them together and sent them out together in the perceived safety of numbers. They were given direction and empowerment.

(2) Jesus gave the disciples prohibition to entitlement. The phrase in verse 3, *take nothing on the way*, seems to be an overarching summary phrase followed by segmented specificity. Jesus' instruction to *take nothing on the way* meant the disciples were to take *neither a walking stick nor a pack*. Jesus' instruction to *take nothing on the way* meant the disciples were to take *neither bread nor money*. Jesus' instructions to *take nothing on the*

way meant the disciples were not to take *two outer garments*. Taken individually, any of the three sub descriptors would leave the reader believing the travelers would be unprepared or unsupported. Taken as a whole, a different tone immerges. The disciples were not to be unprepared; they were to be unconcerned. As apostles, sent to proclaim the kingdom of God, the disciples were to be completely dependent on God for everything that happened. They were to have no inherent authority and power. They only presented that which was given to them to present.

(3) Finally, Jesus prepared the disciples to encounter rejection by providing encouragement. As was seen earlier, Jesus was preparing the disciples for the difficulty of the task. They would be uplifted by their comrades while in common hardship. But this point was too important to leave to innuendo. Accordingly, Jesus told the disciples specifically, "Listen fellows! This is going to get tough." Jesus indicated they would encounter rejection. Anticipation of this ultimate reality in itself helped prepare the disciples. Furthermore, Jesus prescribed their response. "Shake the dust from your feet and go to the next town," said Jesus. The irony of this action was that it was the same activity that a Jewish rabbi took upon returning from a Gentile territory. Although this commissioning took place in Galilee, one can be sure the intended message was understood loud and clear: Jewish rejection of Jesus was no different than the pagan rejection of Yahweh. When the kingdom of God on earth was proclaimed and realized, there would be no distinction between Jew and Gentile, only belief and failure to believe.

Given these three components of Jesus' preparation, one can return to the thesis of the incident. Jesus was engaging his followers in work worth doing. It was a new kind of work. It was work that did not follow constraints of custom. But in the final analysis, it was work that when accomplished engaged the workers in something beyond themselves.

LIKE FATHER, LIKE SON

Luke 9:7–9

⁷When Herod the tetrarch heard all that was happening, he was utterly perplexed because it was being said by some that John was raised from the dead ⁸but by others that Elijah had appeared and by still others that a prophet from long ago had come back to life.

⁹But Herod said, "I myself had John beheaded. Who is this about whom I am hearing?" And Herod sought to see Jesus.

That Jesus' ministry was succeeding was affirmed by the reaction of Herod the tetrarch. One of the sons of Herod the Great, Herod the tetrarch was literally a ruler of a fourth. When Herod the Great died in approximately 4 BC, his kingdom was divided among his sons. Herod the tetrarch ruled in Galilee, and he had a problem. The skyrocketing public acclaim of the "miracle worker from Nazareth" was causing disturbing rumors throughout his reign. Specifically, "Who was this guy, anyway?"

"The apple doesn't fall far from the tree." Perhaps more accurate words have never been spoken. Who has not seen this sage wisdom born out in the relationships of family and friends? It is true today; it was true in Herod's day. Herod the Great heard a rumor; Herod the tetrarch heard a rumor. The father was troubled and all of Judea with him; the son was completely at a loss and utterly perplexed. The Great learned that a legitimate "born" King of the Jews was on the scene, presumably to challenge his right to rule; the tetrarch was told the man he had beheaded was again living. One searched the Scriptures and found Micah 5:2 indicated the Messiah was to be born in Bethlehem. One Herod said, "What if this is the true king?" while the other Herod said, "What if I have killed the long-anticipated prophet?" And for the final comparison, Herod the Great said to the wise men, "Go and search diligently for the young child; and when ye have found him, bring me word again, that I may come and worship him also" (Matt 2:8). Luke recorded that Herod the tetrarch *sought to see Jesus*. Like father like son?

Not all inquiry is honest and open without any ulterior motive. Neither Herod wanted to worship Jesus. They both sought him to kill him, to eliminate him, to remove his positive influence, to ensure the stability of their own control. Sin forces people into the same mode today. Sin is nothing more than seizing control and relegating God to a position of subrogation. We put ourselves in this role and force others to do the same. If Jesus Christ becomes too prominent, we find a way to force him out. Too often, there is a little of Herod in all of us.

FIVE THOUSAND FED

Luke 9:10–17

¹⁰Returning, the apostles told Jesus all they had done. And taking them alongside, Jesus withdrew privately into a city called Bethsaida. ¹¹But learning this, the crowd followed Jesus. He welcomed them, speaking to them about the kingdom of God and healing that which needed to be healed. ¹²But the day began drawing to a close. Coming to him, the Twelve said, "Allow the crowd to leave in order to enter the surrounding villages and countryside so that they may lodge and may find provision, for we are in an isolated place." ¹³But Jesus said to them, "You give them something to eat." They then said, "All we have are five loaves of bread and two fish; we are not expected to go and buy food for all these people, are we?" ¹⁴About five thousand men were there. Jesus said to his disciples, "Tell them to sit in groups of fifty." ¹⁵They did so and made them sit down. ¹⁶Taking the five loaves and two fish and looking up into heaven, Jesus blessed them, broke them into pieces, and gave them to the disciples to distribute to the crowds. ¹⁷The crowds ate and all were satisfied. Twelve baskets of remaining pieces were collected.

The feeding of the five thousand is a story whose details are very well known. As night approached, Jesus urged his disciples to feed the hungry crowd. Sitting in groups of fifty, the crowd was fed with five loaves and two fish, which Jesus broke after he had offered thanksgiving for the Father's provision. Barclay summarized well the two positions that scholars often take to explain the miracle—that either Jesus physically multiplied a small amount of food or as Jesus demonstrated the importance of self-sacrifice, he broke down the selfish nature of the crowd who one by one produced and shared all their hoarded provisions.[43] Regardless of the rhetoric, the event was truly a magnificent, God-inspired, miraculous moment.

But the event was more than just a miracle. The feeding of the five thousand is the only miracle recorded in all four Gospel accounts (Matt 14:13; Mark 6:30; Luke 9:10; John 6:1). All four Gospels consistently fol-

---

43. Barclay, *The Gospel of Luke*, 118.

low the details of the story: It was late, Jesus told the disciples to feed the crowd, the disciples produced only five loaves and two fish, Jesus thanked the Father, and all five thousand men ate to their satisfaction, fifty per group. Furthermore, all four Gospel writers emphasized the underlying consequence of the event, namely, Jesus reached a zenith in his Galilean ministry that would not be surpassed. The miracle to the masses was a turning point in the outward perception of Jesus. The public nature of his ministry was undeniably altered. Jesus was forced into a public prominence he had neither sought nor wished to maintain. The grassroots uprising to identify Jesus as the popular Messiah was undeniable. After all, did the Jews not believe that God would bring a deliverer? Did they not believe that this one would demonstrate God's power? Certainly providing for the welfare of the needy by feeding the hungry was a sign of divine activity.

But for Luke there was even more. Luke's account of the feeding of the five thousand presents a rare Lucan reduction of Mark. Prone to the substitution of numerous synonyms and the elaboration on Mark's basic narrative, Luke's literary style is here uncharacteristically brief, omitting many Marcan details. It is as if Luke were agreeing that the feeding of the five thousand was a watershed moment, but more important to Luke than Jesus' arrival at this moment of public acclaim was how he had arrived at this moment in time—a realization that draws the reader's attention back to Luke's setting.

Before the miracle occurred, several pivotal events were announced. (1) There was validation of the disciples' success. Having been commissioned to go to the cities and villages of the Galilee, the disciples returned with glowing stories of how God had acted on their behalf. The movement of the kingdom had become the purview of the laity. People had come to expect the divine power and presence when Jesus spoke. People were in fact seeking Jesus out to have him heal their sick. People were breaking through ritual taboo to touch even the hem of his garment, expecting God's power at the slightest encounter. But now God was working through ordinary people.

Unnoticed by the general public, one issue that brought Jesus to the pinnacle of his Galilean ministry was the success of the laity. (2) Such success of God's people always draws attention to God. Even though the disciples were excited and encouraged by their recent productivity, it was Jesus' reputation that was bolstered. Kingdom growth always focuses glory and honor on the object of worship, not on the workers whose efforts contributed to the event. (3) Finally, the peak of Jesus' popularity was reached when his response to human need was not reduced by his public acclaim. How many times in today's society has success ruined the person on which it settled? Jesus' response to the crowd demonstrated complete compassion. He welcomed them, and he healed what needed to be healed.

Herein lies the meaning of the text for the church and the Christian seeking to minister to the lost world. Just as a few pieces of bread and fish feed the masses, the efforts of only a few draw attention to the divine. Jesus will give his people all they need to accomplish the tasks placed before them. Simply stated, God's work done in God's way will never lack God's supply.

WILL THE REAL MESSIAH PLEASE STAND UP?

Luke 9:18–27

[18]Now it happened when Jesus was praying alone that the disciples were with him. Jesus asked them saying, "Who are the crowds saying that I am?" [19]They answered him saying, "John the Baptist, others Elijah, still others a prophet from old come back to life." [20]Jesus said to them, "What about you? Who do you say that I am?" Peter answered saying, "The Christ of God." [21]Charging them, Jesus gave strict instruction to tell that to no one at all, [22]adding it was necessary for the Son of man to suffer much, be rejected by the elders and the chief priest and scribes, be killed, and on the third day be raised again. [23]Jesus said to all of them, "If anyone desires to come after me, let him deny himself, take up his cross daily, and follow me. [24]For anyone desiring to save his soul will lose it; but the one losing his soul for my sake will save it. [25]For what does it profit a man if he gains the whole world but destroys or loses himself? [26]Furthermore, the one being ashamed of me and my words, of this one I will be ashamed when I come into my glory and into the glory of the Father and of the angels. [27]I say to you for certain, there are some standing here today who will not experience death before they see the kingdom of God."

The Galilean Beginning 133

In the 1956, CBS television broadcast one of many new nighttime game shows. Hosted by Bud Collyer, a panel of three contemporary celebrities were introduced. Next the imposters arrived. The celebrities asked the contestants, all who claimed to be the same person, questions about their assumed common identity. The premise of the feature was for the celebrities to determine which contestant was the real persona and who were the imposters. This determination was to be based on the contestants' responses to questions directed their way about their identity. Each half-hour segment of *To Tell the Truth* built to the inevitable and much anticipated statement, "Will the real . . . please stand up!"

During Jesus' Galilean ministry, there was a first-century version of *To Tell the Truth* being played; however, the consequences of decisions made were eternal, not temporal; they were life changing, not entertaining. Based on the questions asked and observations made, people were forced to make a decision, "Who was Jesus? Was he the Messiah? What was the Messiah to be?"

Luke followed the Marcan order and duplicated the broad strokes of Mark's literary brush. Jesus asked about the populist view of his earthly ministry. In Matthew, Mark, and Luke, the answer predictably repeated Herod's observation of Jesus' identity: John, Elijah, a great prophet from old. Jesus' retort requested more of the disciples. "Who do you say that I am?" Peter provided the answer for himself and his comrades: "You are the Christ."

The story of Jesus' self-revelation took a dramatic shift at this point of the narrative. Matthew alone recorded Jesus' blessing of Peter for his confession (Matt 16:17–19). Furthermore, Luke omitted Peter's rebuttal of Jesus and Jesus' subsequent rejection of Peter's actions and attitudes (Matt 16:22–23; Mark 8:32–33). All three Synoptic Gospels return to the conditions of discipleship as a conclusion of the narrative and as a transition into the transfiguration event. The Lukan omission will be more important in understanding Matthew and Mark, as will be the inclusion of the Petrine Blessing. For now, the reader should follow Luke's literary argument and notice the popular view, the informed view, and the expanded view.

(1) Jesus first asked the disciples for the popular view of his identity. "Who are the crowds saying I am? You have been there with them. You passed among them during the feeding of the five thousand. You went on your Galilean mission expedition. What did you hear?" All three

Synoptic Gospels used the same word and the same tense, λέγουσιν (*legousin*). The present tense of the verb that means to speak, talk, or say gives the verb the force of continuous action. "What was the scuttlebutt?" Jesus asked. Ministry is never void of a context. While the truth of God's messages remains constant, the level of education, understanding, predisposition, and so forth of the listener always will influence how God seeks to advance the kingdom of heaven. The disciples answered Jesus with a variety of responses, indicating there were numerous views regarding Jesus identity. To be sure, all three answers communicated great respect on the part of the general public. But at best, these opinions were only in the ballpark. The general public's view was limited.

(2) While Jesus wanted to know what the popular view was at the time, he certainly was more concerned with the informed view of the disciples. Had Jesus discussed this matter before? Scripture is silent on that issue. Certainly they had seen the works of Jesus and had the benefit of his additional explanation as with the Parable of the Sower. Certainly the disciples had heard Jesus on numerous occasions tell the recipient of his healing power to go and tell no one what happened. But no doubt the greatest contributing factor to the disciples informed opinion was simply the presence of Jesus. They had lived with him, talked to him, walked with him, observed him, and they had begun to understand. Nothing substitutes for time spent with Jesus.

(3) However, neither the popular view of the people nor the informed view of the disciples was adequate. Jesus chose this moment with his disciples to present the expanded view of the Messiah and what accepting that role meant to him and to those who would follow him.

Jesus' self-designation was that of Daniel's Son of man. According to Daniel, "There was given him dominion, and glory, and a kingdom, that all people, nations, and languages, should serve him: his dominion is an everlasting dominion, which shall not pass away, and his kingdom that which shall not be destroyed" (Dan 7:14). As such, Jesus came to deliver captives from their futile, time-bound limitations. The popular view wanted a temporal king; Jesus gave them an eternal sovereign. The disciples had more knowledge, but still they were looking for an earthly expression of power. The Son of man gave them something that would not pass away.

Yet the cost of receiving such an endless reign was complete submission to the will of the Father. To accomplish all that God intended,

Jesus was to suffer, be rejected, die, and ultimately to rise from the dead. The popular view of the people wanted to alleviate suffering; Jesus accepted suffering. The disciples wanted vindication for their religious understanding; Jesus would not seek to set the record straight with those who would soon control his earthly fate. Jesus offered complete victory, but as he would demonstrate himself, one must die in order to enter this kingdom.

Furthermore, when Jesus stood as the real Messiah, he demonstrated what that reality meant for his followers, both then and now. Three imperatives are given to explain the life commitment of the disciple. One of four modes in the Greek language, the imperative mode affirms the action of the verb as a direct command. Deny ἀρνησάσθω (*arnēsathō*), take up ἀράτω (*aratō*), and follow ἀκολουθείτω (*akoloutheitō*) are commands Jesus gave anyone who would come after him. All three imperative verbs are linked with the Greek conjunction καί (*kai*). When the Greek imperative is listed in a series connected by καί (*kai*), the second imperative is viewed as consequential of the first, and the third imperative becomes durative. Thus the action of denying self-results in the consequence of daily taking up the cross. Following Jesus then ensues as a lifetime of continuous activity. To underscore the meaning of his messianic role, Jesus detailed the futility of pursuing any other means of achieving the freedom offered by kingdom participation. Those who gave up their lives (deny, take up, and follow), would ultimately save their lives via God's salvation. Anyone who sought to achieve meaning, purpose, and eternal security on their on merit would lose all they sought to achieve.

But an understanding of Luke's recollection of Jesus' messianic identification would be incomplete if one misses Luke's setting. While Matthew and Mark focused attention on Jesus' location in Caesarea Philippi, Luke simply stated that Jesus was praying alone while his disciples were with him. Rather than being a contradiction of terms, Luke presented Jesus' motive for revealing his true identity and for explaining the reality of the same for himself and his disciples. The Father told Jesus it was time! Here we see a crystal clear model of prayer in the Christian's life. It did not matter that others were near, that the previous days had been laden with one milestone after another, that his visibility was growing, and that the tide of popular opinion was thrusting him to the forefront of current events. Nothing mattered save Jesus' conversation with the Father. Jesus was praying alone while his disciples were with him. In his epoch work *My Utmost for His Highest*, Oswald Chambers said, "When the Son of God prayers, He has only one consciousness, and that consciousness is of His Father."[44] In Luke's typical, subtle fashion, the reader is given in the opening phrase the clue to the conclusion. If you want to understand the role of Messiah, if you want to understand what that means for you individually, then spend time alone with God.

THE TRANSFIGURATION: INTERRUPTION OR INTENTION

Luke 9:28-36

> [28] It happened that about eight days after these sayings that Jesus went up into the mountain to pray, taking with him Peter and John and James. [29] Now while he was praying, his appearance was altered; even his clothes were glistening white. [30] Suddenly, two men were talking with him, one Moses and the other Elijah. [31] Appearing in glory, they spoke of Jesus' death, which was about to be accomplished in Jerusalem. [32] Peter and those with him had been overcome by sleep; waking up, they saw his glory and that of the two men standing with him. [33] As they were leaving him, Peter said to Jesus, "It is good that we are here; we should make three tabernacles, one for you, one for Moses, and one for Elijah," not knowing what he was saying. [34] As Peter said this, a cloud shrouded them; and they were afraid as they entered the cloud. [35] But then there was a voice from the cloud saying, "This is my son, the one having been chosen. Hear him." [36] After the voice had spoken, Jesus was found alone. They remained silent and did not tell anyone in those days what they saw.

Continuing the theme of Jesus' prayerful dependence on the Father, Luke began his record of the transfiguration with the unique statement that Jesus took his inner circle of disciples up the mountain to pray and that while he was praying, his face was changed to express God's glory. Neither Matthew nor Mark connected the event to prayer; however, for Luke, prayer was the primary context. Additionally, Luke alone added detail to the conversation between Jesus, Moses, and Elijah.

---

44. Chambers, *The Complete Works of Oswald Chambers*, 810.

Specifically, these notables from the past discussed the departure (death) Jesus would soon accomplish at Jerusalem. Used only three times in the New Testament, the word Luke selected for departure, death, or demise is ἔξοδος (*exodos*). The writer of Hebrews used a form of the word to describe "The exodus" when he wrote, "By faith Joseph, when he died, made mention of the departing of the children of Israel; and gave commandment concerning his bones" (Heb 11:22). The only other two uses in the New Testament demonstrate a connection between Peter and the transfiguration event. Here in Luke 9:31, Moses, Elijah, and Jesus discussed the end of Jesus' earthly life. Likewise, in writing to the early church, Peter wrote of his own impending demise, followed immediately by an account of the transfiguration event. In Luke 9:31 and 2 Peter 1:15 and following, the references communicate not only finality but a purposeful and culminating finality. Jesus, and ultimately Peter, saw their deaths as fulfillment of God's plan.

Although Peter reached an understanding of God's glory by the time of his death, he and his friends miserably failed that night on the mountain. Jesus was deeply distressed at the trials about to come his way. Given the severity of the looming test of faith, Jesus did what he had always done: he prayed.

However, this time when Jesus withdrew to seek a moment of prayer, he wanted the disciples to learn something as well. Jesus knew they too would one day face circumstances and decisions that could only be addressed by the empowering presence of almighty God. But they could not stay awake. Jesus was so moved in prayer that Moses and Elijah appeared in a glorified state. But the disciples were overcome with sleep. Peter, James, and John were only inches away from where the laws of the universe were being set aside in time and space, where the eternal literally intersected the temporal, but their fatigue robbed them of the moment. Jesus wanted the disciples to know what the Messiah was to do. Jesus wanted the disciples to understand the necessity of his impending suffering. Jesus wanted the disciples to know that if they relied on their own strength, their own understanding, their own ability, they would indeed fail, a truth disappointingly proven by their slumbering away the opportunity to participate in the transfiguration.

In order to assist the disciples, God provided a miracle. The travel-weary, drowsy disciples awoke from their slumber to see Jesus transfigured into perhaps an earthy version of a glorified body. His face had been changed, and even his clothes were glistening white. Everything God had started to do in the Law and the Prophets, and everything God was going to do through grace and mercy, were present in one remarkable manifestation. Moses and Elijah were speaking to Jesus about his impending death in Jerusalem, just as he had told his disciples. In their presence, the disciples witnessed Moses and Elijah as they validated what Jesus had said about the nature of the Messiah.

Given these facts, is it any wonder Peter did not know what to say? Luke wrote that Peter spoke his thoughts when he encountered this other-worldly event. "We should honor this moment," Peter said. "Let's build tabernacles like the ones constructed in the wilderness when God led his people with his very presence!"

It is at this very point in the narrative that the reader must take great caution not to abuse Luke's literary style by supplying details of a harmonized Gospel. "There goes Peter again! When will he ever learn to keep his mouth shut? He is always speaking when he should be listening!" Admittedly, these statements are typical of contemporary interpretation of Peter. After all, didn't Peter presumptuously jump out of the boat and walk on the water only to take his eyes away from Jesus in a moment of limited faith? Yes, in Matthew 14. Didn't Peter rebuke Jesus for saying the Messiah must suffer, and didn't Jesus compare Peter to Satan saying, "Get behind me"? Yes, in Matthew 16 and in Mark 8. Didn't Peter fall asleep while Jesus was praying in Gethsemane? Yes, in Matthew 26 and Mark 14. Didn't Peter refuse to let Jesus wash his feet and later didn't Peter cut off the ear of the high priest's servant? Yes, in John 13 and 18 respectively.

The point should now be obvious. All of these accurate details about Peter's all too human character were not stories of interest to Luke. If Luke were the sole witness to the Gospel events, the only details about Peter the reader would have had to this point in the narrative would have been these. Peter worshiped Jesus after a miraculous catch of fish (Luke 5:8). He was confused about Jesus' question regarding the widow who touched his garment during a crowded street scene (Luke 8:45). He was present when Jesus raised Jairus's daughter from the dead (Luke 8:51). And finally, Peter grasped, at least in a minimal way, the concept of Messiah when he identified Jesus as the "Christ of God" (Luke 9:20). Nothing is known from Luke that would cast a shadow on Peter's character, his sincerity, or even his devotion. This is extremely important precisely because of what happened next.

The narrative indicates that when the disciples awoke, they viewed the transfiguration of Jesus and the presence of Moses and Elijah. In reaction, Peter spoke and the transfiguration came to a close. Given the stark contrast of the events, traditional interpretation holds that the disappearance of Moses and Elijah, the shrouding of the mountain in a cloud, the voice of God penetrating the moment affirming Jesus and directing the disciples to pay attention to what he was saying are a result of Peter's interruption. This interpretation reads into Luke's biography of Peter the larger characterization that Peter was impetuous, arrogant, and always speaking out of turn. As such, the disciples provide an interruption to the miraculous transfiguration of Jesus.

However, rather than a contrast that called attention to Peter's lack of understanding and assumes facts not presented in Luke about Peter's tendency to "blow it," the reader should hear the voice of God affirming Jesus' messianic identity as a culmination of Jesus' intended instruction to his followers. After all, Luke made it clear that Jesus initiated the discussion of the general public's view of the Messiah, of the disciple's understanding of the same, and of his own explanation that the Messiah was to suffer in order to fulfill the Father's plan. Luke clearly indicated Jesus took the three disciples with him up the mountain to pray, an event that resulted in their seeing Jesus changed and hearing Moses, Elijah, and Jesus discuss the Suffering Servant responsibilities of the Messiah. Finally, Luke placed the disciples in the presence of holy God who covered the mountain and directly presented the divine approval of Jesus' obedience and of God's specific instruction to comply carefully with all that the Christ said. For Luke, the entire scene was one of intention, not interruption, one of validation of Jesus, not of violation by Peter.

One final point bears out this conclusion. After the preliminary discussion, after the prayer, after the transfiguration, after the conversation with Old Testament saints, and after the culmination of divine speech, *Jesus was found alone*. All of the evening's events focused attention on *Jesus, himself, alone*. Nothing else mattered. Jesus alone, his identity, the validation of his teaching, his approval from the Father, was all that mattered. No interruption, only God's intention to glorifying the Son.

THE CONTRAST OF THE NEXT DAY

Luke 9:37–43a

³⁷*Now it happened the very next day as they were going down the mountain that a great crowd met them.* ³⁸*And behold, a man from the crowd shouted saying, "Teacher, I beg you to look carefully upon my son, for he is my only one,* ³⁹*and, listen, a spirit takes him and suddenly shouts out and convulses him with foam; he hardly leaves him alone and breaks him into pieces.* ⁴⁰*I begged your disciples that they may cast him out, but they were not able."* ⁴¹*Jesus answered saying, "Oh you unbelieving and misguided generation! How long will I be with you and tolerate you? Bring your son here!"* ⁴²*While he was still approaching, the demon attacked him and convulsed him. But Jesus rebuked the spirit, cleansing and healing the child and he gave the child back to his father.* ⁴³*All were amazed on account of the magnificence of God.*

Luke captured the full spectrum of human emotion as he emphasized the events of the next day following the transfiguration. From the mountaintop of the moment, Jesus and his disciples descended into daily drudgery of human destitution. Peter spoke his heart when he said, "Let's just stay right here on the mountain." But Jesus knew what was in store in the days ahead. Jesus knew the moment of affirmation and clarification and the undistracted focus on him alone was the only hope the disciples could claim. So Jesus led the three up the mountain to prepare them for the reality of the valley below.

What a contrast! As the four made their way down the mountain, images of the miraculous still intoxicating their senses, they were met with the cruelty of the everyday world. They had experienced unspeakable joy only to face a clamoring crowd. They shared the exuberance of seeing eternity intersect time only to encounter the all too common expression of a disappointed and discouraged parent. They heard God speak of his chosen child only to observe a wounded and stricken child. Perhaps greater contrast could not be found.

Yet this contrast set the stage for a different kind of miracle. Yes, the transfiguration was remarkable; yes the validation of Jesus' role as the Messiah extraordinary; and yes, God's voice was completely unforgettable. But no one else in the world would ever be able to share in that moment. That moment came and went. All of Christianity, from that day until now, can only imagine what it must have been like.

But the contrast exists every day. And just as it unfolded in the first century, it unfolds today. On the one hand there is the potential existence in the presence of God that constantly reflects on Jesus, himself, alone. But on the other hand, there is the fallen world in desperate need of help and hope. In this text, Luke masterfully summarized the tension of this contrast by articulating the cares and concerns of the world, the compassion of Jesus, and the all-consuming greatness of God.

(1) The cares and concerns of the world are enormous, and they are real. Twice in the passage Luke used the word δέομαί (*deomai*). Specifically, the father begged Jesus to examine his son after he had begged the disciples to cast out the convulsing spirit. Common in the New Testament, the word group is used as a courtesy in direct speech. Twice in Acts, Luke used the expression to introduce Paul's statements in formal dialogue. "But Paul said, I am a man which am a Jew of Tarsus, a city in Cilicia, a citizen of no mean city: and, I beseech thee, suffer me to speak unto the people" (Acts 21:39). "Especially because I know thee to be expert in all customs and questions which are among the Jews: wherefore I beseech thee to hear me patiently" (Acts 26:3). The word δέομαί (*deomai*) also is used as a mild command. "But I beseech you, that I may not be bold when I am present with that confidence, wherewith I think to be bold against some, which think of us as if we walked according to the flesh" (2 Cor 10:2). "Brethren, I beseech you, be as I *am*; for I *am* as ye *are*: ye have not injured me at all" (Gal 4:12). "Now then we are ambassadors for Christ, as though God did beseech *you* by us: we pray *you* in Christ's stead, be ye reconciled to God" (2 Cor 5:20).

The word group takes in the meaning of prayer to God. In Acts 10:2, Cornelius was described as a devout man who always prayed to God. In his salutary remarks, Paul indicated his desire to see again the Roman Christians was a prayer to God (Rom. 1:10). Finally, the word meaning includes an impassioned plea for specific action. Such was the case with the Gerasene demoniac who requested not to be tormented (Luke 8:28) and the Macedonians who desired to participate in the famine relief fund (2 Cor 8:4). Likewise, the father of the convulsing child pled for help. These requests were specific: Do not torment, let us participate, heal my son. Furthermore, nothing else mattered to the one making the request. The demoniac preferred anything to being tormented. The Macedonians would prefer going without food themselves than to see the saints in Jerusalem suffer. Likewise, the father would go to any length to aid and assist his stricken child. These are only examples of the countless cares of the world. Assaulted every day with seemingly insurmountable problems, the world struggles to get by, living hand to mouth, one day at a time. They call out for help, specifically and with great passion, setting the stage for the contrast of the moment.

(2) In the face of their care and concerns, the compassion of Jesus arises. There are two aspects of Jesus' comments that indicate the level of his emotional response to the parental suffering presented in the text. First is Jesus' statement. On the surface, the reader knows Jesus identified with the suffering. Furthermore, because the disciples were unable to help the man and his son, Jesus said in frustration, "You are an unbelieving and misguided generation! Had you any faith and had you been paying attention, you would know that I do nothing without the Father. Because of that, what I do, you can do as well. Ask the Father in belief and he will act on your behalf." This view is explained further by the use of the particle ὦ (*ho*) with the vocative case. Specifically, the phrase is translated *Oh faithless generation*. The construction expresses deep emotion. Other examples include Jesus' response to the Canaanite woman who said that even the dogs eat crumbs from the master's table (Matt 15:28) and Paul's outrage at learning of the Galatians' problem when he said, "O foolish Galatians, who hath bewitched you, that ye should not obey the truth, before whose eyes Jesus Christ hath been evidently set forth, crucified among you?" (Gal 3:1). Jesus was so deeply moved by the cares and concerns of those around him that he was himself moved to compassion.

(3) Finally, the reader can see the result of Jesus' compassion exercised on behalf of the concerns of the world is that people focus on the all-consuming greatness of God. After he reprimanded the disciples for their lack of faith, Jesus commanded the boy be brought to him. The lack of detail that accompanies the miracle should lead the reader to understand Luke's emphasis. As important as the healing was, especially for the hurting family, the story is about more. The boy was brought to Jesus mid a convulsing episode. Without fanfare, Jesus rebuked the spirit, healed the boy, and gave him to his father. Luke presented this unexceptional series of events to call attention to the next sentence, which articulates the author's intended outcome; *All were amazed on account*

of the magnificence of God. Though the contrast between the mountain and the valley may seem cruel, when one sees Jesus himself alone, they are drawn to the all-consuming greatness of God.

Luke used an unusual vocabulary to describe this reaction by the crowd. The forms of the word μεγαλειότης (*megaleiotēs*), magnificence, are found only three times in the New Testament, and in each the speaker was calling attention to the greatness of deity. In reaction to Paul's propagating the gospel, a silversmith in Ephesus feared people would not praise the goddess Diana, also known as Artemis, whom the silversmith considered a deity. He said, "So that not only this our craft is in danger to be set at naught; but also that the temple of the great goddess Diana should be despised, and her magnificence should be destroyed, whom all Asia and the world worshipeth" (Acts 19:27). In substantiating the gospel message, Peter wrote to the church saying, "We have not followed cunningly devised fables, when we made known unto you the power and coming of our Lord Jesus Christ, but were eyewitnesses of his majesty" (2 Pet 1:16).

All three passages, including Luke 9:43, should at this point be considered together. All three call attention to the greatness of deity: The people marveled after the healing of the child, the Ephesian silversmith wrongly attributed great worth to a false god, and Peter acknowledged he was an eyewitness to the miraculous transfiguration of Jesus. But even more telling of Luke's literary mastery is the subtle but continued emphasis on contrast. All three references strongly identify an issue of contrast. The silversmith Demetrius contrasted the worship of Artemis with the growing worship of God. Peter contrasted the source of his belief, specifically being an eyewitness to the earthly Jesus with myths and fables. Finally, Luke contrasted the glory of God's presence in the remarkably unique, but unquestionably private transfiguration moment with the belief that allows God's presence to permeate a dark world. It is this reality that Luke proclaimed as the intention of the Messiah and in doing so provided explanation of Jesus' frustration over the disciples' lack of development.

GALILEAN MINISTRY DRAWS TO A CLOSE

Luke 9:43b–50

⁴³ᴮ*While they were marveling at everything he was doing, Jesus said to his disciples,* ⁴⁴*"Place these words for yourselves in your ears; the Son of man is about to be given over to the hands of men."* ⁴⁵*But they failed to understand these words because they were hidden from them so that they would not understand their meaning. Furthermore, they were afraid to ask him about these words.*

⁴⁶*Now there arose a discussion among them as to who was greater.* ⁴⁷*But Jesus knew the thoughts of their hearts. Taking a small child, he placed him in their midst* ⁴⁸*and said to them, "Whoever receives a child in my name, receives me. Furthermore, whoever receives me receives the one sending me. The one being the least among you is the greatest."*

⁴⁹*John answered and said, "Master, we saw someone casting our demons in your name so we attempted to stop him because he is not accompanying us."* ⁵⁰*But Jesus said to him, "Do not forbid him. Whoever is not against us, is for us."*

As Luke's account of the Galilean ministry drew to a close, he included in his record strands of oral and literary tradition that followed closely to the Marcan order. Three story lines are repeated whose connection to Luke's overriding themes do not seem readily apparent. They are a repetition of Jesus' impending suffering, a disagreement about rank and evidence of a para movement of Christianity. Although Luke preserved the Marcan order, these texts represent a rare Lucan contraction of Mark's narrative. Typically, Luke expounded on Mark's narrative, adding needed explanation for his wider audience and often softening Mark's abrupt style. Lack of such evidence should not put in question Luke's inclusion of the material but should press the reader to additional inquiry regarding Luke's intent. Taken separately, these stories seem to add little to the overall movement of Luke's narrative. Taken as a triplet, however, their meaning forges a meaningful idea.

Luke approached the end of the Galilean ministry with an increasing mention of what was going to happen in Jerusalem. Again in this section, the theme is repeated. Luke added the material about the disciples' inability to understand, perhaps to intensify their ultimate comprehension. What these stories in combination add is a reminder that the kingdom of heaven does not operate like anything else on earth. The theme of the Messiah suffering, though reiterated here, is not new; however, the two following stories are. When arguing over who was the greatest in the kingdom of God, a petty and unfortunately all too common occurrence, Jesus said you must be child-like, not childish. When John rehearsed their attempt to banish a "non-authorized" expression of God's power, Jesus explained that one cannot oppose God and work for God simultaneously. Jesus and his disciples were about to leave Galilee and travel to Jerusalem. There the stakes would be high. There the disciples would have little room for error. They were going to Jerusalem, and everything would be different. Maintaining the status quo would not be sufficient. If they were to remain true to Jesus' expressed role and purpose of the Messiah, the disciples would need to be ready to go an entirely different direction than they could ever think or image.

It is interesting to note that all Christians have their own Galilee and own Jerusalem. Each should have a place where they can rest and prepare for the truly difficult challenges that are ahead. Luke's conclusion to the Galilean ministry provides direction. The Christian should forget assumption and pay close attention to God. Get alone with God, even in the midst of the crowd, and hear him. Believers should never allow presupposition and human expectation to rob them of the truly extraordinary presence of God. Embrace the contrast and wait with excitement to see what God will do.

2

Journey to Jerusalem

THE JUDEAN MINISTRY BEGINS

Luke 9:51–56

⁵¹*Now it happened as the days of his assumption drew near, Jesus firmly set his face toward Jerusalem.* ⁵²*Jesus sent messengers ahead of him. They entered into the villages of Samaria to make ready for him.* ⁵³*But the Samaritans would not receive Jesus because he was headed toward Jerusalem.* ⁵⁴*Seeing this, the disciples James and John said, "Lord, do you desire for us to call fire to fall from heaven in order to consume them?"* ⁵⁵*Turning around, Jesus rebuked the disciples.* ⁵⁶*Then they went on to the next village.*

ALTHOUGH THE GOSPEL IS one continuous narrative, Luke divided the material of the Gospel message into four distinctive sections: the birth, infancy, and adolescent narratives (chapters 1 and 2); the early years of Jesus' public life, also known as the Galilean Ministry (5 though 9:50); the Judean Ministry (9:51 through 19:10); and the Jerusalem Ministry (19:11 through end of 24).

By way of reminder, the reader should know the basic premise of Synoptic theory widely held throughout biblical scholarship. Specifically, four components form the literary foundation of Matthew, Mark, and Luke. The first is that of Marcan priority. Both Matthew and Luke followed the basic outline found in the Gospel of Mark. As such, scholarship holds Mark was written first and subsequently used by Matthew and Luke. Second is a document that has become known as "Q." This document consists of sayings of Jesus. Mark and Q are found in both

Matthew and Luke with a high degree of literary dependence. Q is not found in Mark. Accordingly, Matthew and Luke used Mark and Q, the latter not being known to Mark, or if known, not utilized. Finally, three and four are sources of material unique to Matthew and to Luke. For convenience, these have been termed "M" and "L" respectively. This documentary hypothesis results in the conclusion that Mark wrote first. Matthew used Mark, Q, and M while Luke used Mark, Q, and L.

Luke is highly dependent on the source "L" as he recorded the events of the Judean Ministry. According to Bruce Metzger, "It is impossible to determine the exact sequence of Jesus' subsequent journeys, for Luke's special section (9:51–18:14), on which we are mainly dependent for information concerning this period, contains few precise chronological and geographic details."[1]

This comes as no surprise to the student of Luke, who by this point in the narrative is accustomed to finding Luke's thematic approach to be the dominant literary characteristic. More important to Luke than when events occurred was and remains why the selected events took place. Such is the case of the opening words of the Judean Ministry in Luke 9:51: *Jesus set his face toward Jerusalem*. This phrase established the tone not only for the immediate passage but also for Jesus' entire relentless pursuit to fulfill God's plan. Woven throughout Luke's remaining chapters are examples of Jesus' resolve regardless of the consequences and regardless of the reaction of his opponents.

Luke demonstrated Jesus' resolve through a cascading or layered effect. This description formed a series of intensifying expressions. First, Luke indicated Jesus was going to Jerusalem. Specifically, Luke used a genitive infinitive of purpose in the phrase τοῦ πορεύεσθαι εἰς Ἰερουσαλήμ (*tou preuesthai eis Ierousalēm*). This phrase would be translated literally "of the to enter into Jerusalem." Luke's use of the phrase is to call attention to Jesus' direct intention. Jesus was going to go to Jerusalem. Second, Luke employed a literary devise that could be termed a figure of speech in modern linguistics. The phrase τὸ πρόσωπον ἐστήρισεν (*to prosōpon estērisen*) means "to set the face." A similar example is found in the Septuagint, 2 Samuel 17:11, where Absalom was advised to gather all of Israel before initiating a military campaign against his father, King David. Leading the people into battle was described as *the face of you going into the midst of them*. The expression "setting the face" indicated determination and direction. Finally, Luke added the third personal

---

1. Metzger, The New Testament: Its Background, Growth, & Content, 141.

pronoun to the syntax of the sentence. Because all finite Greek verbs indicate the person and number of the subject—*he went*—third person singular would be one word in Greek, the addition of the personal pronoun is not required for the sentence to be complete. Accordingly, the addition of αὐτὸς (*autos*), the third personal pronoun, *he* must be understood as an intentional emphasis. This one word effectively changes the translation from *he was going to Jerusalem* to the translation *he was adamantly resolved to go to Jerusalem*.

One additional comment on Jesus' resolve is needed. Not only does the presence of the personal pronoun add emphasis to the statement but it also clarifies Jesus' decision-making process. Luke indicated "Jesus" set his face—not circumstances, not public opinion, not the discussion even of his closest friends. *Jesus adamantly resolved to set his face toward Jerusalem.*

Notice next Jesus' resolve was unaffected by the reaction of those around him. Luke indicated the Samaritans would not receive Jesus because *his face had been set toward Jerusalem*. Jesus knew all too well the difficulties of the path he had chosen. In 722 BC Assyria conquered the Northern Kingdom, along with its capital at Samaria. The deportation was one of amalgamation, mixing Assyrian captives from one nation with individuals from other captive lands. Accordingly, in the Northern Kingdom, Jews became a mixed race. To the contrary, when Babylon destroyed the Southern Kingdom—in 586 BC, the deportation was a homogeneous process that transported the best and brightest back to Mesopotamia. Although the Southern Kingdom Jews were immersed into a foreign culture, their racial purity remained undisturbed. When Ezra led his return to Palestine in approximately 450 BC, the Samaritan Jews wanted to assist in the rebuilding of the temple. Citing the need for complete purity, Ezra refused their offers of assistance, and the Samaritan rift began. As a result, Samaritans in the first century allowed Jewish passage from Jerusalem to Galilee going north, but the reverse rarely occurred.[2] Passing Mount Gerizim, the holy Samaritan cultic enter, was a slap in the face of the Samaritan. Accordingly, Jews from Galilee would cross the Jordan heading east, pass by Samaria headed south, and then cross back into Judean territory heading west. Jesus knew the social outcry his resolve would create, but he did not hide his intention. Although the pervasive nature of Jesus' purpose would not become apparent until Philip preached the Samaritan Pentecost (Acts 8), Jesus in fact went to

2. Robertson, *Luke*, 139.

Jerusalem to save the Jew and the Samaritan alike. Jesus' resolve was not weakened when those he was going to save did not understand his motivation or level of commitment.

Jesus' resolve was unaffected when those around him wanted to fight for his honor. Believing their actions to be justified, James and John wanted to call down fire from heaven and consume the Samaritans. Knowing their intentions, this too would have been counterintuitive. Why destroy those he came to deliver? Jesus turned, rebuked the Sons of Thunder, and moved on to the next village. Did the sequence of events repeat itself at the next village? Perhaps. If so, the readers can assume from Luke's literary style that Jesus simply turned and went to the next village, always available but never forcing himself on those he came to save.

The life story of William Borden could have been drawn from Jesus' example in Samaria. Heir to a millionaire's fortune, Bill Borden could have enjoyed the luxuries life offered him by his family's dairy empire. Graduating from Yale University in 1909, Borden declined numerous appointments that would have brought him the finest the world had to offer. Accepting neither the benefits of well-born privilege nor the almost certain acclaim of a self-made man in any field of his choosing, Borden instead attended Princeton Seminary in pursuit of God's call on his life into missions. In 1912 Borden sailed for China to serve Muslim populations. Disembarking in Egypt to study Arabic, Borden soon contracted a fatal case of meningitis. Deceased on foreign soil in 1913, many thought his life a waste. Yet short as it was, his few adult years were lived in adamant resolve to serve, a self-imposed obligation he discharged throughout his college and seminary career, or in preparation to serve, an activity that ultimately took his life. Regardless of the cost, Borden lived a life of service to God. Found among his personal effects was his Bible. On the flyleaf was written in Borden's own hand these words: No Reserves; No Retreats; No Regrets.[3]

The reader should notice one final point prior to leaving this passage. While neither was the concept of the Suffering Servant role of Messiah new in Luke's narrative (Luke 9:22,27,31,44) nor was Jesus' commitment to travel to Jerusalem where this suffering would occur difficult to understand (Luke 9:51; 13:22; 17:11), still Luke introduced a new component to the impending suffering. In Luke 9:51, Luke indi-

---

3. Details of Borden's life are included in Mrs. Howard Taylor's *Borden of Yale: The Life that Counts*, published in Philadelphia by the China Inland Mission, 1926.

cated the current narrative occurred when the days of Jesus' assumption were drawing near. The word ἀναλήμψεως (*analēmpseōs*) is used only here in the New Testament. Related words that belong to the same vocabulary family clearly indicate Luke's intention was to convey more than a prediction of Jesus' resurrection, but rather a declaration of Jesus' ascension to the Father.

In Acts 1:2,11,22 Luke clearly used the word group to mean more than the resurrection. While Luke stopped short of full assimilation with the Father, Paul used the same word group to describe Jesus' glorification when he said to Timothy: "And without controversy great is the mystery of godliness: God was manifest in the flesh, justified in the Spirit, seen of angels, preached unto the Gentiles, believed on in the world, received up into glory" (1 Tim 3:16). Jesus was looking to the culmination, even though he could not get there except through suffering.

This new piece of information Luke contributed to the understanding of Jesus' suffering was that the only pathway to glorification was through suffering. Jesus had to go to Jerusalem, endure persecution, and crucifixion. Only then would come the resurrection, ascension, and glorification. Too often Christianity will seek the easy way out, taking the path of least resistance. Yet Jesus told the disciples they would have tribulation but he would be with them, leading them to overcome (John 16:33). While all will not be called on to endure the darkness of the night, the dawn always follows the dark.

WELL-SUITED FOR THE KINGDOM

Luke 9:57–62

⁵⁷As they were going along in the road, a fellow said to Jesus, "I will follow you wherever you may go." ⁵⁸Jesus said to him, "Foxes have lairs and birds of the heavens nests. But the Son of man has nowhere he may lay his head." ⁵⁹Jesus said to another, "Follow me." But that one said, "Allow me to go first to bury my father." ⁶⁰Jesus said to him, "You allow the dead to bury their own dead. You go and proclaim the kingdom of God." ⁶¹Another said, "I will follow you, Lord. But allow me first to bid farewell to the ones of my home." ⁶²But Jesus said, "No one having put his hand to plough who is constantly looking back is well suited for the kingdom of God."

Journey to Jerusalem   151

As the Galilean Ministry drew to a close, Jesus mentioned with increasing regularity the true role of the Messiah—a role that followed neither cultural expectation nor popular acceptance. To the contrary, Jesus' purpose in the kingdom was to suffer and die as a ransom for many. To fulfill that obligation, Jesus would of his own choice lay down his life to save even those who would take his life. Nothing short of ultimate sacrifice would be required for Jesus to fulfill the desires of the Heavenly Father.

As Luke transitioned to the Judean Ministry with its seemingly aimless meandering toward Jerusalem, the topic of discipleship became a frequent focus of his narrative. Moving from village to village, Jesus no doubt attracted a crowd as he had done in his earlier Galilean Ministry. People would move in and out of the company of people that sought Jesus' attention. Certainly the healings continued as did Jesus' teachings about God and the work of the kingdom.

Into this ambiguous scene came three individuals, all pledging their loyalty to the cause of the Christ. Each displayed an interest in what God was doing and a desire to be involved in the same. But each also carried with him baggage that became the subject of Jesus' discussion about discipleship.

But before examining these three would-be disciples, the reader should first see the broad strokes that Luke painted on his literary canvas. When John recorded the conversation between Jesus and Nicodemus in John 3, he used the analogy of entering and seeing the kingdom. Clearly in that context, Jesus was talking to Nicodemus about the initiation of a saving relationship with himself. As such, "seeing and entering the kingdom" were intended as salvation metaphors. From this passage in John originated the evangelical use of the term "born again." Jesus spoke to Nicodemus about beginning a new life in Christ.

Such is not the case with the narrative of the would-be disciples. The term εὔθετός (*euthetos*) is translated in the King James Version as "fit." As such, the reader may mistakenly equate Luke's intention to be similar to that of John's. After all, if a person is not fit for the kingdom of God, doesn't that mean that he cannot get in? If a person is not fit for the kingdom, doesn't that mean he doesn't qualify to enter the kingdom? While the logic of these assertions may stand on their own merit, careful review will reveal a different intent.

The term εὔθετός (*euthetos*) is a compound word that has taken on its own meaning. The compound is formed by the prefix ευ (*eu*), meaning good or well, being added to the verb form τίθημι (*tithēmi*), meaning "to put or to place." The literal meaning would be something that is well placed. Related meanings could be suitable, appropriate, or as translated in the KJV, fit. The word is found only three times in the New Testament. Luke used the term here and in the condemnation of salt that lost its saltiness when he quoted Jesus as teaching, "*It is fit for neither the land nor the landfill. It is cast out. The ones having ears to hear should hear*" (Luke 14:35). Also, the writer of Hebrews wrote that the earth that takes in the rain produces herbs that are useful or appropriate for the ones that they are intended (Heb 6:7). In all three cases, the word means someone or something is well-adapted or well-suited for a particular purpose.

Given this clarification, Luke's description of the discipleship that is appropriate for the kingdom begins to come into focus. At stake in this dichotomy is not salvation or the lack thereof. What is at stake is whether the disciple will behave appropriately or not. The difficulty this understanding presents is that two classes of discipleship immerge: one class that is progressing, learning, growing, and one class that is not or one class that is well-suited for the kingdom and one that is not.

What is more, the three examples of disciples that are not well-suited demonstrate attitudes, priorities, and worldly obligations that simply do not seem unreasonable on their face. Notice the description. When the first man came to pledge his loyalty as a disciple, he prompted Jesus to say, "*Foxes have layers and birds of the heavens nests. But the Son of man has nowhere he may lay his head.*" A cursory examination would lead one to recognize Jesus' response did not match the man's statement. For the dialogue to have made sense, Jesus must have answered the man's attitudes or additional statements not included in the narrative. For Jesus to say to an eager disciple, "Now wait just a moment, young fellow. The Son of man doesn't have the certainty of shelter that is afforded the beasts of the field and the birds of the air," the man must have communicated a degree of careless abandon that caused Jesus to advise counting the cost. Too often there is a class of discipleship that warms to the beckoning of the Spirit and response without any regard for anything. While immediacy in response to the work of the Holy Spirit is taught consistently through Scripture, Jesus also directed his disciples to count the cost, to be a serious follower. Only when people understand the commitment being made are they the class of disciples that weather the storms of life and consistently bring honor and glory to God.

Another premature disciple wanted to acknowledge his responsibility to family prior to making a commitment. While families are God-given and worthy of duty and care, Jesus informed the man that divided loyalties would result in his not being well-suited for the kingdom. As with Abraham and Isaac in Genesis 25 and Jacob and Joseph in Genesis 50, preparation for burial took place long before death occurred. When the man said he would follow Jesus after his father died, he was saying he would get to the kingdom's work on another day, after other more pressing duties had been discharged.

Finally, Jesus told the third pretender to discipleship that starting to accept the responsibilities of the kingdom while remaining in constant view of the prediscipleship way of life would render him unfit. An adverbial phrase, *constantly looking back*, modifies the way the ploughman in the analogy put his hand to the task. Furthermore, the present tense of the participle βλέπων (*blepōn*), "looking," communicates the backward looking was continuous, not intermittent. Moving forward in one direction while constantly looking backward to the past will result in poor progress at best.

In summary, Luke used Jesus' roadway conversation to begin explaining the nature of discipleship. One must count the cost and give the kingdom complete dedication. The uncomfortable reality is there are those among the redeemed who are not fit disciples. Bruce described them like this: "The first case is that of inconsiderate impulse, the second that of conflicting duties, the third of a divided mind."[4] Far from creating an atmosphere of tolerance that would allow one to become complacent with membership in one of these categories, Luke sought to use the narrative to illuminate the nature of true discipleship and thereby encourage maturity into the same.

THE JUDEAN MISSIONARY MOVEMENT OF SEVENTY

Luke 10:1–12

[1] Now after this, the Lord appointed seventy others and sent them two by two ahead of him into all the cities and villages where he was about to go. [2] And Jesus said to them, "The harvest indeed is great, but the workers are few. Pray, therefore, the Lord of the

---

4. Robertson, *Luke*, 143.

harvest, to send out workers into the harvest. ³Go on your way! Behold I am sending you as lambs in the midst of wolves. ⁴Carry neither a money bag, nor a traveler's bag, nor sandals, and salute absolutely no one along the road. ⁵Whichever house you enter, first say, Peace to this house. ⁶And if a son of peace is there, your peace shall be upon him, but if not, your peace shall return to you. ⁷You remain in the house, eating and drinking that which is from them; for a worker is due his wages. Do not move from house into house. ⁸Into whatever town you enter, eat what is provided to you. ⁹Heal those in the city who are sick, and say to them, 'The kingdom of God has come near to you.' ¹⁰But in whatever town you enter that does not receive you, enter into their street and say, ¹¹'We wipe off against you even the dust of your town that sticks to our feet; but again, know this, that the kingdom of God is come near to you.' ¹²I say to you that it will be more bearable for Sodom on that day than for this town."

Far from being a misplaced repetition of Luke 9:1–6 and its Synoptic parallels,[5] the commissioning of the seventy missionaries of the Judean Ministry is a distinctively Lucan narrative that reinforces the gospel's message of universal salvation for all. Specifically, Luke used the phrase *The Lord appointed seventy others* to draw a comparative description that contrasted the Galilean Twelve with the Judean seventy. Furthermore, Luke identified different commissioning events of the two groups. While Luke 9 and the Synoptic parallels portray the disciples as ἀπέστειλεν (*apesteilen*), "sent," the seventy were ἀνέδειξεν (*anedeixen*), "appointed." Used only here and in Acts 1:24, ἀπέστειλεν (*apesteilen*) literally means "to show clearly." In Acts, the disciples asked God to show them who was to replace Judas as one of the Twelve. In both references Luke took care to indicate God was setting people aside for specific tasks. These seventy missionaries were clearly a different group than the Twelve.

Luke's theme of universal acceptance is emphasized in two ways. First is the double meaning of the number seventy. While the historicity of the seventy missionaries should not be doubted, the number was significant in the Jewish milieu. In Genesis 10, the descendants of Noah were listed by their family patriarch. Seventy in all, this list is ended with the following summary statement: "These are the families of the sons

---

5. See Matt 9:55–10:16 and Mark 6:6–13.

of Noah, after their generations, in their nations: and by these were the nations divided in the earth after the flood" (Gen 10:32). Accordingly, the number seventy was equated in popular religion and culture for the entire world, much like the modern expressions "four corners of the earth."

The second means Luke used was the veiled reference to eating unclean food. As the missionaries moved out into the villages of southern Palestine, they were to enter any homes where the occupants were identified as sons of peace. While the reference has no other New Testament occurrence, the phrase is a common Hebraism. For example, the phrases "Son of God" and "Sons of Wrath" both occur throughout the New Testament. They are intended to ascribe to the recipient the characteristics of the phrase. "Son of peace" would be spoken of anyone who sought common good for those in his immediate culture. Clearly, as Jesus dispatched the seventy missionaries, he was not interested in only the "lost sheep of the house of Israel" (Matt 10:6). By using the broader definition, Luke clearly demonstrated Jesus' intent as including all who would peaceably accept the message of the Messiah and of God's kingdom on earth.

If, as the seventy made their way, they came upon those outside the Jewish faith who were receptive to the message, the direction was clear: Do not move from house to house looking for a better offer; eat what is placed before you with thankfulness. Luke repeated this theme in referencing the Peter and Cornelius story in Acts 10. With the seventy, Jesus was saying being unclean was not an issue of nationality but of failing to receive God. "Jesus took the position that being unclean is not a matter of nationality, race, or ritual, but of failure to submit to the rule (kingdom) of God. The kingdom of God is the sovereign rule, and it is not dependent upon man's response. God is King whatever man does."[6]

As Jesus commissioned the seventy, he also prepared them for the task that was to be theirs. Jesus said to the kingdom emissaries, "Don't dilly-dally. Don't dwell on the difficulty. And don't, for even a moment, think those to whom you are sent will not be held accountable!"

(1) Jesus instructed the seventy to be expeditious because there was no time to waste. Specifically, they were relieved of all encumbrance by the prohibition of traveler's amenities—no purse, bag, or extra sandals. Furthermore, they were to salute no one. One example of this is

---

6. Stagg, *Studies in Luke's Gospel*, 78.

provided in story of Elisha and the Shunammite woman. When news reached Elisha that his old friend's son had died, Elisha told his servant Gehazi, "Gird up thy loins, and take my staff in thine hand, and go thy way: if thou meet any man, salute him not; and if any salute thee, answer him not again: and lay my staff upon the face of the child" (2 Kings 4:29). The oriental greeting process often became a social event that consumed enormous amounts of time. The modern reader could compare the Near Eastern greeting to Geoffrey Chaucer's *Canterbury Tales,* where the religious pilgrims meandered on their way, regaling one another with their stories and tales of their exploits. Jesus said, "There simply isn't enough time. The harvest is ready now, and there are too few works. Get Busy!"

(2) Jesus told the seventy their work would not be easy and they would suffer setbacks and defeat. "I am sending you like proverbial lambs among the wolves," Jesus said. "But don't dwell on the difficulty." Jesus reminded them of their own culture that would shake the dust from their feet and clothes, saying metaphorically, "I have discharged my duty." The missions-minded have always been responsible for the process and not the results.

(3) Finally, for the benefit of the seventy, Jesus underscored a frightening reality: The kingdom of God has come and decisions carry eternal consequences. Jesus used a comparison that included an intentional overstatement to make his point. Specifically, Jesus said Sodom would be given greater tolerance than the town who rejected the missionary message of the seventy.

The fate of Sodom and Gomorrah was a staple illustration throughout Scripture of not only wickedness of humanity but of God's decisive and complete judgment against the same. But righteousness, the desired outcome of the missionary proclamation, is not a matter of degree; it is a matter of standing. Jesus soon would die on the cross for those to whom he was sending the seventy. If they trusted God to save them, they would have a new standing or new status before God. Accordingly, the comparison of greater forbearance being extended to Sodom was not intended to be taken literally but figuratively. Jesus was saying if the wicked people of Sodom had seen and heard what the audiences of the seventy were about to see and here, they would have responded in faith. The harvest was white, the time was short, the stakes were high; all was intended to heighten the opportunity of the moment.

COMMISSIONING CONTINUED

Luke 10:13–16

[13] "Woe to Chorazin! Woe to you Bethsaida! If the powerful works accomplish in you had been performed in Tyre and Sidon, they would have repented in sackcloth and ashes long again. [14] Nevertheless, it will be more tolerable in the judgment for Tyre and Sidon than for you. [15] And you, Capernaum, not unto the heavens will be lifted up! Unto Hades you will bring yourself down. [16] The one hearing you hears me. And the one rejecting you rejects me, and the one rejecting me rejects the one having sent me."

There are two important facts demonstrated in this passage that have no direct use in sharing the gospel. Their importance is found in understanding the text and in understanding the process of studying the text. These two facts are that each New Testament writer's literary style was unique and that the gospel genre's was selective in nature.

(1) With respect to the latter, this passage reinforces John's claim, "And there are also many other things which Jesus did, the which, if they should be written every one, I suppose that even the world itself could not contain the books that should be written" (John 21:25). Although John's statement was an intentional exaggeration, the understood meaning is clear. The selected stories recorded in John do not reflect all that Jesus said and did. Although the reader should never doubt the historicity of the Gospel accounts, these accounts should not be understood as a historical record, chronicling everything Jesus said and did. Regarding Luke 10:13–16, Barclay said, "One of the towns on which woe is pronounced is Chorazin. It is implied that Jesus did many might works there. In the gospel history as we have it Chorazin is never even mentioned, and we do not know one thing that Jesus did or one word that Jesus spoke there. Nothing could show so vividly how much we do not know about the life of Jesus. The gospels are not biographies; they are only sketches of the life of Jesus."[7]

Reference by Luke to Jesus' words that have no context does not diminish their importance. Instead, it proves the Gospel messages are highly literary in their nature and the authors of the same selected events

---

7. Barclay, *The Gospel of Luke*, 135.

from the life of Jesus would articulate the message they were seeking to convey. As a result, inspiration is understood as far less mechanical and far more dynamic as God breathed a message into the hearts and souls of the New Testament writers who in turn used their God-given talent and literary ability to accomplish the task.

(2) With respect to the former, this passage demonstrates a distinctive of Luke's literary technique. Specifically, verses 13 through 16 serve as a historical interlude for the progression of the narrative. Rather than sending the seventy to preach in one verse (Luke 10:1–12) and immediately declaring their victorious return in the next (v.17), Luke inserted the woe section associated with the directions to the seventy (vv. 13–17). In so doing, Luke created duration of time.

This is not the only Lucan incident of a mechanism of this nature that effectively condensed or collapsed time. Although more will be discussed in volumes on Galatians and Acts, it is sufficient for explaining this text to identify Acts 9:26–27 as a similar example. In Galatians, Paul's autobiographical account stipulated two journeys to Jerusalem. In Galatians 1:8, Paul went to Jerusalem after his three-year preparation in Arabia. Paul made a second trip to Jerusalem that was recorded in Galatians 2:1 and following. Those who question the historicity of Luke and Acts argue there are only two referenced trips by Paul in Acts, specifically Acts 9 and Acts 15. The argument is that the details of Luke's admittedly secondhand accounts do not parallel well Paul's autobiographical statements.

What this argument fails to recognize is Luke's literary tendency to collapse time. Certainly Acts 9:26–27 reads like a coherent narrative: "And when Saul was come to Jerusalem, he assayed to join himself to the disciples: but they were all afraid of him, and believed not that he was a disciple. But Barnabas took him, and brought him to the apostles, and declared unto them how he had seen the Lord in the way, and that he had spoken to him, and how he had preached boldly at Damascus in the name of Jesus" (Acts 9:26–27). In fact, the critics of Acts would be justified if 9:26–27 were the record of one visit as they would not describe accurately either visit recorded in Galatians. But when the reader knows that Luke was condensing time, specifically fourteen years, verse 26 is viewed as describing Paul's first visit and verse 27 Paul's second.

But more than understanding how God inspired and used the New Testament writers to convey God's message of salvation, this passage indicates salvation is never earned and condemnation is always self-imposed. Through a rhetorical question that demanded a negative response, Jesus indicated all reward is given to a person by God; it is never earned. Three cities were identified as being under judgment. Specifically, Chorazin, Bethsaida, and Capernaum were compared as being worse than Tyre and Sidon, two cities synonymous with vile and ungodly behavior. Jesus said of Capernaum, "You don't expect to be lifted up to heaven, do you?" Beyond the literary device that cast the positive statement in a negative fashion, what is most important is the voice of the verb. By using the passive voice of the verb ὑψωθήσῃ (*hupsōthēsē*), "be lifted up," Jesus indicated no one could achieve righteousness. If anyone reaches heaven, it is because someone else lifted them there.

Furthermore, by means of a similar technique, Jesus indicated everyone who is condemned is in fact self-condemned by their own actions. Luke presented in verse 15 a pair of contrasting statements. The rhetorical question discussed above is paired with the declarative statement, "You will bring yourself down to Hades." Barclay M. Newman, compiler of the *Running Greek-English Dictionary*, located the verb καταβήσῃ (*katabēsē*) as a future middle.[8] Newman's position differs from that of the King James translators who took the verb as a future deponent because the active voice is only found in the present tense. Typically, when a Greek verb ends in the middle passive pronominal suffix, the verb is considered defective or deponent. In those cases, the voice is translated as active, even though the form is middle/passive. Accordingly, the King James Version reads "shalt be thrust down to hell," representing a simple future passive. The strength of Newman's argument is that the verb cannot be future passive as the occurrence would necessarily be based on the aorist stem. Because καταβήσῃ (*katabēsē*) is based on a present stem, it cannot be a passive voice verb and must be considered a middle voice. Given the accuracy of Newman's determination, the verse carries the force of self-condemnation—"you cast yourself down."

There is additional strength given to this position when the reader understands Luke's intent in verse 16. Not only are the seventy to comprehend their responsibility is to proclaim the good news and leave the results to God, but also Luke clearly demonstrated that a decision to reject the disciples is a decision to reject God. The choice was theirs. There was no precondition necessary. Being a Jew was not a require-

---

8. Aland, et al., The UBS Greek New Testament: A Reader's Edition, 194.

ment. Having previous religious experience or prior knowledge of God was not a prerequisite. All they had to do was accept. If they received, the disciples would come in and have fellowship, share the rudiments of the faith, and set the recipient on the path of righteousness to be followed over a lifetime. But if they rejected the message, they were not rejecting the messengers but were rejecting the one who sent the messengers. In so doing, they were choosing destruction.

The same is true in the world today. The good news of God's salvation is offered to all. The status of those who receive is changed. They cannot change themselves; they are changed by another. To the contrary, all who reject God do so at their own peril. Judgment comes as certain to them as salvation does to the penitent. But unlike those who receive life-changing power that is beyond their ability to control, the nonrepentant condemn themselves. Theirs is a self-created damnation. Salvation is never achieved, and condemnation is always self-imposed.

MISSIONARY RESULTS

Luke 10:17–20

> ¹⁷*The seventy returned with great joy, saying, "Lord, even the demons are subjected to us in your name."* ¹⁸*Jesus said to them, "I was watching Satan fall as lightening from heaven.* ¹⁹*Behold, I gave to you authority to trample on snakes and scorpions and all power over the enemy, and nothing will harm you.* ²⁰*But do not take joy in that spirits are subject to you. Take joy in that your names have been written in heaven."*

Several results of the mission of the seventy are of considerable importance. (1) The returning seventy reported that demons were subject to them upon the mention of Jesus' name. The word the King James Version translates "subject" is ὑποτάσσεται (*hupotassetai*). Here in Luke the word is a present middle/passive finite verb. As such, Luke described a reality where the demons were under submission.

There are two approaches to understanding this fully. Because the pronominal suffix for the middle voice is indistinguishable from the pronominal suffix for the passive voice,[9] the translator must determine

---

9. Both are spelled the same way in Greek.

from context how to translate the word. If the verb is passive, the subject receives the action of the verb rather than doing or completing the action of the verb. The meaning in this passage is that demons were placed under submission by someone else. Because the returning seventy referenced Jesus' name, the obvious conclusion was as the seventy faithfully proclaimed Jesus' name and thereby advanced the kingdom, Jesus exercised authority over the powers of the universe and placed the demons under the submission of those who honored the Messiah.

If the verb is in the middle voice, the subject does the action but also receives the action. Translating the middle voice into English will frequently require the reflexive pronoun *myself*. In this passage, if the verb is middle, then Luke was indicating the demons placed themselves under submission of the seventy upon the mention of Jesus' name. Beyond the immediate context, the translator often refers to patterns within the author's own style for subtle distinctions. Unfortunately, ὑποτάσσεται (*hupotassetai*) is not a common word to Luke. There are only three incidences of its use in Luke and Acts: twice in Luke 10 and one more time in reference to Jesus' submitting himself to his parents after the temple narrative (Luke 2:51). While one occurrence does not a pattern make, the voluntary nature of ὑποτάσσεται (*hupotassetai*) is prevalent throughout the New Testament. Accordingly, as the seventy proclaimed the name of Jesus, the powers of the university fell in abeyance.

(2) Additionally, there is the issue of repetition.[10] Unlike the Twelve who were commissioned to have power and authority over disease and demons and to proclaim the message of the kingdom (Luke 9:1–2), the seventy were directed to heal the sick and proclaim the kingdom. It is almost as though the submission of the forces of the universe was an added accomplishment that was secondary to carrying out their assigned task. But even if this were the case, it is important to understand the corollary between proclaiming the name of Jesus and the submission of those who oppose the Messiah. Luke presented the statement in the present tense. As the seventy proclaimed, the demons continued submitting. The durative nature of the present tense communicates an important distinction. It is not the Christian who wields power over Satan. Rather, as the Christian proclaims the gospel message, Jesus *goes on causing* the submission of the forces of evil. Unlike salvation, which is a matter of identity based on the change that God creates and thereby is established

---

10. Robertson, *Luke*, 148.

once for all time, ongoing victory in the Christian's life is a matter of daily discipline. Moment by moment the Christian brings forces into submission to Christ. Regrettably, the antithesis is equally true. Moment by moment the Christian also chooses activities and actions that relegate themselves to a position of weakness, not strength.

In addition to the demons being subject to the seventy, Jesus stated he *was watching Satan fall as lightening from heaven*. The King James Version indicates "I beheld Satan fall" whereas the Revised Standard Version (RSV) and The New International Version (NIV) both have "I saw Satan fall." The verb ἐθεώρουν (*etheōroun*) is in the imperfect tense, which represents continuous action in past time. While the simple past tense of "beheld" and "saw" can be a one-time event or a repetition of events, choosing the English past tense forces the translator to stop and explain that the action of "beholding" and "seeing" was repetitive. More to the point, the reader must decide if Jesus was referring to Satan falling every time the seventy caused the demons to be subject or was Jesus referring to "the fall of Satan." The force of the grammar and the momentum of the immediate context argue for the former, not the latter. While it is true that the aorist tense of ἀστραπὴν (*astrapēn*), "he fell," is frequently used for a particular incident in the past time, "it is not necessary to understand this aorist as connoting the prehistoric, definitive fall of Lucifer; but the aorist may be regarded as a 'global' one embracing the whole process of the defeat of Satan from the fall of Lucifer throughout the whole history of salvation to the full and final victory in the Last Judgment."[11] The reason this distinction is important is to see Jesus invite his disciples, then and now, to join the struggle. Jesus was watching every time the seventy experienced victory, and Jesus is watching now as well. Every time Jesus' name is proclaimed, there is victory. Every time the Christian resists evil, Satan flees (James 4:7).

While it is true that these issues are important, none are more important than the primary result that Luke identified, which was neither the numbers saved nor the foes vanquished. The most important result was the participant's joy. At the conclusion of the mission, Luke indicated the seventy returned with great joy. While Jesus validated their experience of having authority over the demons and the protection from harm, Jesus quickly cautioned the seventy regarding the true reason for joy. It was not success that provided joy. It was not protection that provided

---

11. Zerwick, *Biblical Greek*, 90.

joy. Joy comes from participation in the kingdom. This is immensely important because every experience would not produce the same visible results. Jesus knew that he would suffer an agonizing death in order to be part of God's plan. Jesus knew that with the passing of time reality would call on many who followed him to suffer for the name of Christ. Outward accolades were never to be the motivation for Christian service. The joy of following Jesus is the struggle, the work, the participation.

A PRAYER OF JESUS OR A JOY-FILLED LIFE

Luke 10:21–24

²¹In that same hour, Jesus himself was extremely joyful in the Holy Spirit, and he said, "I praise and thank you, Father, Lord of heaven and earth, that you have hidden these things from those with wisdom and understanding and have revealed them to those who are childlike because it was your gracious will to do so. ²²All things were given to me from the Father. No one at all knows either who the Son is except the Father or who the Father is except the Son and except those to whom the Son desires to reveal him." ²³Turning to his disciples he said privately, "Blessed are the eyes that are seeing what you see. ²⁴For I say to you that many prophets and kings desired to see what you see, but have not seen, and hear what you hear, but did not hear."

"It's just a prayer." That could easily be the reader's initial conclusion about this passage. "After all," one could say, "was not Luke eager to emphasize prayer as one of his dominant themes? Did we not just see the entire transfiguration event unfold as an invitation for the disciples to go away with Jesus and pray? Does the Gospel of John not in fact include a similar prayer in John 17?" Yes would be the appropriate response to all of these questions. But the passage isn't just another prayer. Specifically, the content and context of Jesus' words reveal it is for more; this prayer is the description of why the Spirit-filled life is a joy-filled life.

First is the obvious building of the narrative to the point of culmination. Jesus commissioned the seventy to deliver the gospel message even in the face of opposition. Next Jesus pronounced additional judgment on those who turned from responding to the gospel. Upon the return of the seventy, great success was reported, including Jesus' history encompassing observation about the ultimate and complete demise of evil. Not until Jesus described the victorious nature of true discipleship did he turn in prayer and present the elements of a joyous Spirit-filled life.

(1) The Spirit-filled life is a joy-filled life because it is positional. Luke used the word ἠγαλλιάσατο (ēgalliasato) to indicate Jesus was *extremely joyful in the Holy Spirit*. In the Septuagint ἠγαλλιάσατο (ēgalliasato) translates רָנַן (rānan), the Hebrew word that means cry out or shout out for joy. While its predominant use is in Psalms and Isaiah, רָנַן (rānan) was used to capture the emotion experienced by the children of God as they gained a position of right standing before God via the prescribed sacrificial system. During the Sinai wanderings, Moses commanded the people to prepare themselves and bring animals for a sacrifice so that God could appear before them. Aaron prepared the sacrifice, blessed the people, and entered the tabernacle along with Moses. Upon exiting the tabernacle, Moses and Aaron again blessed the people and God appeared to his people (Lev 9:1–23). Additionally, "there came a fire out from before the Lord, and consumed upon the altar the burnt offering and the fat: which when all the people saw, they shouted, and fell on their faces" (Lev 9:24).

What transpired in that moment was nothing short of transformational for the Hebrew people. They entered into a relationship with God whereby they were pleasing to God. Their shouts of joy were due to the positional change that had taken place. Regarding this passage, William White said that "the joy of Israel at God's saving acts is carried on throughout the OT."[12]

This same positional joy is to be understood in the New Testament use of ἠγαλλιάσατο (ēgalliasato). Furthermore, the term develops an eschatological overtone as the distinction is blurred between the present and future realities of the Christian's new identity in Christ. In John's apocalypse, the corporate nature of the positional joy is viewed in terms of the expectant wedding of Christ and the church. "And I heard as it were the voice of a great multitude, and as the voice of many waters, and as the voice of mighty thunderings, saying, Alleluia: for the Lord God omnipotent reigneth. Let us be glad and rejoice, and give honor to him: for the marriage of the Lamb is come, and his wife hath made herself ready" (Rev 19:6–7). Individually, this positional joy was expressed in

---

12. White, "רָנַן (rānan)," 851.

Luke's recount of Elisabeth's pregnancy. There Elisabeth was said to have joy (Luke 1:14), the infant John leaped for joy at the presence of the earthly Jesus (1:44), causing Mary to say, "My spirit hath rejoiced in God my Savior" (Luke 1:47). Clearly, the joy being described goes beyond the happiness of a moment that fades with time.

The Spirit-filled life is a joy-filled life precisely because of the position the person of faith holds. Rudolf Bultmann addressed the position the Christian holds when he said that ἠγαλλιάσατο (ēgalliasato) "characterizes the consciousness of the community that it is the community of the last time constituted by the saving act of God."[13] The Spirit-filled life is a joy-filled life not because of personal merit but because of the saving act of God. The child of God's only worth is in his or her relationship to Jesus, a position that cannot be changed.

(2) The Spirit-filled life is a joy-filled life because it is confessional. Luke indicated Jesus said, "*I praise and thank you*" in his prayer to his Father. The word used to describe his emotions and his state of mind, ἐξομολογοῦμαί (exomologoumai), dates back to the third century BC, where it had the meaning of admit, confess, or acknowledge. The term ἐξομολογοῦμαί (exomologoumai) is a compound formed from an even earlier word, ὁμολογέω (homologeō), meaning "to speak or say the same thing." The use of ὁμολογέω (homologeō) was common in secular Greek religion and law as early as the fifth century BC Its legal use described a consistent witness, a common understanding where everyone was agreeing to terms; its religious sense was to say the same thing as an accuser, to admit to an accusation or to confess the guilt of an act.[14]

This dual use of ὁμολογέω (homologeō) and ἐξομολογοῦμαί (exomologoumai) are continued well into the Hellenistic and Koine Greek periods. Regarding its New Testament use, ἐξομολογοῦμαί (exomologoumai) is found where it refers to acknowledging the worth of God—praise and adoration—as well as confessing sin to God. No clearer demonstration of this can be found than in Philippians 2:11 and Romans 14:11. In both references, Paul quoted Isaiah who spoke for God saying, "Look unto me, and be ye saved, all the ends of the earth: for I am God, and there is none else. I have sworn by myself, the word is gone out of my mouth in righteousness, and shall not return, that unto me every knee shall bow, every tongue shall swear" (Isa 45:22–23).

---

13. Bultmann, "ἀγαλλιάομαι," 20.
14. Michel, "ὁμολογέω," 199–200.

Writing to the Philippians, Paul used ἐξομολογοῦμαί (*exomologoumai*) to command the worship of God when he said, "Wherefore God also hath highly exalted him, and given him a name which is above every name: That at the name of Jesus every knee should bow, of things in heaven, and things in earth, and things under the earth; And that every tongue should confess that Jesus Christ is Lord, to the glory of God the Father" (Phil 2:9–11). Clearly, Paul intended ἐξομολογοῦμαί (*exomologoumai*), "confess that Jesus Christ is Lord," to be understood as adoration. However, Paul intended ἐξομολογοῦμαί (*exomologoumai*) to be understood as confession of sin when he said to the Romans, "For it is written, *As* I live, saith the Lord, every knee shall bow to me, and every tongue shall confess to God. So then every one of us shall give account of himself to God" (Rom 14:11–12).

The significance of how Paul used the Isaiah passage in general and ἐξομολογοῦμαί (*exomologoumai*) in particular is hard to overstate. Rather than acknowledging what is right or admitting what is wrong, a true confession is both. One cannot affirm the greatness of God without simultaneously confirming the sinfulness of man. Stated differently, without knowledge of God there is no knowledge of right and wrong.[15]

Given this understanding, the reader can return to Jesus' prayer in Luke 10 with the background to grasp fully what Jesus was saying. Luke indicated Jesus was joyful in the Holy Spirit, an experience that led him to confess. As the sinless Son of God, Jesus had done no wrong for which he needed to confess. His statement of adoration and praise exalted his Heavenly Father. But for everyone else, the Spirit-filled life is a joy-filled life precisely because our confession of sin leads to our confession of the greatness of God. There is peace and contentment in knowing that God is greater than our human condition. God's greatness causes us to confess first our sinfulness and next God's wondrous character. Accordingly, the psalmist said,

> "The Lord is my shepherd; I shall not want. He maketh me to lie down in green pastures: he leadeth me beside the still waters. He restoreth my soul: he leadeth me in the paths of righteousness for his name's sake. Yea, though I walk through the valley of the

---

15. The reader should note Paul clearly argued in Romans what can be known about God is plain to all so all are without excuse. Mankind was created in the image of God and inherently knows God exists. What Immanuel Kant called Moral Law acknowledges that God is good, man is sinful, and what is more, we all know it.

shadow of death, I will fear no evil: for thou art with me; thy rod and thy staff they comfort me. Thou preparest a table before me in the presence of mine enemies: thou anointest my head with oil; my cup runneth over. Surely goodness and mercy shall follow me all the days of my life: and I will dwell in the house of the Lord forever" (Ps 23:1–6).

(3) The Spirit-filled life is a joy-filled life because it is relational. Luke again underscored a bedrock principle of the kingdom of God. Nationality did not matter. Family origin did not matter. One was not born into religious privilege like one is sometimes born into financial privilege. Entrance into the kingdom occurred one way and one way only—via relationship with Jesus Christ and through him, with the Heavenly Father. This reality causes the Spirit-filled life to be a joy-filled life for one simple reason. True relationship is established when a person openly and freely chooses to enter into a relationship. Accessibility is a major key to happiness in the Christian walk.

Note the details of Jesus' statement. First he said the Father had given him everything. By association, the person who chooses to relate to Jesus relates to all Jesus has. Obviously this analogy should not be pressed to the point of ascribing false, impure, or ulterior motives to the believer. That being understood, it is easy to see the joy that comes from trusting a person who has control of all created things. Second, Jesus identified himself as one with the Father. Jesus said no one knows the Son except the Father and no one knows the Father except the Son (see John 5). Equality and mutual identity exist between Jesus and his Heavenly Father. Accordingly, as a person chooses to enter relation with Jesus, he or she enters relation with the Father. Third, the Spirit-filled life is a joy-filled life because Jesus exercises sovereign control with the Father over all things. Jesus specifically indicated no one knows the Father except those to whom Jesus has revealed the Father. Furthermore, Jesus' prayer in this passage speaks directly to the Father's sovereign will in this matter. At the risk of trivializing a highly important aspect of God's plan of salvation, Karl Marx was not far from the truth when he said religion was the opiate of the masses. While Marx's motive of stamping out religion was not only improper and ultimately impossible, he inadvertently proclaimed a great truth. Regardless of wealth, status, creature comforts, education, and so forth, relation with Jesus and thereby with the Heavenly Father creates a peace precisely because the believer understands God's sovereign control.

Finally in this passage, Luke returned to one of his fundamental convictions: The universality of the gospel message engages the nameless and faceless crowds that quietly but efficiently go about the kingdom's work. The absence of the articles in the phrase ἀπὸ σοφῶν καὶ συνετῶν (*apo sophōn kai sunetōn*) demands the translation reflect the qualities of people rather than specific people from whom the meaning of the kingdom is hidden. The description of the wise and understanding is paired with the phrase αὐτὰ νηπίοις (*auta nēpiois*). The matters of the kingdom are hidden from those who are wise and understanding, but these same matters are revealed to those who are infants. Positioned as it is in opposition to the wise and understanding, also without the article, the antecedent of infants are those who with childlike qualities simply accept what God is doing. There is no station or rank that predisposes a person to be involved in the things of God.[16]

WHO WAS A NEIGHBOR?

Luke 10:25–37

25 Now there was an expert in the law who, testing Jesus, stood up and said, "Teacher, what must I do to inherit eternal life?" 26 Jesus said to him, "What has been written in the Law? What do you read there?" 27 He answered him saying, "You must love the Lord your God with all your heart, with all your soul, with all your strength, and with all your mind, and your neighbor as yourself." 28 Jesus said to him, "You have answered correctly. Do this and you will live." 29 But desiring to justify himself, he said to Jesus, "Now just who is my neighbor?" 30 Replying, Jesus said, "A man went down from Jerusalem to Jericho, and he fell into the hands of robbers. Stripping and beating him, they departed, leaving him half dead. 31 By coincidence, a priest was coming down the way and seeing him, passed on the other side. 32 In the same way, a

---

16. Not considered in this passage are aspects of Synoptic study that examine the use of "Q" by not only Matthew and Luke but also the Evangelist John. Note the similarities between this passage and Jesus' prayer in John 17; the drawing of the believer to the Father in John 6:4; the joy of Abraham at seeing Jesus in John 8:56; the blessing of seeing and believing in John 20:29.

> *Levite reaching the same place passed in the same way.* ³³*But then a Samaritan who was traveling came upon him and seeing him, took pity on him,* ³⁴*and going to him, dressed his wounds, poured on oil and wine, and placing him on his own beast of burden, brought him to an inn and took care of him.* ³⁵*On the next day, he took out and gave two denarius to the innkeeper and said, 'Take care of him and whatever you spend I will repay to you upon my return.'* ³⁶*"Which of these three demonstrated he was a neighbor to the man who was robbed?"* ³⁷*An he said, "The one who showed mercy." Jesus said to him, "You go and do likewise."*

Luke's Good Samaritan narrative is one of timeless beauty whose details are well rehearsed. A traveler was assaulted on the road between Jerusalem and Jericho. Left by his assailants to die, the man was rescued by an unlikely benefactor after two others valued their own well-being more than that of the victim. The Samaritan not only dressed the man's wounds, an action that placed him in peril if the robbers were still lying in wait, but he also took the man to a place of shelter and paid the expenses of his care. Frank Stagg summarized beautifully the motives of those involved in the narrative. "The robber said, 'What is yours is mine, and I will take it.' The priest and Levite said, 'What is mine is mine, and I will keep it.' The Samaritan said, 'What is mine is yours, and I will give it.' "[17]

More important, however, than the motives of the characters in the parable are the motives of the characters in the narrative. (1) The motive of the arrogant lawyer was to entrap, proving he was better than Jesus. An expert in the Jewish law stood up to entrap Jesus with the question: "What must I do to inherit eternal life?" Though not as obvious of a trap as the woman taken in adultery where the accusers thought Jesus would either forgive and break the law or condemn and break his pattern of compassion, the question of the legal expert was no less without peril. By placing the emphasis on doing acts of the law, the legal expert wanted to place the kingdom of God in a transactional position. Key to this is the understanding of inheritance in Jewish custom. In the Greek legal system a will or testament could name anyone as an heir. But in Jewish law, direct bloodline or descent dictated receipt of property.[18] The fact is the attorney did not think you could "do" anything to receive an in-

---

17. Stagg, *Studies in Luke's Gospel*, 80.
18. Herrmann and Foerster, "κλῆρος," 758–785.

heritance. Luke supported this Jewish belief in the story of the Prodigal Son/Loving Father/Distant Brother story where once the inheritance was divided among legal heirs, it could not be changed. What was to be inherited, in this case eternal life, was of no consequence to the expert, only the means of achieving it. If Jesus said anyone could do anything, he would be in violation of Jewish property law. The expert's motive was entrapment.

(2) The motive of the convicted was to justify his actions, proving he was just as good as Jesus. As was so often the case when people encountered Jesus, assumption faded and preconceived ideas melted away like morning fog. As the narrative unfolded, Jesus' conversation caused introspection. "What do the Scriptures tell you that one must do to inherit eternal life?" Jesus asked. The expert was ready. He responded with a rock-solid answer. "The law says in Deuteronomy 6:5 we are to love the Lord God with all our heart, mind, and soul. Furthermore, the law says in Leviticus 19:18 to love our neighbor as ourselves." "You are correct," Jesus said. "Do that and you will have eternal life."

But instead of ending the dialogue, something happened. Maybe it was the inflection in Jesus' voice, his tone, the nuance. Perhaps it was body language, something Luke could not convey even with his literary mastery. Or maybe it was simply the presence of the Holy Spirit, convincing the world of sin, righteousness, and judgment (see John 16:8). Whatever it was, the expert's anticipated joy at being better than Jesus was no longer there. It had been replaced by worry that perhaps he could not do everything the law commanded—that not only was he not better than Jesus but that he wasn't even as good as Jesus.

It was at this point in the narrative that the inquiry of Jesus' adversary gave all Christianity an extraordinary insight. When false confidence fails, insecurity will increase and minimalism will be the result. "Well, OK. But who is my neighbor? If I must love my neighbor, then who is my neighbor? I mean, I want to be sure that I do what I must do. And besides that, I don't want to do anything that I don't absolutely need to do. Tell me exactly what is required, not a scintilla more." When confronted with the openness of the gospel, the self-serving, self-justifying heart always retreats to that which it believes it can control.

(3) But Jesus' motive was personal, desiring that all, including his then current opponent, would enter the kingdom. Faced with the expert's minimalist question, Jesus told the story of the Good Samaritan.

The obvious hero of the story was an unlikely character. There should be no doubt that Jesus' decision to vilify the Jewish priest and Levite, as well as to praise the Samaritan, were in fact attacks on the man's preconceptions. But the pivotal part of the exchange relates specifically to the question that prompted the parable and the answer that followed. In response to the lawyer's question, "Who is my neighbor," Jesus told the parable and asked a different question, specifically, "Who was a neighbor?" As a result, Jesus eliminated the reductionism that was the basis of the lawyer's approach. The answer to the question, "Who am I obligated to love in order to inherit the kingdom of heaven" was "Anyone who needs your love."

(4) Finally, Luke's motive for including this exchange from Jesus' life was to emphasize both the futility of salvation based on works and the inevitability of the ultimate victory of the rule and reign of God. The former is accomplished by the force of the parable; one can never do enough to merit salvation. The latter is accomplished ever so subtly, yet just as forcibly, by one phrase of the parable. After the traveler was victimized and left on the road to die, the text indicates that by coincidence a priest and a Levite came by. Placed at this point in the narrative, the fact of chance is placed in direct opposition to God's sovereign control, specifically Jesus' statement that God revealed himself to those of his choice (Luke 10:21). By attributing chance to the character who plays a derogatory role, the narrative subtly dismisses chance as even a reality and declares divine intervention and control as a necessity.

THE FUTILITY OF DOING

Luke 10:38–42

38 When the disciples went on their way, they entered a village where there was a woman named Martha who received Jesus as a guest. 39 This woman had a sister called Mary, who was sitting at the feet of Jesus, in order to hear his words. 40 Martha was being distracted by much service so she went to Jesus and said, "Lord! Is it of no concern to you that my sister has abandoned me to serve alone? Tell her she should help me!" 41 The Lord answered and said to her, "Martha, Martha. You are anxious and are becoming troubled over many things, 42 while only one thing is necessary. Mary has chosen the best, and it will not be taken away from her."

"Good. Better. Best. Oh, may I never rest, until my Good is Better and my Better is Best." Even though the primary use of this rhyme may be little more than to teach elementary students the degrees of comparative adjectives, its inherent logic and timeless beauty continue to nudge forward many a driven adult. Ambition is good, and as such should not be discouraged or categorically dismissed. But the advantage of ambition ceases when applied to matters of fellowship with God. Surely that was Luke's intent when placing the account of Jesus, Mary, and Martha in immediate contrast with the works salvation that prompted the Good Samaritan parable. Doing acts of greatness, especially when prompted by personal ambition, gains neither the unbeliever access to God nor the believer greater fellowship with God. Notice in the story the futility of doing.

Luke opened the narrative with a simple statement regarding the setting. Jesus went to a village, and a woman named Martha welcomed him as her houseguest. From the beginning of his Gospel, Luke emphasized the importance of women in the early church. This story is no different. The way Martha is described attributes to her the stature of what the modern Internal Revenue Service code might call the head of the household. Martha greeted Jesus, accepted him as a guest, and shifted to the role of provider and hostess. There were recognized obligations for receiving guests, and Martha attended to those details dutifully.

But Martha also had a sister. The story unfolds to indicate that while Martha was busy with the many details required to perform the responsibilities she had accepted, Mary was with Jesus. Specifically, Mary was sitting at Jesus' feet and hearing his words.

With this, the stage was set for the conflict. Martha was doing while Mary was being. Both had admirable motives. Neither was acting inappropriately. But comparison and conflict were inevitable.

With frustration mounting, Martha reached a boiling point. Constructed as a rhetorical question that expected an affirmative answer, Martha said to Jesus, "Don't you care that Mary has abandoned me to serve alone? I am *doing* all this stuff, and she is just sitting there, *doing nothing!*"

The irony of the story is that Jesus did care. He cared deeply about what was happening. Furthermore, truer words may have never been spoken than those uttered by Martha. Mary was *doing nothing*, and doing nothing was precisely the subject of the superlative of the story. Just like the lawyer, Martha was seeking to achieve a special status with

Jesus based on what she could do and on what she could accomplish. Her attempts were to merit a relationship that was conditional and controllable. Mary, on the other hand, was willing to become completely vulnerable; she approached Jesus unconditionally and without any sense of control. Translated in the King James Version as "the good part," the Semitic force of the expression is actually the superlative.[19] Mary had chosen "the best dish on the table, fellowship with Jesus."[20]

There is one final word about the futility of doing. In her efforts to achieve a works-based relationship with Jesus, Martha only disadvantaged herself. First, there are always more details than can be accomplished. She busied herself with the many things she thought were acceptable, were appropriate, and were required. The reality is there is never an end to what is acceptable, appropriate, and required. Furthermore, Martha initiated a progression that is never healthful. Specifically, she allowed her stress to push her to the point of inappropriate behavior, literally bursting into a social situation and interrupting a conversation. The interruption allowed Jesus to say that being overly anxious ends in being overly agitated. Finally, what could have been a remarkable moment for Martha was forever lost. Hers could have been an example for all time of quietly serving those in need. Instead, she has served as a negative example that has been repeated down through the ages while her sister was rewarded for her desire simply to be with Jesus.

THE MODEL PRAYER

Luke 11:1–4

[1] Now it happened in a certain place that Jesus was praying and when he stopped, his disciples said, "Lord, teach us to pray as John taught his disciples to pray." [2] Jesus said to them, "When you pray, say, 'Father, may your name be made holy; please let your kingdom come; [3] please give to us each day the bread necessary for existence; [4] please forgive us of our sins, for we forgive everyone in our debt; and please do not bring us into temptation."

When the disciples heard Jesus communing with God, they asked him to teach them how to pray. Theirs was not an unusual request. The facts

---

19. Zerwick, *Biblical Greek*, 48.
20. Robertson, *Luke*, 157.

of the text indicate not only did John teach his disciples how to pray but it was known that John had done so. In the Jewish world, "it was the regular custom for a Rabbi to teach his disciples a simple prayer which they might habitually use."[21]

What followed, however, was far from ordinary. As has been seen so many times already in his Gospel, where Luke placed a story, its sequence, is often as important as the story itself. From the beginning of the Judean ministry, Jesus told his disciples what to be more than what to do. Upon their return, Jesus told the seventy missionaries to take joy in the fact that their names were written in the book of life, not that they exercised authority over evil spirits (Luke 10:20). The joy-filled life that is positional, confessional, and relational is more descriptive of who the disciple is than what the disciple does (Luke 10:21–22). While it is true that the Good Samaritan narrative describes love in action, still it carries the overtone of what kind a person the disciple is to be—caring, compassionate, giving, and so forth (Luke 10:25–37). Finally, chapter 10 ends with Jesus cautioning Martha for doing and commending Mary for being (Luke 10:38–42). Placed where it is, the momentum of Luke's narrative would lead the reader to one conclusion about the Model Prayer: Jesus described not a litany but a lifestyle.

If this assumption is correct, the Model Prayer is not simply a pattern to be pedantically repeated. The Model Prayer describes the life of the Christian in two main arenas, one heavenly and one earthly. This duality is not intended to compartmentalize the life of the believer but rather to acknowledge the reality of life in Christ. As a citizen of heaven, the Christian is to be intimate, reverent, and cognizant of God's sovereignty. As a citizen of earth, the Christian is to be forgiven, forgiving, and forever vigilant.

(1) The Model Prayer directs the Christian to be intimate with God. The disciples were to address God as Father. The intimacy of the term was intentional. Conversation with God was to be as open and as frequent as conversations between friends or family members. Luke continued this very point in the story of the neighbor at midnight. There Luke emphasized the image of the Heavenly Father as a loving and caring parent. Prayer was not to be occasional but constant; open and sincere, not contrived.

---

21. Barclay, *The Gospel of Luke*, 145.

(2) The Model Prayer directs the Christian to be reverent. Barclay translated the phrase "hollowed be thy name" as "let your name be held in reverence."[22] Left unchecked, the intimacy of calling God "Father" could lead to a lack of respect. True indeed is the expression that familiarity breeds contempt. However, as Christians relate to the Father with reverence, giving due praise to the God's divine greatness, believers position themselves to understand fully the character of God. When the believer is intimate and reverent, humility results from realizing the God of the universe is near and desires to have a relationship with his creation.

(3) The Model Prayer directs the believer to be cognizant of God's sovereignty. The phrase *please let your kingdom come* initiates the first of four imperative verbs. Most frequently used for a command, the imperative takes on the form of an entreaty when the speaker is engaged in a conversation with a superior, as in prayer.[23] By praying, *please let your kingdom come*, the believer acknowledges the importance of God's rule in the present reality of day-to-day life. Given the nature of the request, the believer is affirming that God can and does control circumstances in the here and now. Furthermore, by wanting the reign and rule of God to be enacted on earth implies that by doing so, God will be recognized. Understanding the kingdom and seeing its reign in the reality of the world is the job of the believer.

One very practical aspect of believing in the sovereignty of God is anticipating that God will provide for even the most basic needs of the believer. Two issues surface in understanding the request for what has been most often translated daily bread. Most debated is the meaning of ἐπιούσιον (*epiousion*). A compound word, the meaning could be simply for the coming day. The translation would be "Give us this day our daily bread." Sounds pretty familiar, doesn't it? However, the compound word can be dissected into a preposition meaning upon and a participial form of the being verb I am. This would push the translation toward the literal meaning upon existence or necessary for existence. Given both possibilities, the force of Luke's literary emphasis on being over doing could lead the translator to the latter meaning. But in either case, Luke showed God wants the believer to apply the understanding of the sovereignty of God to even the most routine details of life.

---

22. Ibid., 145.
23. Brooks and Winbery, Syntax of New Testament Greek, 116.

(4) The Model Prayer directs the believer to be forgiven. While this may appear to be an oversimplification, there are in fact two important aspects to this declarative statement: initiation of belief and continuation of belief. The meaning of both aspects of belief is drawn directly from the tense of the verb. The verb ἄφες (*aphes*) means "I forgive someone or something." Luke used the imperative mode to add the element of pleading for forgiveness. Luke used the aorist tense to emphasize forgiveness past, present, and future. The believer was to be forgiven—a statement that implies there was a point in time when the person acknowledged his or her sin and sought remedy from the only one who could provide it. The believer was to be forgiven—a statement that implies there continues to be an awareness of fallibility that inevitably leads to improper action and activity. In short, no one should be more aware of the need for forgiveness than the one who has received it.

(5) The Model Prayer directs the believer to be forgiving. Given the poetic nature of the prayer, one could easily make the mistake of tying causality to this part of the prayer. While the believer being both forgiven and forgiving certainly are related to the Christian way of life and the reality of serving the God who forgives, God does not forgive us because we forgive other people. All too sadly, the readers of Luke's Gospel through the ages can point to contemporary situations of God's people not acting very godly, forgiven people not being forgiving. It is precisely because of this reality that Jesus instructed his disciples to be forgiven while they live a lifestyle of forgiving. The importance of this distinction relates to credibility. When Christians are not forgiving of others, they fail to represent the power of forgiveness in their own lives. As a result, Jesus made a simple statement: I will forgive you, and you should forgive others.

(6) The Model Prayer directs the believer to be forever vigilant. Rather than the believer asking God to avoid doing something that will cause damage—don't tempt me to sin—the Model Prayer seeks to heighten the believer's awareness of the problem of sin. The aorist verb εἰσενέγκῃς (*eisenegkēs*) should be understood as ingressive, meaning that prayer is a plea to prevent something from starting. "Do not allow me to be tempted." "Place a hedge around me." "Let me be so completely consumed with thoughts of you, O God, that I do not cultivate receptivity to temptation." All of these statements paraphrase and adequately convey the meaning of the King James Translation, "Lead us not into tempta-

tion." Jesus wanted his disciples to be ever aware of their weakness and thereby protected against possible disaster.

THE PERSISTENCE AND PURPOSE OF PRAYER

Luke 11:5–13

> ⁵And he said to them, "Who among you, having a friend, will he go to him at midnight and say to him, 'Friend, loan me three loaves, ⁶for a friend of mine has come to me from the way and I have nothing to put before him.' ⁷This one will answer from within saying, 'Stop bothering me! The door is now shut, and my children are in bed with me. I am not willing to get up and give to you.' ⁸I say to you, he will not get up to give to him because his is a friend, but because of his persistence, he will get up and give whatever he needs. ⁹And I say to you, keep on asking and it will be given to you. Continue seeking, and you will find. Go on knocking, and it will be opened to you. ¹⁰For the one asking receives, the one seeking finds, and to the one knocking it will be opened. ¹¹For who among you if his son asks for a fish will give him instead a snake? ¹²Or if he asks for an egg will he give him a scorpion? ¹³If therefore you who are evil know how to give good gifts to your children, how much more will your Heavenly Father give the Holy Spirit to those that love him?"

As this passage follows on the heels of the Model Prayer, the reader should understand Luke's use of two dominant themes—prayer and the Holy Spirit—as an effort to continue the explanation of the prayer. Specifically, Luke sought to emphasize Jesus' teaching about the persistence of prayer and the true purpose of prayer.

The story of the friend at midnight requires little explanation, its meaning being clear. When a genuine need exists, a person will stop at nothing to address the need. What is more, persistence is the key to acquiring the desired result. The illustration is followed by direct discourse that commands specific action. Ask, seek, and knock are all present imperative verbs. They carry the force not of a single action or activity but rather a description of a lifestyle. Jesus directed his disciples to live lives that were constantly asking, constantly seeking, and constantly knocking. The basic premise of prayer is one of persistence. Those who continually ask, continually seek, and continually knock will find the desired answers.

But a remarkable thing happened in the second part of the narrative. Jesus redefined prayer. Specifically, the object of prayer is the person of the Holy Spirit and nothing else.

Notice the means Jesus used to convey this thought. This passage utilizes a literary device that remains effective today. Perceived logic makes much of western humor actually work. For example, consider the following: Nicholas's father has three sons. One is named Penniless, and one is named Dimeless. What is the third son's name? Perceived logic often will drive the hearer of the riddle to respond, "The third son must be named Quarterless" when in fact the riddle narrative already identified the third son as Nicholas.

Jesus used the same progression of perceived logic when he asked the rhetorical questions, "Who among you would give a serpent to a son who asked for a fish, or a scorpion upon request for an egg?" The grammar of the questions clearly expected a negative answer, "None of us would give something harmful to a child! What kind of parents do you think we are?" Having set the tone, Jesus continued. "If you, who are basically evil, know how to give good things, how much more does your Heavenly Father know how to provide your needs?"

A pause must be made to explain an element of rabbinic argument. Much like modern-day forensic debate, there were first-century rules for intellectual exchange. These often are heard from the teachings of Jesus, as well as the apostle Paul and the writer of the Book of Hebrews. One very common argument was the lesser to the greater. For example, to prove the superiority of Jesus' high priesthood to that of the Levitical priesthood, the writer of Hebrews pointed out that Levi was in the loins of Abraham when Abraham paid tithes to Melchizedek. Because the lesser pays tithes to the greater, Melchizedek was greater than Abraham. By association, the argument goes, because Jesus is like Melchizedek, Jesus' priesthood is superior to Levi's priesthood (Heb 6).

Now back to Jesus' teaching on prayer. Those hearing Jesus that day would have been thoroughly familiar with the flow of argument. The crowd knew exactly where Jesus was going the moment he began the sentence, "If you who are evil . . ." Unlike the modern mind that must pause and wrap its thinking around what was being said, the crowd knew instantly. What is more, they agreed. Given their literary culture, they could do nothing but agree. Obviously if an evil parent knew something, the Heavenly Father would know more. This part of Jesus' teaching carried no surprise.

What did take the crowd off guard and which must be even now the matter of consideration was not the beginning of the argument but its ending. Those hearing Jesus expected him to say, "If you who are evil know how to give good things, how much more does the Heavenly Father know how to give good things?" The perceived logic of what Jesus was teaching created the expectation that the object of the giving would be the same by both the evil parents and the Heavenly Father. But instead, Jesus substituted the object received and thereby taught a tremendous truth about prayer. Prayer is not about getting things. Prayer is about being in fellowship with the Holy Spirit. "How much more," Jesus said, "does the Heavenly Father know how to give not just good things but the best thing—the presence of the Holy Spirit?"

All too often prayer is perceived as a celestial wish list. Like the child on Santa's lap in the retail mall, the believer asks God for stuff. But at the risk of implying that God is unconcerned about the details of the believer's life, the great object of prayer is connecting the believer with God and nothing else. When Christians pray and join the Holy Spirit, they experience the eternal, not the temporal. When this takes place, believers are ushered to a place before the presence of God where everything earthly fades in comparison to things heavenly. At that point, believers understand the only important thing is God, the only important things are those that are eternal, and nothing temporal can in anyway change that reality.

Perhaps no more poetic expression of this truth can be found than is presented in the lyrics of William W. Walford's famous hymn "Sweet Hour of Prayer." A congregational minister in England during the first half of the nineteenth century, Walford published his work in the *New York Observer* in 1845. Included in his verse are these lines that capture the essence of seeking God rather than seeking what God can do.

> *With such I hasten to the place*
> *Where God my savior shows his face,*
> *And gladly take my station there,*
> *And wait for thee, sweet hour of prayer.*
> . . . . .
> *And since He bids me seek His face,*
> *Believe His word, and trust his grace*
> *I'll cast on Him my every care,*
> *And wait for thee, sweet hour of prayer.*[24]

---

24. Walford, "Sweet Hour of Prayer," No. 445.

GATHERING WITH GOD OR SCATTERING WITH SATAN

Luke 11:14–23

¹⁴*Now Jesus was casting out a demon of a man who was unable to speak. When it came to pass that the demon left him, the speechless man spoke and the crowd marveled.* ¹⁵*But some among them said, "He casts out demons by Beelzebub, chief of demons."* ¹⁶*Others, desiring proof, required of him signs from heaven.* ¹⁷*But knowing their thoughts, Jesus said to them, "Every kingdom divided against itself is destroyed, and every house upon house falls.* ¹⁸*If Satan is divided against himself, how will his kingdom stand? You say that I cast out demons by Beelzebub.* ¹⁹*But if I cast out demons by Beelzebub, by whom do your sons cast out demons? For this reason, they will be your judge.* ²⁰*But if I cast out demons by the finger of God, then the kingdom of God has come upon you.* ²¹*When a strong man, being fully armed, guards his own house, his possessions will be in peace.* ²²*But if one who is stronger attacks and conquers him, the stronger carries away the armor upon which the weaker trusted and divides it among the spoils.* ²³*He who is not with me is against me and the one not gathering with me is scattering.*

In this passage, Luke used what appears to be just a miracle story, specifically a demon exorcism, to communicate far more. What simply could have been a Lucan illustration of the growing tension between Jesus and the religious elite became an explanation of an underlying reality of human nature. Though temporal in its current form, humanity is eternal and will either serve or oppose God.

In fairness, a cursory reading of the narrative reveals little more than another miracle, another argument. In fact, that is all this account would be were it not for Luke's inclusion of verses 21 through 23.

Notice the progression through verse 20. Jesus encountered a need—a man without the ability to speak who was also possessed by a demonic presence. Jesus healed the man to the praise of those watching. Not wanting to allow Jesus' popularity to swell, those present with a vested interest in the status quo objected to the miracle. In response, Jesus turned their words against them, forcing the realization that condemning Jesus would logically condemn themselves. End of story. With varying details and settings, the reader of the New Testament has viewed this sequence of events over and over.

But Luke did include 11:21–23. If one assumes that Luke wrote with a literary command rather than simply stringing together unrelated stories and fragments of tradition, one must look for a connection between the initial narrative and the concluding analogy. If Luke had ended the passage with verse 20, the demon exorcism would have been the historic framework for the balance of the all too familiar story. But because Luke continued the narrative through the analogy about the stronger and weaker, the voiceless demoniac was more than just the occasion for the story; the speechless demon-possessed man was the story.

If this is the case, one simply needs to start with the concluding analogy and work backward. Jesus made a statement of a fact that could easily be accepted: A strong man that is well-armed can protect hearth and home. Given agreement with that statement, and one hardly could do otherwise, Jesus presented the full argument, along with its logical conclusion. Only a stronger man could attack and conquer the well-armed, domain-protecting strong man. When that happens, the stronger man takes the possessions of the weaker and makes them the spoils of war. Neither the initial assertion nor the progression of the argument with its conclusion could be contested. The entire argument is accurate on its very face.

But for the analogy to tie back to the preceding story and thereby have any meaning beyond a series of accurate statements, the initial setting must include those who may be identified in the analogy. The first, and most obvious identification with the analogy, is that Jesus was stronger than Satan. The accusation that Jesus cast out demons by the power of Beelzebub provides the bulk of the analogy. A house divided against itself cannot stand. As it was obvious that Jesus did in fact have the power to cast out demons, he was by necessity not in league with demons. Accordingly, Jesus was identified as the stronger who could enter, attack, and conquer the weaker. Satan, it follows, was the character in the analogy that guards well his possession, being himself well-armed. Finally, the speechless, demon-possessed man was the spoils taken by the stronger invader of the weaker.

Unfortunately, nothing to this point is particularly new. Jesus had been in opposition to Satan since the temptation experience. Jesus had demonstrated his power repeatedly and made no secret of his divinity.

The fact that Jesus cared for the less fortunate has been underscored throughout Luke's Gospel. That Jesus would wrestle away from Satan's control the well being of an innocent comes as no surprise.

What makes this more than just another validation of Jesus' divine power, of his eternal authority over Satan, and of his godly compassion for his creation is found in this: The spoils taken away from the weaker by the stronger are specifically identified as the armor upon which the weaker trusted to defend his realm.

This understanding opens up the incident and accompanying analogy to several levels. There should be no mistake that Satan deals in victims. Oppression, sickness, and failure are all part of the satanic intent. Trapped in a spiral that has spun out of control, those whose lives are dominated by sin, death, discouragement, and destruction further Satan's cause. Without them, there would be no momentum to evil. These broken individuals are, in the words of the analogy, armor upon which Satan depends. In short, Satan deals in victims.

Jesus, on the other hand, deals in victors. Without any explanation, without any discussion of detail, Luke stated that Jesus simply removed the demon from a man who could not speak. In so doing, Jesus entered the realm of Satan, and defeating him, took the armor and made it the spoils of war. Among the hundreds of hymns written by Fanny J. Crosby are these fitting lines that describe how Jesus turned victims into victors.

> *Down in the human heart, crush'd by the tempter,*
> *Feelings lie buried that grace can restore;*
> *Touch'd by a loving heart, Waken'd by kindness,*
> *Chords that are broken will vibrate once more.*[25]

In addition to the speechless demoniac, Luke presented those opposing Jesus as the armor on which Satan depends. That something wondrous had taken place is evidenced by two events: The man was healed of his possession and his impediment, and those witnessing the scene marveled. But some in the crowd doubted. They attributed the event to Jesus being in league with Beelzebub. Others questioned the event and wanted a sign from heaven. Neither was moved by the restorative results of Jesus' presence. They had no jubilation at the victim turned victor. In truth, they too were armor on which Satan depended.

25. Crosby, "Rescue the Perishing," No. 559.

Tragically, what this group failed to gain that day was far greater than the receipt of vocal performance. They lost the opportunity to participate in the kingdom of God. Through the logic of the argument, Jesus proved he was not acting on Satan's authority but rather by the finger of God. As a result, Jesus said that the kingdom of God had come upon them. The truth of the same was evident, but they chose to accept a lie. They could have been victim turned victor, but they chose to remain in their own world, deluded about true reality.

The final twist of the narrative is that Jesus invites all to place themselves in the analogy. In a simple declarative statement, Jesus indicated the polarization of all humanity. A person is either with God or against God. There is no in between. All are either gathering in or they are scattering apart. All are either a hollow shell destroyed by Satan or the spoils of war proudly displayed by a conquering savior. All are either victim or victor.

> *Every day they're in the balance;*
> *Every day we make our way*
> *To a people, lost and dying,*
> *To a people God wants to save.*
> *Oh, dear God, may you daily find us*
> *Duty bound to love's refrain;*
> *Always seeking, always serving,*
> *Your dear children you want to save.*[26]

NATURE HATES A VOID

Luke 11:24–26

> [24] When an unclean spirit leaves a man, he travels through waterless places seeking a place to rest, but finds none. Then he says, I will return to my abode from which I departed. [25] Returning, he finds it swept and put in order. [26] Then he goes and brings seven other spirits with him and they enter and abide there, making the last state of the man worse than the former.

That Luke intended to connect the previous passage about the speechless man's healing with Jesus' teaching about the reality of demons is unmistakable. However, it is the meaning of the two stories and not the details of Jesus' instruction that provides the common thread.

---

26. By the author.

Note Jesus' warning. When a demon was disembodied, it searched for a host. Finding none, it returned to its previous host. As the prior residence had been cleaned and put in order, the formerly possessed person made an acceptable receptacle, not only for the original demon but for seven more as well. The result was the ultimate state of the individual was worse than the initial state.

Jesus' illustration is clear. No one is neutral. All are created to be in fellowship with God. Furthermore, when we are not living in relationship with the Heavenly Father, we will in vain seek to fill our emptiness with substitutes that will never satisfy. Regardless of the effort to reform, all will end in tragedy. Only God can fulfill the desires of the heart he placed in the heart. In precisely the same manner, the returning demon narrative reinforces the details of the preceding narrative that stated all are for God or against God; there is no in between.

A PARENT'S BLESSING

Luke 11:27-28

²⁷While Jesus was speaking, a woman's voice shouted out of the crowd, "Blessed is the womb that carried you and the breasts that you nursed." ²⁸But Jesus said to her, "Blessed rather is the one hearing and guarding the word of God."

Heard above the crowd were the words of an exuberant woman. Great worth was attributed to parents by the accomplishments of their children. To that end, this unnamed spokeswoman declared Mary to be blessed in an effort to praise Jesus. Rather than accepting the compliment, Jesus redirected the woman's thought to that of doing God's will. Blessed instead, Jesus said, are those who hear and practice God's Word.

Even with this interruption, Luke continued the theme of the preceding passages. Unlike the dialogue with the crowd where Jesus said those who hear God's Word and do it ποιοῦντες (*poiountes*) were his mother and brothers (Luke 8:21), here Jesus said blessed are those who hear God's Word and keep it φυλάσσοντες (*phulassontes*). This is the same verb Luke used to describe what the strong, well-armed man did with his possessions. He guarded them. He kept them safe. He held them as valuable and most precious. Luke shifted the use of hearing and doing to hearing and guarding and in so doing tied all three stories together.

Journey to Jerusalem 185

No one is independent from God. A person will serve God or oppose God. Simply avoiding evil is not the same as embracing good. Driving out what is wrong will not fill the void of doing what is right. Finally, it is the one who holds these convictions close to heart, incorporating them into the very fiber of their being that will find true contentment is service to God.

UNLIKELY JUDGES

Luke 11:29-32

²⁹As more people crowded in, Jesus began to say, "This generation is an evil generation, always seeking signs. I will give you no sign except the sign of Jonah. ³⁰For just as Jonah was a sign to Nineveh, so will the Son of man be to this generation. ³¹The Queen of the South will rise in the judgment against the men of this generation and condemn them, because she came beyond the boundaries of her land to hear the wisdom of Solomon and I say that one greater than Solomon is here. ³²The men of Nineveh will stand in judgment against this generation and condemn it, because they repented at the message of Jonah and I say that one who is greater than Jonah is here.

Luke's theme of a universally inclusive gospel is displayed in this passage in a rather unique way: Outsiders judging insiders. Not unlike the Marcan technique of placing the affirmation of Jesus on the lips of his enemies—the demon in Capernaum proclaiming Jesus to be the Holy One of God (Mark 1:24) and the Roman centurion's statement at the cross "truly this man was the Son of God" (Mark 15:39)—Luke recorded Jesus' statement that those who responded to less information about God would ultimately condemn those who failed to respond in the presence of far greater information.

Two references are used to make this point: the unnamed Queen of Sheba (2 Chron 9:1-8; 1 Kings 10:1-9) and the penitent recipients of Jonah's proclamation of condemnation (Jonah 3:1-10). The two illustrations differ widely. The Queen of Sheba, most likely from the area of modern Ethiopia, sought an audience with Israel's King Solomon. She arrived in Jerusalem with a royal entourage. Her desire was to trick him with hard questions. Apparently, there was doubt in her mind regarding

Solomon's fame concerning the name of the Lord. Her conclusion after hearing his answers, observing his candor and assessing the loyalty of those who served him was that the half of Solomon's greatness had not been told.

Jonah's story was different. Rather than seeking out the presence of God's messenger, the people of Nineveh were the recipients of the missionary message. Jonah pronounced judgment on all. Without explanation, the biblical reference indicates the people of Nineveh, from the smallest to the greatest, believed God, repented, and initiated acts of penitence intended to turn God's anger.

What both stories have in common is that previously pagan people believed in the reality of God from a limited introduction to the same. It is this point that Jesus used to condemn those of his generation who doubted that he was Messiah and that the new kingdom of heaven was at hand. Using the logic of lesser to greater, Jesus said the very heritage of the present generation would rise to condemn their contemporary actions. If one responded to limited information, a person with greater information should not expect to be excused. With greater opportunity comes greater responsibility.

Jesus' discussion was predicated on his observation that the contemporary obsession with signs would be their undoing. It was, in fact, either the cause or symptom of their being an evil generation. In response, Jesus said his own resurrection would be the only sign they would receive. When that occurred, they could respond in faith or they could continue their doubt. In either case, they would still be held accountable for how they handled the information God graciously supplied.

LIGHT BY DEGREE

Luke 11:33–36

³³No one, lighting a lamp, places it in a hidden place, but on a lamp stand so that all who enter may see the light. ³⁴Your eye is the lamp of the body. If the eye is clear, the entire body is full of light. But if it is evil, your body is in utter darkness. ³⁵Exercise great caution that the light in you will not be darkness. ³⁶If your entire body is full of light, not having any partial darkness, it will be completely full of light, like a lamp gives you light with its illumination.

Jesus' teaching again began with an appeal to an obvious assertion. Here the common starting place is the practice of lighting a room. The reason a person fills a lamp with oil, trims the wick, and ignites the same is for the purpose of lighting a dark space. No one would do otherwise. No one would intentionally conceal a light by hiding it in a secret place.

From this setting, Jesus continued the argument. If, in fact, you do not hide the lamp, what do you do with it? You place it on a prominent place that will enable it to function to the greatest extent possible, to maximize its potential. Again, there is no counter argument. These facts are self-evident.

It is, however, the manner in which the conclusion is stated that truly begins Jesus' instruction. The text indicates the activities of lighting a lamp and placing it in a position of prominence are done in order that a person may see. What can be missed in English grammar is obvious to the Greek. Rather than saying a person *will* see, Jesus indicated a person *may* see. The subjunctive mode was used to indicate the statement contains contingency or uncertainty. What is unknown is whether or not a person will take advantage of the opportunity that the well placed and functioning lamp provides.

This pattern of stating the obvious followed by a contingent statement is repeated. The eyes are the light of the body, the proverbial window to the soul. Again, this statement would have been met with unconditional agreement. But again, there follows a conditional clause. If the eye is cloudy, blurred, or unhealthy, the entire body will suffer.

Jesus, at this point, moved to a direct command, using the imperative mode. Take great care that your light is not mixed with darkness. Only if your light has no part of darkness will it provide light to the soul. Luke used this teaching to return to the dominant theme of this section, specifically that discipleship is an all-or-nothing proposition. If your eyes are cloudy, you will not see. If your light is darkness, your body will be in darkness. If you are not availing yourself to the light that is placed in prominence specifically to shed light, those who responded to less light will condemn your apathy.

JESUS AND THE PHARISEES

Luke 11:37–54

³⁷ After Jesus finished speaking, a Pharisee asked him if he would dine with him. Entering, Jesus sat down at the table. ³⁸ But the Pharisee marveled seeing that Jesus was eating without first washing for the meal. ³⁹ But then the Lord said to him, "Wait a minute! You Pharisees cleanse the outside of the cup and the dish, but inside you are filled with greed and evil. ⁴⁰ You fools! Did not the one creating the outside create also the inside? ⁴¹ If you would give for alms that which is inside, behold everything would be purified for you. ⁴² But woe to the Pharisees, because you tithe the mint and the rue and every garden herb, yet you neglect justice and the love of God; these you ought to have done without neglecting the others. ⁴³ Woe to you, Pharisees, for you love the place of honor in the synagogues and the greetings in the marketplace. ⁴⁴ Woe to you, for you are like unmarked tombs that men unknowingly walk upon." ⁴⁵ One of the Jewish lawyers asked Jesus a question saying, "Teacher, in saying this, you insult us also!" ⁴⁶ Jesus said, "And woe to you lawyers also. You burden men with burdens too heavy to bear, and you lift not a finger to the burden. ⁴⁷ Woe to you, for you build the tombs of the prophets that your fathers killed. ⁴⁸ Therefore, you are witnesses and thereby consent to the works of your fathers, because they indeed killed them and you build their tombs. ⁴⁹ Therefore the wisdom of God said, 'I will send them prophets and apostles, some of whom they will kill and persecute' so that this generation will be held responsible ⁵⁰ for the blood of all the prophets, shed before the foundation of the world, ⁵¹ from the blood of Abel to the blood of Zechariah, who was killed between the altar and the sanctuary. Indeed, I say to you, this generation will be held responsible. ⁵² Woe to you lawyers! For you take away the key to knowledge. You do not enter yourselves and you hinder those who were attempting to enter." ⁵³ And when he departed, the scribes and Pharisees began bearing a grudge against him and provoking him with questions on many issues ⁵⁴ lying in wait to catch him with something he might say.

The harsh condemnation that Jesus delivered to the scribes and Pharisees began and ended with a controversy. The setting was an open dialogue that Jesus was having with the crowd. There is some argument among grammarians whether Luke intended to say the Pharisee invited Jesus to a meal when Jesus finished speaking to the crowds or while Jesus was speaking to the crowds.[27] In either case, Jesus accepted the invitation. As the meal began, the Pharisee was aghast that Jesus did not follow the dictates of accepted religious practice. Ritual cleansings, or baptisms, were practiced prior to eating a meal. Jesus used the opportunity to call attention to the hypocrisy of the Pharisees who were more concerned about the outside of the dish than what was on the inside of the dish. Jesus' condemnation of the empty practice ended in direct instruction from Jesus. Pay attention to what is on the inside, and the outside will take care of itself.

Unfortunately, Jesus' admonition was not received in the manner in which it was intended. Instead of allowing Jesus' directions to reprove them, the Pharisees took offense and increased the animosity between themselves and Jesus. They began lying in wait for him. The expression was one of a predator waiting for its prey. They accosted Jesus with a barrage of questions looking for an opportunity to criticize. They thought that by overcoming him with questions he would slip. Any means would be sufficient for them to discredit Jesus.

But perhaps more than the breech of protocol at the meal, Jesus' open and unqualified condemnation of their behavior was the event that triggered the action of the scribes and Pharisee. Six woes, three to the Pharisees and three to the scribes, showed the unquestionable error of their ways. While the specifics of religion may have changed, these six indictments remain today, challenging believers to live sincere lives.

Legalism abounded in the actions of the Pharisees. They practiced the law to its smallest detail but missed the quality of worship the same law was designed to create. They tithed even the smallest agricultural products but failed to deal mercifully with their fellow man. They sought out prominent places of service, not in order to serve but to be seen in the position. Perhaps most condemning, they actually contributed to people becoming unclean. By being unmarked graves upon which people literally walked around, the Pharisees caused people to come under condemnation (Num 19:16).

27. An argument that may be noticed even among popular modern translations.

Furthermore, the scribes forced burdens upon people that were unbearable. In addition to the prescribed Law of Moses, the scribes were part of creating and codifying the oral traditions of the fathers. These extra laws were viewed as a means to a far greater end but became an end within themselves. But what was more indicting was that the scribes did nothing to assist the general public in keeping any of the laws. They not only did not enter the house of learning but they also saw to it that no one else did either. As a result, they were culpable. Jesus indicated God would require at their hands the innocent blood of the prophets and apostles whom God had sent.

SECRETS PROCLAIMED

Luke 12:1–12

¹Meanwhile, as a countless crowd was gathering together so that they were trampling each other, Jesus began to say first to his disciples, "For your own sakes, beware of the yeast of the Pharisees, which is hypocrisy. ²For there is nothing having been concealed that will not be revealed, nor hidden that will not be made known. ³Therefore, whatever you have spoken in darkness will be heard in the light, and whatever you say privately will be proclaimed upon the housetops. ⁴But I say to you, my friends, stop being afraid of those who are killing the body, but afterward can do nothing else. ⁵I will show you who to fear: Fear the one who after killing has the authority to cast into hell. Yes, indeed, fear him! ⁶Are not five sparrows sold for two silver coins? Yet not one of these is forgotten by God. ⁷Indeed, even the hairs of your head have been counted. Fear not! You are worth more than these. ⁸I say to you, everyone who confesses me before men the Son of man will confess before the angels of God. ⁹But everyone denying me before men I will disown before the angels of God. ¹⁰Everyone who speaks a word against the Son of man, it will be forgiven him. But the one blaspheming the Holy Spirit will not be forgiven. ¹¹But when they bring you before the synagogues and before rulers who have authority, do not start being anxious about how you will defend yourself or about what you will say. ¹²The Holy Spirit will teach you in that very hour what is necessary for you to say."

Journey to Jerusalem 191

Luke opened this section with a temporal reference. The use of expressions such as "meanwhile" or "in the meantime" signal the plot was continuing in more than one physical location. Whether Luke intended to indicate something was developing while Jesus was dinning with the Pharisee or whether the reference was more general is difficult to say. Nothing in the grammar helps the translator make that decision. What is obvious is that there is a coming storm that will pit Jesus against religious power that will have the ability to manipulate and control situations to their benefit, at least on a temporary or earthly basis. The crowd that was increasing beyond the ability to number would first heighten the fear of Jesus' adversaries but would ultimately turn and be used against Jesus. Out of this setting comes Jesus' teachings on sincerity, sparrows, and unforgivable sin, first to the disciples and then to the on-looking crowd.

Steeped in tradition, the Deep South retains many of its cultural charms. Warm hospitality certainly is among its most endearing qualities. After a chance meeting at the local college gymnasium, the new physician found himself sitting on our front porch swing. A native of Los Angeles, California, who had accepted a position in a rural area in part out of principle and in part to expedite repayment of medical school loans, the young doctor listened and laughed for hours while we all sipped sweet tea and talked of life in the South. Upon leaving he remarked he had never been welcomed anywhere so graciously.

Yet hospitality can be an occasion for pretense. As with any gesture, the motive that drives its offering will determine its true worth. Human nature can be genuine and sincere, but it also can be manipulative and hateful.

Knowing his disciples' experience would be similar to his own, Jesus directed them to avoid hypocrisy. The Greek word ὑπόκρισις (*hupokrisis*) has its origin in the theatrical realm. Its basic meaning is that of an actor playing a part in a performance. Jesus warned that what is real and true ultimately will be known. A person can pretend to be something or someone only for so long. Pretense ultimately will fail.

Far from being perfect, every believer should seek to be sincere. No one should believe they can carry out the illusion of being something they are not. Jesus' analogy comparing hypocrisy to leaven should not be overlooked. There are two obvious meanings. First is that a little goes a long way. Second is that yeast cannot be hidden. Buried in a batch of fresh dough, its effects will be known over time. The leaven, literal or metaphoric, will change at a formative level what something is.

Turning to the crowds, Jesus continued his teachings. Even though Jesus' first comments were directed to disciples, one should not assume the crowd was not listening. In fact, understanding the matter of hypocrisy and the importance of seeking sincerity opens up the meaning of the second point. The people that day had a choice. They could choose the Pharisees Jesus had only moments before condemned or they could choose their Heavenly Father. The motive of the Pharisees was to manipulate. The motive of the Father was to love. The Pharisees maintained control by force and intimidation. The use of the imperative verb and the negative particle μὴ φοβηθῆτε (*mē phobēthēte*) is a command to stop fearing. The Pharisees had instilled fear and dread, and they used the same to their advantage. Jesus wanted the people to understand that God's response to them would be tenderness and compassion. Rather than insincerity and manipulation, Jesus was offering a sense of worth. Rather than pawns to be used to an ultimate goal, the people were valued by God who knew the most intimate detail of their lives.

Finally, Jesus turned to the unforgivable sin. A participle translated as blaspheming, the Greek word βλασφημήσαντι (*blasphēmēsanti*) has at its origin the concept of "abusive speech" and means "the strongest form of personal mockery and calumniation."[28] In the Septuagint, the word group is used to translate Hebrew vocabulary that "always refer finally to God, whether in the sense of the disputing of His saving power . . . the desecrating of His name . . . the violation of His glory by derision . . . ungodly speech and action . . . or human arrogance with its implied depreciation of God."[29] Finally, the concept of blasphemy in the New Testament "is controlled throughout by the thought of violation of the power and majesty of God" and "denotes the conscious and wicked rejection of the saving power and grace of God towards man."[30]

Two observations are very important in understanding the setting of this scene. First, it is ironic that the effort of those who hated Jesus to defend the name of God caused them to shut out the opportunity to know God. Second, Jesus elevated the Holy Spirit to position of deity. Jesus said the only sin that could not be forgiven was blaspheming the

28. Beyer, "βλασφημέω," 621.
29. Ibid.
30. Ibid.

Holy Spirit. Because blasphemy always referred only to God, the Holy Spirit had to be one and the same with God.

Furthermore, it is precisely the Holy Spirit's divine role that creates the potential for a person committing the unpardonable sin. Scripture indicates the Holy Spirit convicts people of their sin. When a person shuts out the Holy Spirit, that person shuts out the possibility of conviction. When there is no conviction, there is no remorse, no repentance, and no forgiveness. As Beyer said, "Only the man who sets himself against forgiveness is excluded from it."[31]

BUILDING BIGGER BARNS

Luke 12:13–21

> [13]*One from out of the crowd said to Jesus, "Tell my brother to divide with me the inheritance."* [14]*Jesus said to him, "Man, who made me a judge or arbitrator over you?"* [15]*Jesus said to everyone else, "Be watchful and on your guard against greed, because it is not out of abundance that a man's life exists."* [16]*Jesus then told them a parable, saying, "A rich man's field produced abundantly.* [17]*So he thought to himself, saying, 'What am I to do, seeing that I have no place to gather in my crop?'* [18]*And he said, 'This I will do. I will tear down my barns, and I will build larger ones where I will store all of my grain and goods.* [19]*And then I will say to my soul, Soul, you have goods stored up for many years; Take life easy, eat, drink, and be happy.'* [20]*But God said to him, 'Fool, this very night your soul is required of you; whose will the things you prepared be then?'* [21]*So is anyone who stores up treasures, but is not being rich toward God."*

The purpose of a parable is to present an obvious truth. The story of the rich farmer certainly does that. His land was fertile, and though the story is silent on the detail, the farmer no doubt worked hard to make the land produce. When his harvest was great, he realized he did not have adequate barn space to store all he had produced. Tearing down his old barns, he built bigger ones.

---

31. Ibid.

This story is not a polemic against wealth. Everything to this point would be very admirable. Hard work should produce great results. Furthermore, there is nothing wrong with the protection of wealth that is created. Where the meaning of the story hinges is upon the attitude that follows the rebuilding. The farmer thought his worries were over. He thought nothing could happen to him and his wealth. He did not know his life was being weighed in the balance. He could control when to break the ground, when to plant the crops, when and how to fertilize, and even when to harvest. He could control where and by what means he would store his produce. The one thing he couldn't control was how long he would live. How did his control benefit him when his life was at an end?

Jesus added to this conclusion by stating that everyone who stores up temporal wealth while ignoring eternal wealth will suffer the same fate. The irony of the story is that eternal wealth can be controlled. When a person invests in that which is eternal, it is never taken away. Given the choice to store up treasures on earth or in heaven, human nature will choose the former over the latter. The temporal takes precedence over the eternal. Yet it is the eternal that will last.

SEEKING THE KINGDOM

Luke 12:22-34

[22] And Jesus said to his disciples, "For this reason, I say to you, stop being anxious about your life, what you will eat, or your body, what you will wear. [23] For the soul is more than food and the body is more than clothing. [24] Consider the ravens; they neither sow nor reap, they have neither barns nor storehouses, but God takes care of them. You are worth more than the birds. [25] And who among you is able by worrying to add one cubit to his stature? [26] If you are not able to do a small thing like that, why are you anxious about the rest? [27] Consider the flowers and how they grow. They neither toil nor spin. But I say to you that not even Solomon in all his glory is clothed as one of these. [28] But if God so clothes the grass that is in the field today and tomorrow will be cast into the fire, how much more will He clothe you? Oh, you of little faith! [29] Stop seeking what you will eat and drink. Stop being anxious. [30] All the na-

> *tions of the world are frantically seeking these things. Your Father knows you need these things.* ³¹*Seek his kingdom instead and these things will be given to you.* ³²*Stop being afraid, little flock. It is the Father's good pleasure to give you the kingdom.* ³³*Sell your possessions and give gifts to the needy. Make for yourselves purses that do not wear out, having an inexhaustible treasure in heaven, where neither a thief approaches nor a moth destroys.* ³⁴*Where your treasure is, there your heart will be as well."*

Continuing the theme of laying up provisions, Jesus cautioned his disciples about worry. Repeatedly throughout this passage, Jesus told his followers to stop doing something they were already doing. This is a specific aspect of the grammar that should not be overlooked. Human nature is such that it will fret over the unknown.

But this passage does more than indicate that humans are a worrisome lot. In the inference Jesus made, the reader can understand not only that human nature is prone to worry but also why it worries.

Notice first the commands Jesus issued. Don't worry about your life—what you will eat and drink. Don't worry about your body—what you will wear. Notice second the illustrations. The birds of the air do not worry, work, or fret. The flowers of the field do not struggle for their provision. Notice third the affirmation. God feeds the birds of the air with abundance and clothes the flowers of the field with a glory that is unsurpassed. Finally, notice the logic. If God loves the birds of the air and the flowers of he field, how much more will he love you? If God feeds and clothes those that are here today and gone tomorrow, how much more will he feed and clothe those he created to be in fellowship with himself?

What occurred next in Jesus' discourse reveals why humanity worries. Rather than being like the rest of the nations who frantically seek after food, clothes, and shelter, Jesus directed his disciples to trust God to provide. "Seek the kingdom," Jesus said, "and these also will be provided." It is at this point in his presentation that Jesus revealed the nature of worry. Jesus stated it was God's intent to give his children the kingdom. More than God's intention, it was God's pleasure to give the kingdom. Much like the logic of Luke 11:13, where the anticipated receipt of good things is substituted by receiving the Holy Spirit, the ultimate promise of trusting God's protection is not necessarily food clothing and shelter.

The ultimate promise of trusting God is eternal protection and ultimate meaning and self-worth. We simply want control but go about securing it in the wrong way. "Trust me," God said. "Relinquish control with its feeble ability to secure your peace, and I will give you back control in the form of my peace."

INTEGRITY AND RESPONSIBILITY

Luke 12:35–48

35 "Gird your loins and light your lamps. 36 Furthermore, be like the men waiting for their lord's return from the wedding feast so that when he comes and knocks, they open the door immediately. 37 Blessed are the servants the lord finds awake. Truly, I say to you, the lord will prepare himself, make the servants sit at table, and the lord himself will come and serve them. 38 Blessed indeed are those he so finds in the second or third watch. 39 But know this, if the home owner had known the hour his house would be vandalized, he would not have left his house. 40 You be ready! The Son of man will come when you least expect it." 41 Peter said, "Do you tell this parable for us or for all?" 42 Then the Lord said, "Who then is the faithful and wise household steward that the lord will put in charge over his house servants to give them their food at the appropriate time? 43 Blessed is the servant who the lord finds so doing when he arrives. 44 Surely I say to you the homeowner will put him in charge of all his possessions. 45 But if this servant says in his heart that his lord has delayed his coming and begins to beat the male and female servants and to eat and to drink and to get drunk, 46 the lord of this servant will come in a day that the servant does not expect and in an hour that he does not know and will punish him severely and place him with the unfaithful. 47 The servant who knew the desire of his lord but made neither provision nor acted accordingly will receive a more severe beating. 48 But the one not knowing the desires of his lord and doing what deserved punishment will receive slight punishment. But to whom much has been given, of him much will be required and to whom much is entrusted, of him much will be demanded."

Why does a person do what is right and avoid doing what is wrong? If the answer is fear of punishment, then by necessity an authority exists, be it civil or religious, that mandates certain behavior and prohibits others. While the prospect of retribution certainly provides a meaningful motivation, fear of consequences has its limitations. Will fear motivate a person when there is no immediate threat of retribution? Furthermore, what is a person capable of doing if he or she could act complete anonymously? In such cases, proper behavior will suffer.

Duty, on the other hand, acknowledges a different motivation. With the same restriction in force, a person acting out of duty will act and refrain from acting out of a sense of responsibility to authority. For anyone who has matured beyond avoiding punishment, acting consistently with adopted principles becomes a reward within itself. For these people, integrity, doing what is right simply because it is right, is a way of life.

Jesus introduced this idea to his disciples. The parable and its explanation are straightforward. The wise and faithful servant is always prepared to fulfill his or her duty. No threat is mentioned. They have no other motivation than it is their duty. These servants will be rewarded greatly, being served in person by their master.

Antithetical to a person motivated by duty was the opportunistic servant who took advantage of his master's absence. In his case, fear of repercussion was the motive, even though stated negatively. Because there was no present authority, he did as he pleased. One should not overlook the actions typical of the person who is motivated by fear rather than duty. First, there is a rationalization that one can avoid being caught. Second, there is mistreatment of others as a result of the lifting of authority. Third, there is self-destruction that results specifically from seeking to satiate personal desires.

Instead of applying this teaching of Jesus to the second coming of Messiah as was the case in Matthew 24, Luke coupled the concept of integrity to responsibility. For Luke, it was no accident that a person is in the position to act with integrity in the first place. Notice the illustration hinges on a servant's improper action, specifically not doing what he or she knew was expected of them to do. Those who are expected to act with integrity are those to whom specific instructions have been entrusted. Far from proposing spiritual snobbery, Luke was presenting to his Roman audience a view of Christianity that described its adherents in the most flattering fashion. These were not rouges or brigands. These were people who could be trusted. The warning this position carries, however, is equally as clear: Men have trusted you, and you had better come through for them. Don't let selfish appetites distract you. Stay the course. Discharge your responsibility as a person of integrity.

INTEGRITY AND RESPONSIBILITY ILLUSTRATED

Luke 12:49–59

⁴⁹"I came to cast fire upon the earth, and what I desire is that it already be kindled. ⁵⁰I have a baptism with which to be baptized and how I am distressed until it is completed. ⁵¹Do you suppose that I have come to give peace to the world? No, I say to you, not peace but a division. ⁵²From now on, it will be in one house one against five, three against two, and two against three, ⁵³father divided against son and son against father, mother against daughter and daughter against mother, mother-in-law against daughter-in-law, and daughter-in-law against mother-in-law." ⁵⁴Jesus said to the crowds, "When you see clouds forming in the west, immediately you say that there will be rain, and so it happens. ⁵⁵When a south wind blows, you say that it will be hot, and so it happens. ⁵⁶You hypocrites! You know how to interpret the physical realities of earth and heaven, but you do not know how to interpret the times! ⁵⁷Why do you not judge what is righteous for your selves? ⁵⁸As you are going with a litigant before a judge, make every effort to negotiate the issue while you are still in the way. If you don't, he will drag you before the judge, the judge will deliver you to the jailer, and the jailer will cast you into prison. ⁵⁹I say to you that you will never be released until you repay even the last, smallest coin."

Following his explanation of duty enhanced integrity and responsibility, Jesus illustrated the same with examples from his life and the lives of those around him. Beginning with his own duty, Jesus described the role that Messiah was about to play. Rather than the Prince of Peace, the Messiah was to be a divisive figure. Fire was used throughout the Jewish community as an illustration of judgment. Its use was often to purify that which had mixed content, burning off the unwanted elements. The new world order would not immediately unify all. Instead, members of the same family would be set against one another.

While this may not have been a role of his choosing, Jesus embraced his responsibility with integrity born out of duty. His baptism was to bring an unmistakable watershed moment. From the crucifixion on, there would be no confusing what one had to do: Accept Christ's offer for forgiveness or reject the same. Again, there was no in between. Jesus longed for this baptism to be complete, but he patiently waited until the moment of God's initiation.

Jesus expected those around him to follow his example. They had been given abilities. They could read the signs of God's law in creation and depended on its predictability. Jesus expected the same mental acumen that was being applied to physical laws of the universe to be applied to the spiritual laws of the universe. They had been given much, Jesus told them, but much more was expected of them. They should be connecting the dots and coming to an understanding of how everything God had done in the past was culminating in the presence of the Messiah.

Finally, the civil court should be understood as a veiled reference to God's heavenly court. An obvious conclusion was stated in parabolic format. Specifically, Jesus said if you do not come to terms with your accuser while you have the opportunity, you will find yourself at the complete mercy of the court. Notice further that the accuser is not unjust in the accusation. The Greek word ἀποδῷς (*apodōs*) means "to repay a debt." There is nothing unjust about what was transpiring. The accused stood legitimately charged. Jesus warned that duty motivated responsibility and that integrity demands the repayment of civic debt, but that no less is true about spiritual debt. The Messiah come to accomplish much. Rejection of him would leave the person holding a spiritual debt. If that debt were not paid in time, there would be no recourse. Do what you are required to do. Do not wait for fear to motivate. Do what is right, simply because it is right.

CHARACTERISTICS OF A COMPASSIONATE GOD: REPENTANCE AND FORGIVENESS

Luke 13:1–5

¹Now there were with Jesus at that time those who reported to him about the Galileans whose blood Pilate mixed with their sacrifice. ²Answering them, Jesus said, "Do you suppose these Galileans were more sinful than all other Galileans because of the way they suf-

> fered? ³I say to you, by no means! But if you do not repent, you will all perish in the same way. ⁴Do you suppose those eighteen who died when the tower of Siloam fell on them were worse debtors than all those dwelling in Jerusalem? ⁵I say to you by no means. But if you do not repent, you will all perish in the same way."

First the facts: There was a Tower of Siloam, and Pontius Pilate was the Roman Procurator of Judea from AD 26 to 36. No evidence exists to the contrary. Furthermore, the Tower of Siloam is no longer standing at its archeological cite, so it did in fact fall. Also, recorded Jewish historians Philo and Josephus were not particularly kind to Pilate, showing him to be capable of ruthless atrocities against the Jews. That the Galilean massacre and the loss of life at the Tower's collapse are mentioned only in Luke's Gospel should not call into question the historicity of the events. Luke recounted these events with the conviction of their credibility, and the modern reader should do nothing less. Rather than debate the historicity of Luke, the reader should focus on how Jesus used the conversation to teach those present about the fleeting nature of life and the eternal love of God.

Into the setting came a report of a horrible event: Pilate quelled a rebellion at Jerusalem and in a public display of power mixed the blood of the perpetrators with that of the animal sacrifice at Jerusalem. As unthinkable as this was, one should move past the shock of the report in order to understand the motive of the reporters. There are two likely answers to the question of motive. First, those who came to Jesus were looking to set a trap. Condemning the actions of Pilate could end with the same result. If they could get Jesus to criticize openly the actions of the current administration, perhaps his execution would be next. If not executed, Jesus could be discredited as just another political hack. Either way, the result would be the same—lessening Jesus' influence and control of the general public.

Second, and only slightly more noble, the bearers of the ill news could have viewed this as the trigger event for the coming of Messiah. Popular opinion held that the Messiah would liberate Israel from external control and re-establish theocracy among God's people. Would this public outcry be sufficient to initiate God's rule on earth?

In either case, Jesus did not take the bait. Not uncommon, Jesus answered their question with a question. The crowd asked, "What do you think about the Galilean massacre?" or "Shouldn't something be done about the Romans?" What makes this passage so difficult is that Jesus answered a different question than what the crowd asked. Rather than answer the question, "What is to be done about the Romans?" Jesus answered the question, "Why do unexplainable things happen in the first place?"

The Orthodox Jewish theological response was clear: All sickness and suffering were caused by sin and where therefore by necessity from the hand of God. Such a view is present in the remarks of Job's friend, Eliphaz, when he said, "Remember, I pray thee, who ever perished, being innocent? or where were the righteous cut off? Even as I have seen, they that plow iniquity, and sow wickedness, reap the same. By the blast of God they perish, and by the breath of his nostrils are they consumed" (Job 4:6–9).

But Jesus took exception with that view. To demonstrate his opposition, Jesus posed a second illustration of his point. Common to the crowd was the knowledge of another tragic event. Through no fault of their own, eighteen people died when a public building collapsed. Again, the Orthodox Jew would have reached the same conclusion: No suffering exists except at the hands of God. But by expressing the same contrary view to both situations, one where people were obviously guilty of insurrection and another where people were guilty of nothing more than being at the wrong place at the wrong time, Jesus called attention to their commonalities. Both groups of people lived and then died. All humans live and die. And along the way, suffering sometimes enters their lives.

Jesus' final twist in this exchange was to place the inquisitors in the scene. "Unless you repent" Jesus said, "you will perish in the same way." An obvious dramatic statement, Jesus had to mean something other than "You will be killed by Pilate for insurrection, or you will have a public work fall on you." Jesus' warning was that unless you repent, you will die just like they died, not as a result of calamity but without receiving repentance. Jesus was saying to them that their physical life was fleeting and only the eternal lasts forever. Care must be given to protect that which lasts forever, not that which will inevitably fall. The crowd believed God caused the suffering; Jesus taught God offered forgiveness instead.

CHARACTERISTICS OF A COMPASSIONATE GOD: PATIENCE, PRODUCTIVITY, ACCOUNTABILITY

Luke 13:6–9

⁶Then Jesus told this parable. "A certain person had a fig tree that had been planted in his vineyard. He came looking for fruit on the tree and found none. ⁷The owner said to the gardener, 'Now listen! For three years I have been coming here looking for fruit and finding nothing from this fig tree. Cut it down. Why should it continue using the earth?' ⁸But the gardener answered and said, 'Sir, leave it alone until such a time as I may dig around it and cast manure around it. ⁹Perhaps it will bear fruit in the coming year. If not, you may cut it down.' "

In the parable of the fruitless fig tree, Jesus indicated while God's compassion was without limit, ignoring God's compassion was not without consequence. The parable is easy to follow. (1) There is patient expectation. A vineyard owner looked repeatedly for productivity. Year after year, the landowner came to harvest his crop and take from it a profit. Year after year, the result was the same—no fruit was produced. (2) There was promise without productivity. In order for the landowner to continue expecting a result, there must have been external signs leading him to continue in hope. The tree obviously was not dead. If it were, it would have been removed long before. Furthermore, annual production of foliage gave the anticipation of bud and fruit to come later. (3) There was ultimate accountability. The order was given to cut down the tree. A rhetorical question was asked. "Why should it take up space? Why should it use resources that could be directed to more productive flora with greater promise?" Ultimately, that which was not productive was removed.

From the first portion of the parable, the application is clear. God is patient, loving, and kind. But God's involvement in the lives of his people is designed to be productive. Repeated failure to reproduce leaves the church lacking substance. Activity should not be mistaken for productivity. There can be visible, outward signs that the church is tender, compassionate, and productive; but in reality, it is an illusion. Likewise, the individual Christian can make the right speeches, go through the right motions in a public arena, and never have an intimate relation with the Divine.

The parable continues with the response of the gardener who held out hope. "Delay your action, and I will continue to cultivate the nonproductive part of your garden. You can always remove it later." It is important to understand the accountability was not eliminated, only delayed. Motivated by love, more time was given.

One final caution should be noted. The reader should avoid dichotomizing God in the parable. To identify the landowner as the Heavenly Father and Jesus as the gardener would press the analogy past its original intent. The logic of western culture frequently would necessitate a completely accurate rendering that assigned every aspect of the parable. Doing so champions Jesus against his Heavenly Father, seeking to persuade God not to act. God becomes a vindictive, angry Deity prone to swift and unrelenting punishment. Jesus, on the other hand, is the calm, reasoned force that gives balance to the equation. In reality, nothing could be further from the truth. Adept at the oral transmission of tradition, the near eastern mind heard something different that day. They heard Jesus saying, "The Heavenly Father and I are one. And while we are holy and could demand immediate restitution for all error, we are willing, wanting, waiting. We are willing to give another chance, wanting to be in a relationship where we can share our resources, and waiting patiently for you to receive what we are offering."

CHARACTERISTICS OF A COMPASSIONATE GOD: MORAL NECESSITY

Luke 13:10–17

> [10] Now Jesus was teaching in one of the synagogues on the Sabbath. [11] A woman was there who had a spirit of infirmity for eighteen years that had doubled her over, not allowing her to stand up straight. [12] Seeing her, Jesus called to her and said to her, "Woman, you have been released from your illness," [13] and he placed his hand upon her. Immediately she stood straight up and was praising God. [14] But the leader of the synagogue, being indignant that Jesus had healed on the Sabbath, responded by saying to the crowd, "There are six days in which it is necessary to do work; you ought come on those days to be healed and not on the Sabbath day." [15] But the

> Lord answered him and said, "You hypocrite! Is it not necessary to loose your ox and your donkey and to lead him away to water him on the Sabbath? ¹⁶Ought it not be necessary that this woman, being a daughter of Abraham, who has been bound by Satan for eighteen years be loosed from bondage on the Sabbath?" ¹⁷When Jesus said these things, he put to shame those opposing him, but the crowd rejoiced at the things being done to her.

Luke continued the theme of God's compassion by including in the narrative a Sabbath healing story that had moral necessity as its major theme. An infirmed woman who had suffered with a physical malady for eighteen years introduces the story. When he saw her, Jesus had compassion on her and healed her, saying she had been released from her infirmity.

This action brought a stern reaction from the ruler of the synagogue. He charged the crowd by saying there were six days when it was necessary to work. The grammatical construction uses the accusative case with the particle δεῖ (*dei*). More specifically, the ruler said it was a morally necessity to work on any day other than the Sabbath.

It was the emphasis on moral necessity that was at the heart of Jesus' response. To prove the weakness of the man's statement, Jesus made an observation that appealed to common sense, as well as to acceptable Jewish custom. "Now wait a moment, sir," Jesus said. "Don't you release your livestock on the Sabbath and take them to where there is water? Isn't that a moral necessity? Wouldn't we think a person cruel who caused a helpless animal to suffer or die simply to comply with Sabbath regulations?"

Knowing the answers to these rhetorical questions were obvious, Jesus moved on to the "so what" part of the argument. "If that is the case, and we all know that it is," Jesus said, "then shouldn't I release a daughter of Abraham from her tortuous infirmity? Isn't that in fact also a moral necessity?"

The result of the exchange was twofold: The opposition was put to shame, and the crowd glorified God. Jesus had demonstrated that God's compassion extended to the needs of ordinary people in their ordinary, daily lives. For the legalist who wanted to obey the law blindly, people remained bound in their burdens with no hope of comfort. But Jesus understood that for him there was no higher duty than to release the captives from their burdens of sin and enslaving lifestyles. As a result, the people glorified God because they saw the divine compassion that liberated rather than imprisoned.

KINGDOM OF GOD

Luke 13:18–30

> [18] Then Jesus asked, "What is the kingdom of God like and to what can it be compared? [19] The kingdom of God is like a mustard seed that a man took and sowed in the garden. The seed grew and became a tree where the birds of the heavens came and nested in its branches." [20] Jesus asked again, "To what may I compare the kingdom of God? [21] The kingdom of God is like yeast that a woman mixed onto three measures of flour until it was all leavened." [22] Jesus then made his way through villages and towns, teaching as he went and traveling toward Jerusalem. [23] Those with him asked, "Lord, will few be saved?" Jesus said to them, [24] "You do your best to enter through the narrow gate, for many, I tell you, will seek to enter but will not be able to do so. [25] After the householder has arisen and locked the door, you will be standing at the door, knocking and saying, 'Lord, open for us.' But answering, he will say, 'I do not know from where you have come.' [26] Then you will begin to say, 'We ate with you and drank with you, and you taught in our streets.' [27] He will say again, 'I do not know from where you have come! Get away from me, all you workers of iniquity!' [28] There you will weep and gnash your teeth when you see Abraham, Isaac, Jacob and all the prophets in the kingdom of God, but you yourselves will have been cast out. [29] Men will come from the East, West, North, and South to sit at the table in the kingdom of God. [30] And behold, some will be last who were first and some first who were last."

Having discussed the characteristics of God's compassion, Luke moved on to present the characteristics of God's kingdom. Three analogies are given. Luke used the teachings of Jesus to say the kingdom of God was inauspicious in its beginnings, pervasive in its growth, and accessible in its nature.

(1) The kingdom of God was inauspicious in its beginnings. The kingdom of God was described as being like a mustard seed. As an herb,

the mustard is very small. Yet when planted, the seed becomes one of the largest shrubs or trees in the near eastern garden. The mustard plant becomes large enough that its branches provide shelter for indigenous fauna. This is a recurring theme for Luke. From the beginning of the Gospel presentation, Luke attempted to convey to his non-Jewish reader that the growth of Christian was basically a populist movement. There were no world powers that had to be placated with precise diplomacy. There were no royal deals that had to be verified to make sure allies would not be offended. What started in a stable, witnessed only by those on the lowest of the social ladder, had spread throughout the known world. Like the tiny mustard seed that grew to a sheltering habitat, Christianity grew from an inauspicious beginning to become a recognized world religion.

(2) The kingdom of God was pervasive in its growth. Jesus used the illustration of baker's yeast to describe how the kingdom of God grows until it permeates everything it touches. When leaven is added to bread dough, its results are soon seen. Like yeast in the baking process, the kingdom of God cannot be held back nor its results unnoticed. By including this story in the description of the kingdom, Luke wanted the Roman government to understand that the church will not be stopped by external forces.

(3) The kingdom of God is accessible in its nature. Cast in a negative example, Jesus said anyone can enter the kingdom of God. You need not be wealthy, powerful, or well-born. You need only to be saved in order to enter. Responding to the question, "Will few be saved?" Jesus described those who will not enter the kingdom. Three groups are singled out for exclusion from the kingdom: the unprepared, the presumptuous, and the proud.

Jesus instructed his followers to strive to enter the narrow gate. An athletic or military term, ἀγωνίζεσθε (*agōnizesthe*) describes the struggle of the contest or the battle. Every ounce of strength is to be summoned. "Do your very best," Jesus said, "to enter the kingdom. Make it the priority! Don't think of anything else. Nothing is more important, so get ready! If you are unprepared, you will not enter."

Jesus instructed his followers to avoid presumption. The analogy of the householder who would not open the locked door to those outside warns against trusting a salvation by works. Those who were excluded objected they had worked with and for the one in authority. But Jesus said through the words of the homeowner, "Because I do not know you, your works do not matter. Your presumption will not save you."

Finally, Jesus said the proud would not enter. All would come from the east and the west, from the north and south, to sit at the banquet table. But the first shall be last and the last first. This is not the same analogy as was given about the prominence of John the Baptist (Matt 11:11; Luke 7:28). There Jesus said while no greater human had been born of woman than John, even the least person who was included in the kingdom would be greater than John. Here in Luke, the analogy is one of exclusion. The first who become last will be excluded. Pride will prevent a person from entering the kingdom specifically because pride will prevent a person from acknowledging his or her need of God.

In like manner, the kingdom of God is found in the individual Christian. Small at first, a person recognizes the slight tug of the Holy Spirit. If allowed to germinate, this smallest of beginnings will permeate every aspect of the person's life whereby God becomes accessible.

A STORY OF DESIRE

Luke 13:31–35

³¹At that very moment, certain Pharisees came to Jesus saying, "Leave and depart from here. Herod desires to kill you." ³²Jesus said to them, "You depart and tell the old fox that I am casting out demons and performing healings today tomorrow and on the third day I will be finished. ³³But it is necessary that today and tomorrow and the day after I go on my way. It is not possible that a prophet be killed away from Jerusalem. ³⁴Oh Jerusalem, Jerusalem! You who killed prophets and stoned those sent to you! How often have I desired to gather your children in the same way a hen gathers her young under her wing? But you desired not! ³⁵Behold, your house is deserted and I say to you that you will not see me until you say 'Blessed is he who comes in the name of the Lord.'"

As Jesus taught the crowds about the kingdom of God, he received a disturbing message: "Herod wants to see you dead!" The modern reader should not miss Luke's reason for including this incident. This was not subterfuge on the part of the Pharisees. No one was seeking to trick or trap Jesus. The Pharisees who delivered the message were sincere in their warning. This is important because it sheds light on a frequent misunderstanding. Not all Pharisees opposed Jesus. While the Gospel record clearly indicates there was open hostility to the message and teaching of Jesus on the part of many of the religious leaders, there were those even among the Pharisees who supported Jesus.

That being said, there are three interests that surface in this story, each identified by the Greek word θέλω (*thelō*), meaning "I desire." (1) There was the selfish desire of Herod. It was into the conversation about the kingdom of God that the news came about Herod's desire to kill Jesus. "That kind of talk will get you executed, Jesus," the Pharisees said. "Herod already has made it known he wants you dead!" Selfishness always finds refuge in self-preservation. Herod was protecting his own power and authority. If a pretender to a throne was ever identified, that person's life was in jeopardy. Selfish motives will stop at nothing to protect self-interests.

(2) There was the selfless desire of Jesus. Common sense would demand retreat. Self-preservation would demand a person seek his own safety—run and hide. But Jesus had other motives. His desire was to fulfill the will of the Father. Accordingly, Jesus said, "You go tell Herod exactly where I will be and exactly what I will be doing. I am going to Jerusalem for the good of the kingdom of God." Regardless of its consequence, Jesus selflessly placed the needs of others ahead of his own.

(3) Tragically, there was the self-absorbed desire of the people Jesus came to save. Forever on the fence, the great mass of humanity is too busy with the mundane details of life to see the eternal taking shape all around them. "How often," Jesus said of Jerusalem, "would I have taken you in and enjoyed fellowship and relationship with you? Instead, you eliminated the very things I intended to create covenant." Jesus' statements revealed not only his love and compassion but a long-standing pattern of human indifference to God and to things of the kingdom.

Finally, the reader should notice Jesus' reaction to both extremes and make a contemporary application. On the one hand are defiance and intimidation while on the other hand are indifference and apathy. To open opposition, Jesus affirmed the inevitability of the kingdom. God's plan of salvation will not be stopped. But in response to lack of interest, Jesus showed his broken heart. Regardless of the position, God stands prepared to love and to redeem.

DINING AND DISCIPLESHIP: READY, WILLING, AND ABLE[32]

Luke 14:1-35

¹Now it happened that Jesus went to the home of a ruler from among the Pharisees on the Sabbath to eat. While there, the host and his guests were watching Jesus. ²Suddenly there was before Jesus a man who was suffering from edema. ³Replying, Jesus said to the scribes and Pharisees, "Is it allowed to heal on the Sabbath or not?" ⁴But they were silent. Jesus then took hold of the man, healed him, and sent him away. ⁵Jesus said to those there, "Which one of you will not immediately pull out a son or ox that has fallen into a well on the Sabbath?" ⁶But they were not able to answer him anything. ⁷Jeus then told a parable to those who had been invited, having noticed how they chose the places of honor. ⁸"When someone invites you to a wedding feast, do not sit in the place of honor, lest the host has invited a more important person than yourself ⁹and the host who invited you both will come to you and say yield this place and you will begin with embarrassment to take the last place. ¹⁰Rather, when you re invited, you should go and sit in the last place. Then when the host arrives, he may say to you, 'Friend, you move up to a more prominent seat.' Then you will have the respect of those reclining with you. ¹¹Everyone honoring himself will be humbled while those humbling themselves will be exalted." ¹²Jesus said to the host, "When you give a dinner or banquet, do not invite your friends or your brothers or your family or your rich neighbors so that they will invite you in return and you will have your repayment. ¹³Instead, when you prepare a banquet, you should invite the poor, the crippled, the disabled, and the blind. ¹⁴You will be blessed because they cannot repay you. Instead, you will be repaid at the resurrection of the righteous." ¹⁵Hearing this, one of the guests said, "Blessed is he who shall eat bread in the kingdom of God." ¹⁶Jesus said to him, "A certain man made a great feast and invited many. ¹⁷He sent his

---

32. Author's Note: The following section consists of Luke 14 in its entirety. As the commentary will demonstrate, the chapter is a literary unit. Unlike earlier sections that were divided into small units for the purpose of explaining the text, the follow translation will put the entire thought before the reader, followed by the major themes that constitute the overall thought. This also will be the case in chapter 15.

servant at the time of the banquet to those who had been invited to say, 'Come, everything is ready.' ¹⁸They unanimously, one and all, began making excuses. The first said, 'I have bought a field and have the requirement of going to see it. I beg you, please have me excused.' ¹⁹Another said, 'I bought five teams of ox and must go examine them. I beg you, please have me excused.' ²⁰Another said, 'I have married a woman and am not able to attend.' ²¹Upon returning, the servant reported all to his lord. Becoming outraged, the householder said to his servant, 'Go quickly into the streets and alleys of the city and bring in the poor, the disabled, the blind, and the lame.' ²²But the servant said, 'My lord, we have already done what you command and still there is room.' ²³Then his lord said to the servant, 'Go into the highways and byways and compel them to come, so that my house will be filled. ²⁴For I say to you that not a single one of the men I invited will taste my banquet.'"
²⁵Now a great crowd gathered around him and turning, Jesus said, ²⁶ "If anyone follows me and does not hate his father and his mother and his wife and his brothers and his sisters, indeed even his own soul is not able to be my disciple. ²⁷Whoever does not carry his own cross and follow me is not able to be my disciple. ²⁸Who among you, desiring to build a tower would not first sit down and count the cost, to determine if he has a sufficient amount to complete the task? ²⁹So that onlookers will not ridicule him when having laid the foundation he does not have enough to finish. ³⁰They will say, 'This man began to build and was not able to finish.' ³¹Or what king, going to war against another king, will not first sit down and consider if he is able with ten thousand to oppose one coming against him with twenty thousand? ³²And if indeed he is not, will he not send an offer of peace while he is still far off? ³³In the same manner, any one of you who will not give up his own possessions is not able to be my disciples. ³⁴Salt is good. But if salt has become tasteless, how will its flavor be restored? ³⁵It is fit for neither the land nor the landfill. It is cast out. The ones having ears to hear should hear."

The explanation of this chapter begins not with verse 1 but with an understanding of verse 25. Admittedly, in the middle of the sequence of events, verse 25 provides a transition that becomes the key to comprehending the verses that preceded, the verses that followed, and why both sections should be tied together. Doing so will demonstrate that the verses about dining, Luke 14:-24, and the verses about discipleship, Luke 14:25–35, culminate in Jesus' teaching about the Christian's ability to know and do the work of the kingdom.

As the chapter opens, Jesus was invited to a meal. A common enough experience, the Gospels record numerous such events in Jesus' life. Also unremarkably common, Jesus spoke to the small group who were attending the meal. Included in the setting were scribes and Pharisees, the host himself being a ruler from among the Pharisees, probably a member of the Sanhedrin. Finally, there was a man with a health condition. Frequently translated dropsy, the illness caused the individual to suffer from inflammation and fluid retention. The text indicated the other guests were watching Jesus, and unsurprisingly, the infirmed man happened to show up at this meal on the Sabbath. As such, the stage was set.

Verse 25, however, provides an obvious transition. Departing from the initial setting of the private meal, Jesus turned from speaking to the small crowd at the banquet table and began teaching the multitude who were looking on. This detail introduces a break in the narrative that must be addressed but which also provides the structure for understanding the entire chapter. One of two things happened. Either these two events—Jesus' teaching the guests about dining and Jesus' teaching the multitude about discipleship—were historically sequential or they were not. Either Jesus turned to the onlookers and began discussing discipleship immediately following his teaching at the table or Luke made the connection based on the meaning of Jesus' earlier teaching. Either way, the reader should understand the relation between the two.

Now back to the setting. Luke bracketed the introductory paragraph with a question and a statement about ability that set the tone for the entire passage. Upon seeing the diseased man, who was an obvious plant, Jesus asked if it was lawful to heal on the Sabbath. The word Luke used was ἔξεστιν (*exestin*), a compound word that literally means "it is free." Its use in legal contexts is seen as it often is translated "it is lawful." This context of describing an action allowed by some higher authority is drawn from the basic meaning of something that a person is able to do.[33] In essence, Jesus asked the scribes and Pharisees, "Are you able to heal on the Sabbath?" In response to their silence, Jesus healed the dis-

---

33. Foerster, "ἔξετιν," 560.

eased man, dismissed him from their presence, and asked a rhetorical question structured to anticipate a positive answer. Jesus asked, "When your son or your ox falls in a well on the Sabbath, you immediately lift him out, don't you?" Luke framed their response with the second part of the bracket. Luke indicated no one was able to answer, οὐκ ἴσχυσαν ἀνταποκριθῆναι (*ouk ischusan antapokrithēnai*).

Luke's description of the opening scene, along with the connection between the two halves of the story, provides the reader with the necessary context to proceed. What followed the healing of the man with edema is a description of what the disciple of Jesus, both then and now, is, and is not, able to do.

(1) Jesus' disciple is able to be humble. The description of the seating chart at a public event provided the opportunity for Jesus to direct his disciples to have appropriate humility. Paul underscored this when he wrote, "For I say, through the grace given unto me, to every man that is among you, not to think of himself more highly than he ought to think; but to think soberly, according as God hath dealt to every man the measure of faith" (Rom 12:3).

It was better, Jesus said, to be exalted from a humble position than to be humbled from an exalted position. The Christian should move through this world with a self-image that recognizes a greater reality; this world is temporary, and seeking its fame and recognition does little if anything of eternal significance.

(2) Jesus' disciple is able to be inclusive. A dominant theme for Luke, the universal appeal of the Gospel is not to be taken lightly by the way that Christians live their lives. Jesus said the banquet host had the ability to invite whomever he wished. The common practice was then, and still is now, to invite those who can reciprocate. Jesus said to invite those who could not reciprocate. It has often been said that the measure of a man is taken by how he responds to someone who can do absolutely nothing for him.

(3) Jesus' disciple is able to participate fully in the kingdom of God. As with the universal appeal of the Gospel, the pervasive nature of the kingdom of God is a dominant theme for Luke. In the analogy of the wedding feast, the host invited all to participate. As the plot unfolds, the guests excluded themselves from participation. Three times specific individuals indicated they were not able to participate due to a variety of reasons. The new landowner, the new ox owner, and the new husband all

Journey to Jerusalem 213

offered their excuses and said, "I cannot participate." As such, Luke provided negative illustrations of the disciple's ability to participate. Only self-imposed restrictions will cause a person to lack the ability to participate in God's plan. By choice, people exclude themselves from what God is doing. All are invited, but as the Master said in the parable, *Not a single one of the men I invited will taste my banquet.*

An important subplot in this analogy is the insistence the banquet hall be filled and the anticipation by the slaves of their master's commands. When the invited guests began excluding themselves, the host turned to the masses to fill the dining hall. Nothing short of complete participation would satisfy the patron. Luke's meaning is clear: God will include all who wish to participate. Furthermore, disobedience does not deter the progress of the kingdom; it only changes the names of those involved.

Furthermore, there was no secret to the master's intent. In verse 22 the servant indicated all the master had commanded had been carried out. Specifically, the original guests had been invited and upon their announced regrets, the servant invited others to be guests. In other words, the servant knew the lack of participation would not be acceptable. Knowing the mind of their master, the servant took the initiative to invite others. As such, this part of the narrative provides a illustration of the first point: They were the least that became the first. Even the lowest servant in the kingdom is integrally involved in doing the master's will.

(4) A person is not able to be Jesus' disciple if doing so is not the most important aspect of the person's life. When Jesus turned to the on-looking crowd, he made a harsh statement about discipleship. Jesus told those present that if they did not hate their father, mother, spouse, brother, or sister, then they could not be his disciple. This was intended as an exaggeration meaning nothing should be more important than following Christ. Jesus quoted the Scripture's command to honor one's father and mother (Matt 15:14) and condemned the religious practice of Corban[34] (Mark 7:9–13). The overstatement was intended for its effect. The meaning is that nothing can be more important than following Jesus. This truth is demonstrated throughout each of the family relations available to the disciple. Can a man be a good husband and not be a fol-

---

34. Corban was the practice of dedicating all worldly possessions to the work of God. Once "bankrupt," a person was not obligated to care for parents, even though a person could technically still have access to his or her resources.

lower of Jesus? Yes, he can. He can go to work and provide for his family, paying his bills regularly, saving for children's education, remitting taxes honestly and timely, and do it all with love, devotion, and a kind disposition. But he cannot do any of those things as well as he could if his wife, children, co-workers were second place!

My wife and I are blessed with three perfect daughters. After praying for decades for unnamed suitors, God gave us three wonderful sons. When each requested to marry one of my daughters, I said the same thing, "Only when God is first and my daughter is second will you have the kind of rewarding relationship that God intends." Jesus wanted his disciples to know they were created in the image of God and to be in fellowship with God in order that they could serve God. Only when these matters are in order can anything else be right.

(5) A person is not able to be Jesus' disciple if he or she is not willing first to count the cost. There are three very important aspects to this statement about discipleship. The first is obvious: No one does anything important without an appropriate degree of planning. Discipleship is not an issue one should easily choose. Noncommittal beginnings lead to noncommittal conclusions. As with other important decisions—building a tower or going to war—one should consider the cost of discipleship before making the commitment.

The second aspect is less obvious but more pervasive. Jesus' analogy extended beyond the decision to be a disciple to the consequence of being a bad disciple. Jesus said the builder who runs out of money when only the foundation was laid will be laughed to scorn. Furthermore, the army that battles a superior force will be defeated. More than just the natural consequence of the analogy, Jesus warned that a disciple who cannot stay the course will be ridiculed and ultimately conquered. Recovery from either will be extremely difficult and most unlikely.

Finally, Jesus said the way to prevent these issues was complete abdication of personal control. The way to count the cost and to avoid undesirable consequences of failure was to have nothing at stake. When persons renounce all they are and all they have, then they have counted the cost and then they will finish what they started. When there is no self to protect, the disciple can proceed without impediment.

(6) A person is not able to be Jesus' disciple if he or she has lost the essential quality of discipleship. Great care is to be exercised in understanding this passage. When Jesus compared the disciple's life to insipid

salt, he was addressing effectiveness of the Christian's service, not status as a child of God. Worthlessness will rob the joy from the child of God. Persons who have become jaded are rarely effective in their work for the kingdom. They are good for nothing. They are of no use to the kingdom. Others discard them or dismiss them out of hand. While disciples' salvation is eternally secure, their effectiveness is a matter of practice and daily performance. Jesus warned that one can lose his or her joy, and what a sad reality that is!

EQUALITY[35]

Luke 15:1–32

¹*All the tax collectors and sinners were drawing near to Jesus,* ²*causing the Pharisees and scribes to grumble, saying, "This man welcomes sinners and even eats with them!"* ³*Jesus then spoke to them in a parable.* ⁴*"What man among you, having one hundred sheep and losing one out of them, would not leave the ninety-nine in the wilderness and go search until he found the one that was lost?* ⁵*Furthermore, finding it, he will place it on his shoulder* ⁶*and entering his house will gather his friends and neighbors saying to them, 'Rejoice with me! I found my sheep that was lost!'* ⁷*I say to you that there will be greater joy in heaven over one sinner that repents than over ninety-nine righteous who have no need for repentance.* ⁸*Or what woman, having ten silver coins, if she loses one silver coin, will not light a lamp and sweep the house searching diligently until she finds it?* ⁹*And finding it, she calls together her friends and neighbors, saying 'Rejoice with me! I have found the silver coin that was lost!'* ¹⁰*In the same way, I say to you, there will be joy among God's angels over one sinner that repents."* ¹¹*Then Jesus said, "A certain man had two sons.* ¹²*The younger son said to his father, 'Father, give to me the portion of the property that falls to me.' So the father divided the estate.* ¹³*Not many days later, the younger son gathered all and left for a distant country, squandering his wherewithal by living recklessly.* ¹⁴*But after spending all he had, a severe famine came upon that country, and he found himself to be in need.* ¹⁵*So he went and hired on to a citizen of*

---

35. As with the preceding chapter, Luke 15 is translated together as one literary unit.

that country, who sent him into his fields to tend swine. ¹⁶There he longed to eat even the carob tree foliage that the swine ate, but the owner gave him nothing. ¹⁷Then he said to himself, 'How many of my Father's employees have more than enough bread, but I am being destroyed by hunger? ¹⁸I will get up, and I will go to my father and say, Father, I have sinned against heaven and before you. ¹⁹I am no longer worthy to be called your son, but please, will you treat me as one of your employees?' ²⁰So he arose and went to his father. But while he was a great distance away, his father saw him, had pity on him, ran to him, fell on his neck, and kissed him. ²¹The son said to him, 'Father, I have sinned against heaven and before you and no longer am worthy to be called your son.' ²²But the father said to his servant, 'Go quickly and get a robe, the best one, and put it on him and give a ring for his hands and sandals for his feet. ²³Also, bring the fatted calf and kill it. Let us eat and celebrate, ²⁴because this, my son, was dead and now has come back to life; he was lost and now is found.' ²⁵Now the older son was in the field, and as he come near the house, he heard the music and the dancing. ²⁶So the older brother called the house servant to himself and asked what the noise meant. ²⁷The servant then said, 'Your brother has come, and your father has killed the fatted calf because he returned safely.' ²⁸Becoming angry, the older brother refused to go in. So his father went out to plead with him. ²⁹Responding, the older brother said to his father, 'How long have I served you, never disobeying your commandment, and you never gave even a goat for me to celebrate with my friends? ³⁰But let this son of yours who wasted your livelihood on prostitutes return, and you kill the fatted calf!' ³¹But the father said to him, 'Dear child! You have always been with me and all that I have is yours! ³²But for now, rejoice and be glad because your brother was dead and now is alive; he was lost and now is found.'"

Often titled the "Prodigal Son" or "The Parable of the Loving Father," Luke 15:11–32 is the culmination of a very tightly constructed literary unity that began with a disagreement between Jesus and the religious purists of his day. The setting for the argument is found in verse 1 where Luke indicated that not only were tax collectors and sinners congregating around Jesus but also that they were intent on listening[36] to what he was saying. The first aspect, Jesus' open association with those that were to be avoided, was problematic in itself. But Jesus went beyond casual conversation. Jesus was teaching the socially outcast about the kingdom of God, about repentance, and about new life. Jesus proclaimed to the segment of society who had been excluded that with God they were included. And because these outcasts were included, Jesus was saying they were equals with the religious elite who despised their very existence.

Given this setting, the Pharisees' reaction was not a surprise. Luke recorded they grumbled or murmured. The word choice is important. The word διεγόγγυζον (*diegogguzon*) is found only twice in the New Testament—here and in Luke 19:7 where the Pharisees complained when Jesus ate a meal with the notorious Zacchaeus. The word διεγόγγυζον (*diegogguzon*) is closely related to another term, γογγύζω (*gogguzō*), which is used more frequently, but again, often in context about dietary complaints. The Jews murmured when Jesus said he was the bread of life (John 6:41). There were murmurings when the Hellenist widows were being discriminated against in the daily allotment of food (Acts 6:1). The word group also is used in the Septuagint, most notably when Israel complained about the availability of food during the wilderness wandering (Exod 16:7,8,9,12).

What is difficult to determine from this setting is if the scribes and Pharisees fully comprehended the nature of their hatred or if they were blinded by the same. Rationally, there is a very good reason why the grumbling escalated when Jesus broke barriers surrounding dietary issues. One only sits down to share a common meal with those of equal or greater status. This is evident both on its inherent logic as well as from the progression of Luke's narrative. In chapter 14, the kingdom of God was described in great detail by a variety of banquet analogies, which started with the story of prominence of banquet seating. A socially inferior person certainly would not be included in such a conversation. To allow a sinner to sit at the same table, share the same utensils, and hear the same conversation would imply he was just as good, just as capable of intelligent conversation, and just as equal as everyone else who sat around the table. The religious purist could not accept such a description of God's work.

---

36. The infinitive "to hear" is used in a final clause or purpose clause.

To address these issues, Jesus told three parables, all with the same themes. The parables were of a shepherd, a woman, and a wealthy landowner. The choice of characters for these three parables was intentional. Luke was careful to demonstrate throughout his narrative that Jesus embraced the outcast. That a shepherd and a woman, both living at the bottom of the social ladder, would be the hero and heroine of Jesus' stories probably did nothing to improve the emotions of the moment. The third figure was that of an ideal Jew. The fact that the man had sons and was prosperous underscored for the scribes and Pharisees one thing: This individual was a law-abiding, God-fearing Jew who had consequently been blessed by God. In other words, those complaining about Jesus' actions believed the father of the third story to be their equal. The woman and the shepherd certainly were not.

However, while the religious elite would discriminate between the landowner and those they perceived to be inferior, Jesus demonstrated that the actions of all three were identical. In each parable there was an owner, something owned, that which was owned became lost, and consequently became dirty. Furthermore, in each case, the owners searched for their lost, dirty possessions, themselves becoming dirty in the process. In all three instances, the lost was reclaimed, and there was rejoicing as a result. Notice the similarities in the stories.

The shepherd owned one hundred sheep. When one was lost, he first secured the ninety-nine and then went to search for the one lost sheep. Known for their lack of survival instinct, sheep have little ability to care for themselves. Left unattended, it is not too great an assumption to assert that when found, the one lost sheep was bruised, bloody, wet, and dirty. Rather than herding one sheep, the shepherd, wanting to get back to the ninety-nine, simply picked up the errant sheep and carried it back. At this point, the same filth that was on the sheep contaminated the shepherd.

A woman had ten coins. When one was lost, she lit a lamp and swept her home in a diligent search. Typical construction of a home in the Mediterranean world would lead the reader to assume she lived on a dirt floor. Sweeping the dirt to look for the coin would stir up the dust and dirt, coating the woman in the same.

Common to both of these stories was a celebration. It mattered not what had happened in the past. The lost was found. It mattered not that both the owner and the item owned became dirty in the search. There was joy at their recovery. Finally, Jesus moralized both stories by indicating there was more joy in heaven over one sinner who repents than there is for many righteous who need no repentance.

The first and second parables established the pattern to be followed in the final passage. As with the shepherd and the woman, the loving father lost something he held very dear—his younger son. The pious person listening to the story would have been incensed over the details. When the younger son requested his inheritance, he was in essence telling his father he wished he were already dead. By Jewish property law, the possessions passed to the heirs by right of birth. The child did nothing to earn the wealth. The young man was in fact born into wealth and privilege. The son's actions made him a despicable person in the eyes of the religious crowd.

Worse were the actions that followed. Not only did the young man take his inheritance prematurely but he also left home for a foreign land. Modern culture may romanticize "backpacking through Europe," but the ancients did not. The Jews looked upon their Egyptian sojourn and their time in Babylonian captivity as their darkest of days. The promise of God to give Abraham the land was transferred into a love of home that was inviolate. This action was the first of several events Jesus presented in a cascading fashion that was intended to add insult to injury. Not only did the young man leave home but he also went to a foreign country. Not only did he leave home and go to a foreign country but he also wasted his resources. Not only did he leave home, go to a foreign country, and waste his resources but he did so to experience an immoral lifestyle. No wonder when a famine came upon the land the young man ended up in servitude to a foreigner, tending swine, and so hungry that he was willing to eat pig swill. A fitting end to such a disrespectful, inconsiderate, immature young man!

Or so Jesus' adversaries thought.

Just like the first two stories, the owner became dirty reclaiming that which was owned. As the young man was a long way away, the father saw him approach. Much has been made, and rightly so, about the father's anticipation that each day could afford his wayward son's return. Each day brought another opportunity for the father to pray for his son's health and well-being. Far from the begrudging legalist, the father wanted nothing more than to be reunited. Upon the son's arrival, full emotions overflowed. The father embraced him, kissed him, and in the eyes of the purist, became just as dirty as the young man.

But prior bad acts meant nothing to the loving father. Instead, he rejoiced. He treated his son like royalty. "Give him a robe, shoes, ring," the father commanded. "Get the fatted calf! Prepare a banquet. My son has returned home!"

At this point, the similarity of the three parables ceased. Unlike the first two stories, Jesus added a countereffect in the person of the older brother. Approaching the house, the older brother heard the commotion, requested clarification, and was told his brother had returned to a king's welcome. Infuriated, the older brother refused to participate and caused the father to come to him in explanation of his actions. Luke was very specific in the details of Jesus' story. Service and obedience were the substance of the older brother's argument. "Never have I been rewarded," argued the pouting sibling. To which the father replied, "You have been with me the entire time, and all that I have is yours. But your brother who was dead is now alive, and for that we should rejoice!"

Jesus made two very important points in the addendum of the prodigal son parable. One, it does not cost anything to be inclusive, and two, participation is its own reward. The younger son's return did not mean the older brother would get less. To the contrary—all the father had was the older son's. But more importantly, the older son had the blessing of having always been obedient; he had the blessing of having always served, having always been in relationship, and having never been out of his father's presence.

Far from being a zero sums game where cutting one piece of pie larger means that another slice will be smaller, Jesus was saying God's love is endless. There is not a limited supply of God's grace. Jesus wanted the religious elite to understand that including the downcast in no way reduced God's love for them. Furthermore, what the Jews were missing was that they had always been God's people. There is a joy in the journey that is its own reward.

SHREWD DEALINGS

Luke 16:1–8

¹*Jesus said to his disciples, "There was a certain rich man who had a house manager against whom charges were brought of wasting the house owner's resources. ²The owner called the manager in and said to him, 'What is this I am hearing about you? Give an account of your management because you will no longer be able to be the house manager.' ³The house manager then said to himself, 'What will I do, as my lord is removing from me the house manager position? I am not able to dig and am too ashamed to beg. ⁴I know what I will do so that people will receive me into their homes when I am removed from this house management position.' ⁵So he called to himself each and every one of his master's debtors and said to each, 'How much do you owe my master?' ⁶One said, 'one hundred measures of oil.' The manager said to him, 'Take out your bill and quickly write down fifty.' ⁷To another the manager said, 'How much do you own?' That one said, 'One hundred measures of wheat.' The manager said to him, 'Take out your bill and quickly write down eighty.' ⁸The master commended the unrighteous house manger because he acted shrewdly; for the sons of this age are shrewder in dealing with their own generation than are the sons of light."*

The story of the unrighteous house manager is one that causes the modern reader to scratch his or her head and say, "What?" The passage does not fit the western sense of justice and fair play. In fact, it runs counter to the biblical work ethic that is expected of Scripture. After all, the steward of the house was a reckless individual. His job was to look after the resources of his employer. Not only did he not take care of his responsibility but also the accusations brought against him imply that he embezzled those funds placed under his care. There is no doubt that if this were to occur today, not only would there be an employment termination but there probably would be a felony indictment followed by certain court-ordered restitution. The fact that the story ends with the unethical manager receiving his master's commendation leaves a poor taste in the mouths of the readers, many who simply do not know how to handle such a situation.

In order to understand the passage, the modern reader should first see it for what it is—a story about a person who acted in his own best interest. Without justifying the underlying larceny, note the reactions of the main character. (1) Those who seek their own best interest are realistic. The unethical manager first thought about what would happen next. His self-evaluation determined what he could and could not do. He was unable to farm or perform manual labor and unwilling to beg. (2) Those who seek their own best interest are resourcefully. In order to "feather his nest," the unethical manager involved others in his scheme to defraud. By calling in the land lord's debtors and fraudulently altering their documentation, the main character accomplished two things. One, he curried the favor of those who would later be in a position to assist him. Two, he involved others in the deception. His would not be the only neck in the noose if the entire plan went south. (3) Finally, those who act in their own best interest react quickly to situations. The window of opportunity for action was limited. Once convicted of the allegations, the unethical manager would have lost the wherewithal to accomplish his plan.

Given this understanding, the reader is ready for Jesus' application of the parable. In the final words, Jesus delivered an unexpected indictment. With the commendations of the landowner ringing in the disciples' ears, Jesus said, "You guys are not as savvy as the unethical house manager." The message to the disciples was that they should be at least as involved in seeking the best interest of the kingdom as the unethical manger was in seeking his own best interest. Jesus' disciple should be as realistic about the realities of the present world, as resourceful in engaging the lost, and as quick to react to opportunities that further the kingdom as the villain in the story was to advance his own cause.

AN ILLUSTRATION

Luke 16:9

9 "*And I say to you, make friends by means of unrighteous wealth, so that when it plays out you will be received into the eternal home.*"

What a strange verse! Numerous challenges exist in explaining this teaching of Jesus, not the least of which is in understanding how it fits into Luke's narrative. Does verse 9 belong with the preceding verse regarding the unethical house manager or with the following verses that state wealth is neither to be trusted nor to be served? As will be made clear, verses 1 through 13 will set the context for the latter verses of the chapter. But before yielding to the temptation to see this as nothing more than Luke preserving historic material that would not fit well anywhere else, consider the verse as a simple statement of fact. The disciple should understand there is nothing evil about wealth in and of itself. Wealth can be used to proper ends. Those ends will never allow a person to purchase salvation, but it can be put to moral use. Not unlike the unethical house steward who reacted quickly and resourcefully to his own advantage, Jesus taught that wealth should be used to the advantage of the kingdom.

Many rags to riches stories can be told to illustrate this point. Andrew Carnegie, the industrial steel mogul, said, "The man who dies rich, dies disgraced."[37] J. C. Penney built his apparel empire desiring to live off a tithe and to give the church ninety percent of his wealth. Yet while wealth is fleeting and should never be trusted for the source of contentment, it is a resource of God that is intended to be used.

FAITHFUL IN MUCH

Luke 16:10–13

> [10] "The one being faithful in the smallest things is faithful in great things. The one being dishonest in the smallest things is dishonest in great things. [11] If you have not been faithful in unrighteous wealth, who will trust you with true wealth? [12] If you have not been faithful with another's affairs, who will give to you their own possessions? [13] No servant is able to serve two masters. Either he will hate one and love the other, or he will be loyal to one and despise the other. You are not able to serve God and wealth."

Following the theme of fiscal responsibility, Luke presented Jesus' teaching that could be viewed as the antithesis of the unethical house manager introduced earlier in the chapter. There are two parts to the section.

(1) Integrity knows no limit. This is a simple concept. Faithful service is demonstrated over time and in increasing increments. Employees

---

37. Carnegie, "Wealth," 664.

prove themselves to their employers in small tasks before they are trusted with large tasks. Furthermore, integrity, or the lack thereof, follows a person. Reputations are built on acts of integrity. Two illustrations are given to this point. First is the direct statement that is phrased in a first class condition where "the condition and its consequence are simply stated without reference to whether the condition is in fact fulfilled or not."[38] What this means is that the sentence is written to say if A is true, B also is true. If A is false, B also is false. Categorically, a person who is faithful to a menial task can be trusted with something more important. The inverse also is true. When a person demonstrates unfaithfulness in the one area, he or she indicates a predilection toward failure in others.

(2) While integrity knows no limit, loyalty does. A person cannot be the slave to two masters. Again, Jesus began with a common sense statement that could not be challenged. Slaves obeyed their masters unconditionally. There was no discussion, and there were no questions. There was only obedience. This would become impossible if there were divided loyalty. With two masters, the slave would not know what actions to perform and what actions to predicate upon someone else's approval. The validity of the statement was obvious.

Once his audience was in agreement with the statement, Jesus applied the general truth to a specific situation. You can serve God or you can serve material pursuits, but you cannot serve both. One must take a subordinate position to the other.

It is interesting to note that Luke's use of this teaching of Jesus repeats the theme of looking out for one's own interest. The unethical house servant knew to look after his best interest (16:1–8). Jesus directed the disciples to do the same for the sake of the kingdom (16:8–9). Here (16:10–13), it is taken for granted that the employer tests a potential "promotee" with small assignments before entrusting large assignments precisely because the employer is guarding his own best interest. Clearly there is nothing wrong or inherently evil in wealth.

What is more, one should not overlook the fact that Jesus was looking out after the kingdom's interest. The force of the parable of the foolish farmer in Luke 12 is that he incorrectly assumed he had control. "Who will own what you have made when you die?" asked the parable. The understood answer was that God owned everything before the farmer grew it and owned everything after the farmer harvested it. Here the

---

38. Zerwick, *Biblical Greek*, 102.

question is asked who will trust the untrustworthy with their possessions. If God owns all, then the kingdom is made up of stewards who serve one master. The irony is that while wealth never is the master, it can make one a slave.

CREATING AN ALTERNATE REALITY

Luke 16:14–31

14Hearing all of this and being fond of money, the Pharisees derided Jesus. **15**Jesus then said to them, "You are they who justify themselves before men, but God knows your heart. Speaking of which, what is highly esteemed before men is an abomination before God. **16**The law and the prophets were until John. Since then, the good news of the kingdom of God has been preached freely, as all enter it violently. **17**But it is easier for heaven and earth to pass away than for the smallest stroke of the law to come to an end. **18**Anyone who divorces his wife and marries another commits adultery, and anyone who marries a woman divorced from her husband commits adultery. **19**Now there was a man who was rich. He wore purple and fine linen and faired sumptuously every day. **20**But a poor man, named Lazarus, full of draining sores, had been placed at the rich man's gate, **21**longed to sustain himself with what fell from the table. Not only so, but the dogs licked his open sores. **22**Now it happened that the poor man died and the angels took him to Abraham's bosom. The rich man also died and was buried. **23**But the rich man lifted up his eyes in Hades and being in torment saw Abraham afar off and Lazarus in his bosom. **24**Calling out, the rich man said, 'Father Abraham! Have mercy on me and send Lazarus to dip the tip of his finger in water and cool my tongue, because I am being tormented in these flames.' **25**But Abraham said to the rich man, 'Dear child! Remember that in your life you received good things and Lazarus received evil things. Now Lazarus is being comforted here, and you are being tormented there. **26**But as if all this were not enough, the fact remains that there is a great chasm set between us and you so that those desiring to crossover from here to you are not able and neither are they able to cross from there to us.' **27**Then the

> rich man said, 'I beg you then, Father Abraham, send Lazarus to my father's house, ²⁸that he may sternly warn the five brothers I have, so that they may not come to this place of torment.' ²⁹But Abraham said, 'They have Moses and the prophets; let your brothers hear them.' ³⁰The rich man responded, 'That is not enough, Father Abraham! But they would repent if someone came to them from the dead!' ³¹Then Abraham said, 'If they don't listen to Moses and the prophets, neither will they be persuaded if someone rises from the dead.'"

When Jesus finished his teachings on the true nature of wealth, the Pharisees ridiculed him for his position. Luke indicated their increased hostility was due to the love of money that characterized the Pharisees. Emphasis on wealth, power, and prestige were vital to the Pharisees' system of legalism. Without a public, visible measure of righteousness, there would be no acknowledgment of their perceived worth. For themselves and for those around them, the legalist would have no proof of their compliance with regulation. Accordingly, God's blessing became the obvious means to demonstrate how "good" a person was. Over time, the Jews distorted their belief in God's sovereignty and God's goodness into a system that equated success with God's approval. They believed God's promise to Abraham that "I will bless them that bless thee, and curse him that curseth thee" (Gen 12:3), but ignored the prophet when he said the wicked do in fact prosper (Jer 5:28; 12:1). They believed God rewarded righteous behavior but completely dismissed Jesus when he said God makes the rain to fall on the just and the unjust (Matt 5:45). In order for their legalistic approach of validating their own worth to work, the Pharisees needed a benchmark that was public, visible, and pliable. So it comes as no surprise that Jesus met opposition when he challenged their assumptions that wealth, power, and prestige must be equated with God's approval.

In response to their scornful laughter and comments, Jesus described the Pharisees as men who justify their own actions. The warning associated with such behavior was that the Pharisees made themselves vulnerable to emphasizing outward, visible actions, which on the surface portend great righteousness, but which in reality are motivated by improper intentions and attitudes. "What you think should be highly esteemed by the general public," Jesus said, "actually may be an abomination to God. You are dangerously close to creating an alternate reality where you will not only be condemned for your actions but where you will be so far out of touch with reality that you will not even know that you have been condemned."

It is important to stop at this point in the narrative and understand clearly the ramification of Jesus' accusation. The problem with his opponents' false assumption was that taken to their ultimate conclusion, the legalist will create a false world in which to live. Self-justification, rationalization, and legalism are inherently dangerous because assumption will build upon assumption, and the final outcome will be an alternate reality where everything seems real, but in fact is not. The ultimate conclusion of constant, consistent self-justification is nothing short of complete delusion. The Pharisees had created for themselves a reality where what they espoused as godly and good was in fact aberration and abomination. Note the detail in Jesus' description of the Pharisees.

(2) Their false reality maintained the delusion of control. Jesus indicated that God had spoken through the law and prophets. These were instruments that were appropriate in their time. God used the law to bring about a system of worship. But the law was never intended as the object of worship. The Hebrew people often missed the picture the sacrificial system was attempting to draw. The image of complete surrender that emphasized love and trust was missed in favor of a transactional relationship. The Jews sacrificed items A, B, and C, necessitating that God would respond by saying or providing X, Y, and Z. Unfortunately, the emphasis on obeying the law caused the religious participant to miss the culmination of the law. The message of the transitional prophet, John the Baptist, was that the long-anticipated Messiah finally had come. The good news of the kingdom was proclaimed to all. The gospel was a free gift. There was no longer any transaction to be made, only grace to be received. But this message of hope was wasted on the legalist because of the delusion of control. With grace there was nothing to control. The law did not pass away; it was fulfilled in the person of Jesus. But efforts continued to take the kingdom by force. What Jesus said is plain. The law and the prophets did exactly what they were designed to do: Prepare the way for the gospel. That would never change. Heaven and earth would pass away before that would change. But the Pharisees were stuck in adherence to the law, trapped in a false reality, because of the delusion of control.

(2) Their false reality maintained the delusion of appearance. In their efforts to control the kingdom of God by adherence to and manipulation of the law, the Pharisees relied on what could be observed. For example, the law allowed for divorce if a woman found no favor in the eyes of her husband (Deut 24:1). But this lack of favor was to be due to an indecency or sexual impropriety on the part of the woman. By the first century, however, any type of undesirable behavior or even an honest mistake could be classified as an indecency. Unfortunately, the man was not required to explain his reasons. He simply stated an indecency had occurred. This often left the divorced woman, guilty of impropriety or not, to bear the appearance of an unvirtuous woman.

This entire charade infuriated Jesus. "You are the ones who are divorcing in order to remarry," Jesus said to the Pharisees. "You are the ones who are creating a false appearance about who you are. But you are deluded in your false lives because God sees your heart." They stood condemned, but because of their immersion in a false reality, they didn't even know they were condemned.

(3) Finally, their false reality, with its attempts at control and their reliance on appearance, created a destiny of delusion that locked the Pharisees in a world of their own making that had no bearing on the work of kingdom. Jesus told a parable about two men who died. In the afterlife, the one man who was being punished asked for assistance from Abraham. Receiving none, the man asked a messenger from the dead be sent to his brothers so they would repent of their actions and avoid eternal punishment. Abraham indicated if the man's brothers would not respond to the message of Moses and the prophets, neither would they respond to a messenger from beyond the grave.

Without carefully recreating the entire dialogue, one could conclude the actions of the tormented soul were motivated by benevolence or by compassion. However, noting the contextual statement by Jesus that the Pharisees always sought to justify their own actions and by questioning the likelihood of godly behavior in a place absent of God's presence—compassion on the part of the damned—the reader could easily draw a different conclusion. The reader should note how the story would change if Abraham had agreed to the request. "Well," said Abraham to the tormented person in Hades, "you may have a point there. I think I will do that. Your brothers certainly would benefit from a person rising from the dead and addressing their false assumptions about life, their callous disregard for those around them, and their unrepentant attitudes. Consider it done!" What would have been the next words from the mouth of the rich man who had been consigned to hell for his sinful behavior? If Abraham had granted his request to send a postmortem messenger, the rich man would have had reason for an appeal. "Aha! But Father Abraham, the man in hell would have said, 'No one came to me! You are not being fair! If someone had come to me from the dead, I would have changed!' You are giving them an opportunity I never had!" The rich man in Hades would have rationalized that he should not be held accountable for his actions and immediately restored to life or at least given appropriate reward in the afterlife.

But no justification was allowed. Instead, what was revealed was that there was no way out of the destiny they had created. They had deluded themselves by false efforts of control that relied on false impressions and appearances, and the reality they had created to free themselves was in fact a prison of their own making. Note the details of the parable. The rich man was accustomed to comfort in his life and so wanted comfort in his death. The rich man was served in his life, and so he wanted to be served in his death. He relied on the appearance of godliness. He was wealthy, wearing the finest clothes and eating the best food. He even did God's work by keeping barely alive a person whose appearance demanded a judgment of condemnation. By feeding Lazarus only the scraps from the table, the rich man sustained a sinner so that God could continue to punish the poor wretch. But the rich man woke in torment and was unable to justify his behavior. He was unable to rationalize how what he did was right and proper. He was unable to alter the facts of true reality.

The final warning that must be heard from the story of the rich man and Lazarus is while sinful humanity always seeks to create an alternate reality where self may reign, true reality does not change from one side of the grave to the next. The rich man was the same in life as he was in the afterlife. He was self-righteous, trusting a false reality and ready to justify his actions in life and in the afterlife. Lazarus, on the other hand, was dependent on God's care in one life and was the same in the next. In addition to emphasizing the immortal nature of humanity—all will spend eternity somewhere—the story of the rich man and Lazarus demonstrates the connection between daily action that is temporal and character that is eternal. We practice day by day what we become.

Furthermore, the character that is built now extends into the reward or punishment that is dictated by status in Christ. More than an evangelical passage to warn the lost of the reality of hell, this passage warns the Christian that daily activity cultivates on a daily basis the ability, or lack thereof, to receive what God in fact offers. Undisciplined lives rob the Christian of the blessings God wishes to bestow. Too many Christians simply do not see or understand what God is offering. If that is true in this life, the rich man and Lazarus tell us it will be true in the next. What a tragic reality! To think one could be saved, yet miss the blessings God intends for the children of the kingdom. Yet the love of control, the love of appearance, the propensity of humanity to rationalize and justify will bring one to that very end, deluded about the true reality.

INSTRUCTIONS ON THE JOURNEY: FORGIVENESS

Luke 17:1-4

> ¹*Jesus said to his disciples, "It is impossible that occasions of stumbling will not come, but woe to the one by which they come;* ²*It would be better for him that a millstone be tied around his neck and thrown into the sea than for him to offend one of the least of these.* ³*Pay attention to this! If your brother sins (and he will), you rebuke him, and if he repents (and he will), you forgive him.* ⁴*And if he sins against you seven times a day and turns to you and says, 'Please forgive,' you must forgive him."*

Too often separated by translators and interpreters, Luke purposefully connected the issues of offense (Luke 17:1-2) and forgiveness (Luke 17:3-4). Removed from Matthew's context of offending children who are the model of entrance to the kingdom (Matt 18:1-7) and/or Mark's context of sinning in general (Mark 9:38-48), Luke used the literary force of his vocabulary to build the context of the passage. Two words, the first a noun and the second a verb, construct this context. They are respectively σκάνδαλον (*skandalon*) and σκανδαλίζω (*skandalidzō*).

While the root forms of the word group are not common, neither are they particularly rare. Dating back to third century BC, the verb forms mean to slam shut or to swing back and forth, while the noun was used to describe a thing that slammed shut or swung closed. Continued use began favoring a spring or stick that closed or triggered a snare or trap.³⁹ These words were used in the Septuagint to convey two different Hebrew words with similar meanings. For example, "Our soul is escaped as a bird out of the snare of the fowlers: the snare is broken, and we are escaped" (Ps 124:7). The psalmist said of his enemies, "Let their table become a snare before them: and that which should have been for their welfare, let it become a trap" (Ps 69:22). In addition to a snare or trap, the word group took on the meaning of misfortune or ruin as when the servants of Pharaoh pled, "How long shall this man be a snare unto us? Let the men go, that they may serve the Lord their God: knowest thou not yet that Egypt is destroyed?" (Exod 10:7).

This use led to an increasingly more religious sense in which the snare was an occasion for stumbling or offense as can be seen in the variety of translations of this passage alone. Of the inevitability of the occasion of sin and of the damnability of the action of sin, the King James Version pairs "offenses" and "offend." The Revised Standard Version uses "temptation" and "cause to sin." The New International Version translates the phrases as "things that cause people to sin" and "cause one of these little ones to sin." Clearly, the obstacle in the path and the trigger of the snare are used in the Gospels to describe impediments to the progression of one's faith.

Given this context, the reader should note the reality of sinful human nature. (1) There is the inevitability of sinful human nature. Jesus said occasions for stumbling will come. Stumbling blocks will be placed before you. Snares will abound. Luke used a hapax legomenon,⁴⁰ ἀνένδεκτόν (*anendekton*), to indicate the unavoidable reality of temptation. The word ἀνένδεκτόν (*anendekton*) is a compound word. The root is ἐδέχομαι (*endechomai*), which means "possible" or "allowable." Prefixing a word with the alpha privative reverses the word meaning like the English il, un, or non; legal and illegal, likely and unlikely, applicable and nonapplicable. Luke used ἐδέχομαι (*endechomai*) only one other time in Scripture and that also of his response to Herod's threatening behavior. Jesus said he was going to Jerusalem because it was not possible for a prophet to die away from Jerusalem (Luke 13:33). There Luke used two words, the negative οὐκ (*ouk*) and ἐδέχομαι (*endechomai*), to communicate the same thing as ἀνένδεκτόν (*anendekton*). Every other time Luke sought to com-

---

39. Stählin, "σκάνδαλον, κτλ.," 339–340.

40. A word used only once in a manuscript, document, or genre of literature, in this case, the New Testament.

municate that something was possible or impossible he employed the same technique used by the other New Testament writers, specifically δύναμις (*dunamis*) and ἀδύνατος (*adunatos*). But with respect to Jesus' death in Jerusalem and the unavoidable reality of temptation, it was as if regular vocabulary were not good enough. Somehow these two issues, the sacrificial death of Jesus and that God's people would be tempted, were so inextricably bound to God's plan of salvation that regular conversation would not do them justice. There is a universal, unchangeable, irrevocable, take-it-to-the-bank, and bet-the-ranch kind of reality that just as Jesus died for the sins of all, Christians, by the very nature of sinful humanity, will face temptation.

(2) There is the accountability of sinful human nature. As in the synoptic warning to those who offend children and cause them to stumble, Jesus said the person responsible for causing a person to fall would be held accountable. The image used here and in the parallel passages is that of having a millstone tied to one's neck and having both dropped into the sea. The intended word picture is obvious. There would be no escaping the fate of such a punishment. Furthermore, as the next verse indicates, the sinful person is not given a pass. He or she is rebuked by those who understand the error of the behavior. Those who choose to sin will be held accountable.

(3) Finally, there is the sustainability of faith amidst the predictability of sinful human nature. At this point, Luke again diverged from Matthew and Mark regarding their use of this traditional material. Luke immediately moved to forgiving a brother or sister in Christ who had offended another believer. To convey this, Luke paired two first class conditional sentences in order to show how faith grows even when sin seeks to destroy. A first class conditional sentence is a grammatical construction that creates an "if . . . then" kind of statement. But while there are no specifics associated with this type of "hypothetical statement," the reality of the condition in the statement is assumed to be true or real. "If your brother sins against you, and he will do just that," Jesus told his disciples, "you are to rebuke him for his error."

The next conditional sentence also communicated a reality that was certain. Jesus said, "And by the way, after your brother offends you, if he begs your forgiveness, and I am certain he will, you must forgive him. Even if he sins seven times and repents seven times, you forgive him!" While the first sentence may break the heart of the Christian by reinforcing the inevitability of failure, the second builds up the Christian who by faith continues to struggle to overcome sinful human nature. What is certain is that all sin. The reality of living in a fallen world that has been torn and marred by sin, a God-created world that is waiting itself for full redemption, is that even the believer will stumble and fall. That is certain.

Furthermore, this reality can cause believers to relegate themselves into a marginal Christian existence. Believers know all too well their failures. Believers experience all too often the feelings of remorse that ultimately accompany the realization that the indiscretion, the improper thought or action, the breach of faith, in fact has occurred again. "Me? Be used by God? You must be joking," we have all said to ourselves. "There is no way God can use me!" And so the wounded saint pulls him- or herself out of the game. It is as though someone had taken a millstone, hung it around their neck, and tossed them into the sea. As far as productivity in the kingdom is concerned, the fallen believer is dead already.

But while such a reality causes the child of God to mourn his or her sinful behavior and shamefully withdraw from kingdom service, God still seeks to re-engage and revitalize his child. No one is more cognizant of sin than the one committing the same. In addition to instructing the disciples to forgive their neighbor who sins against them, Jesus commanded the disciples to forgive themselves when they sin. Seven times a day! The writer of Hebrews referred to the sin "which doth so easily beset *us*" (Heb 12:1). In truth, there is no growing Christian who has never said with sorrowful anguish, "I did it again."

When this occurs, children of God will make a choice. They can remove themselves from God's presence and never again seek to fulfill God's call on their lives. Tragically, believers can begin acting as though they had never been born into the kingdom. Or, following Christ's directions, they can rebuke the sinner, in this case themselves, forgive the sinner, in this case themselves, and move forward, knowing that their master is a God of another chance, not just of a second chance.

FAITH'S RESPONSE

Luke 17:5–6

⁵*Then the disciples said to the Lord, "Increase our faith!"* ⁶*But the Lord said to them, "If you have faith as a mustard seed, you may say to this mulberry tree 'be uprooted and planted in the sea,' and it will obey you."*

Hearing Jesus' statements about faith, the disciples were moved to one response; "Give us this kind of faith."

As has been seen repeated in Luke, the sequence is not random. Luke's narrative had just asserted that faith prevents the obstacles or impediments that will come the way of the disciple from being insurmountable. Faith is the key to staying on track and not being diverted toward relentless distractions and blind alleys. Furthermore, by indicating they should be as forgiving of themselves as they are to be of each other, Jesus provided a glimpse of a world where faith rules and human nature is held at bay. In response to such a description of life, the disciples cried out, "Give us that kind of life! Give us the kind of faith that makes these things possible."

Jesus' response used typical language of his day. The modern reader who believes with great conviction in the inspiration and trustworthiness of Scripture runs the risk of pressing this and many other statements in God's Word beyond their original intent. All Scripture is true, but not all Scripture is intended to be understood literally. One should be reminded that the job of the translator is to move an idea from one language to another. Jesus' figurative language was intended to say that in the realm of faith, everything is possible.

Jesus' response to the disciples helps to explain what he meant. "Give us this kind of faith. Make our faith increase," the disciples asked. Jesus said in reply, "You already have enough faith. If you have as much faith as a grain of mustard seed, you have enough. In fact, if you have any faith at all, you have all you need." What Jesus was saying is faith is a characteristic, not a commodity. Faith is not like pixie dust that evaporates when used. Faith is not a weapon that is exhausted when discharged. If it were, a person would be called on to stockpile faith, much like the Hebrews attempted to storehouse extra food sent from heaven. When they did, the extra spoiled. God said to them, "You will always have enough, so stop trying to run the faith world like you run the human world. Trust me, and you will be fine." Rather than being a thing to be used so that believers can do what they want, faith enables believers to trust God who can do whatever he wants. Faith is the medium through which God changes us from unrighteous to righteous. Faith positions us to be involved in whatever God desires to do.

FAITH CONTINUED

Luke 17:7–19

> [7]"Who is there among you who will say to his servant when he comes in from plowing or tending sheep in the field 'Come immediately and sit at the banquet'? [8]To the contrary, will he not say to the servant, 'Prepare something for me to eat and gird yourself and serve me while I eat and drink and then you may eat and drink'? [9]He doesn't give thanks to the servant for doing what was commanded, does he? [10]In the same way, when you have done all that was commanded, you should say, 'We are unprofitable servants; we have done only what we ought to do.'" [11]Now it happened as they traveled between Samaria and Galilee on the way to Jerusalem [12]that ten leprous men came out of a village to meet Jesus. Standing at a distance, [13]they lifted up their voices saying, "Jesus, Master, have mercy on us!" [14]Seeing them, Jesus said, "Go. Show yourselves to the priest." As they went, they were healed. [15]But one of them, seeing that he was healed, returned and with a great voice, glorified God. [16]The healed man fell on his face at the feet of Jesus giving thanks to Jesus. The healed man was a Samaritan. [17]But Jesus asked him, "Were there not ten who were healed? [18]Was there no one found to return and give glory to God except this foreigner?" [19]Jesus said to the healed Samaritan, "Stand up. Go your way. Your faith has saved you."

What again appears to be random events and teachings from the life of Jesus are in fact purposeful aspects of inspiration and literary mastery. Luke continued the current theme of faith and its attributes by connecting the preceding description of the life of faith (17:1–4) and the disciples request for more faith (17:5–7) with a demonstration of what only faith can produce (17:7–19). Only faith fulfills humanity and enables a person to serve without being thanked and to be thankful when being served.

(1) Serving without being thanked is an atypical response for the fallen state of human nature. Even those outside the community of faith expect common courtesy. This is due to the contractual nature of relationships. If you do this, I will do that. For the seventeenth century British philosopher, Thomas Hobbes, this contract was accomplished by and justifies the existence of government. Because Hobbes viewed the state of nature as one of scarcity, he believed all humanity would serve one and only one principle—that being the natural right to protect oneself by any means necessary. To suppress and avoid the inevitable chaos resulting from the scarcity of resources, people acting with enlightened self-interest will form and submit to the government's power. The governmental authority will then enforce common rules and regulations; the government will enforce the social contract. While the social expectations will range widely from one culture to the next, an element of Hobbes's thinking can be seen where any level of polite exchange is expected. Civilized people living in a social order interact with at least a modicum of decency. To repeat the point, fallen humanity expects and depends on common courtesy.

But Jesus instructed his disciples that when they demonstrate true human nature as it was designed to function, the disciples will be able to ignore the expectations of society. Rather than demanding a transactional relationship with those to whom they were sent to serve, the disciples could elevate human nature from its fallen position to its original design by being willing to become vulnerable for the sake of the kingdom.

Two aspects of this passage explain this concept. First there is the debt of true humanity. The second is the design of true humanity. The concept of debt originates from Luke's use of the word ὀφείλω (*opheilō*). In the parable of the unforgiving servant, the debtor who pleaded with the lord for forgiveness of a debt was ultimately punished because he did not show the same forgiveness to a peer who owed him a debt (Matt 18:23–32). Likewise, Jesus taught about forgiveness when he described a king who forgave one servant a larger debt than another (Luke 7:41–43). Both used ὀφείλω (*opheilō*) to indicate owing a monetary debt. However, the same term is used as ought and duty in passages such as "We then that are strong ought to bear the infirmities of the weak, and not to please ourselves" (Rom 15:1) and in Paul's description of the Macedonian contribution to the saints where he said, "Their duty is also to minister unto them" (Rom 15:27). Clearly, the debt true humanity owes is to serve others, support others, forgive others, even as true humanity realizes it has been served, supported, and forgiven. True humanity emboldened by faith can acknowledge and discharge its debt to others.

Second, the original design for true humanity is for its profitability to God. Jesus told his disciples that when they had only discharged their duty, when they had only met the obligations of their debt, they had been unprofitable ἀχρεῖος (*achreios*) servants. Only doing what you are told is insufficient for the person of faith. The term ἀχρεῖος (*achreios*) is used only twice in Scripture. One is here in Luke where Jesus instructed the disciples to go beyond their duty. The other is in the parable of the talents. There the servant who was given only one talent said when called to account, "Lord, I knew thee, that thou art an hard man, reaping where thou hast not sown, and gathering where thou hast not strewed: And I was afraid, and went and hid thy talent in the earth: lo, there thou hast that is thine" (Matt 25:23–24). This servant was described by the lord as wicked and slothful for not doing more with the talent entrusted to his care. The resources the unprofitable servant did have were taken away prior to his dispatch to ultimate punishment. Clearly from these two illustrations, God's design for human nature is to reap a profit, to gather more than that which was sown. God's intent is to use true humanity, even to the point of sacrifice, to draw all people unto himself. Paul's statement about the incarnation was that Jesus became vulnerable when he took on the form of a servant (Phil 2:5–8). God took benefit from Jesus' full and unreserved embracing of true humanity. In keeping with his own example, Jesus told his disciples to put aside their own control, be willing to become vulnerable, and be a benefit to God.

(2) Faith also enables a person to give thanks when he or she has been served. The story line is simple. As Jesus and the disciples passed through Samaria, they encountered ten leprous men, begging to be healed. Jesus healed them, commanding they follow the law that required they present themselves to the priest and follow prescribed actions (Lev 14). Seeing he was healed, one of the ten returned and thanked Jesus. Receiving the praise, Jesus asked, "Where are the others?" The thankfulness of the one prompted another statement by Jesus who said, "Go on your way. Your faith has made you whole."

The key to understanding the connection between faith and thankfulness is the word ἀλλογενὴς (*allogenēs*). Used only here in Scripture, there is a closely related word, ἀλλόφυλος (*allophulos*), which too is used only once, specifically, the story of Peter and Cornelius in Acts 10:28. Both words may be translated stranger or foreigner. Both words imply exclusion. The first was the leper who had been forced to live away from civilized society. The second described anyone who was not Jewish by birth, regardless of belief in God.

One nonbiblical reference to ἀλλογενὴς (*allogenēs*) helps complete the story. The temple in Jerusalem consisted of a series of concentric rectangles, each bearing greater restrictions of access. The inner compartment was the holy of holies, entered only once a year by the high priest. The court of the priests surrounded the holy place and contained the altar of burnt offerings. On rotation, the priests would administer the sacrifices in this part of the temple. Only the purified priest would enter for the daily performance of worship.

Next was the court of Israel, where devout Jewish males came to participate in the religious observance of their faith. Directly in front of the court of Israel was the women's court. Only Jewish women and men were allowed in the court of women. The balance of the temple mount consisted of the court of the Gentiles. Anyone from any nation could enter the court of the Gentiles. It was in this area that temple coinage was exchanged for use in temple gifts and where sacrificial animals were sold to the pilgrims who had traveled great distances to attend worship.

Posted at the entrances to the court of Israel and to the women's court (a Jewish male could enter through the women's court or directly from the court of the Gentiles) were these words: "Let no foreigner ἀλλογενὴς (*allogenēs*) enter within the screen and enclosure surrounding the sanctuary."[41] A constant reminder of class distinction, these postings perpetuated feelings of resentment, inferiority, exclusion, and isolation.

Given Luke's word choice, one begins to wonder about the background of the ten lepers. All outcasts because of their disease, the ten lepers could have had very different backgrounds. For some, being ostracized could have been a new experience. Due to no fault of their own, they were shunned. Once members of a ruling class, they were treated like animals, removed from society, and forced to live an existence that was not in keeping with their background. For these, Jesus' healing was

---

41. Robertson, *Luke,* 228. Italics added.

a sigh of relief: "Finally! At last! I can be restored to my rightful place of honor and worth. I will no longer be excluded from society like a Gentile from the temple!" For the nine, their healing was in their minds more of setting the record straight than a miracle of compassion.

Yet for the one leper, the event took on a far greater meaning than just the removal of a dreaded and ultimately fatal disease. Faith enabled the one leper to understand that for which one should be faithful: inclusion. Somehow the one leper knew though he had been denied access to the court of Israel, he was being granted access to the kingdom of God. Paul faced the same issue when addressing the Ephesians and said,

> "Wherefore remember, that ye being in time past Gentiles in the flesh, who are called Uncircumcision by that which is called the Circumcision in the flesh made by hands; That at that time ye were without Christ, being aliens from the commonwealth of Israel, and strangers from the covenants of promise, having no hope, and without God in the world: But now in Christ Jesus ye who sometimes were far off are made nigh by the blood of Christ. For he is our peace, who hath made both one, and hath broken down the middle wall of partition between us; Having abolished in his flesh the enmity, even the law of commandments contained in ordinances; for to make in himself of twain one new man, so making peace; And that he might reconcile both unto God in one body by the cross, having slain the enmity thereby: And came and preached peace to you which were afar off, and to them that were nigh. For through him we both have access by one Spirit unto the Father. Now therefore ye are no more strangers and foreigners, but fellow citizens with the saints, and of the household of God" (Eph 2:11–19).

LUKE'S APOCALYPSE

Luke 17:20–37

[20]*Being asked by some from the Pharisees as to the coming of the kingdom of God, Jesus answered them and said, "The kingdom of God is not coming with observable signs.* [21]*Neither will they say, 'Look! It is here or it is there' because the kingdom of God is within you."* [22]*Then Jesus said to his disciples, "The days are coming when you will long to see one of the days of the Son of man but will not be able to see it.* [23]*They will say to you, 'Look! Here it is!' or 'Look!*

There it is!' but neither go with them nor follow them. ²⁴ *For just as the lightning flashes and gives light from one side of the heavens to the other, so it will be in the day of the Son of man.* ²⁵*But it is necessary first for him to suffer many things and be rejected by this generation.* ²⁶*And just as it happened in the days of Noah, so shall it be in the days of the Son of man.* ²⁷*They were eating and drinking and marrying and were being given in marriage until the day that Noah entered into the ark and the flood came and destroyed all.* ²⁸*Also, it will be as in the days of Lot. They were eating and drinking and buying and selling and building.* ²⁹*But in the day that Lot left Sodom, fire and brimstone fell from heaven and destroyed all.* ³⁰*So it will be on the day that the Son of man is revealed.* ³¹*On that day, those on the rooftop whose belongings are in the house should not go down to take them. Those working in the field in the same manner should not return to the village.* ³²*You make sure that you remember Lot's wife.* ³³*If anyone seeks to save his own life, he will lose it, but anyone who loses his life will save it.* ³⁴*I say to you that in that night, two people will be in one bed; one will be taken and the other will remain.* ³⁵*Two women will be grinding when one will be taken and the other will remain."*⁴² ³⁷*The disciples responded to Jesus saying, "Where, Lord?" And Jesus said to them, "The eagles will be gathered together where the body is."*

Identifying the participants of Jesus' conversation about the kingdom of God is a crucial first step to understanding Luke's apocalypse. The passage opens with Jesus being questioned by unnamed Pharisees about the kingdom of God. This group asked Jesus what would initiate the kingdom of God. Clearly the question flows from the current thought of the day that God would re-establish a theocracy as in the days of Moses or at least a Davidic styled monarchy. Either would lead to the repulsion of the Romans and better days for an independent Israel.

But the presence of Pharisees should not color Jesus' comments as antagonistic. Unlike the evangelist John who used "the Jews" in an exclusively adversarial role, Luke's "Pharisees" must be examined in each context. True, the Pharisees were described as lovers of money in Luke 16:14. But that statement should not be understood as applying to

---

42. The best ancient manuscripts do not include verse 36, "Two *men* shall be in the field; the one shall be taken, and the other left."

all Pharisees. Jesus told a parable about money, and the Pharisees who heard it scoffed. Jesus said to those Pharisees, who were in fact lovers of money, that a person cannot serve two masters. The reader should remember that it was a group of Pharisees who warned Jesus of Herod's death threats in Luke 13:31. Finally, Luke's own literary thesis of inclusion is sustained when the reader sees people from all walks of life being drawn to the gospel message of Christ. Even though the religious crowd often had great misunderstanding and often very poor motives, not all pious Jews of the day were diametrically opposed to the gospel message of the Christ. Jesus' instruction to these interested Pharisees was that the kingdom of God was not going to be initiated as they thought. The kingdom of God was in fact already present; the kingdom was within each of them.

Care should be given to the translation of this verse. The phrase ἐντὸς ὑμῶν ἐστιν (*entos humōn estin*) is translated "is within you." The only other occurrence in the New Testament of ἐντὸς (*entos*) is in Matthew 23:26. After a lengthy condemnation of hollow, ostentatious practices by the religious elite, Jesus said to the Pharisees, "Clean what is within the cup" and stop worrying about its appearance. Clearly by his use of ἐντὸς (*entos*) Luke intended to capture Jesus' teachings that the kingdom of God was already presence within the hearts of men, even some of the Pharisees.

Jesus turned to his apostles and took the conversation to the next level—the coming of the Son of man. More than a favorite self-designation, Jesus used the phrase Son of man to encourage a re-evaluation of the messianic hope that was common in the observance of Judaism. Here, the "days of the Son of man" is a direct reference to the first century expression *Days of the Messiah*. In verse 25 Jesus associated the Suffering Servant of Isaiah with the reference to the Son of man suffering many things and being rejected by the present generation. With this identification a new idea of the messianic rule is intended. "You will long for the days when I was with you in person," Jesus said to the disciples. "But rather than the messianic rule on earth you though you would have, there will be a messianic rule within you."

Jesus' teaching on this subject of this redefined messianic rule comes in the form of a warning. Jesus said to his disciples then and by way of extension to the church today: Don't accept a counterfeit

Messiah. The real messianic rule will be neither predictable, mistakable, nor escapable.

(1) The real messianic rule will not be predictable. To understand Luke's intent, the reader needs to return to the initial context of Jesus' statements. The Pharisees asked how imminent was the kingdom of God. Jesus said the kingdom of God would come without observation. The term for observation used in Luke 17:20, παρατηρήσεως (*paratērēseōs*), is found only here in the New Testament. The word is a medical reference to the process of diagnosing a disease from presenting symptoms. For example, you can watch a person progress through the stages of leprosy. With an acceptable degree of certainty, you can even predict the onset of the subsequent stages up to and including the fatal last days. This knowledge allowed for an appearance of control. But Jesus said the coming of the messianic rule—the kingdom of God—was beyond human control. The kingdom of God was not run on a human timetable. The kingdom of God takes control suddenly and without warning. Two are walking; one is taken. Two are working and talking; one is taken. There is no predictability.

(2) The real messianic rule will not be mistakable. The very question to Jesus speaks to the common occurrence of messianic pretenders. "Behold, it is here! Behold it is there!" Jesus said mockingly, "Do not be fooled. You will know the real deal when you see it. Just like the lightning flashes from one edge of the sky to the next, so the coming of the messianic rule will be certain."

(3) The real messianic rule will not be escapable. Jesus compared the days of the Son of man to the days of Noah and Lot. The verbs used to describe the daily activity of the people are all imperfect tense verbs. As such, these verbs describe continuing action in past time. The people of Noah's day were eating and drinking and marrying. Likewise, in Lot's day they were eating and drinking and buying and selling. It was business as usual. But then something happened. God closed the ark. God rained down fire and brimstone. God acted, and there was no escape.

Given these realities, there are two specific applications about the coming rule of God. Certainly Jesus spoke of the final consummation of the age where there would be ultimate rule of God. But relegating that understanding to some future point would be most unfortunate. Before indicating that the kingdom of God was neither predictable, mistakable, nor escapable, Jesus said the kingdom is now! It is in the hearts of his people. Furthermore, when God's kingdom is present and active, all other considerations become secondary. The lost world moves in a mun-

Journey to Jerusalem 243

dane sameness day after inexorable day. But for those in the kingdom, every day is an opportunity to participate in the rule of God.

THE PARABLE OF THE UNBIASED JUDGE: PRAYER

Luke 18:1–10

> ¹*Jesus told them a parable how it was necessary always to pray and not give up,* ²*saying, "There was judge in a certain city who neither feared God nor respected men.* ³*But a widow in this city kept coming to him, saying 'Vindicate me against my legal adversary.'* ⁴*For a long time, the judge did not desire to do so. But later he said to himself, 'Even though I neither fear God nor respect men,* ⁵*I will vindicate her because she will pester me to no end by her continual pleading.'* ⁶*And the Lord said, 'Hear what the unjust judge says:* ⁷*Will God not render vindication to his elect who cry to him day and night? Will God be slow to help them?* ⁸*I say to you that God will render vindication quickly.* ⁹*But when the Son of man does come, will he find faith on earth?'"*

Following the discussion of the coming of the kingdom, Jesus turned the disciples' attention to matters of personal devotion that in fact initiate or substantiate that the kingdom has come within men—specifically, prayer, humility, and unreserved commitment.

In the leading verses of chapter 18, Jesus told the disciples a parable about prayer. The typical explanation is that a widow was being oppressed. An easy target of an opportunistic and vile world, the widow could not defend herself and consequently was victimized. She then turned to the local magistrate for appeal. Described by the text as an unjust judge, the reader often concludes the judge may have even been in on the scam. Though inclined to ignore her pleas, the judge acquiesces under the pressure of the widow's constant begging. By comparing God to the unjust judge, the typical interpretation is that persistence pays. The problem with this view of the passage is that it glosses over Luke's description of both the judge and the widow.

First, there is the judge. Twice in the passage Jesus described the judge as neither fearing God nor respecting man. Rather than being unjust, this description applies to one who is completely unbiased. Nothing will prevent an impartial application of the law—not religious conviction, not personal emotion. This judge could not be bought. It was not until the judge reversed his initial opinion and ruled in the widow's favor that the text referred to him as an "unjust judge."

Second, there is the widow. By emphasizing the judge was completely impartial, one comes to a startling understanding. The widow was not being mistreated; she simply had no case. Whatever wrong she alleged had no merit.

Third, there is the application of the analogy that identifies the widow as the disciple, the judge as the Heavenly Father, and pleas for vindication as the prayers of the disciples. By attributing impartiality to the judge and lack of standing to the widow, a true understanding of prayer immerges. When the disciple is at a complete loss, God can act. Too often Christians believe they can cope with the reality of living a spiritual life in a fallen world without the abiding presence of God. What the child of God quickly learns is that such an attempt is completely futile. But when Christians realize they have no means of sustaining their spiritual life and turn to God from a position of complete vulnerability, something remarkable happens. God hears the prayers of the saint and speedily responds. Prayerful entry of this nature initiates the present manifestation of the kingdom.

The final admonition of the story adds an unexpected twist. "Will the Son of man find faith on earth?" asked Jesus. This addendum speaks regrettably to the lack of humility inherent within the human spirit. As such, this assertion both concludes the present section and introduces the next. By posing the question, Jesus made clear there would be some who lack faith. Inevitable is the conclusion that a person cannot go it alone. Like the widow, all will reach the point when the futility of individual ability is realized. All will reach the point where human effort will lack efficacy. Broken and defeated, all come to a point of acknowledging the all-powerful nature of God.

Yet that realization does not equate to salvation. A choice still remains. What will the broken and battered do with the knowledge that they cannot proceed on their own? What follows this decision is the final step of deprivation—knowing God but not choosing God. Only complete humility will lead a person to respond in faith and accept the love, support, and salvation of God.

SINNERS AND CHILDREN: HUMILITY

Luke 18:9–17

⁹Jesus told a parable to those who were convinced they were righteous and who condescended to everyone else. ¹⁰"Two men went up into the temple to pray, one a Pharisee and the other a tax collector. ¹¹The Pharisee stood and prayed before himself in this way, 'O God! I thank you that I am not as other men—greedy, dishonest, adulterous—for example, like this tax collector. ¹²I fast twice each week; I give a tenth of all that I earn.' ¹³But the tax collector stood afar off, not willing even to lift his eyes to heave, but beat his chest saying, 'O God! Have mercy on me, a sinner.' ¹⁴I say to you, this man, the sinner, went down to his house having been justified, not the other. The one exalting himself will be humbled and the one humbling himself will be exalted." ¹⁵Simultaneously, people were bringing even infants to Jesus for him to touch them. Seeing this, the disciples began prohibiting the action. ¹⁶But calling them to himself, Jesus said, "Let the little children come unto me and do not hinder their coming, for to such belongs the kingdom of God. ¹⁷Indeed I say to you, whoever does not receive the kingdom of God as a child does will not enter into the same."

Luke's narrative continued to identify what initiates present manifestations of the kingdom of God by presenting Jesus' teachings on humility typically depicted as two separate incidences. First, Jesus began telling a parable about the self-righteous Pharisee and the self-effacing tax collector. On the one hand, there was a person whose actions and activities provided the appearance of righteousness. The Pharisee stood tall and took pride in his separatist attitude. He rehearsed his accomplishments—fasting, tithing, and avoiding the sins of greed, dishonesty and lust. In short, he based his salvation on those things he could control. On the other hand was one who relinquished even the appearance of control. A tax collector, a despised person, he bowed in humility and acknowledged his sin. All he could do was beg for mercy, offering no merit of his own.

Far from vilifying the tax collector, Jesus praised him. Two men went to the temple, but only one worshiped. "One man," Jesus said, "returned home having been justified." The word Luke used for justified was δεδικαιωμένος *dedikaiōmenos*). The word appears as a perfect passive participle. The perfect tense of the verbal adjective indicates completed action in past time. The passive voice indicates the subject was acted on. The Pharisee thought he would justify himself by his actions. The sinner who begged for mercy did nothing but was justified.

The story ends with the epilogue of humility and exaltation. True humility does not seek its own advantage. True humility is often surprised at being exalted. Jesus' final statement drives home the point of the parable. A person can do nothing to merit inclusion in the kingdom, but humble submission to God initiates its present manifestation.

Into this teaching moment came a living parable. While hanging on every word Jesus spoke, the disciples were rudely interrupted by adults, no doubt many of them parents, who were bringing children and infants to Jesus for his blessing. In order to get control of the situation, the disciples began forbidding the action. Jesus reprimanded the disciples and began beckoning the children to himself. In addition to teaching that humility initiates the present manifestation of the kingdom, Jesus used the moment to create a stark visual depiction. The children desired nothing more than the presence of Jesus. They cared neither for eschatology nor kingdom theology. They wanted to be with Jesus. Simple humility was depicted by simple trust—not ability, not activity—just trust. It was to such that Jesus said the kingdom, both now and in the future, belongs.

THE RICH RULER: ABSOLUTE COMMITMENT

Luke 18:18–30

[18]A ruler asked Jesus, "Good Teacher! What must I do to inherit eternal life?" [19]Jesus said to him, "Why do you call me good? No one is good except God alone. [20]You know the commandments: Do not commit adultery. Do not steal. Do not murder. Do not bear false witness. Honor your father and mother." [21]The ruler answered Jesus, "All of these I have observed since my youth." [22]When Jesus heard this, he said to him, "Only one thing you lack. Sell all that you have and distribute the same to the poor. Then you will have treasure in heaven and you may come follow me!" [23]Hearing this, the ruler became sorrowful for he was very rich. [24]Looking at him, Jesus said, "How difficult indeed it is for one having money to

> enter the kingdom of God. ²⁵It is easier for a camel to go through the eye of a needle than for a rich man to enter the kingdom of God." ²⁶But the ones overhearing this said, "Who then is able to be saved?" ²⁷Jesus said to them, "What is impossible with men is possible with God." ²⁸Then Peter said, "Behold, we have left our homes and have followed you." ²⁹Jesus said to them, "Truly I say to you there is no one who has left house or wife or brothers, or parents, or children, for the sake of the kingdom of God ³⁰who will not receive more in this time and in the coming age, eternal life."

Described only by Luke as a ruler, an affluent, eminent man approached Jesus with a question. In his response, Jesus indicated the third means by which present manifestations of the kingdom of God are initiated. The question posed to Jesus was, "What can a person do in order to inherit eternal life?"

Regarding the inquiry, the reader must first decide if it is in fact a sincere question and not a trick question. From a strictly legal sense, no Jew would think an inheritance could be earned. An inheritance was an issue of birthright. If Jesus said to do such and such, the ruler would then have room for complaint.

However, if the question was sincere, the conversation takes on a different tone. Much like those who prompted the Good Samaritan narrative, this individual appears to be pursing the path of least resistance. "What is the absolute minimum that I must do in order to be assured a place in the kingdom?" the man asked.

In response, Jesus turned the question on itself. "What does the law say on this subject? Well, let's see. There is that adultery thing and that murder thing. Oh and yes, you cannot steal or bear false witness, and finally one must respect parental authority. How about these things?"

This was great news to the prominent citizen. "I have always observed these things! Do you mean that is it?"

"Well, there is one more small detail," Jesus said. "There is that commitment thing."

"Commitment thing? I don't remember studying about any 'commitment thing' in Hebrew school. What are you talking about?"

"Oh, absolutely," Jesus said, "The commitment thing may be the most important of all. It means you are willing to do anything required of you. It means nothing else can be more important. It means you have unqualified, unquestioned, and unrelenting devotion to God."

"Are you sure?" said the man.

"I am quite sure," said Jesus. "And what is more, the commitment thing is different for every disciple. What God asks of one may not be asked of another. For example, Peter over there is going to be asked to relinquish control of his ability so that the Father can work. Thomas here is going to be asked to give up his dependence on his extraordinary intellect. And you, God wants you to forego reliance on wealth. So, go. Sell all you have. Then go about distributing those proceeds to the poor. Then you will be able to come and follow me."

What follows in the text is Jesus' commentary on the scene. Seeing the man's great disappointment, Jesus indicated dependence on wealth and creature comforts is a tremendous barrier to complete commitment. Most people of wealth have accrued the same by making its acquisition the driving force in their lives. As such, they are reluctant to relinquish the control their station, rank, and accumulated wealth allow them to maintain. Not being able to become vulnerable and trust anyone other than themselves, they also are not able to trust God. The statement "It is easier for a camel to pass through the eye of a needle" is misleading as Jesus intended it as a superlative and not a comparative statement as the English translation implies. It is in fact impossible for a camel to pass through the eye of a needle. In the same way, it is impossible for someone who trusts anything or anyone other than God to enter into the kingdom of heaven.

But to return to the current theme of acts of discipleship that enables present manifestations of the kingdom, Jesus said anyone who had sacrificed anything for the sake of the kingdom would receive much more in return. Specifically, Jesus said they would receive more in the kingdom now and eternal life in the kingdom to come. Only complete dedication that holds nothing in reserve will enable a person to participate in what occurs in the kingdom of God.

One last aspect of Luke's rich ruler narrative must be examined. In the context of demonstrating complete and unreserved commitment to God, it is important to stress that God uniquely enables a person to fulfill this charge of discipleship. In directing the man to give all his possessions, Luke recorded διάδος (*diados*), meaning distribute, rather than Matthew's and Mark's δὸς (*dos*), meaning give. Jesus did not simply want the man to divest himself of his wealth; Jesus wanted him to participate in giving it to the poor. Knowing God never asks his disciples to do anything he does not equip them to do, one must conclude this young ruler had great compassion for people. Yet that skill had somehow been suppressed in favor of the crass task of amassing wealth. The irony of the exchange was even more discouraging to the man as he heard Jesus say, "Anyone can make money, but not just anyone can care for people. Why did you sell out your gift? What you thought was important, what you thought would bring you happiness, has robbed you of true joy that not only brings God's kingdom into the here and now but which also lasts for all eternity."

THE CLOSE OF THE JUDEAN MINISTRY AND IMPENDING SUFFERING

Luke 18:31–34

³¹Taking the Twelve aside, Jesus said to them, "Listen carefully. We are going up unto Jerusalem, and all that has been written in the prophets about the Son of man will be fulfilled; ³²for he will be delivered to the Gentiles to be ridiculed, insulted, and spit upon; ³³and being beaten with a whip, they will kill him, but on the third day he will raise himself up." ³⁴But the disciples understood none of these things because these words were hidden from them. They did not comprehend what was being said.

As in the final days of the Galilean Ministry (Luke 9:44–45), Jesus signaled the closing moments of the Judean Ministry by returning to the theme of the imminent suffering of the Son of man. The significance of the repetition should be understood as a matter of focus. At every major intersection of his life, Jesus remained dedicated to fulfilling the plan of salvation set before him. Though always deemed worth the effort in retrospect, discipleship always bears a cost in human terms.

But Luke signaled more than just the closing of the itinerate ministry of Jesus. For the third time in his Gospel, Luke recorded Jesus' statements about the suffering of the Messiah. After Peter's confession of Jesus' identity as the Christ, Jesus said the Son of man must suffer many things, be rejected, and killed (Luke 9:22). Only eight days later, following the transfiguration, Jesus again told the disciples the Son of man would be handed over to the authorities (Luke 9:44). The third prediction of his suffering came at the end of the Judean Ministry when Jesus called his disciples aside and indicated the suffering of the Messiah was in fulfillment of Scripture (Luke 18:31–35).

Rather than seeing these as three separate events, Luke twice recorded a statement that drew the events together. As the Galilean and Judean ministries drew to a close, Jesus made a statement or statements about the purpose of the incarnation, followed by an explanatory comment about the disciples' understanding. In Luke 9:45 and again in Luke 18:34, Luke stated that they *understood none of these things*. What is even more telling, given Luke's literary mastery, is the repetition within the statement. At the end of the Galilean Ministry and at the end of the Judean Ministry, Luke indicated not once but twice that the disciples did not comprehend what Jesus was saying.

Taken separately, this could be viewed as Luke's propensity to provide detail in the description of the settings. But taken as a pattern, a far more beautiful meaning emerges.

(1) Jesus told the disciples difficult days were ahead. There should never be the misconception in the life of the child of God that living a godly life in an ungodly and fallen world will always be easy. Doing so will always be worth the effort but frequently will test the endurance of the saints. By nature of the very fact that the Christian seeks to be a force for good in a world system gone terribly bad, struggles will come. Of this one thing, Jesus wanted his disciples to be sure.

(2) But beyond anticipating difficulty, Luke captured a detail of discipleship that dare not be missed. In addition to enduring struggles, trials, and difficulty, the disciple often is called on to do so without an understanding as to why the events are taking place. And that is OK! It is as if Jesus were saying, "I am going to suffer as part of God's will, and that's OK. You will not understand why, and that's OK. Furthermore, as I was persecuted, so will you be. When that happens, you probably will not understand, and that's OK. What is not OK is turning in the face of difficulty to your own understanding and when that understanding fails, you walk away from the kingdom's service. So, stay the course. Trust what you do know. Trust me."

(3) Finally, the reason the disciple can trust without understanding is because God always is in control. Both references to the coming persecution include Jesus' discussion related to dying and living again.

The resurrection is never out of sight of the crucifixion. Furthermore, Luke's recording of Jesus' statement is very important. At the end of the Galilean Ministry, Jesus said the Son of man would be handed over and killed. But afterward he would ἐγερθῆναι (*egerthēnai*), "be raised" (Luke 9:22). The word ἐγερθῆναι (*egerthēnai*) is an aorist passive infinitive. The passive voice indicates another will act upon the subject. Jesus said that even though he was going to die, God would raise him from the dead.

In a related fashion at the end of the Judean Ministry, Jesus said the Son of man would be flogged and killed and on the third day ἀναστήσεται (*anastēsetai*), "raise himself up" (Luke 18:33). The term ἀναστήσεται (*anastēsetai*) is a future indicative middle verb. Unlike the passive voice that receives the action of the verb, the middle voice completes and receives the action of the verb. Thus Jesus indicated he would raise himself. Though entombed in the earth, Jesus was neither dead nor absent. One with the Father, Jesus was in complete control. It is no wonder that when describing Jesus' power over death that Paul shouted, "O death, where is thy sting? O grave, where is thy victory?" (1 Cor 15:55). Christ overcame the defeat of the present world and accomplished all the Father required of him. Is it any wonder Luke wanted the early church to understand the power of this reality? Yes, there would be difficulties. Yes, there would be disappointments and struggles. But the child of God need not worry nor even understand. God has overcome and is in complete control.

A BLIND MAN SEES JESUS

Luke 18:35–43

³⁵Now a blind man was sitting near the roadside begging as Jesus drew near to Jericho. ³⁶Hearing a crowd passing by, he asked what was happening. ³⁷Those from among the crowd told him that Jesus of Nazareth was passing by. ³⁸So the blind man shouted, saying, "Jesus, Son of David! Have mercy on me!" ³⁹Those who were in front of Jesus rebuked the blind man that he should be silent, but the blind man cried out all the more, "Son of David! Have mercy on me!" ⁴⁰Stopping the procession, Jesus ordered the blind man should be brought to him. As he approached, Jesus asked him, ⁴¹"What do you desire that I should do for you?" To which he answered, "Lord, that I may be able to see." ⁴²Then Jesus said,

"Receive your sight; your faith has saved you." ⁴³*Immediately, the blind man received his sight and began following Jesus, glorifying God.* ⁴⁴*Seeing this, all the people gave praise to God.*

To understand the beauty of this incident in the life of Jesus, one must begin with the end in mind. As the scene drew to a conclusion, Jesus said to the blind man, "Receive your sight; your faith has saved you." Translated by the New International Version and the Revised Standard Version as "healed you" and "made you well" respectively, σωζω (sōzō) means to save someone from harm, to rescue a person from danger, or to prevent one from suffering by healing them of disease. In the current passage, the implication is the blind man received more than sight. The text indicates he began following Jesus. The extent of the discipleship is left unanswered. But without a doubt something remarkable happened to the blind beggar that day on the road to Jericho; his life intersected the life of Jesus, and his body and his personality were never the same again.

It is the degree of this "saving faith" that becomes the subject of the balance of the passage. What creates saving faith? What moves a person beyond curiosity to belief? What kind of interest wells up within a person's soul that causes him or her to reach out and receive what God has to offer? The text suggests there are four attributes that generate and sustain saving faith.

(1) Saving faith is prompt. From limited involvement with compassionate donors, the blind beggar followed current events. What was happening in the lives of his small circle of family and friends no doubt was part of his basic human experience. To an unknown degree, the man would have knowledge about town affairs, as people stopped to pass the time. Unable to do anything else, the man also simply listened to the conversation of those passing by. It is therefore not too great an assumption to assert at least a limited knowledge of Jesus. When a commotion was obvious, the beggar asked what was happening. The text indicated the crowd was passing by. As such, there would not have been time to research the identity of this Jesus of Nazareth. To the contrary, the beggar was ready to respond instantly to the opportunity. "Strike while the iron is hot" and "make hay while the sun is shining" are not only accurate axioms for productive metal workers and farmers. These phrases carry the wisdom of the ages that opportunity waits for no one. Given

the movement of the crowd, a delay on the part of the beggar would have been devastating. He had no time to debate, no time to think, no time to worry about the consequences of his action. He only had time to trust. Saving faith is prompt.

(2) Saving faith is persistent. When the beggar cried out for mercy, those who were going before Jesus sought to silence him. If Jesus had been a 21st century politician, these individuals might have been called "handlers." They went out on "the rope line" to eliminate any obstacle. They had an interest in getting Jesus to his destination and no consideration for any impediment. This blind beggar was a distraction they did not need.

But opposition does not dissuade saving faith. The more they attempted to quell his cries for help, the louder he became. When nothing else will do except to be with Jesus, faith breaks through to miraculous results.

(3) Saving faith always is full of praise. The term δοξάζων (*doxazōn*) is a present active participle that modifies how the blind man began following Jesus. The tense of the participle conveys a continuous action. He began following Jesus, also in a continuous fashion, but as he did, he was constantly glorifying God for what Jesus had done. What is more, saving faith that is full of praise is contagious, causing a ground swell of involvement. The crowds who saw what had happened gave glory to God. In short, the praise that accompanies saving faith expands in every increasing, concentric circles, encompassing all that it pervades.

(4) Saving faith is pervasive. It is on this final point, the universality of the gospel message of saving faith, that one last lesson must not be overlooked. Only three times in his Gospel did Luke use the phrase "Jesus of Nazareth." Jesus was rejected in Nazareth after delivering his message of inclusion (Luke 4:18–28). From there, Jesus traveled to Capernaum where a demon proclaimed in the synagogue, *What does this have to do with you and us? Have you come to destroy us? We know who you are, the Holy Son of God* (Luke 4:34). Here in this passage, the crowd announced to the beggar that the commotion was due to the presence of "Jesus of Nazareth" (Luke 18:37). Finally, when Jesus joined the two disciples on the road to Emmaus, he asked them what caused the disturbance in Jerusalem, to which they replied, "Jesus of Nazareth" (Luke 24:19). In all three incidences, recognition of Jesus was by the relatively uniformed. Those closest to Jesus may have known more about Jesus, may

have known more about God's plan for the Son of man, but that did not stop the greater public from knowing enough about Jesus to propagate the gospel. Those nearest to Jesus may have had the benefit of intimate communion, growing ever closer and closer with each precious moment spent with the Master, but that did not mean the masses had no part in the invasive spread of the good news. Once started, once encouraged by the slightest belief, saving faith is pervasive.

A BAD MAN MAKES GOOD: FAITH IN ACTION

Luke 19:1-10

¹Then Jesus entered and was passing Jericho. ²Now there was a man whose name was called Zacchaeus, who was a tax-collecting executive; he was rich. ³Zacchaeus was seeking to see who Jesus was but was not able because of the crowd; his stature was small. ⁴So, running ahead of the crowd, he climbed up a sycamore tree in order that he might see Jesus as he was about to pass by that way. ⁵As he came to that place, Jesus looked up and said to him, "Zacchaeus, climb down quickly. It is necessary for me to stay in your house today." ⁶Zacchaeus climbed down quickly and joyfully welcomed Jesus as a house guest. ⁷But seeing this, everyone grumbled, saying "This man enters as a guest of sinners!" ⁸But standing, Zacchaeus said to the Lord, "Half of all my possessions, Lord, I will give to the poor. Furthermore, if I have cheated anyone, I will restore it fourfold." ⁹Jesus said to Zacchaeus, "Today salvation has come to this house because he too is a son of Abraham. ¹⁰For the Son of man came to seek and to save that which had been lost."

Immediately following his discussion of the attributes of saving faith, Luke presented an incident from Jesus' life that complemented the preceding narrative. Two aspects of the story are highly significant—the continued open manner in which Jesus embraced his destiny and the open manner in which Zacchaeus demonstrated faith in action.

Paramount to understanding the Zacchaeus story is Jesus' conclusion. Regarding the entire encounter with Zacchaeus, Jesus said salvation had come to the house. Furthermore, that announcement was accompanied by the affirmation that Zacchaeus was in fact a son of Abraham. Caution should be exercised in understanding Jesus' statement. John the

Baptist had specifically excluded the empty religious expressions of the Pharisees claiming God could raise up children of Abraham from the multiple indigenous stones of Palestine (Luke 3:8). Just being a Jew did not automatically correlate to being pleasing to God, but neither, however, did being a Jew preclude a person from being in right relationship to God. The interesting twist in the story is that in the eyes of popular culture, Zacchaeus's activity had excluded him from his native citizenry. Because he chose to participate with the Roman government as a tax collector, Zaachaeus was a man without a country. Jesus' statement made it clear that a person's identity, while demonstrated by his actions, is in fact distinct and different from the sum total of his or her actions.

Given Jesus' statement about Zacchaeus's identity as a son of Abraham and given that salvation had come to his home, Zacchaeus's action become more understandable. Zacchaeus was a person of faith whose chosen profession placed him in a compromised position. Able to extort those who were subject to him, greed began dictating his actions. Yet his interaction with Jesus indicates there was more to him than the collection of bad behavior. While his actions and activities were inconsistent with a person of faith, there remained within him something that pushed him forward. Perhaps it was that Zacchaeus had been taught as a child to love God and obey the law. Perhaps the desire to be pleasing to God was not extinguished by the ambition to amass wealth. Even though his poor choices had quieted the inner voice that cried out to God, evident from the details of the story is that it had not been silenced. Something was still there, deep within, yearning to break free from the bondage of self-imposed chains, something that could be seen in Zacchaeus's faith in action.

(1) Faith in action reaches out to know Jesus. Created in the image of God, all humanity longs to return to its maker. Unfortunately, in an increasingly secular world, the competition for the soul of humanity is great. Immediate gratification, intense experience, justification of anything that "feels good" are part of a universe gone bad. Satan continues to lure people away from the worship of and fellowship with God.

But remaining within each person is the awareness that only God can satisfy their deepest longings. Such was the urge that prompted Zacchaeus to find out more about Jesus. The text indicates he desired to know just exactly who was this Jesus. He no doubt had heard the stories about healing and teaching. Maybe Zacchaeus even scoffed publicly when hearing of a possible Messiah while quietly and privately he hoped this was the moment in time when God would reveal himself. Regardless of the details, Zacchaeus began overcoming the obstacles that stood between him and Jesus. He could not get through the crowd so he ran ahead of it. He was too short to see over the crowd, so he climbed a tree that lined Jesus' path. Because faith is a divinely imparted attribute, even the smallest amount will seek out God.

(2) Faith in action reacts quickly when presented the opportunity to learn more about Jesus. Had this been an event driven by intellectual curiously alone, perhaps the events would have unfolded differently. Zacchaeus wanted firsthand information. Climbing a tree produced the physical evidence; he wanted to see and he saw. That ends that.

But that is not how the day unfolded. Faith in action will respond obediently to the call. Jesus commanded Zacchaeus come down quickly, and the text indicates he climbed down quickly. Far from empty repetition, Luke's literary ability was designed to reflect the degree to which faith prompts obedience.

(3) Faith in action responds to conviction. If all that faith accomplishes in a person is to place him or her in right relationship with God, its outward manifestations would be virtually nonexistent. To the contrary, right relation with God always demands responsible relation with mankind. The Ten Commandments are routinely explained as being divided between vertical issues, humanity's relation to God, and horizontal issues, humanity's relation to humanity. Without ethical demands for right living and acceptable conduct, religion would be hollow indeed.

Accordingly, as a man seeking to be in right relation to God, Zacchaeus demonstrated his faith in action by confessing his sin and by seeking to make restitution, actions that were prescribed by law. "And the Lord spake unto Moses, saying, Speak unto the children of Israel, When a man or woman shall commit any sin that men commit, to do a trespass against the Lord, and that person be guilty; then they shall confess their sin which they have done: and he shall recompense his trespass with the principal thereof, and add unto it the fifth part thereof, and give it unto him against whom he hath trespassed" (Num 5:5–7). Furthermore, "If a man shall steal an ox, or a sheep, and kill it, or sell it; he shall restore five oxen for an ox, and four sheep for a sheep" (Exod 22:1). When Zacchaeus gave half of his possessions to the poor and repaid fourfold those he swindled, he proved the sincerity of his faith.

Beyond showing Zacchaeus's faith, the narrative demonstrates the open acceptance on the part of Jesus of his role as the suffering Messiah. Jesus knew that reaching out to a sinner, especially one as notorious as a chief tax collector for the Roman government, would draw criticism. Precisely on cue, the crowd grumbled at the notion that Jesus would be his house guest. After all, the acceptable crowd had succeeded in ostracizing Zacchaeus. The people prohibited Zacchaeus from gaining access to Jesus in the public forum just like they had prohibited his access to every other social circle of any importance. Jesus knew his actions would speak volumes to the superficial crowd.

But Jesus was willing to accept their scorn in order to accomplish his purpose. Two comments indicate his intention. One, salvation had come to the house of a son of Abraham, and two, the Son of man came to seek and to save the lost. By enabling Zacchaeus's faith in action, Jesus accomplished the Father's will.

The same remains the unrelenting task of the church today. Regardless of the cost, citizens of the kingdom should seek to engage the lost in the conversations that lead them to Jesus. Created with a longing to be in fellowship and in perfect harmony with their God, all humanity has the opportunity to respond and to place their own faith in action.

THE PARABLE OF THE POUNDS

Luke 19:11–27

[11] As they heard these things, Jesus proceeded to tell them a parable because they were drawing near to Jerusalem and because they all supposed the kingdom of God would appear immediately. [12] Jesus said, "A nobleman went to a distant land to receive a kingdom and then to return. [13] Calling ten of his servants, the nobleman gave to each of the ten a mina [a golden Greek coin worth approximately one hundred day wages] and he said to each of them, 'Conduct business until I return.' [14] But his own people hated him and sent an envoy after him saying, 'We do not desire you to rule over us!' [15] Upon his return, after he had received his kingdom, he summoned the servants to whom he had given the money to find out what the entrusted money had earned. [16] Coming to the noble man, the first one said, 'Lord, your one mina has made ten mina.'

> ¹⁷ The nobleman said to the servant, 'Well done, good servant! You have been faithful over the smallest; now you are in authority over ten cities.' ¹⁸ A second servant came to the nobleman saying, 'Your one mina, Lord, has made five mina.' ¹⁹ The nobleman said to the servant, 'Be over five cities.' ²⁰ Another servant came saying, 'Lord, behold your mina which I keep stored safely in a napkin; ²¹ for I was afraid of you, because you are a hard man, taking up what you did not put down and reaping what you did not sow.' ²² The nobleman said to this servant, 'I will judge you by your own words, wicked servant! You knew that I am a hard man, taking up what I did not put down and reaping what I did not sow. ²³ Why did you not put my money in the bank? Then upon my return, I would have collected it with interest.' ²⁴ Then the nobleman said to the ones standing by, 'Take the mina from him and give it to the one having ten mina.'" ²⁵ Jesus' disciples reacted saying, "But Lord, he already has ten!" ²⁶ To which Jesus responded, "I say to you, to everyone who has more will be given and from those who do not have, even what they have will be taken away. ²⁷ But back to the parable, the nobleman said, 'But as for my enemies who did not desire that I rule over them, bring them in and execute them before me.'"

As the final incident in the Galilean Ministry, the parable of the pounds has several obvious themes. There is the theme that God invests in the lives of his children, expecting to gain more in return. Furthermore, there is the theme that faithfulness leads to greater responsibility. Finally, the parable teaches there are consequences for tentative behavior and those who fail to recognize the gravity of the eternal nature of kingdom issues are in fact punished for their disobedience and lack of engagement.

Unique to the Gospels of Matthew and Luke, the parable of the talents (Matthew) and the parable of the pounds (Luke) have many similarities. In both, the master of the story entrusts his resources to his servants prior to departing on a journey. During the master's absence, the servants were expected to invest through whatever means necessary to yield a return. No details are given as to the manner by which two of the servants made these investments. The narrative only indicates that upon accounting, the wise servants produced more than they were originally given. The only clue as to a possible method is seen from the master's comments to the fearful servant that the money could have been placed with the bankers and an interest exacted. While no specific instructions were presented to the servants other than to "do business until I return," it is obvious they were expected to use the entrusted resources wisely.

Regarding the nature of the reward presented to the faithful servants, one should understand that only those who looked after their master's interest received the blessing, "Well done, good and faithful servant." Unspoken in the parable is the concept of stewardship. Without being told, the faithful and wicked servant alike understood the deposited resources were not their own. They knew they had been given a trust. They knew they were only managers of something that was not theirs. What was uncertain was how much like their master they would be in furthering his cause. Two from the story acted in a way in keeping with the character of their master. They either knew what he would have done with his assets or at least what he was likely to have done. Such knowledge no doubt would have been enhanced by having spent time with the master, observing even the smallest of tendencies. The third servant admittedly knew the traits of his master but allowed fear of failure to influence negatively his action. The wicked servant did not seek to advance his master's cause.

But perhaps the most compelling theme of the parable is understood by properly identifying those who reacted to Jesus' parable. The grammar of verse 25 is ambiguous, leaving the reader to decide the antecedent of the third personal pronoun "they." Those objecting to the nobleman giving the one mina to the servant who had ten mina must have been those listening to the parable and not characters in the parable. The strength of the reaction identifies a key component to the narrative that is heightened by their objection. *You must be kidding! Where is the fairness in that? Where is the forgiveness in that?* they must have thought.

Jesus paused telling the parable to explain that more would be given to those who had and those who did not have would get even less. The stark objection indicates disciples of all ages often mistakenly equate the never-ending love of God that extends salvation to all regardless of their circumstances with an all-patient permissiveness that will allow a child of God to continue to err and continue to live a life of disobedience that does not take seriously the charge to look to the master's business. Salvation and discipleship are two different things. Freely offered by God, salvation is a gift. Discipleship is a commitment that costs the Christian everything. When this principle is lived out in the lives of kingdom citizens, a class gap opens into an enormous chasm. There are those who look to the master's interests, learning from constant fellowship, implementing character traits learned from Jesus and accomplishing great things for the sake of the kingdom. Sadly, there are those who in timidity and fear hide resources entrusted to them—assets intended to be used to advance the cause of Christ. These find that being a disciple exacts a toil. They see others experiencing joy and victory they scarcely if ever have known. As Barclay claimed, "There is no such thing as standing still in the Christian life. We either get more or lose what we had. We either advance to greater heights or slip back every day."[43]

Luke's inclusion in his narrative of this event from Jesus' life is highly intentional. Jesus himself lived out this parable as he faced his final assignment. Jesus too had been entrusted with assets intended to be used for the Father's cause. For Jesus, discipleship was about to cost him his life. In fear, doubt and selfish preservation, Jesus could have turned away, the cost of which would have been the opportunity to accomplish God's will. This story stands at the pentacle of not only the Galilean Ministry. It stands also at the precipice of the incarnation itself.

---

43. Barclay, *The Gospel of Luke*, 248.

3

Jerusalem and Beyond

THE ROYAL ENTRY[1]

Luke 19:28–40

²⁸*Having said this, Jesus went ahead, going up to Jerusalem. ²⁹It happened as he drew near to Bethphage and Bethany at the place called the Mount of Olives that he sent two of his disciples ³⁰saying, "Go into the village and upon entering you will find a tied donkey, upon which no man has ever sat. Turn it loose and bring it here. ³¹If anyone says to you, 'What are you doing?' say 'The Lord has need of it.' ³²Those having been sent went away and found things just as Jesus told them. ³³As they were loosening the donkey its owner said to them, "Why are you untying the donkey?" ³⁴So they said, "The Lord has need of it." ³⁵They brought the donkey to Jesus and throwing their garments the donkey, they sat Jesus upon him. ³⁶As they rode along, they also spread their garments upon the way. ³⁷As Jesus drew near the descent of the Mount of Olives the entire host of disciples began rejoicing and praising God with a great voice for all the mighty works they had seen, ³⁸saying, "Blessed is the King who comes in the name of the Lord! Peace in heaven! Glory on high!" ³⁹When this happened, some of the Pharisees in the multitude said to Jesus, "Teacher!*

---

1. Beginning with the journey to Jerusalem and throughout the balance of the Gospel, there is a noticeable change in Luke's literary tone. It is as if Luke were seeking to capture in the narrative the same momentum that was carrying Jesus forward to the culmination of this ministry as Savior of the world. In like fashion, the commentary on these sections are brief and to the point, seeking to honor the intent of the Gospel writer.

Rebuke your disciples!" ⁴⁰*But Jesus answered them, "I say to you, If they become silent, the very stones would cry out!"*

As was true of the final days of the Judean ministry, the first event of the Jerusalem Passion ministry continued to define the nature of Messiah and the identity of Jesus as the same. Often mislabeled as a "triumphant" entry to Jerusalem, the image of Jesus descending the Mount of Olives and entering Jerusalem is correctly understood as a coronation or royal entry.

In a triumphant entry the returning warrior was seated on a noble steed. Paraded with the ruler were the conquests of the battle: slaves, captured war implements, and often strange bounty from far away places. Included in the processional would be the military entourage that facilitated the king's victory. After a successful campaign against the Philistines, King Saul returned to exuberant crowds who sang the praises of Saul and David in true triumphant entry fashion (1 Sam 18:6–7).

But Jesus did not enter Jerusalem as a military force poised to capture a kingdom and subjugate its citizens under the auspices of a new king. When Zadok the priest and Nathan the prophet confirmed Solomon in a coronation, they were following King David's directions. Solomon was the true heir to the throne and had been named by David as his successor (1 Kings 1:32–40). So too Jesus entered Jerusalem as the rightful sovereign of the kingdom of God. When Solomon was coroneted, the people sang, "Long live King Solomon!" "And all the people came up after him, and the people piped with pipes, and rejoiced with great joy, so that the earth rent with the sound of them" (1 Kings 1:40). So too when Jesus entered Jerusalem the people cried, "Blessed is the King who comes in the name of the Lord! Peace in heaven! Glory on high!" Jesus came to claim his true place as Lord of lords and King of kings. But Jesus did so through an invitation, not through an invasion.

A PRIVATE MOMENT IN A PUBLIC EVENT

Luke 19:41–44

⁴¹*Seeing the city as he drew near, Jesus wept over Jerusalem* ⁴²*saying, "If only you knew even today that which brings peace; but even now it is hid from your eyes.* ⁴³*The days are coming when your enemies will put up an embankment and surround you and*

> hem you up on all sides, **44**and dash you and your children within you to the ground. They will not leave stone upon stone within you because you did not know the time of your visitation.

More than just a prediction of the destruction of Jerusalem, Jesus' emotional outpouring as he descended the Mount of Olives provides a unique view of the Messiah. Jesus was compassionate regardless of the cost. Jesus knew that going to Jerusalem would seal his fate. He would not escape the venom of those who sought his life. As early as the Galilean ministry, Jesus intended to fulfill the Father's will in Jerusalem. Yet even knowing what awaited him there, Jesus still was moved to compassion at the site of the great city teaming with activity and motion that spanned the full range of human experience. Jesus knew that before him lay the purpose of the incarnation.

In Calvin Miller's wonderful parody of the life of Jesus, the Singer learned that the Father-Spirit had given him the Ancient Star-Song and was calling him to spread its life-giving melody of love and hope. After the baptism by the River-Singer and temptation by the World-Hater, the Troubadour returned to his childhood home where he encountered Mary. They spoke of his true identity as the Singer. Then Mary asked,

> "You know the final verse?"
> "I know it all," he answered back. "But I'll not sing it here. I'll wait till I am on the wall. Then alone the melody will fall upon thick ears."
> "They will not like the final verse," she said.
> "They will not like it, for its music is beyond their empty days and makes them trade their littleness for life."
> "The self of every singer of the song must die to know its music?"
> "They all must die, and ever does the self die hard. It screams and begs in pity not to go. Nor can it bear to let the Father-Spirit own the soul."
> He turned the thoughts methodically within his mind then spoke again, "Mother, I shall sing the song while I move out to seek more singers who like me are quite content to sing, then die."
> She knew that he was right, but found it hard to talk of joyous life and painful death at the same time. How odd the song born on Earthmaker's breath should lead his only Troubadour to death.
> "I cannot bear to see you die. Let all the world go by. Don't sing upon the wall. At least don't sing the hell-bound ancient curse. If you must sing of life leave off the final verse."
> "I go," he said. "God give me strength to sing upon the wall—the Great Walled City of the Ancient King."

> He turned.
> She cried.
> "Leave off the final verse and not upon the wall."
> He kissed her.
> "I can't ignore the Father-Spirit's call so I will sing it there, and I will sing it all."[2]

Not only was Jesus compassionate regardless of the cost but his presence also offered peace until the very end. Luke used a second-class conditional sentence to record Jesus' longing for those of Jerusalem. "If even today you knew that it was my visitation that held the key to your peace, you could embrace me and inherit the kingdom," Jesus said emotionally. The significance of the second-class statement is that it presents a condition that is undetermined. "Even today," Jesus said, "You could choose to accept what I came to offer." Though time is unpredictable and no one knows its extent, the opportunity to accept is ever present. Jesus said that his visitation is the key to the peace that the world seeks and that anyone at anytime can accept his offer of peace. The problem with open opportunity is that humanity inevitably will delay. Unfortunately, with time comes callous, cold behavior that hardens the soul and deafens the ear to God's call. Events were set in motion in Jerusalem that day that would not change. Though some experienced God's presence by what was to occur before their very eyes, most lived through the single most important moment in history without any notice. They had set a course that caused them to march pedantically past the very thing they sought without even the slightest notice. Only God's presence gives God's peace. While mankind may become incapable of receiving, God never fails to provide.

CLEANSING THE TEMPLE: THE POINT OF NO RETURN

Luke 19:45–48

> ⁴⁵As Jesus entered the temple, he began casting out the moneychangers, ⁴⁶saying, "It is written, My house is a house of prayer, but you have made it a robbers' hideout." ⁴⁷Afterward, he was teaching every day in the temple during which time the chief priests, scribes, and other leading people were seeking to kill him; ⁴⁸but could not find anything to do because the people hung on his every word.

---

2. Miller, *The Singer*, 44–45.

A routine procedure in criminal investigation is to "follow the money." Though criminals certainly are capable of random acts of violence simply because of their base behavior, there tends to be method in their madness. Crimes are committed to further other means; the higher the crime, the greater possible pecuniary gain. Because of the profit motive, there will be a money trail within the crime that leads inexorably back to the perpetrator.

When Jesus descended the Mount of Olives and ascended to the temple mount in Jerusalem, he encountered the lowest depth of human depravity. The crassness of man's inhumanity to man always is demonstrated when those who can take advantage of others do take advantage of others. Since the time of the exodus, every Jewish male over twenty paid an annual tax of one-half shekel (Exod 30:11–16). Such was the tax collected from Jesus at Capernaum (Matt 17:24–27). Matthew identified the specific tax as the Didrachma, a silver Roman coin. However, Jewish custom forbade the carrying of any graven image in the temple. Accordingly, the Jews struck a separate coinage that bore agricultural and religious symbols rather than the customary images of governmental officials. The need for this specific temple coinage created the opportunity for corruption. Those without the temple coinage could not pay their tax in the temple. They were forced to exchange their Roman currency for the temple currency. Furthermore, having the corner on the market, those in charge could charge any exchange rate they desired.

As if this greed-driven, excessive profiteering was not enough to infuriate Jesus, this system of abuse took place in the outer court, the court of the Gentiles. A series of porches and colonnades, the court of the Gentiles surrounded the temple on all three sides. Only here could non-Jews, male or female, from any country or nationality, congregate to worship God. Therefore, as Jesus arrived, he viewed not only crass commercialism in the most sacred of all human places but also those being abused were those with the least ability to alter their present condition and assert even their most basic human rights of inquiry to the divine. Arguably, those being abused in the court of the Gentiles had come to Jerusalem looking for hope and found none. Instead, what they found was a system that further disadvantaged people, a system operated by the very people who should have known better.

Seeing what probably could best be described as an Oriental bazaar filled with moneychangers, tax collectors, and the sale of sacrificial animals, Jesus thought of God's intention for the temple and God's desire to incorporate all nations into the kingdom. Quoting Isaiah, Jesus said, "My house is a house of prayer." The entire quotation is

> Thus saith the Lord, Keep ye judgment, and do justice: for my salvation is near to come, and my righteousness to be revealed. Blessed is the man that doeth this, and the son of man that layeth hold on it; that keepeth the sabbath from polluting it, and keepeth his hand from doing any evil. Neither let the son of the stranger, that hath joined himself to the Lord, speak, saying, The Lord hath utterly separated me from his people: neither let the eunuch say, Behold, I am a dry tree. For thus saith the Lord unto the eunuchs that keep my sabbaths, and choose the things that please me, and take hold of my covenant; Even unto them will I give in mine house and within my walls a place and a name better than of sons and of daughters: I will give them an everlasting name, that shall not be cut off. Also the sons of the stranger, that join themselves to the Lord, to serve him, and to love the name of the Lord, to be his servants, every one that keepeth the sabbath from polluting it, and taketh hold of my covenant; Even them will I bring to my holy mountain, and make them joyful in my house of prayer: their burnt offerings and their sacrifices shall be accepted upon mine altar; for mine house shall be called an house of prayer for all people (Isa 56:1–7).

Beyond the obvious care for the sacredness of the temple, the passage presents God as intentionally reaching out to the disenfranchised, the stranger, and the eunuch so that they may be included. Such action is doing justice and demonstrating God's righteousness.

As far as "follow the money," Luke included the perpetrators of these atrocities in his narrative. The chief priests, scribes, and other leaders among the people began seeking an opportunity to destroy Jesus. Theirs was the greed that put these events in motion, and Jesus was about to uncover their scheme. In simple terms, Jesus had to go!

THE AUTHORITIES ON AUTHORITY

Luke 20:1–8

¹One day while Jesus was teaching in the temple and preaching the good news, the chief priests, scribes, and elders approached him ²and speaking they said to Jesus, "By what authority to do you do the things you do? Who gave you this authority?" ³Answering,

> Jesus said to them, "Well, I too will ask you a question, so tell me, ⁴was the baptism of John of heaven or of men?" ⁵*Conferring with themselves, they said, "If we say 'John's baptism was of heaven,' he will say, 'Then why did you not believe him?' ⁶But if we say 'John's baptism was of men,' all these people will stone us for they believed John as a prophet." ⁷So they answered Jesus by saying that they did not know the origin of John's baptism. ⁸Then Jesus said to them, "Neither will I tell you by what authority I do what I do."*

Following his public entrance to Jerusalem as the legitimate liege and sovereign Savior and following the unrestrained opposition to the abusive establishment, a confrontation between Jesus and the Sanhedrin was inevitable. Described by Luke as "chief priests, scribes, and elders," the group no doubt was an envoy from the ruling religious body. Aloof and above any public fray, the seventy of the Sanhedrin held that their roots traced back to Jethro's (Ruel) suggestion to Moses that he should appoint notable persons to assist his leadership of the people. While there certainly are references to noble men, elders, and councils throughout the Old Testament, the consolidation of the Sanhedrin as a priestly aristocracy did not appear consistently until the second century BC. Entrusted by the Roman government to oversee local religious affairs, the Sanhedrin dispatched the group of examiners much like a revenue commissioner would issue a business license. Jesus was not part of the established religious order. He was not a recognized Sadducee or Pharisee. He had no formal training and, most condemning of all, had not bothered to ask their permission. Furthermore, if a person claimed political dependence from the Roman government, the Sanhedrin's entire house of cards could fall. Officially, the Jews detested Roman rule. But human nature will protect the status quo over principle nine times out of ten. "Better the devil you know," the sage would say. So the Sanhedrin tipped their hat to Rome, accepted the limited control that was offered, and proceeded to protect their own interests.

But Jesus was not interested in furthering their hold over the people whom God created and whom he had come to save. Recognizing the inquiry for what it was—a feeble attempt to maintain control—Jesus refused to play along. Knowing the pretense of their power, Jesus turned the examination on the chief priests, scribes, and elders. Jesus knew that the message of John the Baptist fell on deaf ears among the religious elite. But Jesus also knew that the people recognized the breath of God in the words and work of John. Finally, Jesus knew that as his message and motive was the same as John's, he also would share John's fate.

But not on that day. On that day, Jesus had more to say, more to do. His time had not come. Rather than hasten the inevitable, Jesus turned the moment against the inquisitors. Rather than admit they thought John a fraud and risk causing a riot and threatening their own system, they chose to drop the issue. The confrontation would have to wait.

THE PARABLE OF THE VINEYARD: INCARNATION ILLUSTRATED

Luke 20:9-18

⁹Then Jesus began to tell the people this parable. "A man planted a vineyard, rented it out to a farmer, and departed for a long time. ¹⁰After a while, the man sent one of his servants to the farmer so that the farmer would give to the owner his portion of the fruit. But the tenant farmers beat the servant and drove him out empty handed. ¹¹The owner then proceeded to send another servant whom the sharecroppers abused and sent away empty handed. ¹²The owner then sent a third; this one was injured and expelled. ¹³Then the owner of the vineyard said, 'What will I do? I will send my beloved son. Maybe they will respect him.' ¹⁴But seeing the owner's son, the farmers said to each other, 'This is the heir! Let us kill him so that the property will become ours!' ¹⁵So they killed the owner's son and cast him out of the vineyard. What will the lord of the vineyard do to the tenant farmers then? ¹⁶He will come and kill the farmers and give the vineyard to someone else." But hearing this, the people reacted saying, "May it never be." ¹⁷But Jesus looked at them and said, "What then is the meaning of that which was written, 'The stone that the builders rejected will become the chief corner stone'? ¹⁸Furthermore, everyone that trips on this stone will be broken to pieces; and anyone upon which this stone falls will be completely crushed."

The parable of the vineyard should be considered in two parts. The first is the parable itself. The second is the crowd's reaction to the parable and Jesus' continued explanation.

In the parable, a wealthy investor planted a vineyard and entrusted its care to tenant farmers prior to departing upon distant travels. When the owner sent servants to collect a portion of the produce, the sharecroppers beat each servant. Finally, the owner sent his own son, believing that the tenant farmers surely would honor him. Rather than honor the owner's son, the wicked husbandmen killed the son in an effort to seize control of the owner's property and the son's inheritance.

The lessons of this incarnation narrative are clear. (1) God is the Creator of everything and therefore is the owner of everything. (2) God entrusts the care of his creation to those who are only stewards of his resources. Ownership is never transferred. (3) God intends to receive a profit from the divine investment in creation. A harvest is expected. (4) God progressively increased divine revelation that culminated in God taking on human form and living among men in the person of his divine Son. (5) Humanity's greed knows no end and will stop at nothing, even seeking to eliminate God, in order to seize control of all that God controls. Man seeks to be divine. (6) Finally, God never relinquishes control. While humanity often destroys itself seeking to usurp God's control, the divine work never goes untended. God simply includes others who are willing to work obediently in the vineyard.

While the telling of the parable is in itself beautifully instructive, understanding the reaction of the hearers brings a level of indictment that cuts to the heart of the human condition itself. To this point in his ministry Jesus had avoided the crowded thoroughfare of metropolitan areas. As a basically rural, itinerant ministry, Jesus had moved through the villages and towns of Galilee and Judea. His reputation grew and people went to him. Surrounded for the most part by those who chose to hear him because of their belief or desire to believe, Jesus largely was insulated against those who would attack him.

But when Jesus embraced Zacchaeus in Jericho and allowed the pomp of the royal entry into Jerusalem, public scrutiny changed. Jesus no longer enjoyed the luxury or relative anonymity. With the increase in the size of the crowd came increased numbers of those who opposed Jesus or who, in apathy, simply did not care. Emboldened by those who had no opinion about Jesus and who in essence placed Jesus' supporters in a minority, those in opposition to Jesus had the upper hand. They could begin swaying the masses. They could use the court of public opinion to their advantage. "Do you really want Rome to think there is an insurrectionist on the loose?" the Pharisees suggested. "Don't you think we should handle this for you?" the scribes whispered. "Haven't we always looked out after your best interest?" the members of the Sanhedrin counseled. And with each innuendo and each subtle suggestion, the die was cast against Jesus.

This phenomenon is presented in Luke's telling of the parable and the incidents that followed. Seeing where the parable was leading, there were those in the crowd that day who reacted strongly and vocally, probably to four aspects of the parable's conclusion. First, they scoffed at the character list that equated Jesus as the Son of God. Second, they resented the implication that they did not own the vineyard. Third, they were incensed that God would punish them for the manner in which they had discharged their duties. But fourth, and perhaps most importantly, they were outraged and livid at the mere suggestion that the vineyard would be entrusted to someone else's care. With this final twist of the parable, Jesus had struck at the heart of their problem: arrogance that led not only to exclusivity but also to the unspoken belief that by following carefully prescribed ritual they had ultimate control and were answerable to no one, not even to God.

Less this last point seem overstated, the reader should note Jesus' addendum to the reaction of his opponents. "God forbid," they cried at the suggestion that the vineyard be handed over to others. "May it never be!" Jesus countered with a question: "What then is the meaning of Psalm 118:22? The stone that the builders rejected will become the chief cornerstone."

The word ἀποδοκιμάδζω (apodokimadzō) means "to declare as useless" or "to reject after close scrutiny." The word was used throughout Greek literature to describe the process a stone mason used to select stones for building purposes. A mortarless process, the mason would interlock stones in such a fashion that the wall being constructed would become structurally sound. The Roman arch may provide the most common example of the process where each stone is pulled down by gravity but cannot fall because of the stone next to it. Accordingly, each stone had to be perfect in size and in shape. Knowing the predetermined pattern, the mason examined each stone before its use. If, according to the mason, the stone did not match the preconceived structural need, it was discarded as useless to the process.

Jesus' use of Psalm 118 reinforced the meaning of the parable. Not only was God in control of all, not only were the religious leaders of the Jews the "hired help," not only did they kill the prophets and seek to gain control of God's resources, but they held Jesus up to a predetermined mold and declared, "He doesn't fit; throw him away!" The recipients of the incarnation were given a most remarkable opportunity. They were allowed to examine, to look at, to converse with, to handle, to turn over in every direction, the very presence of God. Sadly, when given that chance, rather than embracing the presence of the person of their worship, they elevated objects of their own design to that very status. They chose their own interpretation of what God should be over what God, in the flesh and standing before them, actually was.

Finally, the last chapter of this parable continues to be written. Every day the living, breathing, incarnate God comes to everyone. And everyone is given the same choice: Accept God or reject God. Though human nature would rationalize the choices made as valid because of this reason or that, the reality is the same. When a person rejects Jesus, it is for one reason and one reason only: Jesus didn't fit the mold, the pattern, and the preconceived idea of what God should be and what God should do. In the final act of insurrection, the choice that is made seeks to exercise a pretense of control. Sadly, the only thing that will follow is that life will spin helplessly out of control. The conclusion of Psalm 118:22 is that those who reject will be crushed and scattered. Only when God is accepted and trusted can the person, Christian and non-Christian alike, avoid a demise of his or her own making.

TAXES

Luke 20:19–26

[19] *The scribes and chief priests sought to lay hands upon Jesus in that very hour, but feared the people who knew that Jesus had told the parable about the religious leaders.* [20] *Watching Jesus closely, these same leaders then sent spies pretending to be sincere, in order that they might catch Jesus in his words and have reason to deliver him to the authority and jurisdiction of the governor.* [21] *Accordingly, they asked Jesus saying, "Teacher, we know that you speak rightly and justly, showing no favoritism, but always teaching the truth and the way of God.* [22] *Is it or is it not lawful*

for us to pay taxes to Caesar?" ²³*Discerning their deceit, Jesus said to them,* ²⁴*"Show me a denarius. Whose likeness and inscription does it have?" They replied, "Caesar's."* ²⁵*Jesus said to them, "Well then, give to Caesar that which is Caesar's, but to God that which is God's."* ²⁶*So the spies were not able to trap Jesus in his words in the presence of the people, but marveling in his reply, held their peace.*

The conflict between Jesus and the religious authorities continued at a feverish pitch. It is no surprise that the contest turned to subterfuge and deceit. Human nature often disguises its true intention. The spies sent to trap Jesus used a fool-proof approach. Regardless of Jesus' answer, He would be criticized and discredited. If Jesus said, "Pay the tax," he would suffer the anger of the people heavily burdened by a corrupt tax system. If Jesus said, "Don't pay the tax," he would be guilty of insurrection and arrested accordingly. Either way, Jesus would be marginalized and removed from the public eye.

What the spies did not anticipate was the discernment of Jesus. Knowing their intention, Jesus did not take the bait. Rather than choosing sides between God's law and man's law, Jesus legitimized both. "Render to each," Jesus said, "what is their due."

In different ways, all three Synoptic Gospels conclude the parable with the same teaching. The spies were stunned. They marveled and were dumbstruck. The lesson is clear: Doing the right thing silences the critic. When a person is above reproach, small-minded people are left with little to say. Ultimately the futility of such attempts at trickery turned to perjury and collusion. But for the moment, Jesus was willing to confuse his accusers and move on. Though right had the upper hand, there was nothing to be gained that day in forcing the issue. Further humiliation of the spies would have made matters worse, not better. Jesus kept his attention focused on the goal and refused to accept a lesser challenge.

CHRISTIAN APOLOGY

Luke 20:27–40

²⁷*Now certain Sadducees, those denying the reality of the resurrection, came up to Jesus* ²⁸*saying, "Teacher, Moses wrote to us that if a man's brother dies having a wife but no children, that*

> man should take his brother's wife and raise up children for his brother. ²⁹Now what if there were seven brothers, one of who took a wife and died without having children. ³⁰The second ³¹and third brothers took her, as well as the others, none of whom left any children before they died. ³²Then the woman died. ³³Whose wife will she be in the resurrection? She was the wife of all seven?" ³⁴Jesus said to them, "The sons of this age marry and are given in marriage. ³⁵But the ones being counted worthy to attain that age and the resurrection from the dead will neither marry nor be given in marriage. ³⁶They are not able to die for they are angle-like, being sons of God and sons of the resurrection. ³⁷But regarding the raising of the dead, Moses demonstrated such in the passage about the bush when he said the Lord was the God of Abraham and the God of Isaac and the God of Jacob. ³⁸But God is not the God of the dead, but of the living, for all live to him." ³⁹Some of the scribes answered and said, "Teacher, you have spoken well." ⁴⁰They no longer were willing to ask him anything.

Luke included the story of the Sadducees' conversation with Jesus to continue the pattern of public opposition to Jesus. It is unclear if the conversation was part of a planned assault by the Sanhedrin, a group known to include Sadducees, or if the encounter with Jesus was more of an impromptu meeting. What is clear is that this was not a sincere question. This was an open attempt to ridicule and discredit Jesus.

The Sadducees traced their origins to the Ezra/Nehemiah returns to Jerusalem. Having suffered the humiliation of the temple destruction, an event that pious Jews believed impossible, those who returned brought with them an ardent defense of the law. It was commonly held that the relaxed attitude on obedience by their forebears had caused the fall of the Southern Kingdom. Accordingly, those who believed they had been given a second chance took no shortcuts on adherence to the law, regardless of how extreme its application. Examples include the divorce of foreign wives (Ezra 10:3) and exclusion of the indigenous half-Jewish population in the rebuilding process because of their racial impurity (Ezra 4:1–3).

One unintended limitation of the Sadducees' insistence on following the law was that at some point they limited their canon to the Pentateuch. In the first century, the Hebrew Scriptures were divided into three categories: law, prophets, and writings. Jesus quoted from all three.

But the Sadducees only held to the law. Consequently, if the law did not address an issue, the Sadducees disregarded the idea's validity.

Such was the case of the resurrection from the dead. Nowhere in the first five books of the Scripture, the Law of Moses, is the resurrection of the dead mentioned—no after-life, no eternal reward nor punishment. All of these are ideas that taught through God's progressive revelation to his people.

Therefore, the Sadducees' question to Jesus that day was a farce. It was intended to ridicule the commonly held position of an after-life. Furthermore, the Sadducees' very high view of Scripture would have caused them to believe that Scripture does not contradict itself. And so the stock and trade rebuttal to the doctrine of the resurrection was born. Deuteronomy 25:5 prescribes Levirate marriage. If your brother died without preserving his family name, you had a duty to take his wife as your wife and bear children with her for him. If that were to happen to seven brothers, all who died without fathering a child and then were resurrected, who would be married to whom? Because the Sadducees knew that Scripture commands Levirate marriage, how could resurrection be possible?

Jesus responded on two fronts. First, the Sadducees's assumption about marriage in heaven was incorrect. Jesus said to them that they were applying earthly limitations to a heavenly reality. "Things will not work exactly the same in heaven," Jesus said. "You are attempting to superimpose earthly restrictions to the after-life." Second, Jesus addressed their misunderstanding of Scripture. Knowing they only believed the first five books of the Hebrew canon, Jesus used a reference from the life of Moses. At the burning bush, Yahweh God spoke to Moses and said he was the God of Abraham, of Isaac, and of Jacob (Exod. 3:6). Jesus then clarified that Yahweh was not God of the dead but the living. Accordingly, Abraham, Isaac, and Jacob must have been resurrected from the dead.

Too often readers take away from this passage a cryptic reference to the reality of heaven. All will be angel-like. There will be no marriage. For many dedicated Christian spouses, this is a bittersweet teaching from Scripture that they simply accept as a matter of belief in Scripture and trust in God. They cannot imagine eternity without the life partner they believe was given to them by God. But convinced of the inspiration of Scripture, they accept and trust God to prepare them for how God intends to use them.

However, there is more in this passage than a limited description of heaven. Here the reader sees Jesus as the first Christian apologist. While the concept of the after-life is limited in the teachings of the Old Testament, it is none-the-less present. The witch at Endow raised Samuel to speak to Saul (1 Sam 28:7–25). King David wrote of his soul hiding in Sheol, the abode of the dead (Ps 139:8). Jesus could have used many references to explain the reality of reward and punishment in the life to come. But he didn't. Rather than quoting Scripture from the prophets and the writings that Jesus knew would not be accepted by the Sadducees, Jesus referred to the teaching of the after-life that was found in the Torah. And in so doing, Jesus became the first Christian apologist.

Three important aspects of Jesus' interaction should be noted. (1) Jesus cared enough to know there was nothing to be gained by being argumentative. There were certainly circumstances in the life of Jesus that demanded he be argumentative. Open abuse of the helpless in the temple caused Jesus to act with careless abandon. Veiled deceit on the part of many who came to him led him to oppose openly something that was said or being done. But in an apology, in an effort to persuade with reason, there is no room for name calling. Jesus saw the Sadducees as fellow Jews who could help shape the fledgling movement if they would only trust God and discard their preconceived ideas. Jesus was not soft-peddling the message because he knew they were politically connected and could have him arrested at any moment. Jesus cared enough to seek to engage them where they were and to lead them to where they needed to be.

(2) Jesus cared enough to listen. By demonstrating compassion for those who meant him harm, Jesus earned the opportunity to continue the conversation. Jesus listened intently to what was being said as well as what was being implied. Only after determining how he could possible assist his foes did he begin to speak. Oliver Wendell Holmes once said, "It is the providence of knowledge to speak, but it is the privilege of wisdom to listen."[3] Jesus knew when to speak and when to listen.

(3) Jesus cared enough to respond from a position of mutual agreement. By quoting Moses, Jesus pulled the teeth out of the Sadducees' argument. The Torah did in fact allude to after-life. Building his apology, his defense of *his* faith, upon mutually agreed upon assumptions, Jesus kept alive the possibility of further conversation and ministry. By

---

3. Holmes, *The Poet at the Breakfast Table*, 264.

meeting people where they were and gently moving them to where they needed to be, Jesus gave all of Christianity a model for ministry and interaction in a hostile world.

Nothing else is said about the Sadducees who spoke to Jesus that day. Nothing is known of their continued success or their demise. But is it possible that Jesus reached even one of those who came to him in self-righteous indignation? Could it be that just one left with his heart warmed and his mind opened?

Luke alone of the Synoptic writers concluded that the Sadducees "dared not to question Jesus further." Mark concluded the episode abruptly with the statement about the burning bush and the evidence of the eternal life of Abraham, Isaac, and Jacob. Matthew added that the people marveled. Only Luke addressed the attitude of the scribes who acknowledged Jesus' answer.

Luke's use of the phrase οὐκέτι γὰρ ἐτόλμων (*ouketi gar etolmōn*), "dare not," sheds light on the shifting mental thought of the Sadducees. In its classical Greek use, ἐτόλμων *(etolmōn)* meant "to endure" or "to suffer," but became to be used as "to dare." "The transition 'to dare' is plain here. The ref. (sic) is to perception of a danger and the courage to accept it. What is at issue is whether one will expose themselves to the danger or not."[4] Could Luke have been communicating that there were those among the Sadducees that day who were swayed by Jesus? that Jesus' words "dared" them to believe? If so what was the threat? Where was the perception of danger that had to be endured?

An additional reference to ἐτόλμων *(etolmōn)* in the New Testament portrays a similar crisis in belief. After Jesus' death, Joseph of Arimathea, a member of the Sanhedrin, requested to take possession of the body for burial. Mark indicated that Joseph of Arimathea "dared" to go to Pilate to request the body (Mark 15:43). As it was Roman custom to release the body of an executed criminal to an acquaintance,[5] where was the perception of danger that had to be overcome in order to accept the consequences of his actions? Was it fear of retribution from the Romans? No. It was fear of identifying with the Christian movement. It was fear of being ostracized by the Sanhedrin, and if he had been a member, of the Sadducee party itself. Yet Joseph had the courage to accept the perceived danger and overcame that fear of the possible consequences of his actions.

4. Fitzer, "τολμάω, κτλ.," 181.
5. Ibid., 183.

Was Joseph of Arimathea among the Sadducees that day? Was he one of these who dared not ask anything further? There is no way to know. What is known is that those listening to Jesus perceived a danger so great that they ceased their inquiry.

But of what were they afraid? Did Jesus threaten their way of life? Had they approached Jesus certain they had the upper hand only to have their argument handed back? Had their conviction been challenged? Did Jesus' apology succeed? Did the fact that Jesus cared enough to avoid an argument, to listen sincerely, and to speak from common assumptions begin to break down the harsh edifice of an opponent and reshape it as a warm receptive student? While ironically these answers may never be known this side of the "resurrection from the dead," the possibility certainly fits Luke's literary intent to demonstrate the universal appeal and inclusion of the Gospel.

BALANCE

Luke 20:41–47

41 Then Jesus said to them, "How is it that they say 'the Christ is the Son of David?' 42 Did not David say in the book of the Psalms, 'The Lord said to my Lord, Sit at my right hand 43 until I make your enemies your footstool'? 44 David called the Messiah Lord; how is the Messiah David's Son?" 45 Jesus then said to his disciples in the hearing of all the people, 46 "Beware the scribes, the ones desiring to walk around in long robes and loving eloquent greetings in the market place and the front seat in the Synagogues, and the place of honor at banquets. 47 They cheat the house of widows and in pretense make long prayers. They will receive greater condemnation."

Following his dialogue with the Sadducees where he dismantled an absurd argument, Jesus turned to his disciples, who no doubt had been listening, to say, "This is not the only abuse that is prevalent in our society." Jesus proceeded to unmask another rabbinic argument that was in essence a "tempest in a teapot."

Rabbinic arguments typically took two opposing views and named a learned orator to each view. They would then debate the merits of the case. Over time, parameters for these debates evolved. Certain aspects of logic became accepted axioms of these debates. For example, quoting a noble rabbi of the past would trump the opinion of a younger rabbi. They also argued from the lesser to the greater. If a certain offense required a certain punishment, a greater offense would require a greater punishment.

To show the futility of such banter, Jesus applied the rabbinic argument to himself. Born into the house of David, Jesus served as his family progenitor. Yet in a psalm ascribed to David, the great king called the Messiah "Lord." If the lesser serves the greater, how can King David call the Messiah "Lord"? How can the Messiah come from the loins of David and also lead David?

Showing the weakness of this circular logic, Jesus turned to more concrete and damaging examples of religious abuse. Many among the religious elite took advantage of the weak and helpless through pretense. They used their learned position to peddle influence. With such corruption came a host of travesties. They advanced themselves at the expense of others. Then in a turn of the phrase, Jesus gave the scribes a dose of their own medicine. Because theirs was the greater opportunities, theirs was the greater condemnation for squandering those opportunities. God had given the Jewish leaders a sacred trust. With the messianic expectation on the very brink of realization, the religious establishment was choosing their own understanding over trust in God.

INEVITABLE TRUTH

Luke 21:1–36

¹Looking up, Jesus saw the wealthy casting their gifts into the collection box. ²He also saw a poor widow casting in two leptons, the smallest copper coin. ³Jesus then said, "I say to you that this poor widow has put in more than all the rest. ⁴They gave out of their abundance, but she gave her livelihood out of her poverty." ⁵As some were speaking about the temple, how it was decorated with beautiful stones and offerings, Jesus said, ⁶"These things which you see? The day is coming when one stone will not be left upon another that is not torn down." ⁷They asked him saying, "Teacher, when will this be and what will be the signs that it is about to occur?" ⁸Then Jesus said, "Beware that you are not led astray. Many will come in my name same saying, 'I am the one!' and 'The time is near!' Do not follow them. ⁹And when you hear of wars and uprisings, do not be afraid. It is necessary for these things to occur first. But the end will not be imminent." ¹⁰Then Jesus said to them, "They will rise, nation against nation and kingdom against kingdom. ¹¹There will be great earthquakes, famine, and plagues. There will be dreadful events and great signs from heaven. ¹²But before these things, they will seize you and persecute you and hand you over to the synagogues and prisons, leading you away to kings and governors for my name's sake. ¹³This will result in your bearing witness. ¹⁴You should put it in your heart not to premeditate an answer; ¹⁵for I will give you a mouth and wisdom to which no enemy will be able to contradict. ¹⁶You will be handed over by your parents and your brothers and your relatives and your friends who will kill some of you. ¹⁷You will be hated by all for my name's sake. ¹⁸But not a hair on your head will be destroyed. ¹⁹You will gain your life by your patient endurance. ²⁰But you will know that destruction is near when you see armies surrounding Jerusalem. ²¹At that moment, those in Judea should run to the mountains. Those in the city should depart and those in the country should not return. ²²These are the days of punishment that fulfill what has been written. ²³Woe to those who are pregnant or nursing a child during those days. There will be great trouble upon the earth and wrath upon the people. ²⁴They will be killed by the edge of the sword and led captive unto the nations. Jerusalem will be trampled by the nations until the time of the nations is fulfilled. ²⁵There will be signs in the sun and the moon and the stars. Upon earth the nations will be perplexed at the sound of the tides. ²⁶Men will faint with fear and expectation regarding what is coming upon the world. The powers of the heavens will be shaken. ²⁷Then they will see the Son of man coming in the clouds with power and much glory. ²⁸When these events begin to take place, you should raise your heads for your redemption is about to occur." ²⁹Then Jesus told them a parable. "Observe the fig tree and all the fruit trees. ³⁰When they put on their leaves, you see and know for yourselves that summer is near. ³¹In the same way, when you see these things taking place you know that the kingdom of God is near. ³²Truly I say that this generation will not pass away *until these things have occurred. ³³Heaven and earth may pass away, but my word will never pass away. ³⁴You should pay close attention that you not burden your heart with dissipation and drunkenness and concerns pertaining to everyday life and that day come upon you suddenly and trap you like a snare. ³⁵That day is coming to everyone who lives upon the face of the earth. ³⁶Be alert at all times; pray for strength to escape these things that will take place so that you will stand before the Son of man."*

As Jesus watched the wealthy and poor of society participate in temple ritual, he began to instruct the disciples about the futility of human systems. Jesus indicated that all the finery of the temple would soon come to an end. Jesus observed mankind placing their trust in things of their own making and calling them sacred. But none of these human assumptions would prevent Rome from destroying the temple in AD 69–70. "Learn the lesson from the fig tree," Jesus said. "Watch the times, and don't be led astray. When you see armies surrounding Jerusalem, flee! Don't think that the temple will save you."

Jesus included other predictions as well. He indicated the times were coming when the disciples would suffer for their faith. They would be sold out even by family and friends.

The form of Jesus' teachings was Jewish apocalyptic literature. Common in the first century, modern readers since the mid-nineteenth century have struggled to grasp its picturesque meanings. Cataclysmic upheaval of even the very laws of the universe will mark the days when God will intervene in history and make his divine presence known. The modern proclivity to dissect, boil down, analyze, and synthesize have led many to miss a very simple truth. Even though there will be wars and rumors of wars, even though nation will rise against nations, even though Jerusalem will be surrounded, the temple destroyed, and the disciples persecuted, the Son of man will return. God will conclude the divine plan of salvation for all history. Regardless of what happens, man never is alone and God always is sovereign.

THE BEGINNING OF THE END

Luke 21:37-38

³⁷Every day, Jesus was teaching in the temple, but at night, he spent the evening on the Mount of Olives. ³⁸Then early in the morning, all the people would come to the temple to hear him.

Jesus' final days on earth began much like his first days of the Galilean ministry. Following his self-declared purpose sermon in the synagogue, Jesus went to Capernaum. There He rose early in the morning and withdrew to a lonely place. His prayerful respite was soon disrupted by those who sought his attention (Luke 4:42). Furthermore, both in Galilee and in Jerusalem, Jesus' private time of communion with God was followed by service to mankind. As the final moment of his incarnational purpose drew near, receiving divine direction was essential. Only with a sense of divine appointment will the human heart be able to face the challenges that serving God will bring.

BETRAYAL

Luke 22:1-6

¹As the Feast of Unleavened Bread, also called Passover, drew near, ²the chief priests and scribes sought to get rid of Jesus, for they feared the people. ³Satan entered into Judas Iscariot, one of the Twelve. ⁴Judas went away to speak to the chief priests and officers regarding how he could hand over Jesus to them. ⁵They were glad for the opportunity and agreed to give Judas money. ⁶Judas consented and sought a good chance to hand over Jesus to them away from the crowds.

Throughout his ministry, Jesus had grown accustomed to the attacks of the religious establishment. He challenged their control of a system that abused innocent people, potentially at every turn exposing his adversaries as frauds. These typically had been poorly veiled attempts to discredit his growing popularity by trapping him in his own words. But every attempt had failed.

The time had come for more drastic measures. When trickery and innuendo failed, open defiance was all that was left. Someone had to betray Jesus. Judas was that person. Bought and paid for, Judas would seek an opportunity to deliver into their hands the Son of God.

Yet as the events unfolded, one question continued to surface. Why did the chief priests need Judas at all? Jesus was openly preaching and teaching in the temple every day. His whereabouts were common. Furthermore, the bogus charges against Jesus would stand or fall at any time, with or without Judas.

There truly was only one reason that Judas was needed. The religious leaders feared the people. Ironically, it was those whom Jesus sought to free from the oppressing perversion of religion that stood between the high priest and the restoration of order that Jesus had disturbed. Judas was to betray Jesus in solitude, away from the crowd that could spin out of control. The betrayal of Jesus would not stand the light of day. Only in the shadow of deceit and collusion could Jesus be whisked away, hopefully never to be heard from again.

PASSOVER PREPARATION AND THE LORD'S SUPPER

Luke 22:7–23

⁷The day of the Feast of Unleavened Bread arrived when it was necessary to sacrifice the Passover lamb. ⁸Jesus sent Peter and John saying, "Go. Prepare a place where we may eat the Passover." ⁹Peter and John said to Jesus, "Where would you like us to make these preparations?" ¹⁰Jesus said to them, "Upon entering the city, you will meet a man carrying a jar of water. Follow him to the house that he enters. ¹¹Say to the home owner, 'The Teacher says to you, Where is the guestroom where I may eat the Passover with my disciples?' ¹²He will show you a large, furnished, upstairs room. Make preparations there." ¹³Peter and John went and finding everything just as Jesus told them, they made preparations. ¹⁴When the hour arrived, Jesus sat at the table with his apostles. ¹⁵Then Jesus said to them, "I deeply desire to eat this Passover with you prior to my suffering. ¹⁶For I say to you that I will in no way eat it before it is fulfilled in the kingdom of God." ¹⁷Taking a cup, Jesus gave thanks saying, "Take this and divide it among yourselves.

> ¹⁸ For I say to you that from now on I will by no means drink the fruit of the vine until the kingdom of God comes. ¹⁹ Taking bread, Jesus gave thanks, broke it, and gave it to them saying, "This is my body that is given for you. Do this in remembrance of me." ²⁰ In the same way with the cup, after the meal, Jesus said, "This cup, being poured out for you, is the new covenant in my blood. ²¹ But even now the hand that will betray me is on this table with me. ²² Indeed the Son of man goes as it has been determined, but woe to the one by whom the Son of man is betrayed." ²³ Then the disciples began to question each other, which one of them it was that would do such a thing.

Luke's Passover and Lord's Supper narratives are a continuation of dominant themes from his Gospel. From the beginning, God had a plan of salvation that was set aside for Jesus to complete. There was never a time during Jesus' earthly ministry that this moment was not the goal. Luke alone placed the statement regarding the providential suffering of the Son of man at the conclusion of the meal. By doing so, the narrative builds to the moment of Jesus' affirmation that God is sovereign and that God's directions are a joy to fulfill. Additionally, Luke alone recorded that the Son of man goes "as it was determined"— ὡρισμένον (*hōrismenon*)—rather than "as it was written"—γέγραπται (*gegraptai*).[6] By doing so, Luke reiterated that the plan of salvation was God's plan. Jesus' death was neither chance nor fate. The crucifixion was in fact Jesus' preordained duty that Jesus was glad to fulfill.

HUMAN REACTION TO PRESSURE

Luke 22:24-46

> ²⁴ Then an argument happened between the disciples as to who was regarded as the greatest. ²⁵ Jesus said to them, "The Gentile kings exercise lordship over each other and the ones having authority are called benefactors. ²⁶ But you are not such. Rather, the greatest among you should become as the youngest and the ruler as one who serves. ²⁷ Who is greater—the one who seated himself at the table, or the one who is serving? Is it not the one who is seated?

---

6. Compare to Mark 14:21.

But I am the one among you who is the servant. ²⁸You are the ones who have remained with me during my time of trouble. ²⁹I will give to you the same kingdom my Father gave to me ³⁰so that you may eat and drink at my table in my kingdom and sit upon thrones as you judge the twelve tribes of Israel. ³¹Listen to me, Simon. Satan demands to sift all of you like grain. ³²But I have prayed for you, Peter, that your faith will not fail. When you have turned, strengthen your brothers." ³³Peter said to Jesus, "Lord, I am ready to go to prison and even death with you." ³⁴Jesus said to him, "Peter, I tell you the rooster will not crow today until you have denied knowing me three times." ³⁵Jesus said to all of them, "When I sent you out without having a purse, bag, or extra sandals, what did you lack?" The disciples replied, "Nothing." ³⁶Then Jesus said to the disciples, "Well, let him who has a purse take it and likewise a bag. Anyone who does not have a sword should sell his mantle and buy a sword. ³⁷I say to you that what has been written must be fulfilled in me that 'he was reckoned with transgressors'; what was written has a fulfillment. ³⁸The disciples said, "Lord, here are two swords." Jesus said to the disciples, "That will be sufficient." ³⁹Then Jesus came out and went to the Mount of Olives as was his custom. His disciples went with him. ⁴⁰Having come to the place, Jesus said to them, "Pray that you will not enter temptation." ⁴¹Jesus then went a stone's throw away from the disciples and knelt down and prayed ⁴²saying, "Father, if you are willing, take this cup away from me. Nevertheless, not my will, but your will be done."⁷ ⁴⁵Rising from his prayer, and returning to the disciples, Jesus found them being asleep with sorrow. ⁴⁶Jesus said to them, "Why are you sleeping? Rise and pray that you not enter temptation."

Given the extraordinary details of the preceding conversation that included the new covenant, the broken body, the poured out blood, and the betrayal, it is not hard to understand that the human emotions of the disciples were running a bit wild. Why a dispute erupted between

---

7. The oldest and best manuscripts do not include verses 43 and 44. "And there appeared an angel unto him from heaven, strengthening him. And being in agony he prayed more earnestly: and his sweat was as it were great drops of blood falling down to the ground."

the disciples is a matter of speculation. Perhaps one stood to take charge of an internal investigation to identify the betrayer. Such an effort could have led to a first-century version of the twentieth-century vernacular "Who died and made you the big cheese? Maybe you should go sit in the grocery store so everyone can know you're the big cheese!" Who knows what happened?

What is known is that Jesus directed the disciples to have appropriate attitudes. Rather than behaving like the Gentiles whose system of laws were amoral at best, Jesus said that each person should value others more than self. The least shall be the greatest. The servant of all will ultimately rule all. Jesus reminded the disciples that he was prepared to give them the same kingdom benefits that the Father had given him. They would lead when they realized that true leadership starts and ends with service.

Out of this remarkable narrative emerge two extraordinary events that must dominate the thoughts of the interpreter. One, Jesus prayed specifically for Peter. Two, Jesus repeated his command to the disciples that they pray to avoid temptation.

While it comes as no surprise that prayer is again a major theme in Luke's work, these two references have far-reaching consequences. Out of the argument that arose at the Last Supper, Jesus centered on a conversation with Peter. From Luke's narrative, the reader cannot know if Jesus turned to Peter because he was the instigator or the potential reconciler. Either way, Jesus drew a contrast. Specific to Luke's narrative are different words for the second personal pronoun in Luke 22:31–32. Luke recorded ὑμᾶς (*humas*), second person plural, when Jesus said, *Satan demands to sift all of you*. This declarative statement was followed by the encouragement of the ages. Luke recorded σοῦ (*sou*), second person singular, when Jesus said, "But Peter, I am praying for you." Jesus said that Satan wanted to devour each of the disciples, that there was a categorical contempt for all things godly, and Satan wanted it gone. Destroyed! But Jesus' response to that very real and very dangerous reality was to invest in Peter in a way that would counter Satan's darts through all eternity. "But Peter," Jesus said, "I am praying for you by name."

Not only should the Christian be uplifted by the thought of eternal God interceding on behalf of the individual but comfort also is taken from the message of the prayer. One should watch closely the sequence of the narrative. Jesus had not yet revealed that Peter would deny Christ.

Long before the moment of crisis, Jesus was praying for Peter. But amazingly, Jesus was praying for what would happen after Peter's inevitable failure. Sinful human nature being what it is, Peter would stumble and fall. But in the face of his inevitable failure was another undeniable certainty: Peter would repent. Jesus' prayer was that Peter would not lose heart nor would he become so discouraged that he would quit. Identity always trumps behavior. The Christian will fail. The child of God will disappoint the one he or she loves the most. But improper behavior, acting out of character, does not change a person's identity in Christ; it does not alter who a person is. Jesus said to Peter, "You are my dear child. I am praying for your continued strength so that after you fail, after you realize you failed, after you weep bitter tears of shame and disappointment, you will turn and strengthen those around you." Regardless of how the child of God falters, nothing changes his or her identity in Christ.

The second extraordinary aspect of this passage is the repetition of Jesus' command to the disciples. Other than Jesus' threefold reinstatement of Peter on the seashore following the resurrection where Jesus instructed Peter to feed the flock (John 20:15–19), there is no other reference in the New Testament where Jesus repeated a command. When Jesus sought the solitude of prayer with the Father, he instructed the disciples to "pray that they not enter temptation." Returning to find them asleep, Jesus again directed the disciples to "pray that they not enter temptation." Matthew and Mark record only the second of these commands in Matthew 26:41 and in Mark 14:38. Only Luke recorded the first imperative as well.

Why the repetition? Why did Matthew and Mark condense the event to the second command? For Luke the answer was simple: Jesus was telling the disciples that prayer really does work. Jesus knew the difficulties they were about to face. He knew the moments ahead would test their faith. Jesus also knew that the presence of the Holy Spirit places a person in a different arena. Prayer enables a person to see circumstances from God's perspective and enables the faith required to trust God to act in and through even the worst circumstances. Prayer positions a person to resist temptation, eliminating for at least the moment, the need to beg for forgiveness.

This reality is presented by the psalmist who made a subtle distinction about sin and forgiveness that is easily overlooked. In describing the human condition and its need for redemption, the psalmist wrote, "Blessed is he whose transgression is forgiven, whose sin is covered" (Ps 32:1). How wonderful it is when a person trusts God to do what only God can do; forgive a person of his sins and make that person new! But the psalmist continued by writing, "Blessed is the man unto whom the Lord imputeth not iniquity, and in whose spirit there is no guile" (Ps 32:2).

While one could interpret the passage as a typical Hebrew parallel where one concept is presented in two slightly different consecutive presentations, the psalmist here seems to be describing two different groups. First are those who have sought God's forgiveness for their disobedience. Without question, those who have sinned and who consequently need forgiveness includes all of humanity. As Paul wrote, *All sin and go on falling short of the glory of God* (Romans 3:23). But equally without question is that God intends for his children to live victorious, overcoming lives, freed from the power of sin. Paul also wrote,

> For if we have been united with him in a death like his, we shall certainly be united with him in a resurrection like his. We know that our old self was crucified with him so that the sinful body might be destroyed, and we might no longer be enslaved to sin. For he who has died is freed from sin. But if we have died with Christ, we believe that we shall also live with him. For we know that Christ being raised from the dead will never die again; death no longer has dominion over him. The death he died he died to sin, once for all, but the life he lives he lives to God. So you also must consider yourselves dead to sin and alive to God in Christ Jesus. Let not sin therefore reign in your mortal bodies, to make you obey their passions. Do not yield your members to sin as instruments of wickedness, but yield yourselves to God as men who have been brought from death to life, and your members to God as instruments of righteousness. For sin will have no dominion over you, since you are not under law but under grace (Romans 6:5–14).[8]

To this second group, those who have died to sin, were buried with Christ, over whom sin hath no dominion, who have been cleansed of their sin and who for the moment at least are living a victorious Christian life, "God imputeth no iniquity." To these two groups of believers, the psalmist would say, "It is great to be forgiven, but it is even better not to need it."

8. RSV.

It is to this purpose that Luke repeated Jesus' command to the disciples that they should pray to avoid temptation. "Stay awake! Pay attention!" Jesus must have been saying. "Don't you realize that through the power of prayer you can escape the misery of sin? Can't you see that by prayer you remain connected to the one that can give you victory? Only through an obedient relationship with the Father can you avoid the corruption of the flesh. And while there always will be an endless supply of my grace and forgiveness available to you when you fall, I would spare you the pain of disappointing me. So pray, and keep on praying because while it is great to be forgiven, it is better not to need it!"

THE ARREST OF JESUS

Luke 22:47–53

⁴⁷As Jesus was speaking, a crowd arrived that was led by the disciple called Judas. This same Judas approached Jesus and kissed him. ⁴⁸Jesus said to Judas, "Do you deliver up the Son of man with a kiss?" ⁴⁹Seeing what was about to happen, the disciples said, "Lord? Are we to strike with the sword?" ⁵⁰Then one of the disciples cut off the ear of the high priest's servant. ⁵¹Responding, Jesus said, "Enough of this!" Jesus touched the man's ear and healed him. ⁵²Then Jesus said to those who had come with chief priests, temple officers, and elders, "Why have you come to me as a thief, with swords and clubs? ⁵³When I was with you daily in the temple, you could have reached out and touched me. Instead, this is your hour and the power of darkness."

Exactly on time, Judas arrived at the garden retreat to have Jesus arrested. As planned, Judas approached Jesus and kissed him. The treason was complete; Jesus had been betrayed.

What was not expected was Jesus' response. "Why did you select a kiss as your means of identifying me?" Jesus asked Judas. It was as if Jesus were saying, "How ironic. I came to love and to show God's love. Is that why you chose an expression of affection to betray me?"

But more important than the means of identification was the method of the incarceration. In tow behind Judas were the chief priests, temple officials, and elders, along with a mob of enforcers whose weapons of choice were clubs and swords. So overly armed were they that

Jesus could not help but comment on their inappropriate anticipation of hostility. Furthermore, Jesus' statement gives the reader a better understanding of the mental anguish he suffered during his final days. "You have come here prepared to apprehend a felon who would resist arrest by force when in fact, I have been yielding myself to you openly in the temple," Jesus said.

The reader already knows the motivation of the religious leaders. Wanting to protect their system of worship and their way of life, those in charge sought to eliminate Jesus in such a way as to avoid public outcry. Accordingly, Judas agreed to show the chief priests and others where Jesus would be out of the public eye.

Jesus' comments, however, revealed that he not only anticipated being arrested but that He was surprised it had taken so long. Jesus had openly explained to his disciples that he was going to Jerusalem where he would be persecuted and ultimately executed. Jesus said on three different occasions that the Son of man was to suffer at the hands of those who thought they were doing God's service. With everything building to that point, Jesus made his way to Jerusalem amidst public shouts of praises to God and the anticipation of certain incarceration. But no arrest came. Jesus simply continued to preach the good news of the kingdom. Every day in the temple Jesus stood in public view and without any hesitation declared indictments against a religious system gone astray, but there was no arrest. His message was not one of righteousness through ritual but of hope for the burdened and broken, one of peace and security in simple acceptance of God's love. Day after day Jesus stood in the presence of those he knew wanted to arrest him, but no arrest was made.

How must Jesus have felt when, kneeling in the garden, he asked his Heavenly Father to take the cup away? Did his human emotion ever bring clouds of doubt? Could he have wondered if he was right about the Son of man suffering? After all, Jesus did go to Jerusalem, he did preach the gospel openly, and he made no secret of his beliefs. Yet those in charge never made a move against him. In his humanity, Jesus must have been forced into a crisis of belief where he wondered if he understood God's will. Understandably, out of that moment Jesus cried, "You take charge. Your will be done."

Presented in the garden prayer that is enhanced by Jesus' comments during his arrest is a parable for all who seek to live out God's will in their lives. Once a vision is given there should be no hesitation.

Occasionally God pulls back the veil of time and shows his child the way. When presented with such an opportunity, the child of God should never falter from following that path. Even when resolution does not come, never falter from the path. Even when doubts assail, never falter from the path. God will accomplish his plan in ways we do not understand and at moments we do not expect.

PETER'S DENIAL: A PROGRESSION OF DISCONNECTION

Luke 22:54–62

⁵⁴They arrested Jesus, led him away, and brought him to the house of the high priest. Peter followed at a safe distance. ⁵⁵Those around kindled a fire in the midst of the courtyard where they sat down together and Peter sat down among them. ⁵⁶Seeing Peter by fire light, a little servant girl gazed at him and said, "You also were with him." ⁵⁷Peter denied saying, "I do not know him, young lady." ⁵⁸A little while later, someone else saw Peter and said, "You are from their group." But Peter said, "Fellow, I am not!" ⁵⁹After about an hour, another insisted saying, "Surely you are with him. After all, you are a Galilean." ⁶⁰Listen man, I don't know what you are talking about!" And while Peter was still speaking, the rooster crowed. ⁶¹Turning, the Lord looked at him and Peter remembered the words of the Lord that Jesus said to Peter—that before the rooster crows today you will deny me three times. ⁶²Then Peter went out and wept bitterly.

According to A. T. Robertson, "It is almost impossible to co-ordinate the three denials in the four accounts unless we conceive of several joining in when one leads off."[9] What Robertson was describing was a setting where people were moving in and out of the courtyard, hearing different things, speaking at different times. All four Gospel accounts are accurate in their detail, yet all form unique perspectives.

To understand Luke's perspective, one must realize two important differences between his account and the other three Gospel records. First, Matthew, Mark, and John depict the denial as part of the court case before the high priest. This is most noticeable in John where the denial

---

9. Robertson, *Luke*, 275.

is interwoven into the elements of the interrogation (John 18:12–26). In Matthew and Mark, Peter followed the arrest party from a safe distance and entered the high priest's courtyard where he could see and hear what was about to transpire (Matt 26:57–57; Mark 14:53–72). But this positioning of Peter was interrupted by the flow of the questioning by the high priest. To the contrary, Luke placed Peter in the courtyard and immediately proceeded with Peter's threefold denial of Jesus. The literary force of this structure is to compel the reader to continue to focus on Peter's denial. At that moment, nothing was more important than what was happening between servant and master neither the trial nor the false accusations nor Jesus' response, not even the impending execution. Nothing was more important than the relationship between Peter and Jesus.

The second major difference between Luke and the other three Gospels is the progression of the dialogue. Only Luke recorded the progression of Peter's three statements without commentary. John and Mark include the summary statement that Peter "denied knowing Jesus." Matthew did not use this technique but repeated Peter's words, "I don't know the man." Only Luke recorded three separate statements in progression.

The conclusion to draw from these two differences is that Luke's narrative was designed to force the readers to focus on a specific message. This is not simply a historic narrative intended to convey data or information. Luke's record of the event calls attention to the consequences born by any child of God who disavows his or her relationship with Christ. Peter's words present a progression of disconnection that is born by all who, because of pressure, circumstance, or apathy, turn their backs on Jesus.

(1) Peter said, "I don't know him." Once in the courtyard, Peter attempted to blend in with the crowd. He did what everyone else was doing; he tried to stay warm by the fire. But the flames that gave warmth also gave light. A young slave girl noticed Peter and asked, "Hey, weren't you with this guy who is being tried up there?" Peter's response was to say he did not know Jesus. The first step of the progression of disconnection was to sever the relationship with the Master. Perhaps out of fear, perhaps out of a desire to maintain anonymity, Peter undercut the source of his identity. Tragically, in the moment where all he had was his identity, Peter chose to rely on himself and on his own ability to perform.

Somehow there is rooted deep in the human soul this belief that the individual can handle disappointment, pain, and crisis. But ironically, these moments should call forth the greatest dependence on God, not the opposite. The Christian can never achieve his or her way to right standing with God. Only as personal identity is tied to who God is, rather than to what the individual can do, will the child of God be able to negotiate the trauma of living in a sinful and fallen world.

(2) Peter said, "I am not part of his group." A little while later, a person that Luke did not name made the same identification. "Aren't you one of those who were following him?" Peter's response was similar to his first. "No. I am not part of his group." Once Peter's identity was no longer based in Jesus, an association with like-minded people became not only unnecessary but counterproductive.

While it is true that a child of God who is wrestling with identity issues may from time to time continue to hang out in the same old circles, the truth is that the separation is continuing, even though it may well be hidden. The Christian knows how to act, what to say, when to stand, and when to sit. But the child of God who is not depending on the only identity that matters, the identity that is based on God's righteousness, is a miserable person. The joy is gone. The front may appear connected, but the tie has been severed. And further separation is only a crisis away.

(3) Peter said, "I don't know anything about what you are saying." When asked the third time if he was a disciple of Jesus, Peter denied any knowledge of Jesus' activity. Peter moved from a loss of identity in Christ to a loss of belonging in the body of Christ to finally a loss of knowledge about anything God was doing in history at all.

This final stage of the progression of disconnection completes the process of severing the Christian from his or her source of fulfillment and victory. Only when our identity is based in Christ can we experience belonging among likeminded believers. Only as a member of the body of Christ can we cultivate the ability and skills to understand what God is doing in his kingdom. Peter's denial was more than a tragic moment in one disciple's life; it was a warning to all who follow. The only way to see God's hand at work is to mature through the body of Christ as one whose identity is based in Christ.

Not only did Luke present aspects of Peter's denial that enable every Christian to benefit from Peter's devastating experience but Luke also revealed that God was constantly working to bring about his plan of salvation. For Luke, every aspect of the passion was carefully orchestrated by the ever-present hand of God. In addition to Peter's culminating denial that occurred at precisely the predicted moment of the rooster's call, Luke added a pivotal detail. Using the aorist passive participle, Luke said that Jesus, having been turned, gazed at Peter. Not only did Luke alone record the penetrating stare of Christ that coincided with Peter's remembrance of Jesus' prediction but Luke also indicated that the shared moment was possible only because Jesus had been turned toward Peter. In his sovereignty, God reached down to control even the physical elements of the salvation process and gave Peter a convicting moment with his Lord. Jesus did not turn to look at Peter. Jesus was turned by those who were incarcerating him, which allowed him to gaze at his disciple in that moment of crushing reality.

THE ARREST CONTINUES

Luke 22:63–71

63 Now the men detaining Jesus derided him and beat him. 64 They blindfolded him and asked him saying, "Prophesy! Who is it that hit you?" 65 They said many other blasphemous things to Jesus. 66 When it became day, the elders of the people gathered together, with the high priests and the scribes, and they led Jesus away to their council 67 saying, "If you are indeed the Christ, tell us." But Jesus said to them, "If I tell you, you will not believe me. 68 And if I question you, you will not respond. 69 But from now on, the Son of man will be seated at God's right hand of power." 70 Then they all said, "Are you the Son of God?" And Jesus said, "As you say, I am." 71 To which they responded, "What more witness do we need? We have heard it ourselves from his own mouth!"

In Jesus' trial before the Sanhedrin, Luke continued the theme of Jesus' submission to earthly authority. But instead of repetition, Luke enhanced the theme of Jesus' willing obedience to God's plan by emphasizing three important attributes of Jesus—his humanity, his deity, and his definition of the Messiah.

The theme of Jesus' willingness to submit to the will of the Father, even at the cost of suffering at the hands of the authorities, is seen in Jesus' response to their question, "Are you the Son of God?" While a literal translation, "You say that I am," could be viewed as a nonanswer, when understood as a vernacular expression or idiom, it is a clear response, "Yes, I am."[10] Jesus did not try to hide his identity. He willingly laid down his life to bring salvation to all humanity, even to those who were persecuting him.

But equally as important to Jesus' affirmation was the progression of his self-identification. When asked if he was the Messiah, Jesus shifted the conversation to his humanity. (1) Jesus acknowledged that he was fully human by evoking the Son of man imagery. A leader would come from among the people to bring them back to God. Jesus' willingness to die for the sins of the world began with the incarnation, God becoming fully human. (2) Jesus' emphasis on his humanity is followed by his asserting his deity. As already demonstrated, Jesus made no attempt to veil his deity. When asked if he was the Son of God, his response was clear, "Yes, I am." The incarnation that did not start with eternal God would have been hollow and empty, a mere pretender or charlatan. Without being fully God, Jesus would have been exactly what the authorities were seeking to prove—just another would be a savior that when pressed would fade and fail. But the incarnation was not hollow, not empty. Eternal God chose to empty self and become fully human. (3) As divine and human, as God and man, the Messiah would enable the complete plan of salvation. "From this point forward," Jesus said, "You will see the Son of man seated at God's right hand of power." Messiah, the one who would bring all to God, would rule the hearts of man from the side of God the Heavenly Father. What Jesus did was take the concept of the Messiah and change it from one that the religious leaders would anticipate using to their advantage and defined the role as one that has ultimate authority and control.

Finally, the reader should not miss Luke's intended message to his Gentile audience. Messiah was not just a Jewish figure. The God that came to earth to live a perfect example in the form of man did not do so to fulfill a narrowly defined, preconceived religious role. Messiah was enthroned on high, endued with power, and available to all. There was nothing that the Christian, regardless of background, could not do in the power of God. A new age truly was dawning.

---

10. Ibid., 277.

THE TRIAL OF JESUS: THEY PREVAILED

Luke 23:1-25

¹At that moment, the entire Sanhedrin arose and led Jesus to Pilate. ²There they began accusing Jesus saying, "We have found that this man is misleading our nation and forbidding the rendering of taxes to Caesar, and saying himself to be Christ the King." ³Pilate asked Jesus saying, "Are you the King of the Jews?' Jesus replied to Pilate, "You say." ⁴Pilate then said to the high priests and to the crowd, "I find no basis for a criminal complaint in this man." ⁵But the delegation insisted saying, "He stirs up the people teaching throughout all of Judea, beginning in Galilee and continuing to even this place." ⁶When Pilate heard this, he asked if the man was from Galilee, ⁷and knowing that to be under Herod's jurisdiction, Pilate send Jesus to Herod, who was in Jerusalem at that time. ⁸Herod was very glad when he saw Jesus. Herod had desired for some time to see Jesus, because he had heard about Jesus and was hoping to see Jesus perform some kind of sign. ⁹Herod Antipas questioned Jesus at length, but Jesus gave no answer, ¹⁰all the while the chief priests and scribes stood by vigorously accusing Jesus. ¹¹Then Herod, along with his soldiers, treated Jesus with contempt and ridicule, placing fine robes on him before he sent Jesus back to Pilate. ¹²Herod and Pilate became friends that very day; before they had been at odds with each other. ¹³Assembling the chief priests, the rulers, and the people, ¹⁴Pilate said to them, "You brought to me a man accused of misleading the people. But after examining him before you, I find no basis for the allegations brought against him. ¹⁵Neither did Herod who immediately sent him back to us. ¹⁶I will beat him and release him."[11] ¹⁸But the mob began shouting together saying, "Kill this man, Jesus, and release to us Barabbas" ¹⁹who was an incarcerated murderer and insurrectionist. ²⁰Pilate addressed the mob again desiring to release Jesus. ²¹But they shouted, "Crucify him, crucify him." ²²Then for the third time, Pilate asked the mob, "Why? What evil works has he done?" ²³But they kept on insisting with loud voices, demand-

---

11. Some ancient manuscripts include verse 17 "For of necessity he must release one unto them at the feast."

ing that Jesus be crucified. And their loud voices won. ²⁴Therefore, Pilate rendered his verdict that their demands be granted. ²⁵Pilate released the one that the mob demanded, who had been thrown into prison for rebellion and murder. But he gave up Jesus to their desire.

Jesus' trial is recorded by all four Gospel writers, each bringing his own literary style and audience needs to the presentation. Matthew follows Mark closely but added details about Barabbas and Pilate's hand-washing gesture. John included the more lengthy conversation between Jesus and Pilate. Luke alone recorded that Jesus was sent before Herod, given that Herod was in Jerusalem and that Jesus was from Galilee, the jurisdiction of Herod Antipas. By incorporating the Herod event, Luke revealed a literary progression to the numerous subplots that were unfolding. There was the obvious pragmatic shift in the accusations of Sanhedrin from religious violations to allegations of civil insurrection. This was necessary for the Jewish leaders to secure the capital punishment they sought. Another subplot was the validation of Jesus' innocence by Pilate, the Roman official who three times said to the crowd that Jesus was innocent. Writing to the Roman official Theophilis, Luke remained true to his intent to show that Christianity was no threat to the Empire.

But more important than these issues, Luke sought to position his readers in the narrative by subtly asking the question, "What would you do with Jesus?" Presented in the trial narratives are three responses to Jesus. There was Pilate, there was Herod, and there was the mob, each with different motives that drove very different responses. Pilate treated Jesus with indifference, Herod with disdain. But the people of the mob treated Jesus with control.

(1) When presented with the allegations of civil unrest and insurrection, Pilate questioned Jesus about the matter. "Are you the King of the Jews?" asked Pilate. "Are you seeking to assert your claims to the throne of this people and thereby overthrow the Roman authorities?" The grammar of Jesus' response leads to an ambiguous English translation. The phrase σὺ λέγεις *(su legeis)* is translated literally as "you, you say," and can simply mean "yes." It also is possible that Jesus answered a question with a question, a technique he was known to use. If this is a question, Jesus' response to Pilate took on an entirely different tone. "Are you the King of the Jews," Pilate asked. Jesus responded, "Who is asking—

you or the people who are making this false accusation? If you are only mouthing their ludicrous claims, then I am not going to dignify them with an answer. If, on the other hand, you as the legitimate civil authority are asking me honestly if I am a political figure bent on overthrowing the existing government in order to replace it with my own monarchy, then the answer is no. I am not a political figure. I have made that clear over and over again." Regardless of whether this was a statement or a question, Pilate's response to Jesus was the same. Pilate met Jesus with indifference. Pilate returned to the Jews and said, "This is an innocent man. He is no more guilty of insurrection than I am." But even though Pilate had reached the correct conclusion about Jesus, he did nothing to take a stand with Jesus. Pilate simply let the moment pass. Three times Pilate reiterated that Jesus had done nothing wrong. But at no time did Pilate's belief translate into action; he simply was indifferent.

(2) Herod had quite a different reaction. Herod treated Jesus with disdain. Herod had heard of Jesus and had longed to meet him in order to be entertained. Herod viewed Jesus like one views a carnival sideshow—with curiosity and amusement. Herod listened as Jesus' accusers perjured themselves. Herod taunted Jesus by giving the accusations even a measure of credibility. But Jesus did not respond. Jesus knew that Herod's interest was nothing more than a facade. Finally, Herod began mocking Jesus, placing royal garments on him and parading him around as a newly enthroned king. Herod looked at Jesus like one watches a court jester whose sole purpose is to amuse and entertain. Herod treated Jesus with disdain.

(3) Finally, and most tragically, the people treated Jesus with control. Pilate repeatedly attempted to vindicate Jesus and release him as the innocent man that he was. But the cries of the crowd grew larger. The more Pilate insisted Jesus had done nothing deserving capital punishment, the more the rabble grew incensed at the idea that they were not calling the shots. The conclave grew at a feverish pitch until, as Luke described the scene, "their great voices prevailed." The word κατίσχυον (*katischuon*) is translated "prevailed" and appears only three times in the New Testament. The occurrences are here, in Luke 21:36 where Jesus warned the disciples that they would need strength to escape the cataclysmic destruction of Jerusalem, and in Peter's confession at Caesarea Philippi in Matthew 16:18, where Jesus said the gates of Hades could not prevail against the church that would be built upon Peter's confession.

All three of these uses of κατίσχυον (*katischuon*) are in keeping with its word group origin, specifically ισχυω (*ischuō*), ισχυρος (*ischuros*), and ισχυς (*ischus*). "The word group ἰσχυ- has the meaning "to be able," to be capable," "capacity," "power," "strength." It is largely co-extensive with δυνα-, and the derivatives overlap. In the case of ἰσχυ- there is more emphasis on the actual power implied in ability or capacity."[12] Accordingly, the disciples would have inherent within themselves the ability to flee the destruction of Jerusalem (Luke 21:36) and the church has the ability and strength to withstand the power of sin and death (Matthew 16:18). But to the point of Jesus' trail, the mob, fomented by the angry shouts, had the power to do with Jesus as they desired.

Luke pressed the point further by recording as an omniscient narrator Pilate's final action of the trial. When he concluded that the angry mob would not be dissuaded, Pilate *gave up Jesus to their desire*. Often translated as "delivered," the word παρέδωκεν (*paredōken*) literally means "gave over." The resulting idea of the word is to hand over to someone, to deliver into someone's care or custody, to place a person or thing under the control of another. Pilate conceded the argument and let the people have what they wanted most—to be in control of Jesus.

With these two mechanisms, the prevailing great voices and Pilate's giving control to the mob, Luke focused the attention of the trial on the larger issue of the death of Christ for the sins of all mankind. Inherent within the actions of the crowd is the key to understanding the atonement of Christ in God's plan of salvation. At its heart, sin is about who is in control—God or self. Each person throughout time has been given the ability to choose. The depth of mankind's depravity is viewed painfully in the trial of Jesus. Given the opportunity to embrace God, mankind instead took God and killed his earthly form on a cruel cross. In so doing, God stopped at nothing to provide an opportunity for salvation. Regardless of whatever else is true about the sacrificial death of Christ, this certainly is true. The death of Christ demonstrates the extent to which mankind is willing go to be in control and the extent to which God is willing to go to be redemptive.

---

12. Grundmann, "ἰσχύω," 397.

THE CRUCIFIXION OF JESUS

Luke 23:26–49

²⁶*As they led Jesus away, they seized Simon of Cyrene who was coming in from the country and made him bear the cross to carry it behind Jesus.* ²⁷*A great crowd of people and women followed him, mourning and weeping.* ²⁸*Turning to them, Jesus said, "Daughters of Jerusalem, do not weep for me. Weep for yourselves and for your children.* ²⁹*For the day is coming when they will say, 'Blessed are the barren and the wombs that never bore and the breasts that never nursed.'* ³⁰*Then they will begin to say to the mountains, 'Fall on us,' and to the hills, 'hide us.'* ³¹*For if they do this when the wood is green, what will they do when the wood is dry?"* ³²*Two criminals were led away to be executed with Jesus.* ³³*When they came to the place called The Skull, they crucified Jesus with the criminals, one on the right and one on the left.* ³⁴*Jesus said, "Father, forgive them. They do not know what they do." Then they divided his clothes by casting lots.* ³⁵*The people stood by, watching.* ³⁶*The soldiers ridiculed Jesus, coming up and offering vinegar* ³⁷*saying, "If you are the King of the Jews, save yourself."* ³⁸*There was an inscription above him that said, "The King of the Jews."* ³⁹*One of the criminals that was hanging there began blaspheming, saying, "Are you not the Christ? Save yourself and save us."* ⁴⁰*But the other criminal responded, rebuking him and saying, "Do you not even fear God, knowing you are under the same condemnation?* ⁴¹*We are justly accused and deserve what we are getting. But this man is innocent of all wrongdoing."* ⁴²*Then he said, "Jesus, remember me when you come into your kingdom."* ⁴³*Jesus said to the thief, "Truly I say, today you will be with me in paradise."* ⁴⁴*Now it was about the sixth hour when darkness came upon the entire land and lasted until the ninth hour.* ⁴⁵*The sun's light faded, and the veil in the temple was torn in half.* ⁴⁶*Then Jesus cried out in a loud voice saying, "Father, unto your hands I commit my spirit." After saying this, Jesus died.* ⁴⁷*Seeing all of this, the Roman soldier began praising God saying, "Indeed this man was righteous!"* ⁴⁸*Now the crowd that had assembled together to see the sight, when they saw what had happened, they lamented, returning to their homes*

> beating their chests. ⁴⁹All those that knew Jesus and the women who had followed him from Galilee stood at a distance and saw all these things.

Two details emerge from this text when the reader focuses on the unique contributions of Luke's crucifixion narrative. While Matthew and Mark both recorded the conscription of Simon of Cyrene to bear Jesus' cross to Calvary, only Luke included the comments Jesus made to the crowd that were enabled by his turning to address them. Additionally, all four Gospels indicate that Jesus was executed between two common criminals, but only Luke recorded their conversation during the crucifixion. Luke used both of these conversations to emphasize again the reality of the human condition. When man's feeble efforts to save himself inevitably fail, God lovingly provides a way of escape.

While it is obvious that the comments Jesus made on the way to the cross were not just another conversation, Jesus' use of sarcasm and exaggeration signal he did not intend his comments to be taken literally. First, Jesus reversed a typical or common blessing. Childbirth was considered one of God's greatest gifts. Life was sacred and to be cherished. The Bible is replete with tales of women seeking God's blessing through childbirth. For Jesus to say that the barren and the childless were to be blessed was a contradiction in terms.

Because of the obvious disconnection from reality, some interpreters have taken the statement as a prediction of the impending Roman invasion of Jerusalem. Jesus had spoken of this before. Like the statement in the little apocalypse that said there would be woe to the woman who was nursing at that time, some take this passage to describe the carnage that was to come with the destruction of the temple. This view is supported by two important facts. The first is Jesus' use of the parable that if you burn green wood, what will you do with dry wood? The imagery is plain. Green wood is not a good fuel. The sap causes the wood to be wet and therefore fire resistant. A fire hot enough to burn wet wood will consume dry wood in an instant. Likewise, if an authority would convict and ultimately execute an innocent person, what would the authority do to a truly guilty person? Second, Jesus was, in fact, an innocent man. If the Romans could so easily mistreat and execute an innocent man during what to the Romans was just another day, what would they do during a time of open military conflict?

While this approach certainly has merit, it seems to miss one very important point. Luke sought to demonstrate that the Christian movement was peaceable, that its adherents were law-abiding citizens who answered to civil and divine authority and was thereby absolutely no threat to the Roman Empire. This view is born out in Luke's unique recording of the Roman centurion's statement. While Matthew and Mark recorded the statement "Surely this was the Son of God," Luke alone included the proclamation by the Roman officer who carried out the execution, "This is an innocent man."

Assuming that Jesus' statements were not intended as an anti-Roman polemic, Luke's message becomes clear with an understanding of Jesus' quotation of Hosea 10:8, "And they shall say to the mountains, 'Cover us,' and to the hills, 'Fall on us.' " Rather than a narrow apocalyptic reference, the reader should understand Jesus' remembrance of the entire thought of Hosea. Roy L. Honeycutt, Jr. said of Hosea 10 that "the whole of the narrative is an excellent commentary on the inevitable accomplishment of a broken faith."[13] Though they prospered and acknowledged God through increasingly more opulent worship, their hearts were false. Furthermore, because they did not fear the Lord, the efforts of a king were futile and bound to fail. Ineffectual covenants were established with empty oaths. The fertile land, which when blessed by God brought them prosperity, would yield only poisonous harvests. Rather than turning to God in contrition, they turned to idols until in ultimate shame they would cry for the mountains to fall and the hills to cover them from the sight of a righteous and judging God.

Taken with the figurative blessing and the exaggeration of the innocent being swept away with the guilty, the Hosea passage drives home the point that human effort inevitably fails. There is no efficacy in man's righteousness. Rather than actually achieving salvation, man's righteousness actually gets in the way of what God alone can do. Jesus' comments on the way to the cross were intended to heighten the awareness of those listening that only by turning to God can there be any hope and assurance of salvation.

The second unique aspect of Luke's crucifixion narrative relates to the exchange between Jesus and one of the dying thieves who hung by his side. "Save yourself," cried the executioners. "Save yourself and us," begged one of the thieves who was dying as well. But without explana-

---

13. Honeycutt, Hosea-Malachi, 45.

tion, one of the criminals made a remarkable observation. Speaking to his fellow malcontent he said, "Do you not even fear God? You and I are condemned for what we did. We lied, we stole, we murdered, we broke man's law and God's law as well. We deserve to die for our transgressions. But this man has done nothing. This man is innocent."

Luke provided no rationale for the man's spontaneous remarks. Had the thief seen Jesus perform a miracle? Had he heard Jesus speak to the crowds? Did the dying thief have a friend or relative who had been touched by Jesus? Or was it simply the moment? Perhaps the man dying for just cause saw through his vile nature to recognize eternal God. If so, Luke's use of Jesus' quotation of Hosea can be understood as building to a climactic moment; "Remember me," the sinner said to Jesus, "When you come into your kingdom." When mankind's efforts fail, when all human hope is abandoned, when that moment of final realization comes that there is nothing anyone can do to save him or herself, then one turns to God to hear the words of redemption, "I will remember you. Today you will be with me in paradise."

No modern thought may express better the inevitable failure of man's feeble efforts to save himself than the 18th century Englishman, William Cowper, who wrote,

> *The dying thief rejoiced to see*
> *the fountain in his day;*
> *And there may I, though vile as he,*
> *Wash all my sins away.*

Not only did Cowper capture the joy of salvation found by the sin-sick soul but his lines also articulate the very essence of faith's access to God, both for salvation and life eternal with the divine.

> *E're since by faith I saw the stream*
> *Thy flowing wounds supply,*
> *Redeeming love has been my theme,*
> *And shall be till I die.*[14]

Luke's crucifixion narrative goes beyond mere detail, his intent exceeding the desire to rehearse the facts. Luke's narrative cast the whole of salvation in the light of God's eternal plan.

---

14. Cowper, "*There Is a Fountain*," Public Domain.

SEEING GOD WHEN NO ONE ELSE DOES

Luke 23:50–56

⁵⁰⁻⁵¹*Now there was a man named Joseph who was a Jew from the city of Arimathea. Although he was a member of the council, he agreed with neither their plan nor their action. He was good and righteous, looking for the kingdom of God.* ⁵²*Joseph went to Pilate and requested the body of Jesus.* ⁵³*Taking Jesus down, Joseph wrapped him in linen cloth and laid him in a tomb, hewn from a rock, in which no one had ever been laid.* ⁵⁴*It was the day of preparation and the Sabbath was beginning.* ⁵⁵*The women who had come with Jesus out of Galilee followed and saw the tomb and the manner in which Jesus had been placed there.* ⁵⁶*Then they returned to prepare spices and ointments.*

As Luke concluded the crucifixion narrative, a new character was introduced. A member of the Sanhedrin, Joseph of Arimathea was described as opposing the plans to accuse falsely and ultimately execute Jesus. One obvious reason for Luke's inclusion of the Joseph episode was to avoid vilifying the entire Jewish race. Many Jews followed Jesus and were in sympathy with his message of forgiveness, love, and hope. Not every Jew in Jerusalem that day committed perjury, calling for the death of an innocent man. Furthermore, in the aftermath of the tragedy of epic proportion, not every Jew fled from the moment in confusion and sorrow as did many of Jesus' closest disciples. Many stayed, addressed the needs of the moment, and by so doing set an example for all of Christendom.

Such people were typified by Joseph, who buried Jesus at his own expense. Described as good, righteous, and looking for the kingdom of God, Joseph helped conclude Jesus' earthly life in much the same way it had begun. When Jesus was taken as an infant to the temple for the rights of purification, he was greeted by Simeon. Described as righteous, devout, and looking for the consolation of Israel, Simeon recognized Jesus for who he was: the Savior of the world. "Now I can depart in peace," Simeon said in praise to God, "for my own eyes have seen your salvation." Both men were called righteous. Simeon was devout and righteous. Joseph was good and righteous.

When used of a human in a religious context, the word δίκαιος (*dikaios*) is translated as "righteousness," and carries the meaning of "not violating the sovereignty of God"[15] or "conforming to the standard, will or character of God."[16] As a result, a righteous person is thought to be good, just, fair, upright, honest, and innocent, or more to the point, pleasing to God.

Too often, however, the necessity of righteousness is considered only with regard to eternal security. As Isaiah proclaimed, "But we are all as an unclean thing, and all our righteousnesses are as filthy rags; and we all do fade as a leaf; and our iniquities, like the wind, have taken us away" (Isa 64:6). Paul said to the Roman church, "There is none righteous, no, not one" (Rom 3:10). What is more, the main message of Romans is clear: Mankind's only true righteousness is the righteousness of God imparted to mankind by faith.

Such is the meaning of the words of 19th century songwriter Edward Mote who penned the final verse of "The Solid Rock".

> *When he shall come with trumpet sound,*
> *Oh, may I then in him be found;*
> *Dressed in his righteousness alone,*
> *Faultless to stand before the throne.*[17]

But the Christian's desire to be pleasing to God, to be in compliance with God's character, to be righteous, should reach beyond the need for salvation. The lives of Simeon and Joseph send a clear call to the church that God desires to impart righteousness so that in obedience his children live lives that expect God to act. Righteous and devout, righteous and good, both Simeon and Joseph were looking for God to act on humanity's behalf and for humanity's benefit. It is this final quality that is the key to understanding God's desire for the church.

In the temple at Jesus' purification and in Jerusalem during the moments after the crucifixion were people who loved God, people who trusted God, people who had faith that God could and would save. But only two were given opportunities that by their very nature were completely unique. Only one would hold an infant in his arms and announce in praise to God that the Savior had arrived. Only one would take a lifeless body from the cross of that same Savior and lay it lovingly in an unused tomb. Righteous and devout, righteous and good were the

---

15. BDAG 195.
16. Newman, A Concise Greek-English Dictionary of the New Testament, 46.
17. Mote, "The Solid Rock," Public domain.

qualities that caused Simeon and Joseph to live their lives in expectation of what God would do. And it was that expectation that God utilized, allowing these two friends of God to see something remarkable, to see something no one else saw. They saw God intervene into history in a personal way.

Insights of this nature rarely go without an indictment. What a wonderful opportunity righteousness brought to Simeon and to Joseph! How marvelous to be used by God in such a way! But how tragic that they alone experienced what God was doing. How condemning it is when a child of God doesn't move from righteousness to expectation to seeing what no one else sees. How sad when the believer uses the incredible gift of right relationship with God only for personal security rather than to live a life, daily expecting God to act. It is this anticipation that unlocks a rarely considered view of salvation: God wants to save his child to live eternally with him, starting right here, starting right now.

THE RESURRECTION

Luke 24:1-12

On the Sabbath, the women rested according to the Commandments. ¹But on the first day of the week, they went to the tomb, carrying the embalming spices that they had prepared. ²There they found the stone rolled away from the tomb, ³but going inside the tomb, they did not find the body of the Lord Jesus. ⁴While they were perplexed concerning these matters, they saw two men in shining clothing. ⁵The women were frightened and were bowing their faces to the earth. So the men said to them, "Why are you seeking the living among the dead? ⁶He is not here. Get up! Remember what he told you while he was still in Galilee, ⁷saying that it was necessary for the Son of man to be delivered into the hands of sinful men, be crucified, and on the third day be resurrected." ⁸Then the women remembered Jesus' words. ⁹Returning from the tomb, the women told these things to the Eleven and to all the rest. ¹⁰Now it was Mary Magdalene, Jo-Anna, Mary the mother of James, and the other women who told these things to the apostles. ¹¹But their words seemed like nonsense to the apostles, who did not believe them. ¹²But Peter arose, ran to the tomb, stooped down and

> *looked in, and saw the burial clothes alone. Then he went home wondering what had happened.*

Luke's resurrection narrative is short and to the point. There is no wondering about how the stone was rolled away, there is no questioning of the angelic forms. The women arrived with their spices to honor the body of Jesus. Finding the tomb empty, they were astonished by the appearance of the angels and by the message that was delivered. Departing, they told the eleven remaining disciples.[18] Considering it foolishness, the apostles dismissed the report.

Luke's intent in recording the resurrection narratives seems to be simply the inclusion of female characters in the propagation of the gospel. The facts of Jesus' resurrection were well established in the Christian community by the time of Luke's writing, even though they were unfolding for the first time for Theophilus. By emphasizing the women's role, Luke again painted a portrait of inclusion for all who hear the gospel. Introduced here, though, is a literary devise that Luke repeated in his unique record of the road to Emmaus.

But beyond Luke's inclusion of women as the first postresurrections apostles, there is a lesson to be learned about ministry. Specifically, the women at the tomb show that ministry is born out of love. Because of their love and devotion to Jesus, they returned to the tomb to anoint the lifeless body of the one they believed had been the Messiah. Their love drove them to serve even though they must have wondered about access to the tomb. Their love drove them to serve even though at that moment they must have thought they had been wrong about Jesus being the Christ. When ministry is born out of love, reason does not always apply.

The incident also informs the reader about ministry in a broken and fallen world.

(1) Uncertainty is inevitable. Unspoken in Luke's narrative was the concern about removing the stone and accessing the body. Luke chose the moment of the empty tomb to express the confusion that can follow even the best intended act of kindness. Translated as "perplexed," ἀπορεω (*aporeō*) and its related words carry the meaning of being at a loss for words. It must have been one of those head-scratching, "this

---

18. This is the only inference to Judas's demise in Luke's account. See also Luke 24:33.

sure is peculiar" type of moments. These same word groups were used by Luke to describe Herod's reaction to the news about Jesus after having executed John the Baptist (Luke 9:7) and Peter's reaction to his roof-top vision of being commanded to eat that which was unclean (Acts 10:17). John used these related words to describe the disciples' reaction at the Last Supper to Jesus' announcement that his betrayer was in their midst (John 13:22). Bewilderment, confusion, uncertainty, and ambiguity all are adjectives that could describe the state of being at a loss. All could apply to the inevitable moment in ministry when the person must relinquish the all too human desire to understand and to simply "keep on moving." (2) Too often confusion gives way to fear. While the women were at a loss as to what had happened and as to what they should do, they encountered the two angelic forms that told them of the resurrection. Understandably, the women fell prostrate in fear. When ministry is allowed to stay in the bewilderment stage, too many things can happen that cause fear to take control. Ironically, the message was sent to affirm and instruct. But even that which God intends for the Christian's benefit can strangely become the source of more frustration and increased anxiety. (3) But joyfully, ambiguity, and apprehension fade away in the presence of the God's recalled word. The child of God intent on fulfilling love's obligation of service need only to cherish God's direction. The angels delivered the message that the Christ had arisen from the dead after being persecuted and executed, just as he had said he would. Luke indicated that the women remembered Jesus' words and returned from the tomb to tell all that had happened. Ministry should be guided constantly by the realization that nothing escapes God's notice and that divine providence follows those who serve. God knows the paths down which he sends his servants and has prepared the way for success.

THE ROAD TO EMMAUS: FAULTY ASSUMPTIONS

Luke 24:13-35

13 That same day, two of the disciples were going to a village about seven miles from Jerusalem that was known as Emmaus 14and they were talking to each other about everything that had happened. 15 While they were talking to each other and discussing these things, Jesus approached them and began walking with them. ¹⁶*But their eyes were restrained so as to not recognize Jesus.* ¹⁷*Then Jesus said to them, "What are these words concerning that you are exchanging with each other?" And they stood still looking saddened.* ¹⁸*The one named Cleopas answered and said, "Are you the only person living in Jerusalem that does not know the things that have been happening in these days?"* ¹⁹*Jesus said to him, "What things?" Cleopas then said to Jesus, "Concerning Jesus of Nazareth, a prophet who was powerful in work and word, in the sight of God and all the people;* ²⁰*how our chief priests and rulers delivered him to a judgment of death and crucified him.* ²¹*But we had hope that he was about to redeem Israel; and even now it is the third day since all of these things took place.* ²²*Furthermore, some of the women of our group astonished us. They were at the tomb early this morning* ²³*and not finding his body they came talking about seeing visions of angels who said Jesus was alive.* ²⁴*Some of our company went to the tomb and found matters just as the women had said, but did not see Jesus."* ²⁵*Then Jesus said, "O, ye foolish men, and slow of heart to believe all that the prophets have spoken.* ²⁶*Was it not necessary for the Christ to suffer in order to enter into his glory?"* ²⁷*Then Jesus began to explain all the Scriptures had to say concerning himself, beginning with Moses through all the prophets.*

Immediately following the story of the women at the tomb, Luke included a unique narrative about two disciples walking on the road that led to Emmaus. In the aftermath of the eventful Passover, the disciples were doing what comes all too normally: They were sorting out the events as best they could. They were so consumed by their efforts that even Jesus' approach did not break their concentration. They were shocked to hear Jesus express a lack of knowledge about the topic of their conversation. Surely, they thought, what concerns us should concern everyone.

As the conversation continued, the error of the disciples' assumptions began emerging. First, the Emmaus-bound disciples attributed to Jesus the status of mighty prophet. While this certainly was a true statement, it was not a complete statement. Jesus had made no secret about his filial relationship with the Heavenly Father. Proof of Jesus' self-proclaimed divinity was a major part of the accusations that led to his execution. To assume that Jesus was only a prophet was a gross understatement. Second, the disciples continued to misunderstand and to misrepresent the true nature and purpose of the Messiah. Luke indicated that the disciples thought Jesus would be the one to redeem Israel. The word λυτροῦσθαι (*lutrousthai*) literally means "he set free." The concept of redemption was that of buying back one's freedom or releasing one from the bondage of another. Far from understanding the role of the kingdom of God on earth, the disciples incorrectly assumed that had he been the Messiah, Jesus would have eliminated the Roman occupation of Israel. Third, the near end of the third day without confirmation of their self-constructed resolution had to mean only one thing: Jesus was not the Christ.

Fortunately, God does not deal in mankind's faulty assumption. Mankind incorrectly thinks that when God does not act on cue, God must not be acting at all. To the contrary, the Messiah had come, the redemption on Israel had been accomplished, and God's kingdom on earth had begun to reign in the hearts of men.

YEARNING TO UNDERSTAND SCRIPTURE

Luke 24:28–35

28 As they drew near the village where they were going, it appeared that Jesus was going to proceed farther. 29 But they urged Jesus saying, "Abide with us, for it is about evening, and the day is drawing to a close." So Jesus stayed with them. 30 Now it happened that Jesus sat down to eat with them and taking bread, he blessed it, and gave it to them. 31 Then their eyes were opened and they recognized Jesus, who then became invisible before them. 32 But they said to each other, "Did not our hearts burn as he spoke to us in the way and explained to us the Scriptures?" 33 They arose that very hour and returned to Jerusalem and found the Eleven gathered together, and they were with them 34 who had said, "The Lord has risen indeed and appeared to Simon." 35 So they told them all that had happened in the way and how Jesus had become known to them in the breaking of the bread.

In sequential stories, Luke incorporated an important detail about living the Christian life: Human disappointment can temporarily rob the child of God of the joy of the Lord. When the women went to the tomb, they encountered an empty grave. Rather than remembering that Jesus had said he must suffer at the hands of sinful men and then be resurrected, the women were astonished and fell down in fear at the angel's announcement that Jesus was not dead. Their grief over their apparent loss caused them to discount all that Jesus had predicted about the moment.

Likewise, the two disciples who walked with Jesus were so sorrowful about the events of the past week that they did not recognize Jesus. Even with the encouragement of Jesus' recitation of all that Scripture indicated about the role the Messiah must play, they could not get past their personal sense of loss. Only when Jesus blessed, broke, and distributed the bread did the two men recognize him.

Tucked away in the road to Emmaus narrative was the statement of the disciples' reaction to Jesus' instruction. "Didn't our hearts burn within us when he opened our minds to the Scriptures?" said the two to each other. Created in the image of God, all humanity yearns to be in fellowship with the divine. Unfortunately, because of our fallen sinful nature, we too often enthrone the wrongs things to the object of our worship. Attempting to be in control, we are not willing to admit we have a need that we cannot fulfill. Only as we are submissive to God can there come the seasons of refreshing that wash over our souls. Without realizing the stranger was Jesus, the disciples knew there was something about what he was saying. In retrospect, they understood why they were so satisfied by Jesus' comments. Only the words of Christ can calm the spirit and nurture the soul.

FAITH TRUMPS REASON

Luke 24:36–43

[36] While they were speaking these things, Jesus appeared in their midst and said to them, "Peace to you." [37] Now they were all astonished and became fearful, thinking they saw a spirit. [38] But Jesus said to them, "Why are your troubled and give rise to questions in your heart? [39] Look at my hands and my feet. It is indeed I. Touch me and see. A spirit does not have flesh and bones as you see I have." [40] Jesus showed them his hands and his feet as he said these things. [41] While they were still disbelieving in joy and amazement, Jesus said to them, "Do you have anything to eat?" [42] The disciples

gave Jesus a piece of broiled fish **⁴³***and he ate it before them.*

Following the twin narratives about how human emotion runs contrary to the sustained joy of service to the risen Christ, Luke included Jesus' conversation to reinforce the point of the previous stories. Straight to the point, Jesus asked the disciples why they were troubled and why they questioned in their hearts that the events were unfolding exactly as he had said they would.

Recognizing their difficulty, Jesus lovingly met the disciples at their point of need. Rather than insisting that faith allows a comprehension that supersedes rational thought, Jesus allowed a rare moment of accommodation. It was as if Jesus said to them, "OK, you want a physical Jesus? Then go ahead and touch me. If seeing and touching is believing, then gaze on my wounds and touch my scars. Examine me to see that I have flesh and bones. I am not a spirit. I really did die. I really was buried. I really, really did raise from the dead just like I said I would."

But the question that Luke's narrative begs will not be answered in his first volume. While Jesus agreed to a physical verification by the disciples, Luke will make the point in his second volume, The Acts of the Apostles, that the first true test of the fledgling Christian movement was could there be a church without a physical Jesus. The answer will be a resounding yes!

FINAL INSTRUCTIONS AND ASCENSION

Luke 24:44–53

⁴⁴*Then Jesus said to them, "These are my words that I spoke to you while I was with you; that it was necessary to fulfill all the writings in the Law of Moses and in the prophets and the psalms concerning me."* **⁴⁵***Then Jesus opened their minds to comprehend the Scriptures,* **⁴⁶***and said to them, "In such a way, it was written that the Christ must suffer and be resurrected from the dead on the third day,* **⁴⁷***and that repentance and forgiveness should be preached in his name to all nations, beginning in Jerusalem.* **⁴⁸***You are my witnesses.* **⁴⁹***Now I send the promise of my Father upon you. But remain in the city until you are clothed in power from heaven."* **⁵⁰***Then Jesus led the disciples to Bethany, and lifting up his hands, he blessed them.* **⁵¹***Now it happened while Jesus*

> was blessing them that he parted from them and was taken into heaven. ⁵²Worshiping, the disciples returned to Jerusalem with great joy, ⁵³and were continually in the temple praising God.

When Jesus met with the disciples for the last time, he delivered a very important message. First, Jesus reiterated that there was nothing new about his message. What Jesus said in his final hours was no different from what he had been saying all along. God's message to his people, whether it be written, proclaimed, or simply felt, is always the same

Second, as he recorded the event, Luke indicated that Jesus opened the minds of the disciples to the Scriptures. Luke used διήνοιξεν (*diēnoixen*), meaning "he opened," here and previously in verses 31 and 32 where, on the road to Emmaus, Jesus opened the eyes of the disciples to the meaning of Scripture. Though circumstances certainly were heightened in the hours before Jesus' ascension, Luke gave the people of God an extraordinary insight: As Jesus is the standard by which Scripture is interpreted, only he can open the heart of the believer to the truths of Scripture.

Once this takes place, once the soul has been enlightened and is in harmony with Christ's urging, three things occur. (1) The believer becomes a witness. Jesus made a simple declaration. "You are my witnesses." By the power of the promised presence of the Heavenly Father, all believers who hear the words of Scripture opened by the person of Christ are by their very nature witnesses to the life-changing power of God. (2) The believer becomes a true worshiper. Immediately following Jesus' ascension, the disciples began returning to Jerusalem, worshiping as they went. True worship occurs spontaneously in the life of the believer whose heart has been opened to the truth of Scripture by the presence of Jesus Christ. (3) Finally, the believer becomes a constant source of praise to God. Continually in the temple, the disciples were giving εὐλογοῦντες (*eulogountes*), "good words," to God. Praise, glory, adoration, and honor all belong to God and are constantly on the thoughts and hearts of those whose lives have been changed by the power, presence, and person of Jesus Christ.

Bibliography

Aland, Barbara, Kurt Aland, Johannes Karavidopoulos, Carlo M. Martini, and Bruce M. Metzger. *The UBS Greek New Testament: A Reader's Edition. Running Greek-English Dictionary*, Compiled by Barclay M. Newman. Germany: Deutsche Bibelgesellschaft, Stuttgart, 2007.

Aland, Kurt. *Synopsis Quattuor Evangeliorum: Locis Parallelis Evangeliorum Apocryphorum et Patrum Adhibitis Edidit.* Germany: Deutsche Bibelgesellschaft Stuttgart, 1985.

Barclay, William. *The Gospel of Luke*. Philadelphia: Westminster, 1953.

Bauer, Walter, Frederick W. Danker, William F. Arndt, and F. Wilbur Gingrich. *A Greek-English Lexicon of The New Testament and Other Early Christian Literature*. Chicago: The University of Chicago Press, 1979.

Beyer, Hermann Wolfgang. "βλασφημεᴆω." In *TDNT* 1:621.

Brooks, James A., and Carlton L. Winbery. *Syntax of New Testament Greek*. Washington, D.C.: University Press of America, 1979.

Bultmann, Rudolf. "ἀγαλλιάομαι." In *TDNT* 1:20.

Carnegie, Andrew. "Wealth." *North American Review*, June (1889) 664.

Chambers, Oswald. *The Complete Works of Oswald Chambers*. Grand Rapids: Discovery House, 2000.

Crosby, Fanny. "Rescue the Perishing." In *The Baptist Hymnal*. Nashville: Genevox, 1991.

Dana, H. E., and Julius R. Mantey. *A Manual Grammar of the Greek New Testament*. New York: The MacMillan Company, 1962.

Davis, William Hersey. *Beginner's Grammar of the Greek New Testament*. New York: Harper & Row Publishers, 1923.

Fitzer, Gottfried. "τολμάω, κτλ." In *TDNT* 8:181–186.

Foerster, Werner. "ἔξεστιν." In *TDNT* 2:560.

Grundmann, Walter. "ἰσχύω." In *TDNT* 3:397–402.

Herrmann, Johannes and Werner Foerster. "κλῆρος." In *TDNT* 3:758–785.

Holmes, Oliver Wendell. *The Poet at the Breakfast Table*. Boston: Houghton, Mifflin & Company, 1892.

Honeycutt Jr., Roy L. *BBC*. Vol. 7, *Hosea-Malachi*. Nashville: Broadman, 1972.

Josephus, Flavius. *Complete Works of Flavius Josephus*. Translated by William Whiston. 1867. Reprint, Kregel, 1984.

McCasland, S. V. "Education, NT." In *IDB* 2:34–38.

Metzger, Bruce M. *A Textual Commentary on the Greek New Testament*. New York: United Bible Societies, 1975.

———. *The New Testament: Its Background, Growth, & Content*, 3rd ed. Nashville: Abingdon, 2003.

Michel, Otto. "ὁμολογέω." In *TDNT* 5:199–200.

Miller, Calvin. *The Singer*. Downers Grove: InterVarsity, 1975.
Moulton, Harold K. *The Analytical Greek Lexicon Revised*. Grand Rapids: The Zondervan Corporation, 1982.
Newman Jr., Barclay. *A Concise Greek-English Dictionary of the New Testament*. United States: United Bible Societies, 1971.
Rahlfs, Alfred. Editor. *Septuaginta: Id est Vetus Testamentum Graece Iuxa LXX Interpretes*. Germany: Duetsche Bibelgesellschaft Stuttgart.
Richardson, L. D. J. "ΥΠΗΡΕΤΗΣ." *The Classical Quarterly* 37 (1943) 55–61.
Robertson, A. T. *A Grammar of the Greek New Testament*. Nashville: Broadman, 1934.
———. *WPNT*. Vol. 2, *Luke*. Nashville: Broadman, 1930.
Schmoller, Alfred. *Concordantiae: Novi Tetamenti Graeci*. Germany: Duetsche Bibelgesellschaft Stuttgart, 1982.
Skinner, J. *The Book of the Prophet Isaiah Chapters XL-LXVI*. In *The Cambridge Bible for Schools and Colleges*. Cambridge: University Press, 1917.
Smart, James D. *The Strange Silence of the Bible in the Church*. Philadelphia: Westminster, 1970.
Stagg, Frank. *Studies in Luke's Gospel*. Nashville: Convention, 1967.
Stählin, Gustav. "σκάνδαλον, κτλ." In *TDNT* 7:339–340.
Taylor, Mrs. Howard (Mary). *Borden of Yale: The Life that Counts*. Philadelphia: China Inland Missions, 1926.
Throckmorton Jr., Burton H. *Gospel Parallels: A Synopsis of the First Three Gospels*. Nashville: Thomas Nelson Inc., 1979.
Walford, William. "Sweet Hour of Prayer." In *The Baptist Hymnal*. Nashville: Genevox, 1991.
White, William. "רָנַן (rānan)." In *TWOT* 2:851.
Zerwick, Maximilian. *Biblical Greek: Illustrated by Examples*. Rome: *Editrice Pontificio Instituto Biblico, 1963*.
Zerwick, Maximilian, and Mary Grosvenor, Mary. *A Grammatical Analysis of the New Testament*. Rome: Biblical Institute Press, 1981.

Scripture Index

OLD TESTAMENT

Genesis

1:2	9
2:2–3	75
6:3	9
10:32	155
12:3	226
24:31	43
25	153
41:38	9
50	153

Exodus

3:6	274
10:7	231
11:25–29	9
13:2	34
16:7–12	217
20:8–11	75
22:1	256
30:11–16	265
35:2–3	75

Leviticus

9:1–23	164
9:24	164
13:45–46	65
14	237
14:36	43
19:18	170
25:8–17	57

Numbers

5:5–7	256
6	10
18:15–18	34
19:16	189
24:2	9
27:18	9

Deuteronomy

6:5	170
8:3	6
24:1	228
25:5	274

Joshua

1:8	53
24:15	19

Judges

13	10

1 Samuel

28:7–25	275

2 Samuel

8	14
17:11	147

1 Kings

10:1–9	185
17:8	58

2 Kings

4	98
4:18–37	98
4:29	156
5	58

1 Chronicles

23:3	4
24	4
28:11–19	4

2 Chronicles

9:1–8	185
23:8	4
35:21	60

Ezra

2:36–39	4
4:1–3	273
10:3	273

Nehemiah

13:30	4

Job

4:6–9	201

Psalms

16:11	10
23:1–6	167
32:1–2	287
51:10–12	8
69:22	231
118:22	270, 271
119	ix
119:11	53
124:7	231
139:8	275

Isaiah

7	14
40:3–5	43
45:22–23	165
54:1	7
58:6	57
61:1	57
61:1–2a	42
63:10–11	9
64:6	304

Jeremiah

5:28	226
12:1	226

Daniel

7:14	134

Hosea

10:8	301

Jonah

3:1–10	185

Micah

5:2	129

Malachi

3:1	43
4:5-6	102

NEW TESTAMENT

Matthew

2:8	129
2:10	13
3:4	42
3:7	46
3:14	49
4:8	63
4:24—5:2	83
5:45	226
5:12	13
5:25	2
5:17	88
8:23–27	115
8:27	95, 116
9:1	68
9:8	95
9:17	30
9:31	57
9:36	98
9:55—10:16	154
10	127
10:1–4	81
10:6	155
10:7	5
10:34–38	26
11:2–6	100
11:11	207
13:21	109
14	138
14:3–12	101
14:13	130
14:14	98
15:14	213
15:28	142
15:32	98
16	138
16:17–19	133
16:18	297, 298
16:22–23	133
17:24–27	265
18:1–7	230
18:13	13
18:23–32	236
18:27	98
20:19	70
20:34	98
21:20	95
22:22	95
23:26	241
24	197
25	86
25:23–24	237
25:35–36	53
26	138
26:6–13	104
26:41	286
26:58	2
27:14	95

Mark

1:41	98
1:24	185
2:1	68
3:2	77
3:13–19	81
3:19–22	114
4:17	109
4:35–41	115
5:1-20	59
5:33	124, 125
5:38	30
6:6–13	154
6:7	127
6:17–29	101
6:20	31
6:30	130
6:34	98
7:9–13	213
8	138
8:2	98
8:32–33	133
9:22	98

Scripture Index 317

Mark - continued

9:38–48	230
12:17	95
14	138
14:3–9	104
14:11	13
14:21	283
14:38	286
14:54	2
14:65	2
15:5	95
15:39	185
15:43	276

Luke

(Additional references not presented in their narrative context)

1–2	146
1	103
1:1–4	22, 100
1:14	165
1:21	95
1:36	7
1:41	8, 10
1:44	165
147	165
1:63	95
1:67	8, 10
1:68–79	17
1:68	21, 99
1:78	99
2:9	37
2:29–32	17
2:33	95
2:41–52	98
2:51	161
3:3	72
3:8	255
3:19–20	101
4:1	58
4:16–21	72
4:16	2
4:18–28	253
4:18–19	42, 66
4:34	253
4:37	66
4:38–39	81
4:39	106
4:42	281
5:1—9:50	146
5:1–11	81
5:1	66
5:8	138
5:17	80
5:20	108
5:24	80
5:27–28	81
5:33–39	81
6:47	46
7:9–10	108
7:16	20, 21
7:28	207
7:41–43	236
7:50	109
8:21	184
8:28	141
8:45	138
8:48	105, 109
8:51	138
9:1–6	154
9:1–2	161
9:7	307
9:20	138
9:22	149, 249, 251
9:27	149
9:31	149
9:44–45	249
9:44	149, 250
9:45	250
9:51—18:14	147
9:51—19:10	146
10:1–12	158
10:17	158
10:20	174
10:21–22	174

Scripture Index

10:21	171	13:22	307		
10:25–37	174	16:33	150		
10:33	99	16:8	170		
10:38–42	174	17	163, 168		
10:40	37	18	138		
11:13	195	18:3	2		
12:5	46	18:12	2		
13:22	149	18:18	2		
13:31	241	18:22	2		
13:33	231	18:36	2		
14	217	19:6	2		
14:1	77	20:15–19	286		
14:31	31	20:29	168		
14:35	152	21:25	157		
15:20	99				
16:14	240				
17:11	149	**Acts**			
18:42	109	1:2	150		
19:7	217	1:11	150		
19:11—24:53	146	1:22	150		
20:20	77	1:24	154		
20:26	95	2:4	8, 9		
21:36	297, 298	2:5	35		
23:29	7	2:7	95		
24:19	253	4:8	8, 10		
24:33	306	4:13	95		
24:36	105	4:15	31		
		4:31	8, 10		
		6:1	217		
John		7:23	21		
1:14	3	8	148		
2:4	60	8:2	35		
3	36, 151	9	158		
4:27	95	9:16	46		
5	167	9:17	8, 10		
6:1	63, 130	9:24	77		
6:4	168	9:26–27	158		
6:41	217	10	155		
7:15	95	10:2	141		
7:45	2	10:17	307		
8:51	77	10:28	238		
8:56	168	12:6	77		
13	138	13:9	8, 10		

Acts - continued

13:52	8, 10
15	158
15:36	21
16:11–18	1
17:18	31
18:27	31
19:27	143
20:14	31
20:35	46
21:4	29
21:39	141
22:12	35
26:3	141

Romans

1:10	141
3:10	304
3:23	287
6:5–14	287
12:3	212
12:12	13
14:11–12	166
14:11	165
15:1	236
15:27	237

1 Corinthians

1:12	28
4:1	2
5:4–5	69
10:13	54
15:55	251
15:58	xiv

2 Corinthians

5:19	21
5:20	141
8:4	141
10:2	141
11:26	116

Galatians

1:8	158
2:1	158
3:1	142
4:10	77
4:12	141
4:27	7
5:22–23	10
6:7	111

Ephesians

2:11–19	239
4:24	22

Philippians

2:5–8	237
2:9–11	166
2:11	165

Colossians

3:13	5
4:14	1

1 Thessalonians

2:10	22

1 Timothy

3:16	150
5:8	53

2 Timothy

2:15	53

Titus

1:8	22

Hebrews

2:3	3
2:6–7	21
4:15	55
6	178
6:7	152
11:22	137
12:1	233

James

1:36	21
4:7	54, 162

2 Peter

1:15	137
1:16	143

1 John

1:1	3

Revelation

1:3	77
19:6–7	164